THE SNYDER COUNTY PIONEERS

BY

DR. CHARLES A. FISHER

CLEARFIELD

Originally published
Selinsgrove, Pennsylvania, 1938

Reprinted for
Clearfield Company, Inc. by
Genealogical Publishing Co., Inc.
Baltimore, Maryland
1991, 2001

International Standard Book Number: 0-8063-5060-1
Made in the United States of America

DEDICATION

——◆—●—◆——

This work is dedicated to those hardy
pioneers, our ancestors, who made possible
a goodly heritage, and a pleasant place for
us to live.

CHARLES A. FISHER.

Selinsgrove, Penna.
August 22, 1938.

As historian of the Fisher and Herrold families I learned that no work giving a record of all the people who lived in what is now Snyder County, prior to 1800, was in existence. Fragments of data on this one and that one could be found at different places, but no combined information existed any where except in the tax and military lists of the Pennsylania Archives, and usually these gave only the name and no additional information. So I decided to compile, for public use, such biographical information as I was able to find of the various persons whose names appeared on the tax and military rolls prior to 1800, in what is today Snyder County, from such sources as were available.

Errors may have crept into the work, and whenever a reader discovers an error, I trust he will be so kind as to inform me of it.

In order to better understand this work, certain introductory remarks are necessary. Prior to 1772, roughly, that part of Snyder County lying south of the Middle Creek was part of Cumberland County. The general section between the Middle and the Mahantango creeks, and south of the latter was known as "Penns Manor" and on other old maps as "Pennsboro." The first tax list of this section was compiled in 1768 and contained twenty-three names showing that not many settlers had located in the section. The part north of Middle Creek belonged to Berks County. Some of the people on the 1768 tax list probably lived in what was then Berks County. In 1772 Northumberland was formed and the southern boundry of the new county, west of the Susquehanna River, was the Mahantango Creek, and what is now Snyder County, except Monroe Township, became in 1772, Penn Township of Northumberland County. The "New Purchase" of lands beyond the mountains was made in 1769, and immediately settlers from the southeastern and eastern sections began to move beyond the mountains and across the Susquehanna, in numbers. The tax list of Penn Township for 1772 contained about fifty names and that of 1776 at least three hundred, and although the Indians harrassed the settlers so much that some returned to their old homes, others came on, and pushed up into the Penns, Middle Creek, Nittany and Bald Eagle valleys. In 1787, the western part of Penn Township was cut off, and named Beaver Township, and in 1796, the southern part of Penn Township was formed into Mahantango Township. This new township comprised largely what is today Union, Chapman, Washing-

ton, Perry and West Perry Townships. What is today Monroe Township, was then part of Buffalo Township but later became part of Penn and about 1843 became known as Monroe Township. Other townships were formed from time to time from the three townships, Beaver, Penn, and Mahantango, which existed prior to 1800, and by 1819, Mahantango had disappeared entirely, becoming, Perry, Chapman and Washington.

In the compilation of this work the following were used:

Snyder County Annals.
Selinsgrove Chronology.
History of the Juniata and Susquehanna Valleys.
Linn's Annals of the Buffalo Valley.
Meginnis' Work.
Various family histories.
Private Papers.
County records of wills; deeds, etc., at Lewisburg, Bellefonte, Carlisle, Sunbury and Middleburg.
Tombstone inscriptions in various cemeteries.
Various local historical pamphlets, and records of historical societies.
Church marriage and baptismal records.
The Pennsylvania Archives.
Federal and state military records.
Miscellaneous sources.

The compiler has attempted, whenever possible, to give the date of birth and death of the subject, with place of birth and burial, known children, various places at which the subject of the sketch lived and when, what he did, and property owned by him, with such other data as he was able to locate, including military service, if any.

GEORGE ADAMS was listed on the Penn Township tax list for the first time in 1774. In 1767 and 1768, he was a laborer and single, and lived in Tulpehocken Township, Berks Co., Pa. In 1781 and 1782 he was assessed with 50 acres of land and personal property in Penn Twp. He died in the year 1785. The tax list of 1791 in Penn Township contained the names of Widow Adams and John Adams, probably the wife and son of the above. During part of the Revolution he seems to have served as a Fifer in the 8th Pennsylvaia Regiment, Continental Line (Regular Army.) His widow was named Catharine. and Jacob and John are supposed to have been his sons. George Troutner was administrator of his estate.

JOHN ADAMS was probably the son of George Adams, mentioned above. It is believed that he was born in Tulpehocken Township, Berks County, Pa. He was first as-

sessed in Penn Township in 1791. His wife was Christina, daughter of Adam Ewig, Sr. John paid toward the erection of the First Lutheran Church in 1801.

FREDERICK ALBRIGHT (also Albrecht, Allbrite, Albert, etc.) was an early settler in the vicinity of Freeburg, Pa., and his name appeared on the Penn Township tax list for the first time in 1771. He lived in Flint Valley about a mile south of Freeburg and owned 159 acres part of this land he sold to his son-in-law, Adam Stahl in 1800. Frederick was a Fence Viewer in Penn Township in 1787 and on various occasions was appointed to boards of viewers for various purposes. Frederick died in the year of 1816, and in his will, on record at Lewisburg, Pa., he mentions two daughters, Elizabeth and Susanna (Mrs. Adam Stahl), and a granddaughter, Catherine Helwig, daughter of Susanna. Catherine married Francis Ludwig Brenner. Ludwig and his father, Francis Peter Brenner, came to Philadelphia, from Rotterdam in the British ship "Pennsylvania, Packet" on November 12, 1768, and took the oath of allegiance there. Jacob and Andrew were probably brothers of Frederick. Frederick received depreciation pay for services in the Northumberland County Militia during the Revolutionary War. In June 1780, he served 14 days in Lieutenant Simon Herrold's Company of Rangers on the frontier. Frederick was a son of Mathias and Magdalene Albright of Heidelberg Township, Lancaster County.

FREDERICK ALBRIGHT, JR., was assessed in Mahantango Township for the first time in 1796. If he ed above, he was not mentioned in his will. Some of the military service attributed to Frederick, may have been performed by Frederick, Junior. About 1800 he moved to Miles Twp., Center Co., where he seems to have died before his father.

JACOB ALBRIGHT, SENIOR, probably came to what is now Snyder County, from Berks County, Pa. On November 20, 1772, he was granted a warrant to survey for 150 acres in Northumberland (now Snyder County). His name appeared on the Penn Township tax list for the first time in 1776, and continued thereon until the formation of Beaver Township in 1787, when his name appeared at the head of the tax list there. He died in the year 1801, in Beaver Township, and his will is on record at Sunbury. Pa. His children were Jacob, Jr., Peter, Christopher (Stophel), Julia Ann. Catherine, Christina Wilson and Rachel Moar. Andrew and Frederick are believed to have been brothers of his. The U. S. Census of 1790, lists his wife and him as the only members of the family.

JACOB ALBRIGHT, JUNIOR. was the son of Jacob, Senior, and a brother of Christopher and Peter. He lived in Beaver Township prior to 1800 and died there in 1813. His will, which is on record at Lewisburg, Pa., mentions the following; Mary (wife), Margaret Albright (cousin), Julia Ann (sister), Christina Wilson (sister), Rachael Moor (sister, Christopher (brother), and Peter (brother). Of Peter, he states in the will, he had heard nothing for thirty years. It is evident that Jacob left no children. The compiler believes that he is the Jacob Albright who founded the Evangelical church, an offspring of the Methodist church, and for whom Albright College at Reading, Pa., is named. He may have served as a Sergeant in Capt. Wilson's Company of the 1st Penna. Regiment.

JOHN ALBRIGHT. A John Albright lived in Donegal Township Lancaster County, Pa., in 1773 and thereafter for some years, and another lived in Douglas Township of Berks County in 1784. It is believed that the John of this sketch is the latter. He was taxed in Mahantango Township for the first time in 1796. It is believed that he was a relative of Fred and the other Albrights of what is now Snyder County. Several Pennsylvania men of this name served in the Revolution.

MICHAEL ALBRIGHT was a resident of Mahantango Township. The date of his first residence there is unknown to the compiler, but it surely was before 1800. It is believed that he previously lived in Lancaster County. His will was probated at Lewisburg, Pa., on July 14, 1815. It mentions his wife, Catherine Elizabeth Bauer and their two children, Emanuel and Ann Elizabeth wife of Simon Ritter. Henry Holtapple, father of Jacob and John was a nephew of Mihacel Albright. When Henry died in 1802. Michael was the executor of his will. It is believed that Michael was a Revolutionary soldier.

STOPHEL (CHRISTOPHER) ALBRIGHT, was a son of Jacob Albright, Senior, who lived in Beaver Township in 1801, and a brother of Jacob, Junior, and Peter Albright. Christopher lived in Penn Township as early as 1776. Little is known concerning his early life, but his military record as a full one having served during the greater part of the Revolution in militia or ranger organizations from Northampton County. He served as a Private in

Captain John Moll's Company; Captain John Black's Company; Captain Michael Motz's Company; and on May 13, 1780 in Captain John Snyder's Company. At another time he served in Lieutenant John Coleman's Party; Ensign Simon Herrold's Party, and Lieutenant Jacob Spee's Company of Rangers. Probably no other man in the county had such a varied military career during the period.

THOMAS ALLEN was born in Ireland. The time of his coming to America is unknown to the compiler. On May 30, 1757, he enlisted as a batteau man in the service of the Province of Pennsylvania. Later, at the age of 23, on May 6,——, he enlisted in Captain Samuel Neilson's Pennsylvania Regiment of Foot at Sunbury. Pa. The enlistment record states that he had pale hair and pale complexion, and that he was slender limbed, and that his trade was that of tailor. No doubt he remained in the vicinity after the expiration of his term of service, because his name appeared on the Penn Township tax list for the year 1771. On June 4, 1762, he was granted a warrant of survey for 130 acres of land in Cumberland County (all south of the Middle Creek in Snyder County belonged to Cumberland County at that date). He seems also to have received grants for land in Dauphin, Huntingdon, and Northumberland counties. A Thomas Al-¹ n served in the Revolution from what is now Dauphin County (then Lancaster County).

JACOB ANDERSON, innkeeper of Selinsgrove, was probably the son of William Anderson, who lived in Penn Township at an earlier date. Jacob was assessed in Penn Township for the first time in 1799. He died in the year 1800, and is probably buried in the Old Lutheran cemetery in Selinsgrove. His will is recorded at Sunbury and mentions his wife, Jennie; his mother, Anna Catherine, and his daughters, Susanna and Elizabeth. No military record found.

WLLIAM ANDERSON was a tanner, and a resident, but not a land owner in Leacock Township, Lancaster County, Pa., in 1771. He was assessed in Penn Township for the first time in 1778 and at that time was taxed with 50 acres of land and personal property. When Mahantango Township was formed from the lower part of Penn in 1796, he was assessed there. William Anderson, Senior, and William Anderson, Junior, served in the 4th Company, 6th Battalion of the Lancaster Co., Militia, the former in the 6th class, and the latter in the 2nd class. The

compiler does not know which of these two men came to what is now Snyder County. One of them received a pension for having served in the Northumberland County Rangers during the Revolution. In 1778 he asked for tax exemption.

MATHIAS APP was born on October 33, 1761, and died on March 14, 1826. He came to what is now Snyder County about the year 1790, from Northampton County, locating near Selinsgrove. In 1796 he was one of the road supervisors of Penn Township, in 1800 he was one of the viewers for a road across the Isle of Que from Selinsgrove to the river, in 1801 he was one of the building committee for the erection of the Lutheran and Reformed church in Selinsgrove, in 1807, he was again a road supervisor in Penn Township, in 1815 he was a viewer for a bridge across the Penns Creek at Pine Street, Selinsgrove, and in 1823 he was an overseer of the poor for Penn Township. He was a large landholder in Penn and Monroe Townships, some of which is still owned by members of the App family. His will is recorded at Lewisburg, Pa., and mentions his wife, Elizabeth and the following children; Mathias, Jr.; Leonard (who had a son Mathias); John, Frederick (whose wife was Eve); Elizabeth (Mrs. Peter Born); Susanna (Mrs. Daniel Gross); Catherine (Mrs. Henry Uhls or Ulsh); Regina (Mrs. John Kleckner; Mary (Mrs. Bernard Bach, whose children were, Mathias Bach, John Bach, George Bach, Bernard Bach, Jr., Leonard Bach and Catherine Bach) Mary App Bach died before her father. Mothias (Mathias) App was a private, 5th class, in the 7th Company of the 3rd Battalion, Northampton County Militia in 1782. It is supposed that he is buried in the old Lutheran cemetery in Selinsgrove.

JONAS APPLE was a resident, but not a landholder in Pine Grove Township, Berks County, Pa., in 1784. He was assessed in Penn Township for the first time in 1785 and in 1787 was taxed with 200 acres of land and personal property. He was a relative of, if not a son of John or Henry Apple. No military record was found. A Henry Apple lived in Center Twp. in 1800.

PETER APPLE (also Apfel, Auple, Appfel, etc) was assessed in Beaver Township for the first time in 1789, and in the same year was granted 40 acres of land there. In 1798 he was granted an additional 50 acres in Northumberland (now Snyder) Co. He was an innkeeper and was assessed in Penn Township for the first time in 1799. It is believed that he was a relative of Jonas Apple who came from Berks County in 1785. Peter served as a substitute in the Berks County Militia for two months in the year 1777. In 1790, his family consisted of one male over and one under 16 years and one female. He lived in Center Twp. in 1800.

FREDERICK ARBOGAST (also Arbengast, Armagast, Armogast, Armagost, Arbegast, etc), was probably a brother of John Arbogast who was an early settler in Penn Township. Frederick lived in Penn as early as 1782, because in that year his daughter, Eva Susanna, was baptized at at the old Zion Lutheran church, about a mile north of Freeburg, and Andrew and Susanna Weddemier (probably Wittenmeyer) were the sponsors. In the same year, Frederick and his wife, Margaret, were the sponsors for Elizabeth Barbara, daughter of George (Weis) and wife, at the same church, and the next year they were sponsors for Jacob Frederick Freiberger, son of Frederick and Dorothea Freiberger. The Frederick Arbogasts must have moved on, as nothing further concerning them could be found.

JOHN ARBOGAST, was born in Germany and sailed for America from Rotterdam, Holland in the British ship "Edinburgh," James Russell, master, and landed at Philadelphia, Pa., where he took the oath of allegiance to England on September 16, 1751. In 1768 he was assessed with 25 acres of land and personal property in Heidelberg Township, Berks County, Pa., and with 60 acres and personalty in 1784. In 1785 he was assessed with 160 acres in Penn Township, but seems not to have lived there at the time, however, it is believed that he became a resident of Snyder County before 1790. He died in 1811 and his will is recorded at Sunbury, Pa. He mentions his wife (Catherine), and the following children; Nicholas; Peter; John, Jr.; Ludwig (Lewis); William; Catherine (Mrs. Christopher Shotzberger); Anna Maria (Mrs. Jacob Felmly), and Barbara (Mrs. John Zwally.) Lewis married Gertrude, daughter of Phillip Mertz. She was born in 1787.

NICHOLAS ARBOGAST was born in Heidelberg Township, Berks Co., Pa., on October 7, 1771. He came to what is now Snyder County with his parents prior to 1790, and died in Perry Township on July 3, 1851. His wife was Eva, a daughter of Philip and Eva Mertz in Penn Township. Philip Mertz died in Penn Township in 1804. Samuel, son of Nicholas and Eva Mertz Arbogast was baptized at the old Zion Lutheran church, north of Freeburg, in 1807. Nicholas and wife are buried in St. John's cemetery at Fremont. The names of his brothers and sisters will be found in John Arbogast's sketch. Nicholas was the oldest son of John.

ADAM ARNOLD was born about the year 1760. His name appeared on the Penn Township tax list for the first time in 1782, the same year that that of widow Arnold disappears. He was taxed for the same amount of land, and that leads the compiler to believe that he was the son of Lorentz (Lawrence) Arnold who died in 1781 in Penn Township. Adam's name appears regularly on the Penn Township tax list until 1790, but does not appear on that of the Mahantango or Penn in 1796, so he must have removed from the district. Angeline, wife of an Adam Arnold is buried in the old Hassinger cemetery, west of Middleburg. She was born April 24, 1782, and died December 7, 1849. No military service in the Revolution was located for this man. In 1790, his family had one male over and three under 16, and three females.

CASPER ARNOLD, SENIOR, was probably a native of Berks Co., Pa. In the summer of 1934, Benjamin F. Arnold, Freeburg, Pa., then aged 93 years, told the compiler the following: "When the pioneer, John George Herrold, settled near where the village of Chapman now stands in 1771, he discovered the need and location for a gristmill, so he sent word down to Heidelberg Township, Lancaster Co., his former place of abode, for someone to send him a millwright to build a mill. In due time, Casper Arnold, Sr., arrived, built the mill fell in love with his employers daughter, Anna Maria Herrold. Later they were married. Mr. Arnold is a great-grandson of this couple. Casper was born about 1747, and was assessed in Penn Township for the first time in 1776. In 1781 he was taxed with 100 acres and personal property, and in 1786 with a sawmill in addition. In 1795, he was one of the viewers appointed by the court to locate a road between Selinsgrove and Freeburg. In 1796, when Mahantango Township was formed from the lower part of Penn Township, he was assessed in the new district. In 1808, he still owned a sawmill, about one-fourth mile west of the present Susquehanna Trail at the village of Independence in Chapman Township. It is believed that he is buried in the St. John's Cemetery at Chapman, but if so, his grave is unmarked. Anna Maria Herrold, his wife, daughter of the pioneer, John George Herrold, was born in Heidelberg Township, Berks Co., Pa.

on December 27, 1752. She was confirmed as a member of the Tulpehocken (Christ) Lutheran church in 1766, and accompanied her parents to what is now Snyder County about 1770, where she later met and married, Casper, as above mentioned. She died on April 26, 1820 and is buried in the St. John's Cemetery at Chapman, and her grave is marked. Tradition has it that the Arnolds had five sons and two daughters, of these, the compiler has been able to definitely identify only two; George Arnold (1773-1848), and Casper, Junior (1787-1859). Peter (1793-1873), a soldier in the War of 1812, was possibly a son. No military record was found for Casper, but it is believed that he served during the Revolution. John who married a Gaugler and left four young children, may have been a son.

In 1790, his family had one male over and four under 16; and three females. Casper was baptized at Hain's Reformed Church, June 7, 1747. His sponsor was Casper Hain, son of George Hain, founder of the church.

GEORGE ARNOLD was the oldest son of Casper Arnold, Senior and his wife, Anna Maria, oldest daughter of the pioneer, John George Herrold. The subject of this sketch was named for his maternal grandfather, and was born in what is today Chapman Township, Snyder County, Pa., on August 9, 1773, and died in the same section on March 11, 1848. His wife, Marie E. Strayer, was born on February 7, 1775 and died on May 23, 1857. Both are interred in the old part of the Grubb's church cemetery in Chapman Township. Marie (Mary) Strayer was the daughter, or granddaughter of Mathias Strayer, a Revolutionary soldier, who died in Beaver Township in 1791. The Arnolds were members of the Lutheran congregation at Grubb's church. Elizabeth, a daughter of George and Maria Arnold, was born on Feb. 24, 1799 at Grubb's church on August 11 of the same year. Andrew and Elizabeth Strayer, parents of the mother were the sponsors for the child. The children of George Arnold and his wife were: Elizabeth (1799-1878).; George (1800-1878) Jr. (1803-1865)., who married Mary —; John S. (1808-1857), who married Elizabeth, Catherine; Magdalene; Mary, Benjamin, and Samuel (1815-1851).

LORENTZ (LAWRENCE) ARNOLD was born in Germany and embarked for America at Amsterdam, Holland, on the British ship "Good Intent," John Lasly, master, and arrived at Philadelphia where he took the oath of allegiance to the English government on October 23, 1754. In

1771 and 1772, he was a resident, but not a property owner in Heidelberg Township, Lancaster Co., Pa. It is believed that he came to what is now Chapman Township in the year 1773, and his name appears on the Penn Township tax lists until 1780, when the name of Widow Arnold appears instead. He died in 1781 and in 1782 letters of administration in his estate were granted to Mary Arnold, evidently his widow. Philip Aumiller was her surety. It is believed that Lawrence was the brother of Casper Arnold, Senior, who lived in the same section at that time. Adam Arnold was probably his son. Lawrence served in the militia and as a ranger during the Revolution, and at one time was a private in Captain Michael Motz's Company from Northumberland County.

GEORGE AULT (also Alt, Oldt, Olt, Old, Awlt, etc) was probably a son of Michael Ault, a Revolutionary soldier who was first assessed in Penn Township in 1776. In 1796, when Mahantango Township was formed he was assessed there, the name of Michael having disappeared from the Penn lists by that time. He may have been the George Ault who was assessed in Buffalo Township as early as 1782.

MICHAEL AULT probably came from Berks County. His name appears for the first time on the Penn Township tax list in 1776, and regularly thereafter for a number of years. From 1781 to 1787 he was assessed with 50 acres and personal property. In 1796, when Mahantango Township was formed from the southern part of Penn, his name had disappeared and that of George, believed to have been his son, appeared. Michael lived in what is today Perry Township. During the Revolution he served as a private in Captain John Snyder's Company and Lieutenant Jacob Bard's Party of Rangers from Northumberland Co. Michael evidently was born in Germany and embarked for America at the British ship "Janet," William Cunningham, master, arriving at the port of Philadelphia, Pa., where he took the oath of allegiance on October 7, 1751. In 1790, his family consisted of one male over and four under 16, and six females. He petitioned for tax exemption in 1778.

JOHN HIRONIMUS AUGUSTINE was born in Germany and embarked for America at Rotterdam, Holland, on the British ship "Sally," John Osman, master. He arrived at Philadelphia, Pa., where he took the oath of allegiance to the English government on October 23, 1767. On August 16, 1773, he was granted a warrant of survey for 100 acres in Northumberland (now Snyder) County, on April 16, 1776 he was granted 70 acres, in 1786, 125 acres and in 1793, 75 acres, making him one of the large landholders of the section. His name appeared on the Penn Township tax list for the first time in 1776. In 1787 he was assessed with 450 acres and personal property, and in 1800 was still living in Selinsgrove and his occupation listed as tailor. He had a long military career during the Revolution in the rangers and militia, he served in Captain John Clark's Company, Captain Michael Motz's Company, Captain John Moll's Company, Captain John Snyder's Company, and Lieutenant Jacob Spees Company, all of Northumberland Co. In 1790, his family consisted of one male over and one under 16, and four females.

JOHN AUMILLER. A John and a Conrad Aumiller arrived at Philadelphia on the British ship "Good Intent" and took the oath of allegiance there on October 3, 1754. They embarked at Amsterdam, Holland. In 1766, John was a resident, but not a land owner in Heidelberg Township, Berks County, Pa. In the same year, his name appeared on the tax list of the Pennsboro district, Cumberland (now Chapman Township, Snyder) County. He had not been assessed in Heidelberg Township in 1767, so his residence there was probably short. Northumberland County was formed in 1772, and on November 27th of that year he was granted a warrant of survey for 50 acres in the new county. On April 5, 1776, he enlisted as a private in Captain Casper Weitzel's Company at Sunbury, and served in the Continental Line at Marcus Hook, King's Bridge, and Harlem Heights, where he was ill. The following year he was on the roll of Captain John Robb's Company at Red Bank, New Jersey, on May 9th. It is believed that he may have returned to Heidelberg Township for a period after his military service, because in 1780, he was assessed with 15 acres and personal property there. In 1782, he was assessed with 250 acres, but nothing else, an evidence that he did not live there at the time. In 1787, he was again taxed with land and personal property in Penn Township, and his name had disappeared from the Heidelberg Township list. It was not an unusual happening for settlers to return to the eastern and southern counties during the Revolution because of the Indian ravages. On November 7 and 8th 1788, he was granted warrants of survey for 25 acres and 109 acres, respectively in Northumberland (now Snyder) County.

He was the son of Phillip Conrad Aumiller who lived in Penn Township as early as 1768. It is believed that the John and Conrad mentioned in this sketch were brothers, and that they followed their father to America at an interval of some three years. The Revolutionary Soldier, Conrad Aumiller, was either his father or brother. John died in what is now Snyder County in 1815. Two of his children were probably George and John. The Subject of this sketch was an overseer of the Poor in Penn Township from March 25, 1790 to March 25, 1793. In 1790, his family consisted of two males over and three under 16, and three females.

PHILIP CONRAD AUMILLER was born in Germany. The name is also given as Owmiller, Awmiller, etc. He embarked for America at Rotterdam, Holland, on the British ship "Edinburg" and arrived at Philadelphia, Pa., where he took the oath of allegiance to the English Government on August 13, 1751. It is believed that John George Aumiller who came in the ship "Anderson" on August 25, 1751, and John and Conrad Aumiller, who came in the ship "Good Intent" on October 23, 1754, were his sons. On June 5, 1755, Philip Conrad Aumiller was granted a warrant for a land survey in Cumberland (now Snyder County). A George Aumiller, probably his son who came over in 1751, was granted some at the same time. This, no doubt, is the land they occupied in 1768, when the first tax list of that section was made. In 1774 and 1775 Philip Conrad was an overseer of the poor in Penn Township and on Mar, 25, 1779, he was appointed Constable. In 1780 he was one of the largest land owners in Penn township, and in 1781 was assessed with 300 acres and personal property. He remained on the tax list until his death in the spring of 1787. The Aumiller holdings were in either Perry or Chapman Township. A Conrad Aumiller served in Lieutenant John Coleman's Company from Northumberland County. Some of the early Aumillers lived in the present Penn Township.

CONRAD AUMILLER, believed to have been the son of Philip Conrad, came to America in 1754. He was assessed in Penn Township in 1778. He may have been the Conrad who served in Lieutenant John Coleman's Company of the Northumberland County Militia.

DANIEL AURAND was assessed in Maxatawney Township, Berks Co., Pa., with 200 acres and personal property. About 1780 he became the non-resident owner of 300 acres in

Buffalo Township (now Union Co.) He was assessed in Penn Township for the first time in 1793, and in 1799 lived in Beaver Township. It is believed that he was a son of John Aurand and his wife, Mary Elizabeth Pontius. In 1790, his family had one male over and one under 16, and four females.

GEORGE AURAND, probably a brother of Daniel, and if so, a son of John Aurand ad Mary Elizabeth Pontius, who lived in what is now Union County. He was assessed in Beaver Township for the first time in 1794, and prior to that lived in Buffalo Township of Union County. On June 16, 1794, he was granted a warrant of survey for 200 acres in Northumberland (now Snyder) County. George was born on November 16, 1769, and died July 18, 1850. His wife, Mary Barbara—— who was born on August 9, 1766, and died on March 8, 1829. It is believed that he had a second wife, n..med Mary ——, who was born on October 6, 1777, and died on October 17, 1848. All three are buried in the Old Hassinger Cemetery, west of Middleburg, Pa.

HENRY AURAND, probably a brother of George and Daniel, mentioned above, was a son of John Aurand (1725-1807) and his wife Mary Elizabeth Pontius. Henry's father was born in Strasseberstadt, Germany, and during the war was a member of the committee of safety from Buffalo Township. Henry lived in Buffalo Township between 1775 and 1787, wad was assessed in Beaver Township for the first time in 1794. Henry died in what is now Snyder County. He was a Private in Captain John Forster's Company of Rangers from Northumberland County.

JACOB AURAND, believed to have been a brother of the above men, and possibly a son of John. He lived in Penn Township for a short time and died in 1788, prior to coming to Penn Township, he lived in Buffalo. He served as a Private in the Northumberland County Militia during the Revolution.

GEORGE BADER was a native of the Berks County and was assessed for the first time in Penn Township in 1773, but he evidently returned to Berks Co., for a period, because in the years 1784 and 1785 he was assessed with 200 acres and personal property in Maxatawney Township of Berks County. His name again appeared on the Penn Township list in 1786. He received Depreciation Pay for service in the Berks County Militia. In 1790, he had a wife and two daughters.

WILLIAM BAKER, Senior, was assessed for the first time in Penn Township in 1776, and remained until 1780. The following year it was found on the list of Augusta Township in which Sunbury was then located, and after two years it disappeared from the Augusta Township list. On May 14, 1773 he was granted 200 acres in Northumberland (now Snyder) County, and in 1776 he was granted lot No. 231 in the town of Sunbury.

WILLIAM BAKER, Junior was born July 12, 1765 and died September 26, 1863, being more than 98 years old at the time of his death. He is buried in the Bakers Cemetery in West Beaver Township, Snyder Co., Pa. He was the son of William Baker, Senior, and at the age of sixteen years took his fathers place in the Revolutionary forces. He is the William Baker Private, whose name was found on the list of New Levies.

NICHOLAS BALLIET, tanner, was assessed in Penn Township for the first time in 1799. He was born in Whitehall Township, Northampton County, Pa., about the year 1768 and died in Selinsgrove, now Snyder Co., Pa., in 1808. It is supposed that he is buried in the old Lutheran Cemetery in an unmarked grave. He was the youngest son, and ninth child of Paul Balliet. Paul Balliet was born in the province of Alsace in France in 1717 and died in Whitehall Township, Northampton County, Pa., on March 19, 1777. It is said that he descended from Tancred le Balyard, commander of the army of Shlodwig, King of France, about 500 A. D. Paul seemingly was a Huguenot and came to America for the purpose of obtaining religious freedom. He sailed from Rotterdam, Holland, in the British ship "Robert and Alice," Captain Walter Goodman, master, and arrived at the port of Philadelphia, Pa., where he took the oath of allegiance to the English government on September 11, 1738. His name on the ship list was "Paulus Buliut." Paul settled in Whitehall Township, Northampton, now Lehigh Co., Pa., before September 23, 1740. He was a large landholder in that section and on April 10, 1759 was naturalized as a British citizen. On June 22, 1756, he was granted a license to run the Whitehall Tavern. In 1749, he married Mary Magdelene Worting or Wotring, who was born in the province of Lorraine in 1727, and died in Whitehall Township in 1802. She was a daughter of Abraham Wotring. The issue of this marriage was Jacob, born December 23, 1750 and died in infancy; Mary Catherine,

born July 28, 1752, and died on January 28, 1823 (she married Adam, son of Adam and Appolonia Deshler, who was born on October 1, 1745, and died on Feb. 24, 1790. Adam, Jr. was a Revolutionary soldier. Mary Catherine's second husband was Christian Deily, whom she married Sept. 13, 1798. She had one son and seven daughters by her first husband). The third child of Paul Balliet was Stephen, born in 1753 and died near the place of his birth in Whitehall Township on August 4, 1821. (Stephen was a Lieutenant-Colonel in the Northampton County Militia in 1776, agent for forfeited Tory estates in 1778, member of the Supreme Executive Council of Pennsylvania in 1783, and member of the General Assembly of Pennsylvania in 1788. He married Magdalena, daughter of Peter Burkhalter. She was born on April 17, 1765, and died on ——1805. They had two sons and one daughter) 4th. Susanna, born in 1755 and still living in 1811. (She married John Baer and some time after 1794 moved to Hampshire Co., in Virginia) 5th. Eva, born in 1760, and died March 20, 1797. (On April 10, 1781, she married Nicholas Saeger). 6th. John, born November 31, 1761, and died November 2, 1837. (He was a Revolutionary soldier. He settled in the Sugarloaf Valley of Northampton or Northumberland County in 1784, and later moved to Turbot Township, Northumberland Co., Pa. In 1786, he married Catherine M., daughter of John Jacob Mickley. She was born on March 28, 1764 and died on January 2 1835. They had one son and one daughter. 7th. Magdalena, born about 1764. (She married Christian Troxell). 8th. Paul was born May 24, 1766 and died on February 17, 1845. (On December 19, 1819, he married Mary Elizabeth, daughter of David and Susanna Deshler, of Salisbury Township, Northampton County, Pa. At the time of her marriage she was the widow of Christian Mickley. She was born on March 27, 1775, and died on December 17, 1840. Her first husband, Christian, was born in 1767, and died in 1812). The compiler has a genealogy of the male members of this family.

ADAM BALT (also Bald, Baolt, etc.) was assessed for the first time in Penn Township in 1776 and his name seems to have disappeared from the tax lists after 1782. In 1781 he was assessed with 100 acres and personal property. It is believed that he moved to some other district. He died in the year 1792 according to a record at Sunbury. No military record was found for Adam, but John

Balt, probably a son, served in Captain Snyder's Company of the Northumberland County Militia in 1780.

JACOB BADER lived in Beaver Township in 1790. His family consisted of himself and wife, two sons under 16, and a daughter.

JOHN BALT was probably a son of Adam Balt who was first assessed in Penn Township in 1776, and died in 1792. Later tax records do not contain the name of John, so it is evident that he moved on to some other locality. John served as a private in Captain John Snyder's Company of the Northumberland County Militia. On Aug. 29, 1792, John bought from Anthony Selin the land of Leonard Dell in Beaver Township. Anthony had bought same at a tax sale.

LIEUTENANT JACOB BARD (also Bart, Baird, etc.) was listed as a freeman in Strasburg Township, Lancaster County, Pa., in 1778. He was assessed in Penn Township for the first time in 1774 and in 1785 was taxed with 100 acres and personal property. In 1793, he was granted a warrant of survey for 200 acres, and in 1793 for 200 acres additional. He was listed as a skin dresser in Penn Township in 1799. It is believed that he was a relative of Peter Bard who was commissary at Fort Augusta on September 4, 1756. In 1780 Jacob was a second lieutenant in Lieutenant Jacob Spees' Company of Rangers from Northumberland County. In 1790, Bard's family had one male over and four under 16, and three females. On April 24, 1785, he was Ensign in the 3rd Company, 1st Battalion of the Northumberland County Militia.

JOSEPH BARGER (also Berger) was listed as a resident, but not a landowner in Maiden Creek Township, Berks County, Pa., in 1768. Soon there after it seems he became a resident of Coventry Township, Chester County. He was assessed in Penn Township for the first time in 1798, and at that time operated a sawmill. In Berks County he was listed as a carpenter. In 1781 and 1782, he served as a private in Captain Mordecai Morgan's 8th Company, 4th Battalion of the Chester County Militia.

JACOB BARLET was probably a native of Berks County. He was assessed in Beaver Township for the first time in 1799. No military record was found. His family had one male over and two under 16, and four females in 1790.

JOHN BARNES was assessed in Beaver Township for the first time in 1789. Several men of this name

from various parts of Pennsylvania, served in the Revolution. This man probably served in Captain Jack's Company of the Cumberland County Militia in 1781. In 1790, one male and three females composed his family.

HENRY BARNHART was assessed in Mahantango Township for the first time in 1796. He later moved to Center County, and on January 26, 1833 he or a relative of the same name, was granted a warrant of survey for 216 acres of land in that county. A Henry Barnhart served in the Revolution from Pennsylvania.

CHRISTOPHER BARTGES (Stophel Bartes on some records) was assessed in Penn Township for the first time in 1774. In 1781 he was taxed with 50 acres and personal property. He died in the year 1782, possibly in the service of his country. He served as a Private in Captain John Moll's Company of the Northumberland County Militia. George Bartges, who died in Mahantango Township in 1815, is believed to have been his son. George left a will which is recorded at Lewisburg, Pa. It mentions his wife, Rebecca, and their children: Elizabeth, Jacob, George, Adam, and Barbara. It is believed that Christopher is buried in Chapman Township in an unmarked grave.

GEORGE BASSLER (also Bossler) was a resident, but not a landowner in Windsor Township, Berks County, Pa., in 1779 and 1780. His given occupation at the time was that of weaver. He was assessed for the first time in Penn Township in 1785, and was then taxed with 50 acres of land and personal property. His wife was named Mary, and they had a son named Jonathan, who was baptized at the old Zion Lutheran church, north of Freeburg, in 1789. George Bassler died in 1805 and is probably buried in the old Zion cemetery. Some of his descendants still live in Freeburg.

DANIEL BASTIAN was assessed with 300 acres of land and personal property in Mahoning Township, Northumberland County, Pa., in 1785, and appeared on the Penn Township tax list for the first time in 1793. In 1801, he contributed to the fund for the erection of the Lutheran and Reformed church in Selinsgrove.

GEORGE BASTIAN was assessed with 280 acres, personal property and a gristmill in Allen Township, Northampton County, Pa., in 1785 and thereafter for several years. His name appeared on the Penn Township tax list for the first time in 1793, It is believed that he was a relative of Daniel Bastian. In 1801, he contributed to the fund for the erection of the Lutheran and Reformed church in Selinsgrove. He served as a Private, 8th class, in the 2nd Company, 4th Battalion of the Northampton County Militia in May of 1778.

MICHAEL BASTIAN, laborer, lived in Upper Milford Township, Northampton County, Pa., in 1772. From 1786 to 1788 he was assessed with 75 acres of land and personal property in Macungie Township of the same county. His name appeared on the tax list of Penn Township for the first time in 1793. In 1801, he contributed to the fund for the erection of the Lutheran and Reformed church in Selinsgrove, Pa. He served as a private in the 7th Company, 2nd Battalion of the Northampton County Militia. It is believed that he was a relative of the Bastians mentioned above.

PETER BAUM (also Bum, Bawm), sawmill owner and operator, was assessed in Cumru Township, Berks County, Pa., in 1785. His name appeared on the Penn Township tax list for the first time in 1799. It is believed that he was the Peter Baum who was a private in Captain Daniel DeTurck's Company of the Berks County Association in July, 1776.

JOHN BAY probably came from Londonderry Township, Lancaster County, Pa. He was assessed in Mahantango Township for the first time in 1796. A John Bay was a private in Captain John Bankson's Company, 2nd Pennsylvania Regiment, Continental Line, on September 8, 1778. In 1790, his family consisted of one male over and three under 16, and two females. The name was also written "Beh."

FREDERICK BEAK was probably a native of Lancaster County, Pa., and was assessed in Beaver Township for the first time in 1789. No military record was found.

JACOB BEAR was granted a warrant of survey for 200 acres of land in Northumberland (now Snyder) County in 1773, and his name appeared on the tax list for the first time in 1776. In 1782, he was taxed with 300 acres and personal property, and in 1787 he was taxed in Beaver Township. On March 28, 1793, he was granted a warrant for an additional 100 acres in Northumberland (now Snyder) County. He died in Beaver Township in 1809. Isaac Bear is supposed to have been his son. Not less than three men of this name served in the Revolution from York, Chester, and Northampton Counties. Jacob's land lay in Center Twp. His wife was named Susanna and prior to 1815, she married Jost Althouse. The Bear children were: Isaac, Benjamin, Jacob, Samuel, Frances (Mrs. Christian Bubacher), and Kate, (Mrs. Christian Beaver.)

WILLIAM BEARD (also Baird, Bard, etc.) was assessed in Penn Township only in the year 1780. In 1785 he was taxed in Armagh Township, Cumberland (now Mifflin) County. He is supposed to have died in the year 1792. He received depreciation pay for services in the Cumberland County Militia, and may also have served in Captain Thomas Robinson's Company of Rangers.

HUGH BEATTY was a son of Alexander Beatty who died in 1787. He was born in 1752 and still living in 1833. He is supposed to have lived within the present bounds of Snyder County for a short time. He served in the Northumberland County Militia and received a pension. He lived near New Berlin and is supposed to have been buried there.

JOHN BEATTY was a brother of Hugh. He, too, lived near New Berlin and may be buried there. His sojourn in Snyder County was short. He served in Captain John Clark's Company of Associators and in Robinson's Rangers.

JOHN MICHAEL BEAVER (also Beiver, Bieber, Bever, Bevor, etc.) was a grandson of John Bieber who was born in Germany about 1700, and arrived in Philadelphia, Pa., on the British ship "Friendship" and took the oath of allegiance there on November 2, 1744. He settled in Oley Township, Berks County, Pa. He was murdered between his home and Philadelphia, while he was returning from the city where he had sold a load of grain. His son John Jacob Bieber, was born in Germany on December 24, 1731, and came to America with his parents in 1744. "Jacob" Bieber as he was commonly called lived with his parents on their land in Oley Township, where on November 7, 1758, he married Catherine, daughter of Michael Steinbrenner. Jacob was not satisfied with his small land holdings in Oley Township, no additional land being obtainable, began to seek a larger tract on which to raise his large family. He found what he wanted in what was then Northampton County, but now West Salisbury Township, Lehigh Co. Pa., Here he bought a tract of 460 acres for 2300 pounds in 1786. Jacob and his wife died here, the former on October 16, 1798, and they are buried in the cemetery of the Jerusalem Lutheran church in W.

Salisbury Township. The names and dates of birth and dates of baptism of their children are recorded on the records of the Lutheran church at Dryville, Berks County, Pa. The evidence indicates that Jacob became a resident of Northampton County prior to the Revolution, but that at first he may not have been a landholder there. On June 27, 1778, he served as a private in Captain John Stahl's Company of the Northampton County Militia, and at an other time he was a private in the 8th Company, 3rd Battalion of the same county. His children were named; Dewald, Jacob, John, Christian, John Michael (subject of this sketch), Conrad, Christian, Abraham, John George and Catherine.

John Michael Beaver, commonly called "Michael," was born June 17, 1769, and died on January —, 1848. His wife was Susanna, daughter of the pioneer and Revolutionary soldier, John George Ott (1745-1814). Susanna was born in Salisbury Township, Northampton County, Pa., on March 16, 1770 and died near Selinsgrove, Pa., on July 3, 1845. She is buried in the old Lutheran cemetery in Selinsgrove, and it is supposed that her husband is buried there also. Her grave is marked. Michael was probably born in Oley Township, Berks County, moved to Northampton County with his parents and married there. His name appears on the Penn Township tax list for the first time in 1795. On July 7, 1795, Michael Beaver bought his first land in Snyder County from Conrad Hain, an early settler in the section, east of Kratzerville. In 1801, Michael contributed to the fund for the erection of the Lutheran and Reformed church in Selinsgrove. Michael in addition to being a farmer was also a pumpmaker. Michael during thirty-five years residence in Snyder Co., secured large land holdings in what is now Snyder and Union counties. These he disposed of June 6, 1831 to George Beaver (a son), Simon Beaver (a son), and William Wagner, (son of Yost Wagner), a son-in-law. The land sold to the sons lay in either Union Township, Union County, or Monroe Township, Snyder County, or part in both. The land sold to his son-in-law, William Wagner, lay in the then Beaver Township. Michael was married to Susanna Ott in 1787, and the dates of birth of some of their children are recorded in the West Salisbury Reformed church in Lehigh County, Pa. The names of their children were: Sarah (Mrs. Isaac Brobst), born November 26, 1789; Susanna (second wife of John Oldt), born January 25, 1792; Jacob (who

married Magdalena, daughter of Yost Wagner), born January 14, 1794; Mary (Mrs. Michael Engle); Hannah (Mrs. John Moyer); Simon (who married Elizabeth, daughter of John Oldt), who was born on August 26, 1803, and died Nov. 25, 1881;—— (who married William, son of Yost Wagner), and George (who married Sarah——), who was born on June 2, 1788 and died February 15, 1865. Several of the children of Michael Beaver rest in the old cemetery at Kratzerville, Pa.

GEORGE BELL was probably a native of Lancaster County, Pa. He was assessed in Beaver Township for the first time in 1799. Several men of this name served in the Revolution, one of them, believed to have been the subject of this sketch, served in Captain McCallen's Company, 1st Battalion of the Lancaster Co. Militia. In the 1790 U. S. census there were two males over 16 and three females in his family.

ADAM BENDER (also Bander, Binder, etc) was assessed in Penn Township for the first time in 1776. It is believed that he was a native of Warwick Township, Lancaster Co., Pa., and that during the Indian uprisings in the then more remote Penn Township, he returned to Lancaster County, where in 1779, he was assessed with 7 acres and personal property. The records seem to indicate no Snyder County, but as people of the name Bender lived in the now Chapman Township early in the nineteenth century, either he or some of his descendants returned. John Bender of Perry Township, who died in 1829 was probably a son of Adam. John left a will and mentions his wife, Catherine, and the following children: John, Jonas, Susanna, (Mrs. Philip Arbogast), (Mrs. Jacob Mitterling), and Elizabeth. In 1782, Adam Bender was a private, 4th class in the 3rd Company, 3rd Battalion of the Lancaster County Militia. In 1786 he was still a member of the militia.

JOHN GEORGE BENFER (also given as Benford, Binford, etc) was born in Germany on March 21, 1745 and embarked for America in the British ship "Betsy," John Osmond, master, at Rotterdam, Holland, enroute they touched Cowes, Isle of Wight, arriving at Philadelphia, where he took the oath of allegiance to the English government on October 13, 1766. He was assessed in Penn Township for the first time in 1778, and in 1787 was taxed with 150 acres and personal property. He probably lived on the south side of the Penns Creek in what is now Jackson Township of Snyder County. In 1793, he was one of the officials of Penn

Township. "George" as he was commonly called, married Maria Magdalene Miller, who was born in 1764 and died in 1832. She may have been his second wife. George died on April 23, 1818, and he and wife are buried in the old cemetery at New Berlin, Pa. George Benfer served as a private in Lieut. James McElvey's Company and Captain James Boevard's Company of Rangers from Northumberland County. In a will made in 1815, George mentions his children, as follows: George (1777-1854), Henry, John, Daniel, Frederick, Teany (a daughter), Elizabeth, Eva, Magdalene, Barbara, Michael and Andrew. In 1790, had one male over and five under 16, and three females. Mary Magadalene Miller, was a daughter of Frederick Miller, a pioneer in the Salem section of the present Penn Township.

SEBASTIAN BERGER, weaver, was assessed in Penn Township for the first time in 1799. It is believed that he was a son of Joseph "Barger" who became a resident of Penn Township in 1798. No military record was found for Sebastian. Bergers live at Centerville in Snyder county at the present time.

FREDERICK BERRY was probably a brother of John Berry and possibly a son of Jacob Berry who lived in the vicinity of Freeburg. Frederick lived in Penn Township as early as 1784, because in that year, Anna Catherine, daughter of Frederick and Catherine Berry, was baptized at the old Zion Lutheran church, north of Freeburg. Their residence in that section must not have been long as nothing additional concerning them could be found.

JACOB BERRY was assessed with 100 acres and personal property in Haverford Township, Chester Co., Pa., in 1780. In 1782 his name was listed as the owner of 25 acres in Heidelberg Township, Berks County, but there is no indication that he lived there. He was assessed in Penn Township for the first time in 1791. The Jacob Berry, age 21, 5 feet 9 inches tall, dark complexion, shoemaker, who on April 6, 1788 enlisted in Captain Zeigler's Company for federal service under General Harmar, may have been his son. A Jacob Berry and his wife, Christina, had their daughter, Christina, baptized at the old Zion Lutheran church, a mile north of Freeburg, in 1789, and a daughter Barbara at the same place in 1794.

JOHN BERRY was probably from Berks County, Pa. He was assessed in Penn Township for the first time

in 1799. His wife was Catherine Elizabeth Brenner, daughter of John Daniel Brenner, who may have died in Penn Township in 1792, and granddaughter of Francis Peter Brenner, who died in Penn Township in 1807. Francis Peter was a Revolutionary soldier, and it is possible that John Daniel was also. Catherine Elizabeth, the wife of John Berry, was born on March 6th, 1775, and died July 15, 1853, and is buried in St. Peters cemetery in Freeburg. It is believed that John is buried there in an unmarked grave. Anna Mary, daughter of John and Elizabeth Berry was baptized at the old Zion Lutheran church, north of Freeburg, in 1804. Another of their children was Henry Berry (1812-1885). Henry had two wives, the first was Elizabeth———(1814-1837, and the second was Mary———) A John Berry served as a private in the Northumberland County Militia during the Revolution. The compiler believes that John Berry, the Revolutionary soldier, was the father of Frederick, John, and Jacob, mentioned above.

ROBERT BEVOR (probably meant for Beaver- lived in Penn Township around the year 1780, but no other information seems available, except that he served as a private in Captain Charles Moyer's Company of the Northumberland County Militia or Rangers.

PETER BERST was listed as a landowner in Derry Township, Lancaster (now Dauphin) County, Pa., in 1773. His name appeared on the Penn Township tax list for the first time in 1776, and in 1781 he was listed as a non-resident landowner in Penn Township, and by 1783 his name had disappeared from the tax lists. No military record was located.

BENJAMIN BERTCH (also Bertsch, Berch, Burch, etc) was first assessed in Penn Township in 1789. No military record was found. In the 19th century some Bertches lived in Chapman Township, and at present at least one family of the name lives in Freeburg, Pa.

JOHN BICKHART (also Bickard, Bickhardt, etc) was assessed in Penn Township for the first time in 1776, and was still living in 1796, when Mahantango Township was formed from the southern part of Penn. It is believed that he was the first of his name in the county, and several families of the name still exist in various sections of Snyder. He may have come from Chester County, because a John Bickhart or Pickard served in Captain Joseph Gardiner's Company of the Chester County Militia. The name was also used as Bi-

gart in early days. In 1790, his family had one male over and two under 16 years of age, and three females. He was unmarried in 1776.

CHRISTOPHER or CHRISTIAN BICKEL (also Pickel, Bickle, Bickle, Pickle, Buckel, Bidel, etc.) was probably a brother of Henry Bickel who lived in Buffalo Township as early as 1778, or he may have been a son of Tobias Bickel, Senior, and early resident of Penn Township. Christopher or Christian (name uncertain) was a private in Captain Michael Motz's Company and at another time he served in Captain Charles Meyer's Company of the Northumberland County Militia. If he was a son of Tobias, Sr., he died before his father, because he is not mentioned in his will.

JACOB BICKEL (also Bickle, Pickle, Buckel, Bidel, Biggle, etc.) was a son of Tobias Bickel, Sr. He was born on April 24, 1757, probably in North Heidelberg Township, Berks County, Pa., and died in or near Kratzerville, Union (now Snyder) County, Pa., on September 9, 1852. His wife was Maria Magdalena Ulrich, who died at the age of 92 years. Both are buried in the old Lutheran and Reformed Cemetery at Kratzerville, Pa. It is said that he was the oldest person buried in that particular cemetery. Jacob's father became a resident of Penn Township as early as the year 1770, when Jacob was 13 years old. Jacob was assessed in Penn Township for the first time in 1780. His brothers were Henry, John, Simon, Thomas, Tobias, Jr. In 1781 Jacob was assesse with 100 acres and personal property, and it is believed he lived all his life in what is today Jackson Township, at least he spent his declining years on a farm in that section once owned by the late Samuel Ulrich, and later by John Kline. Jacob Bickel served in Lieutenant John Coleman's Party of Rangers, and in Captain John Snyder's Company, and Captain Michael Weaver's Company, all of them being Northumberland County organizations. A Jacob Bickel served as a private in Captain Martin Weaver's Company of the Lancaster County Militia on November 5, 1777, but it is believed that this was another man of the same name. Jacob brought his musket, uniform, and accoutrements home from the war and kept them as relics. On February 2, 1833, at the age of 75, he applied for a pension, which was granted. In 1840 his name still appeared on the pension rolls, and his residence was given as Union (now Snyder) County. His name appeared on some military rolls as "Jacob Bidel." In 1790, his family consisted of himself and three females.

JOHN BICKEL was a son of Tobias Bickel, Sr., and a brother Jacob mentioned above as well as of Thos. Tobias, Jr., Simon, and Henry. He was born March 16th. 1744, probably in North Heidelberg Township, Berks County, Pa. In 1770 he came with his parents to what is now Snyder County, and he was assessed in Penn Township for the first time in 1774. In 1782 he was taxed with 150 acres of land and personal property. His wife was Catherine (probably a daughter of Peter Witmer, Sr.) John died in Penn Township in 1805. John Bickel, a son of John and Catherine, was baptized at the old Zion Lutheran church, a mile north of Freeburg in 1781, and Peter Witmer was the sponsor. John and all of his brothers, with the possible exception of Henry, served in the Revolution. John was a private in Captain John Snyder's Company of Northumberland Co. His brothers, Jacob, Tobias, and Simon were also members of this organization. In the U. S. Census of 1790, his family had two males over and four under 16 and three females.

SIMON BICKEL was a son of Tobias Bickel, Sr., and a brother of John and Jacob, mentioned above. Simon was born in February, 1750 probably in North Heidelberg Township, Berks County, Pa. About 1770, he came to what is now Snyder County with his parents. He was assessed in Penn Township for the first time in 1776. In 1787 he was taxed with 100 acres, personal property and a sawmill. In 1801, he contributed to a fund for the erection of the first Lutheran church of Selinsgrove, Pa. In 1810, he was one of the overseers of the poor in Penn Township. In 1783, he and his wife, Elizabeth had a daughter named Rosina baptized at the old Zion Luthern church, north of Freeburg. The sponsors were Michael Treaster and his wife, Rosina. In 1780, he was a member of Captain John Snyder's Company of Northumberland County. His brothers Tobias, John and Jacob also served in this organization. Simon died in Penn Township in 1824. In 1790, his family consisted of one male over and three under 16. and five females.

THOMAS BICKEL was one of the six sons of Tobias Bickel, Sr. He was born October 20, 1752, probably in North Heidelberg Township, Berks County, Pa. He came to what is now Snyder County with his parents about the year 1770. He was as-

sessed in Penn Township for the first time in 1778. In 1781 he was taxed with 250 acres of land and personal property. It is believed that Thomas' wife was Catherine Barbara, daughter of Andrew and Catherine Elizabeth Shaffer, who lived in the vicinity of Salem in Penn Township. Mary Julia, a daughter of Thomas and Barbara Bickel was baptized at the old Zion Lutheran church, about a mile north of Freeburg, in 1783. Thomas and his brother, Jacob, served in Captain Michael Beaver's Company of the Northumberland Militia. At an other period, Thomas served in Lieutenant Jacob Spees Company of Rangers. In 1790, he lived in what is now Union County and his family consisted of one male over and three under 16. and three females. In 1803, he lived in Miles Twp., Center Co.

TOBIAS BICKEL, Jr., was a son of Tobias Bickel, Sr. He was born about the year 1748, probably in North Heidelberg Township, Berks County, Pa. He came to what is now Snyder County with his parents about the year 1770. He was assessed in Penn Township for the first time in 1771. In 1775, he was one of the constables of Penn Township. After the war he moved to the vicinity of Rebersburg, or Madisonburg in Center County, Penna., where he died in 1814. On January 30 1777, he was a private in Captain Benjamin Weiser's Company, German Regt. Continental tal line, stationed at Philadelphia. In May of 1780, he served in Captain John Snyder's Company of the Northumberland County Rangers (or militia). In 1790, his family had four males over and three under 16, four females, and one other person.

TOBIAS BICKEL, SR. (sometimes given as Boeckel) was born in Germany about the year 1718. He died in what is now Penn Township, Snyder County, Pa., in 1792. The immigration lists show that Christopher Bickel, aged 48; George Felte Bickel, aged 32; and John Philip Bickel, aged 16, arrived at Philadelphia, Pa., from Rotterdam, Holland, but last from Cowes, Isle of Wight, in the F itish ship "Mary," John Gray, master. and that they took the oath of allegiance on September 26, 1732. They were designated as Palatines. It is believed that Christopher and George were brothers, and that John Philip was a son of Christopher, and that Tobias was a son of either Christopher or George, probably the former. Tobias' ancestors evidently settled in Berks County, Pa., because in 1744 Tobias was a resident of North Heidelberg Township in that

county. In his younger days, Tobias was associated with the Moravian church, and in 1744, he donated land in North Heidelberg Township, Berks County, about five miles northeasst of Robesonia, on which the Heidelberg Moravian church was built. It was a log structure, and the congregation was never very large, eventually the congregation moved to other sections, and the church now is, used by the Lutherans and Reformeds The third or fourth building now and for a century or more has been occupies the site donated by Tobias nearly two hundred years ago. Frederick Bickel, a brother of Tobias, was the first elder of the congregation. Tobias and his family became residents of what is now Snyder County in 1770, at the same time that a number of others, including the Herrolds and Reichenbachs, came into the section from Berks and Lancaster counties. He was assessed in Penn Township for the first time in 1771. The Bickels had large land holdings in Penn Township, and at one time also owned a gristmill, sawmill, and tannery in addition. Some of the Bickels continued to own land in Heidelberg Township as late as 1785. Tobias died in 1792 and his will is recorded at Sunbury, Pa. The will mentions the following children: Henry, Tobias, Jr., John Simon, Thomas, Jacob, Catherine, Margaret Elizabeth, Marie Margaret, Anna Maria, and Rosina, Mrs. Michael Treaster). It is believed that Tobias, Sr., may have served in the Revolution, and that some of the service credited to his son, Tobias, Jr., may have been his. The compiler believes that the subject of this sketch may be buried in the Row's (Salem) cemetery in an unmarked grave. At least five of Tobias' sons served in the Revolutionary War. Tobias, Sr., had two wives. Some of his children were baptized at Christ Lutheran Church. Stouchsburg, Pa. His daughter Margaret was born Mar. 22, 1746, Anna Maria, Apr.—, 1751, and Rosina, Mar. 13, 1755.

ANTHONY BIERLY (also Byerly, Byerley, Bierley, Biarley, Beerly, etc) was a son of Melchoir Bherly, who immigrated from Barvaria, Germany, prior to the Revolution. Melchoir was married in the old country, and it is supposed that most of his children were born there. Anthony was granted a warrant of survey for 200 acres in Northumberland, now Snyder County, on December 5, 1772, and was assessed in Penn Township for the first time in 1778. It seems that he did not actually become a resident of Penn Township until 1785. In 1787, he was taxed with 250 acres and personal property, and lived some where along the Mahantango Creek. Melchoir and his wife, in their latter days, lived with or were close neighbors to their son. It is believed that they previously lived in either Berks or Lancaster County. During the Indian troubles they fled to the lower counties, and the old couple never returned. It is said that Anthony's mother was an invalid, and that she was removed with difficulty. The elder Bierlys had two sons, Nicholas and Anthony. Nicholas moved to Ohio. Anthony married Anna Maria Warner, who was born on November 15, 1752, and died on April 3, 1841. Her husband was born in 1743, and died on April 7, 1825. Both are buried in the cemetery at Rebersburg, Pa. Eva, one of the twelve children of this pair was born September 7, 1791, and baptized at Grubb's Church in Chapman Township, on April 14, 1792. The names of their children were: Margaret (Mrs. John Philips and later Mrs. Peter Greninger); Nicholas, who married Lucy Buchtel (daughter of John); Elizabeth (Mrs. Peter Berry); Catherine; John, who married Catherine Berry; Sarah (Mrs. H. Greninger, later Mrs. Geo. Lesh); Eva (Mrs. Michael Ketner); Rosina (Mrs. Christian Gramley); Barbara (Mrs. Frederick Womelsdorf; Anthony, Jr., who married Maria Crotzer; Ann (Mrs. Philip Glantz; and Mary (Mrs. Michael Kahl). In 1790, Anthony's family consisted of one male over and three under 16, and seven females. Anthony and his family moved to Brush Valley, Center County, Pa., in 1792, and settled about a half mile northeast of the present site of Rebersburg. The compiler did not find a military record for Anthony, but feels sure he served in the Revolution.

ABRAHAM BILLMAN was assessed in Penn Township for the first time in 1771, no further information concerning him could be located.

FREDERICK BINGAMAN was the son of John Jost Bingaman and his wife, Juliana Ort. The parents came from Germany, arriving at Philadelphia, Pa., on the British ship "Edinborough" James Russell, master. John Jost took the oath of allegiance to the English government on September 30, 1754. The Bingemans (also spelled Bingaman) were of Palatine or Wurtemburg ancestry. John Jost Bingeman died in July, 1755, just a few months after the birth of his son. Frederick was born in Berks County, Pa., on January 15 1755, and died in what is now Snyder County, Pa., on October 30, 1845, aged nearly 91 years. On April 6,

1779, he married Maria Christina Hufnagle, daughter of John Christian Hufnagle, and his wife, Maria Elizabeth, of Ruscomb Manor Township, Berks County, Pa. She was born on May 3, 1758, and died in what is now Adams Township, Snyder County, Pa., on April 12, 1818. Both are buried in the cemetery of St. Henry's church at Troxelville. In the U. S. Census of 1790, Frederick was assessed in Ruscomb Manor Township of Berks County, and there were in the family one male over 16, and two males under 16, and two females under sixteen. The exact date of Frederick's coming to what is now Snyder County is unknown, but it was prior to 1800, probably in 1794 or 1795. Frederick was assessed in Ruscomb Manor Township in 1779, but owned no land at the time there. In 1781 he was taxed with 81 acres and personal property in that district. Due to the fact that Frederick on one occasion refers in his writings to Maria Hufnagle as his "first wife" he was evidently twice married. There were twelve children in the Bingman family, six sons and six daughters, and it is supposed that all, or most of the twelve accompanied their parents when they came to what is now Snyder County. Henry Bingman (1794-1861) was a son of Frederick. Henry married Christina Moyer and they had at least ten children (names are found on page 243, vol. 1, Snyder County Annals). It is said that Henry served in the War of 1812. Frederick served in the militia during the Revolution, and is said to have been in the battle at the Brandywine. The Rev. Dr. Ira W. Bingaman, President of Carthage College, Carthage Illinois, is a descendant of the subject of this sketch

JOHN BINKOMER was assessed in Penn Township for the first time in 1798. He was a merchant. No military record was located.

JACOB BISHOP (also Bischoff, Bishopp, etc). Several men of this name lived in Pennsylvania prior to 1800. It is believed that the subject of this sketch was the man who was assessed with 90 acres and personal property in Upper Milford Township, Northampton County, Pa., in 1785 and 1786. His name appeared on the Penn Township tax list for the first time in the year 1791. He died in Center Township in 1814. It is believed that his wife's name was Catherine, and that one of their children was named John. Jacob was a private in Captain William Heyser's Company, German Regiment, Continental Line, on May 22, 1777. A Jacob Bishop was captain of the 7th Company, 1st Battalion,

Berks County Militia, on May 12, 1783. In 1790, his family consisted of two adult males and four females. He was one of the petitioners for the formation of Mahantango Twp., in 1795.

CAPTAIN JOHN BLACK (This name may have been Schwartz originally, Schwartz is the German for Black. The name Schwartz today is usually spelled Swartz) lived in what is now Snyder County prior to 1780. He came originally from Northampton County or Lancaster County. His residence in Penn Township may not have been long, because in 1781 and in subsequent years a John Black was assessed with 120 acres and personal property in Mahoning Township of Northumberland Co., and in 1782 a John Black was a resident of Augusta Township, same county. The John Black of Mahoning Township was a large landholder in other sections. The compiler is unable to tell which one of these men served in the Revolution, probably both of them. The John Black of this sketch was captain of a company of militia or rangers from Northumberland County about the year 1780. The members of his company lived in what today comprises Beaver, Franklin, Center, Penn, Union, and Chapman Townships of Snyder County. In 1790, his family consisted of two males over and two under 16, and four females.

MARTIN BLACK (See explanation above) is believed to have been a relative of Captain John Black. He seems never to have been assessed in Penn Township, but the fact that he served in the militia from the section indicates that he lived here for a short time at least. Martin was a private in Captain John Moll's (Mull's) Company from Northumberland County. Peter, given below, may have been a brother.

PETER BLACK is believed to have been a brother of Martin, and a relative of Captain John Black. The fact that he served in the militia from Penn Township indicates that for a short time at least he must have been a resident in the district. Peter and Martin were both privates in Captain John Mcll's Company of Northumberland County. It is believed that the Blacks came from Lancaster Co. As Black is the English for the German Schwartz, and as there are none of the former, but many of the latter (now spelled Swartz) living in Snyder County, the compiler believes that the translation was only a temporary situation.

JOHN BLASSER was probably

SNYDER COUNTY PIONEERS 11

the son of Abraham Blasser of
Hopewell Township, York County,
Pa. In the years 1781 and 1783 a
John Blasser was assessed in that
township, and the records state that
there were eleven in the family at
that time. John was assessed in Mahantango Township for the first
time in 1796. He, or his son, of the
same name, built the large stone
mansion house on the west side of
the Susquehanna Trail, about a
mile south of Port Trevorton. Abraham Blosser, probably a son of
John, was one of the viewers for
the location of Bough Street in Selinsgrove in 1822. The Blassers were
neighbors of the Herrolds and intermarried with them. Colonel William G. Herrold married Mary
(Polly) Blasser. In 1802, John Blasser was one of the three witnesses
to the will of John George Herrold.
Captain Simon Herrold in his will
made in 1827, states that he and
John Blasser (probably John Jr.)
were partners in a shad fishery in
the Susquehanna river. Simon also
mentions that he owned land on the
east bank of the Susquehanna adjoining that of John Blasser. The
Herrolds and the Blassers both lived on the west bank. The compiler
believes that the Blasser's are buried on the now almost forgotten
plot, opposite the lower Herrold's
school house in Union Township.
This cemetery is on the farm once
owned by the Blassers.

CONRAD BLOMPTON (or Blom-
pon) was assessed in Beaver Township for the first time in 1799. He
operated a gristmill at that time.
No military record was located.

HENRY BLOOM was assessed as
a laborer in Lower Smithfield
Township, Northampton County,
Pa., in 1772. He was assessed in
Penn Township for the first time
in 1799, and his occupation designated as a weaver. He probably had
a military record, but the compiler
did not find it.

JOHN BLOOM was assessed as a
tenant farmer in Penn Twp. in 1774.
The 1776 list does not contain his
name. It is possible that Henry,
mentioned above, was his son.

DAVID BLYLER, millwright, was
assessed in Penn Township for the
first time in 1799. It is believed
that he was of the same family that
later lived in Union County. No military record was found.

LIEUTENANT WILLIAM BLYTHE
was one of the very earliest residents
of what is now Snyder County. He
lived at the mouth of the Middle
Creek as early as 1768. On February
3, 1755, he was granted a warrant
for 50 acres of land in Cumberland

County, in that section south of the
Middle Creek, which is now Snyder
County. Prior to the French and Indian War, he was an Indian trader
at Shippensburg. On November 1,
1756, he was an Ensign in the 2nd
Battalion of the 2nd Regiment of the
Pennsylvania State Troops. On December 24, 1757, he was a Lieutenant
in the Pennsylvania Regiment of
Foot, and he remained in active service until after the Bouquet expedition to Ohio. During the years 1758
and 1759, he was a Lieutenant in the
Militia, west of the Susquehanna River, and in August, 1763, he was an
officer in Colonel John Penn's Pennsylvania Regiment. On June 10, 1765,
he was one of the officers stationed
at Fort Augusta (Sunbury). For his
services in the French and Indian
War he, with other officers, was
granted some land in the Buffalo
Valley. At the time Frederick Stump
murdered White Mingo and several
other indians, Lieutenant Blythe
lived on the banks of the Middle
Creek, and it was he, on January 19,
1768, reported the matter to the Colonial Council in Philadelphia. Just
how long he remained a resident of
Penn Township is not known. The
tax lists of White Deer Township
(now in Union County) gave him as
a land owner in that district from
1778 to 1784, with the exception of
1781, when he was assessed in Mahoning Township of Northumberland
County. It is believed that he died
before 1793.

CHARLES BOATMAN lived in
Penn Township for a short time
around 1792, where he came from, or
where he is buried is unknown. He
died in the township because in August of that year, letters of administration were granted to his son, Chas.
Boatman, Jr. Since no military re-
ord could be found, it is believed he
was too old to serve in the Revolution
No one of the name of Boatman has
lived in Snyder County for many
years.

JOHN CONRAD BOBB (also Bopp,
Bop, Bob, Bub Bupe, Bube, Bubb,
etc.) was born in one of the Palatine
provinces of Germany on Feb. 5,
1740, and died near Middleburg, Pa.,
on Feb. 5, 1809, and is buried in the
Hassinger old cemetery, west of Middleburg. His parents were John Bobb
and Eleanor Klein. The elder Bobb
and his wife sailed from Rotterdam,
Holland, and arrived at the port of
Philadelphia, where he took the oath
of allegiance to England on Sept.
5, 1743. They sailed in the British
ship "Charlotta." John Bobb was
born about 1715, and died in Berks
County, Pa., in 1779. His wife, Elean-
or Klein, was born on February 5,

1719, and died near Middleburg, Pa.,
on March 5, 1801. She is buried in
the same cemetery as her son, mentioned above, and her daughter, Eva
Catherine, wife of John Hassinger.
The elder Bobb settled in Berks Co.,
but when Conrad grew up he seems
to have settled in Breaknock Township, Lancaster County, where in
1771, he was assessed with 100 acres
and personal property. His father
having died in 1779, he moved to his
mother's property in Berks County,
and nine or ten years later to what
is now Snyder County. He was assessed in Beaver Township for the
first time in 1789. Conrad operated a
hemp mill in Beaver Township for
some time. His wife was Elizabeth
Nelson. Their known children were:
Conrad, John, Peter, and two daughters. It is believed that they had other
children, because in the U. S. Census
of 1790, his family consisted of three
males over, and three under 16, and
six females. "Conrad" as he was
commonly known, served in Captain
John Rutherford's Company, 4th
Battalion of the Lancaster County
Militia. His sons, John and Conrad
are said to have served in the same
company during the War of 1812.

ADAM BOLLENDER, Sr., was born
in Germany and embarked for America at Amsterdam, Holland, in the
British ship "Good Intent," John
Lasly, Master. He arrived at Philadelphia, Pa., where he took the oath
of allegiance to the English government on October 23, 1754. Before
coming to what is now Snyder
County it is believed that he lived in
Lancaster County. He was assessed
in Penn Township for the first time
in 1774. In 1781 and thereafter for
a number of years, he was assessed
with 300 acres and personal property. In 1786 and 1787 he was
a constable in Penn Township.
In 1791 he was one of a board
of viewers appointed by the court to
locate a road from John Adam Fisher's ferry across the Isle of Que and
up the Penn's Valley. From 1799 to
1801, he was a road supervisor in
Penn Township. Adam, Jr., Fred, and
John were his sons. In 1776, he was
a member of the Committee of Safety from Penn Township, and he may
have had other services in the Revolution. His three sons were Revolutionary soldiers. He lived in Center
Twp., in 1800. His son, Adam, Jr.,
also lived there.

ADAM BOLLENDER, JR., was the
son of Adam Bollender, Sr. The name
is also given as Ballander, Ballinger,
Bollinger, Bolander, etc. Adam, Jr.,
was assessed in Penn Township for

the first time in 1778. He did not own any land at the time. Adam's wife was Magdalena Morr, daughter of Andrew Morr, Jr., of the Freeburg section. Andrew Morr, Jr. died in the year 1801, and his father, Andrew Sr. in the year 1771 in Penn Township. John Philip, son of Adam and Magdalena Bollender was baptized at the old Zion Lutheran church, north of Freeburg in 1787. Adam served as a private in Captain William Weirick's Company and in Captain Michael Motz's Company of Northumberland County. His brothers John and Frederick, and his father-in-law, were Revolutionary soldiers. In 1790, his family consisted of himself, wife, two sons and three daughters.

HENRY BOLLENDER lived in Penn Township in 1790. He had a wife but no children then.

JOHN FREDERICK BOLLENDER, commonly called "Fred," was a son of Adam Bollender, Sr. Fred was born on March 16, 1761, and died on January 13, 1832. His wife, Elizabeth—— was born on September 18, 1761, and died March 17, 1839. Both are buried in the Hassinger old cemetery, west of Middleburg. Frederick was assessed in Penn Township for the first time in 1785, with personal property only. Frederick served in Lieutenant Jacob Speeses' Party of Rangers from Northumberland County. His brothers Adam and John also served in the Revolution. In 1790, his family consisted of himself and five females.

JOHN BOLLENDER was a son of Adam Bollender, Sr. He was born about the year 1759. He was assessed in Penn Township for the first time in 1783 but evidently moved to some other section soon after the Revolution. Like his brothers, he served his country in the military forces. He served in Captain William Weirick's Company, and at another time in Captain John Moll's Company of the Northumberland County Militia. In 1790, his family had one male over and two under 16, and two females. In 1804, John was a Captain in the 77th Regiment, Penna. Militia. He lived in Center Twp. in 1800

GEORGE BOMBACH (also Bumbach) was born in Germany in 1717, and died in Penn Township in the year 1780. He embarked for America at Rotterdam, Holland, in the British ship "Samuel", Hugh Percy, master, and arrived at the port of Philadelphia, Pa., where he took the oath of allegiance to the English government on December 3, 1740. He was assessed in Penn Township for the first time in 1776. His widow and some

children survived him. No military record was found, but it is believed that he may have served during the Revolution.

JOHN BOMBERGER was a resident not a landowner in Paxton Township, Lancaster County, Pa., in 1772. The next year he was assessed as a freeman in Warwick Township of the same county. He was taxed in Penn Township for the first time in 1774. He must have returned to Lancaster County during the Indian uprisings, because in 1779, we find him again assessed in Warwick Township. He served as a private in the 3rd Co., 3rd Battalion of the Lancaster Co. Militia in 1780.

JOHN BONER was a native of York County. His stay in Penn Township did not last long. He served as a private in Captain Michael Motz's Company from Northumberland County.

GEORGE BOOP (also Boob, Bub, Bupe, Bube, etc.) was assessed in Penn Township for the first time in 1783. In 1785, he was granted a warrant of survey for 60 acres in Northumberland county (now Snyder County). In 1787, he was taxed with 50 acres and personal property. He served as a Private in Captain Patrick Watsons Company of the Northumberland County Militia, and probably lived in Buffalo Township, before becoming a resident of Penn.

ANTHONY BOUTCH (also Bouch, Boush, etc.) was assessed as a distiller in Beaver Township in 1789. His name seems not to have appeared before in what is now Snyder County. He was probably a native of Berks County, and is believed to have been a relative of Peter Bouch, who lived in Penn Township at an earlier date. No military record was found for Anthony. In 1790, he had four sons and three daughters.

PETER BOUCH, probably a relative of Anthony, mentioned above, lived in Penn Township around the year 1790. He probably came from Berks County and it is believed that he returned there. There are indications that he was a descendant of John Michael Boush, a German, who sailed for America from Rotterdam, Holland, in the British ship "Robert and Alice", arriving at Philadelphia, Pa., where he took the oath of allegiance to the English government on December 3, 1740. Peter served as a private in Lieutenant Jacob Spees' Party of Rangers from Northumberland County.

DANIEL BOWER was assessed as a single freeman in Penn Township for the first time in 1781. It is thought that he was a relative of

Henry, Peter, and Philip Bower who lived in Penn Township during and after the Revolution. In 1796, when Mahantango Township was formed from the lower part of Penn, he was assessed in the new district. His wife was named Sabilla ——. Their daughters Catherine, born February 23, 1791; Anna Maria, born September 3, 1793, and Agnes, born March 12, 1795, were baptized at Botschaft's (Grubb's) Church in Mahantango (now Chapman) Township. Due to the fact that the Sheterly and the Gottshall's stood sponsors for these children, it is believed that they were relatives of Daniel, or his wife. In 1781, Daniel served forty days as private in Lieutenant Peter Grove's Party of Robinson's Rangers from Northumberland County. A copy of the receipt which he gave Lieutenant Grove for his pay is now part of the Pennsylvania Archives.

HENRY BOWER was assessed in Penn Township for the first time in 1771. On July 11, 1746, a Henry Bower enlisted in Captain John Diemer's Company then in the service of the Province of Pennsylvania. His age was given as 22 years, and his occupation as cooper. The list of 1771 makes no distinction between residents and non-residents, and as later lists designate him as a non-resident landowner, he may never have lived in Penn Township. His holdings in the township totalled 200 acres, and it is believed that some of his descendants occupied them after the Revolution. He was probably a native of Northampton County. On June 15, 1782, a Henry Bower was a private, 7th class, in Captain Felix Good's 7th Company, 4th Battalion of the Northampton County Militia.

JACOB BOWER was born in or near Lancaster, Pa., in 1764 or 1765, and died in Butler County, Kentucky, in 1837. He was assessed as a single freeman in Penn Township in 1785, and later he received a pension under the name of "Jacob Borah", and in his application for a pension stated that he enlisted at Sunbury, Pa., and that he served under two captains, one of them named Weaver. The supposition is that prior to becoming of age he lived in Penn Twp., and served as a ranger of militiaman under Capt. Michael Weaver, who time and again led the militia aginst the Indians in the Buffalo and Penns Valleys.

PETER BOWER in 1771 and 1772 was listed as a freeman in Donegal Twp., Lancaster Co., Pa. His name appeared on the Penn Twp. tax list for the first time in 1774 but for a number of years he was designated as

SNYDER COUNTY PIONEERS

13

a non-resident landowner. In 1787, he was granted a warrant of survey for 300 acres in Northumberland (now Snyder) County, and it is believed that he became a permanent resident of Penn Township from that date on. Due to the fact that he served as a private in Captain Michael Weaver's Company of the Northumberland County Militia, it is believed that he lived in the township for a while, and then returned to Lancaster County, and later again came back to this section. Peter Bower's wife was named Catherine ———. They had a daughter named Anna Catherine, who was born on Jan. 6, 1792, and baptized on March 17, of the same year at the Botshcaft's (Grubb's) Church, in the now Chapman Township. He probably was a son of Peter Bower who died in Penn Twp. in 1785, and some of this sketch may apply to the older Peter.

PHILIP BOWER, innkeeper, was assessed in Penn Township for the first time in 1799. It is believed that he was the same Philip Bower who died in West Buffalo Township (now Union County) in 1816. In his will, recorded at Lewisburg, he mentions his wife, Mary, a son, John, and refers to other children but gives no names. In the year 1786, a Philip Bower was assessed with 400 acres and personal property in Mahoning Township, Northumberland County. The same or an other of the same name, was assessed with 50 acres and personal property in Augusta Township in same county, in 1787. A Philip Bower from Berks County, and one from Washington County, served in the military forces during the Revolution. A Casper Bower (Bauer) died in Northumberland County in 1794.

GEORGE BOWERMAN (also Bauerman, Bauermann, Bowermann, Bourman, etc.) was probably a non-resident landowner in Penn Township. His name appears on the tax list for the first time in 1771. John and Peter may have been his sons, and were probably tenants on his land in what is now Snyder Co. In 1785, George was a resident of Weisenberg Township, Northumberland County, and was taxed there with 150 acres and personal property. In 1787, he was still designated as a non-resident land owner in Penn Township. No military record was found for him, but the compiler believes that he served in the Northampton County Militia. The U. S. census of 1790, stated that his family had three males over and two under 16, and four females; and that he lived in Penn Township. He asked for tax exemption in 1778, because the ene-

my was destroying property and crops.

JOHN BOWERMAN is believed to have been a son of George Bowerman of Weisenberg Township, Northampton County, Pa. He was assessed in Penn Township for the first time in 1778, and was probably a tenant on his father's land. For a number of years from 1781, he was taxed with 150 acres and personal property. Peter may have been his brother. In 1780, John was a private in Lieutenant Jacob Bard's Party of Rangers from Northumberland Co.

PETER BOWERMAN was probably a son of George, and brother of John, mentioned above. He was assessed in Penn Township for the first time in 1782, and since it was only for personal property, it is believed that he was a tenant on some of George's land. No military record was found for him, but it is believed that he had one.

GEORGE A. BOWERSOX (also Bauersox, Bauersax, Bowersocks Boursax, etc.) was a son of Paul Bowersox, a Revolutionary soldier, who died in 1806. George was born on April 1, 1774, and died on March 29, 1852. His wife, Marie———, was born in 1776, and died on March 24, 1860. Both are buried in the Salem cemetery in Center Township, Snyder County, Pa. George was a mason and was assessed in Penn Township for the first time in 1799. He had five brothers.

PAUL BOWERSOX (also Bauersachs) was born in Germany probably about the year 1745. He embarked for America in the British ship "Betsey," Andrew Bryson, master, probably from the port of Rotterdam, Holland, but last from London. He arrived at Philadelphia, where he took the oath of allegiance to the English government on December 4, 1771. It is supposed that he lived in an eastern county for a few years. He was assessed in Penn Township for the first time in 1778. In 1787, he was assessed with 100 acres and personal property. He died near Middleburg, Pa., in 1806, and is buried in the Hassinger old cemetery, west of Middleburg. His grave is marked with a stone marker with the initials "P. B." His sons were George A., Michael, Benjamin, David, John, and Jacob. Paul served in Captain William Weirick's Company of the Northumberalnd County Militia. In 1790, his family consisted of himself, three sons under 16, and four females.

JACOB BOWMAN was assessed in Mahantango Township for the first time in 1796. In 1788, a Jacob Bowman, tailor, was assessed in Low-

hill Township, Northampton Co. Maybe they were the same person. No less then three men of this name served in the military forces from Pennsylvania during the Revolution, several of them from Lancaster Co., but the compiler is unable to separately identify them.

ROBERT BOYD was first assessed in Penn Township in 1771. It is believed that he was a native of Lancaster County. Several men of this name served in the Revolution, one of them was a private in the 9th Pennsylvania Regiment, Continental Line.

CHRISTIAN BOYER was born on March 16, 1759, and died on November 16, 1839. His wife's name was Christina. They are buried in the St. Peters Cemetery in Freeburg. Some claim Christian's first name was Christopher, but the compiler doubts this. Indications are that he came from Berks County, where we find a Christian Boyer a resident of Bern Township in 1779. A Christian Boyer, carpenter, lived in Reading in 1785. Records indicate that Christian Boyer opened a store about a mile north of Freeburg, near the old Zion Lutheran church in the year 1789, and in 1797 he opened a store in the village of Freeburg. He built the house in Freeburg which was owned by the late F. C. Moyer. Some claim that he came from Northampton Co., or from Berks, adjoining the Northampton County line. He was probably a brother of Philip (1746-1832), who also settled in the Freeburg section. These men are the first of this name to settle in the locality. In 1804, Sarah, a daughter of Christian and Christiana Boyer was baptized at the old Zion Lutheran church, north of Freeburg. Christian Boyer received depreciation pay for services in the Northampton County Militia, during the Revolution.

JOHN BOYER, was a relative of Christian Boyer, mentioned above. He was assessed in Penn Township for the first time in 1799. He was a blacksmith by trade. Several men of this name served in the Revolution.

PHILIP BOYER was born on July 3, 1746, and died on March 24, 1832. His wife was Catherine———, who was born on January 29, 1762, and died on January 8, 1835. Both are buried in St. Peters cemetery in Freeburg. Philip is supposed to have come from Lancaster County. Francis (1790-1876) was probably a son of his. Philip Boyer came to what is now Snyder County around the year of 1800. He served as a private in Captain Martin Weybright's Company, 8th Battalion of the Lancaster County Militia.

PHILIP BREINER was probably a son of John Breiner of Lynn Twp., Northampton County, Pa. Philip was assessed for the first time in Lynn Township in 1785. He owned no land then. In 1789 he was assessed in Beaver Township for the first time. A Philip Breiner served as a private, 3rd class, in the 6th Company, 6th Battalion of the Northampton Co. Militia.

FRANCIS PETER BRENNER (Brenner is the German for Burner, which may have been corrupted to Burns) was born in Germany about the year 1725. He sailed from London, England, in the British ship "Pennsylvania Packet," Robert Gill, master, arriving at Philadelphia, Pa., where he took the oath of allegiance to the English government on November 12, 1768. For a time Francis lived in the vicinity of Stouchsburg, Berks County, Pa., and on October 30, 1772, he received a warrant of survey for 100 acres in Northumberland (now Snyder) County. He was assessed in Penn Township for the first time in 1774. In 1785. he was granted a warrant for additional land, and in 1787 he was taxed with 400 acres and personal property. Francis Peter Brenner's wife was Mary Catherine Elizabeth———, and they were the parents of two children; Francis Ludwig Brenner, and John Daniel Brenner. The Brenners lived in the vicinity of Freeburg and may have been related to the Albrights. Francis Peter died in 1807, and left a will which is recorded at Sunbury, Pa. Francis Peter served as a private in Captain James Boevard's Company of Militia (or Rangers) from Northumberland County. In 1790, his family consisted of two males over 16 and two females.

FRANCIS LUDWIG BRENNER, son of Francis Peter Brenner, mentioned above, was born in Germany about the year 1750, and died in what is now Snyder County in 1787. He arrived on the same ship with his father and took the oath of allegiance at Philadelphia, Pa., on November 12, 1768. Francis Ludwig married Catherine Elizabeth Helwig and they had a daughter named Catherine. It is believed that Francis Ludwig served in the Revolution, but the compiler was unable to locate his record, probably due to the fact that the name was variously spelled as Brenard, Bernard, Barnard, Brannar, Branner, etc. He was assessed as a single freeman in Penn Township in 1781. His wife and Frederick Albright were administrators of his estate. Frederick was the grandfather of Catherine Elizabeth.

JOHN DANIEL BRENNER, son of Francis Peter Brenner, and brother of Francis Ludwig, was born in Germany in 1756, and accompanied his parents to America in 1768. On Whitsunday, 1772, he was confirmed as a member of the Tulpehocken (Christ) Lutheran Church, near Stouchsburg, Pa. He came to what is now Snyder County prior to or during the Revolution. John Daniel was married, and had one daughter. Her name was Catherine Elizabeth, and she married John Berry (See his sketch in this work). John Daniel may have been the John Brenner who died in Penn Township in 1792. It is believed that John Daniel was a Revolutionary soldier.

NICHOLAS BRESSLER was assessed in Penn Township only in the year 1776, and may never have actually lived in Snyder County. In 1779, a Nicholas Bressler lived in Lampeter Township, Lancaster Co., Pa., and from 1781 he was assessed in Pine Grove Township in Berks Co. In August and September, 1780, a Nicholas Bressler was a private in Captain Conrad Shierman's Company, 6th Battalion, Berks County Militia. A man of the same name, and probably the same man, in 1776, was a private in Captain John Lesher's Company, Patton's Battalion of Berks Co. An older Nicholas Bressler was a private, 6th class, 6th Company, 1st Battalion of the Lancaster County Militia in 1782. He was born in 1754. In 1840, at the age of 86 years, he was a pensioner in Haines Twp., Center County, Pa. His father was probably Philip Bressler.

JOHN BRIGHT was probably a native of Bern Township, Berks Co., Pa. His name appears on the Penn Township tax list for the first time in 1774 and on some later lists he is designated as a non-resident landowner. The exact date of his first residence is unknown to the compiler, but he died in Washington Township, Union (now Snyder) Co., Pa., and his will was recorded at Lewisburg, Pa., on April 16, 1820. Daniel and Michael were probably his sons. He served during the Revolution and his record may be found on page 23, vol. 13, 2nd series of the Pennsylvania Archives. John Bright's wife was Margaret, daughter of Alexander Schaffer, founder of Schaefferstown, Lebanon Co., Pa.

DANIEL BRIGHT, probably a son of John Bright, mentioned above, was assessed in Penn Township for the first time in 1774. At that time he may have been a tenant on his father's land. It is believed that he

was a Revolutionary soldier, but no record was found for him. John and Daniel were non-residents in 1774.

MICHAEL BRIGHT is believed to have been a relative of the Brights mentioned above. Some think he was a native of Philadelphia Co., Pa. He was a non-resident owner of 300 acres of land in Penn Township as early as 1781, and was assessed as a resident for the first time in 1787. When Mahantango was formed from part of Penn in 1796, he was assessed there. In the 1790 census his family consisted of himself, four sons under sixteen years, and three females, one of whom was his wife. The Pennsylvania Archives state that he was a private in the Flying Camp during the Revolution.

JOSEPH BRITTON was born on March 7, 1755 in Bucks or Montgomery Co., Pa., and died in what is now Chapman Township, Snyder Co., Pa., on September 26, 1830. He became a resident of what is now Chapman Township prior to 1800, and followed the occupation of farming. In 1820, he had a wife and two daughters. His will was recorded at Lewisburg, Pa., on October 10, 1830. His will mentions two daughters; Mary (Polly), married to William Carwell, and Anna, married to Benjamin Borris (maybe Bertch). He was a pensioner. In the spring of 1776, at John Stetlers Tavern, Limerick Township, Montgomery Co., Pa., he enlisted in Captain Caleb North's Company of Colonel Anthony Wayne's Regiment, Pennsylvania Line, and marched with same to Fort Ticonderoga. He and his wife are buried in the old part of the cemetery at Grubb's church in Chapman Township.

DANIEL BROSIUS seems to have been a resident of Penn Township for a short time during the Revolution. He probably was a brother of Nicholas, Jr., and George, both Revolutionary soldiers. In 1787, he was assessed with a sawmill and personal property in Mahantango Township of Northumberland Co. He served as a private in Captain John Molles Company from Northumberland Co. In 1790, his family consisted of two males over and two under 16; and three females.

GEORGE BROSIUS seems to have been the son of Nicholas Brosius, Sr., of Mahanoy Township, and a brother of Nicholas, Jr., and Daniel. If they did not live in Penn Township, they at least served with those who did. In 1781, and thereafter, he was assessed with 50 acres and personal property in Mahanoy Township of Northumberland Co. At one time he was a private in Captain William Weirick's Company of the Northumberland County Militia, and on January 30, 1777, he was a member of Captain Benjamin Weiser's Company of the German Regiment, Continental Line, stationed at Philadelphia. Weiser's company was largely raised in what is now Snyder County. In 1790, his family consisted of two males over and one under 16, and one female.

NICHOLAS BROSIUS seems to have been a son of Nicholas Brosius, Sr., and a brother of Daniel and George, mentioned above. During the early days of the Revolution it is believed he lived in what is now Snyder County. He was assessed in Mahanoy Township for the first time in 1778, and for a number of years thereafter. He too, served as a private in Captain Benjamin Weiser's Company of the German Regiment, Continental Line, and was stationed at Philadelphia on January 30, 1777. In 1790, his family had one male over and two under 16, and four females.

DANIEL BROUGHT (also Braucht, Braught, etc.) was granted a warrant of survey for 100 acres in Cumberland County in 1773, but since the county lines were not definitely located at that time, it is believed that this land lay within the confines of what is now Snyder Co. His name appeared on the Penn Township tax list from 1776 to 1782, and it is evident that he was a non-resident landowner during the period. In 1773, he was assessed with 100 acres and personal property in Paxton Township, Lancaster (now Dauphin) Co. He was a private, 8th class, 2nd Company, 8th Battalion of the Lancaster County Militia.

ADAM BROUSE (also Brause, Braus, Brous, Brauss, Browse, etc.) was assessed with 175 acres and personal property in Macungie Twp., Northampton Co., Pa. He was assessed for the first time in Penn Twp., in 1798, and in that year was taxed with a sawmill, gristmill, and still. He died in 1802 and is buried at Kratzerville, Pa., but his grave seems to be unmarked. Abraham and John were probably sons of his. Adam was a private, 4th class, 6th Co., 1st Battalion of the Northampton County Militia on November 1, 1781.

JOHN BROUSE was granted a warrant of survey for 100 acres in Cumberland County on February 6, 1755. Part of Penn Township was attached to Cumberland County then. John's name appeared on the Penn Township tax list for the first time in 1774. The 1781 list designated him as a non-resident landowner. It is

doubtful if he ever lived here. The compiler believes he was Adam's father. No military record was found for John.

LUDWIG BROWER evidently lived in Penn Township for a short time around the year 1785. His wife was named Elizabeth, and their daugther, Catherine Elizabeth Brower was baptized that year at the old Zion Lutheran church, north of Freeburg. No military record was found.

GEORGE BRUMBACH (maybe Bumbach, or Bombach) was assessed in Mahantango Township for the first time in 1796. The compiler thinks the name was "Bombach" rather than "Brumbach," and that he was the son of George Bombach who died in Penn Twp. in 1780. The widow of the George who died in 1780, was assessed in Penn Township for a number of years. A George Brumbach lived in Frankstown Township, Bedford Co., Pa., in 1783. No military record was found.

GEORGE BRYAN, blacksmith, was assessed for the first time in Penn Township in 1799. At least three men of this name served in the Revolution, from Pennsylvania.

PHILIP BRUNER lived in Beaver Township in 1790. There were six males and four females in his family then.

FREDERICK BUBB (also Bub, Bube, Boob, Bobb, Boop, etc.) was assessed in Penn Township for the first time in 1782. He was taxed with personal property only, at the time. In 1787 the same condition existed. No military record was found. In 1790, his family consisted of one male over and two under 16 and three females.

DANIEL BUCHANAN (also Buckannon, Buckhannon, etc.) lived in Penn Township at some period during the Revolution. No record of his assessment was located. He received depreciation pay for services in the Northumberland County Militia.

JAMES BUCHANAN may have been a brother of Daniel mentioned above. In 1781, he was assessed as the non-resident owner of 300 acres in White Deer Township, and it is believed that at that time he was a resident of Penn Township. In 1783, he was taxed as a resident of White Deer Township (now Union County). It is believed that James Jr. and David were sons of his. He received depreciation pay for services in the Northumberland County Militia. He lived in Penn Township in 1790, and his family had one male over 16, and two females.

JOHN BUCHER, blacksmith, was assessed as a single freeman in Augusta Township, Northumberland Co., Pa., in 1785. He was assessed in Penn Township for the first time in 1799. He was married about the year 1788. No less than three people of his name served in the Revolution from Pennsylvania.

JOHN BUCHTEL (also Buchtol, Buchtil Buchtill, Booktill, Booktel, etc.) was born in Wurtenberg, Germany about the year 1730. He embarked for America at Rotterdam, Holland, on the British ship "Edinburgh," James Russell, master. He arrived at the port of Philadelphia, Pa., where he took the oath of allegiance to the English Government on September 14, 1753. Buchtel, like many other immigrants of that period, was unable to pay for his passage across the ocean, and was therefor bound out to the person who had bought his services, until the debt was cancelled. While serving his indenture he met a young woman of the neighborhood, who was also in servitude, and they were subsequently married. He was assessed in Penn Township for the first time in 1774, and it is stated that he lived at or near McKees Half Falls. In 1786, he was assessed with 250 acres of land and personal property. Prior to coming to what is now Snyder County, he lived in Exeter Township, Berks County. In 1791, he became a resident of Haines Township (now Centre County, Pa.,) and in 1797 he lived in the Brush Valley, Miles Township, Center County, where he died in 1809. He is buried at Rebersburg, Pa. In 1790, his family consisted of his wife and himself. After his death about 1812, some of their children moved to Ohio, settling around Uniontown and Akron. They took their aged mother with them, and she died there some years later. The Buchtels had nine children: John (who married Catherine Snyder); Martin (who married Eva Walter); Peter (who married Margaret Kreamer); Solomon (who married Marie Reber); Lucy (who married Nicholas Bierly, son of Melchoir); Agnes (who married Michael Meyer, or Moyer, son of Jacob); Elizabeth who married John George Meyer, now Moyer, son of Jacob, and brother of Michael, mentioned above); Catherine (who married Simon Bickel, son of Tobias Bickel, Sr.,) and Maria (who married Abraham Kreamer). John Buchtel served as a private in the 5th Company, 3rd Battalion of the Berks County Militia, during the early days of the Revolution, and it is believed that he also served in the

Northumberland County Militia. Several of his sons and sons-in-law also were Revolutionary soldiers. One of his great-grandsons, John R. Buchtel, founded Buchtel College, now the University of Akron, at Akron, Ohio. The compiler has a rather complete genealogy of the elder generations of this family, and of some of the families with whom they intermarried.

NICHOLAS BULL, (or BUSH) tailor, was a resident, but not a landowner in Warwick Township, Lancaster County, Pa., in 1771. He was assessed in Penn Township for the first time in 1789. The compiler found no military record for him, but believes he served in the Revolution.

In 1790, the Nicholas Bush family had one male over and two under 16, and four females. They lived in Penn Township at the time.

ABRAHAM BUNKER was a resident of Middletown, Lancaster (now Duphin) County, Pa., in 1773. He was assessed in Penn Township for the first time in 1776. In 1782, he lived in Jack Township, Cumberland (now Juniata) County. In the earlier days that section was considered part of Penn Township. In 1796, he was granted a warrant of survey for 100 acres in Cumberland County. The village of Bunkertown, Juniata County, was probably founded by, or named for this man. An Abraham Bunker also lived in Reading in 1784. No military record was found under this name.

WILLIAM BURCHARD (also Birchard) was assessed on the Penn Township list of 1771. He probably came from Lancaster County, and later returned here. A man of his name served in the 1st Battalion of the Lancaster County militia, during the Revolution.

CHARLES BURCHFIELD (also Birchfield) was granted a warrant of survey for 25 acres in Northumberland (now Snyder) County, on November 7, 1792. His name appeared on the Penn Township list for the first time in 1793. When Mahantango Township was formed from the southern part in 1793, he was assessed there. No military record was found for him.

PHILIP BUNKHART, Sr., (also Bockhart, Burckhart, etc.) in 1799 was a resident of the Mulberry Ward, east part, city of Philadelphia. In 1782, he was a trustee of the estate of Sarah Thompson there. He was assessed in Mahantango Township for the first time in 1796. He was evidently an attorney, or at least a justice of the peace, because he is

mentioned in a number of old wills as the executor, and on various occasions was appointed an administrator. He was also a witness on a number of wills and judging from the similarity of the penmanship, he was the writer of them. One of these wills was that of Captain Simon Herrold, made in 1827. He must have been a close friend and neighbor of the Herrolds, and is buried in the same cemetery as the older members of this pioneer family, namely, the old, and now almost forgotten cemetery across the road from the Lower Herrold's school house, south of Port Trevorton, Union Township, Snyder County. His tombstone, a common field stone, is the only one remaining in this cemetery which contains an inscription. The inscription is merely his name and the date of his death either 1835 or 1836. Philip, Jr. (buried in the old Lutheran Cemetery in Selinsgrove), Jacob, Benjamin, and Wendell were probably his sons. It is believed that he served in the Philadelphia County Militia, but the compiler did not find a service record for him. Later data indicates that he lived in East District Township, Berks County Pa., at the time of the U. S. Census of 1790. He was single, and may have been the son of Jacob Burkhart of the same township. He served in the Revolution and his grave is marked.

CONRAD BUSSINGER (also Businger, Bisinger, Breisinger, etc.) was a native of Northampton County. He was assessed in Penn Township for the first time in 1785, and in that year owned personal property only. On May 2, 1787, he was granted a warrant of survey for 100 acres in Northumberland, (now Snyder) Co. This land lay in the western part of the county, because in 1789 he was taxed with land and personal property in Beaver Township. In 1778, he was a corporal in the 3rd Company, 3rd Battalion, and in 1782, a private 3rd class, in the 3rd Company, 6th Battalion of the Northampton Co. Militia.

He was born in 1752, moved to Ravenna, Ohio, from what is now Snyder County, in 1801, and to Tallmadge, Summitt County, Ohio, in 1809. He is buried in a private cemetery at Tallmadge. He married Barbara Yancer, who was born in Pennsylvania on December 18, 1753, and died on March 16, 1816.

GEORGE CABLE seems to have been a resident of Penn Township for a short period. He may have been the same man who was granted a warrant of survey for 400 acres of land in Westmoreland County, Pa.,

on April 4, 1794. He was a private in Captain John Moll's Company of the Northumberland County Militia.

LIEUTENANT CLARY CAMPBELL was assessed as a tenant on the land of Charles Gemberling in Penn Township in 1781. He previously resided in the Bald Eagle settlement and it is believed that he returned there. His name did not appear on the Penn Township list after 1781. He died near Howard, Center County, Pa., in 1809. In 1778, he was a lieutenant in the Northumberland County Militia under Colonel Cookson Long. He also served in Robinson's Rangers.

PETER CAMPBELL was probably a son of Clary Campbell, mentioned above. The Campbells had lived in the Bald Eagle settlement, but left there and temporarily lived in Penn Township, during the worst of the Indian raids. A Peter Campbell was granted a warrant of survey for 400 acres in Westmoreland County in 1793. The Peter of this sketch, served as a private in Captain John Black's Company from Northumberland County, during the Revolution. A Peter Campbell served in the Washington County Rangers.

JACOB CARPENTER was listed on the Penn Township tax list of 1768, but the name disappeared several years later, and it is believed that he returned to either Earl or Lampeter Township, Lancaster Co., Pa. On June 2, 1774, he was granted a warrant of survey for 300 acres in Northumberland, now Snyder Co., but there is no evidence showing that he ever lived on this land. A J.cob Carpenter was Sub-Lieutenant for Lancaster County on April 1, 1780, and on August 6th of the same year he was a Lieutenant-Colonel, in command of the 5th Battalion of the Lancaster County Militia. He was still in command of this battalion in 1781.

FREDERICK CARROLL (also Carol, Carel, Carrell, Karel, Karol, Karroll, Karoll, etc.) was assessed in Beaver Township for the first time in 1789. It is believed that he was a son of Hugh Carroll, a Revolutionary soldier, who lived in Beaver Township at the same time. No military record was found for Frederick.

HUGH CARROLL was assessed in Penn Township for the first time in 1778, and may have lived elsewhere for a while after 1781, but in 1789 he lived in Beaver Township. In 1781, he was taxed with personal property and 50 acres of land. Frederick, mentioned above, may have been his son. In the U. S. Census of 1790, Hugh's family consisted of one male over, and four under 16 years, and four females.

and four females. Hugh served in Capt. Michael Motz's Company of the Northumberland Co. Militia.

GEORGE CATHERMAN lived in what is now Snyder County for part of the Revolutionary period. In 1786, he was taxed as a single freeman in Buffalo Township (now Union County). It is believed that he was a relative of Jacob Catherman. Both were soldiers. George served as a private in Captain John Moll's Co., from Northumberland County.

JACOB CHATHAM was assessed in Beaver Township in 1790. At that time his family consisted of two sons under 16, one daughter, his wife and himself.

JAMES CHRISTY was probably a native of Cumberland County. He was assessed in Beaver Township for the first time in 1789. A James Christy was granted 400 acres of land in Bedford County in 1794. A James Christy served as a private, 8th class, in Captain Joshua Brown's Company, 8th Battalion of the Cumberland County Militia. In 1790, he lived in Mifflin County, south of the Juniata River, and his family consisted of two males over and three under 16, and two females.

JAMES CLARK was probably a native of Lancaster County. He was assessed in Penn Township for the first time in 1787, and in 1789 he lived in Beaver Township. In the beginning he was assessed with personal property only. A James Clark was a Sergeant in the 7th Pennsylvania Regiment, Continental Line, and the same, or an other of the same name was a First Lieutenant in the 4th Battalion of the Lancaster County Militia in 1777. In 1790, his family consisted of one son under 16, three daughters, his wife, and himself.

ABRAHAM CLEMENS (also Clemmens, Clemmence, Clemence, Clemence, Clements, Clemmons, etc.) was assessed in Penn Twp., for the first time in 1772, but it seems that his name did not appear again. Because there was no distinction made in the earlier lists between resident and non-resident landowners, the compiler is not sure that this man ever lived in the county. In 1799, an Abraham Clemens, carpenter, lived in the city of Reading, and his name continued there for some years. Edward, Michael and Peter, who lived in the county (Snyder) were possibly relatives of his. An Abraham Clement served with the New Levies, and also in the 9th Pennsylvania Regiment, Continental Line.

EDWARD CLEMENS was prob-

ably a son or brother of Abraham. He was assessed in Penn Township for the first time in 1781. In that year he was taxed with 50 acres of land and personal property. No military record was found, but it is believed that he served during the Revolutionary period.

PETER CLEMENS was born in the year 1757, and died in what is now Chapman Township, Snyder County, Pa., on March 19, 1841. Before the Revolution Peter seems to have lived in Maiden Creek Township, Berks County, Pa. He was assessed in Penn Township for the first time in 1787, and was then designated as a single freeman. At one time he was a tenant on some of the Hehhodl holdings in Chapman or Union Township. Elizabeth, wife of Peter Clemens died in 1820. A Peter Clements served in both the 1st and 3rd Pennsylvania Regiments of the Continental Line. A Peter Clements aged 74, of Union (now Snyder) Co., was granted a federal pension July 21, 1819. This age and the one given above do not check, that there were two Peter Clements or Clemens. The Peter of Maiden Creek Township was listed as a single man in 1767, and the Peter who was 74 years old in 1819, must have been born in 1745, and in 1757, would have been 22 years old and probably single. There may have been two Peter Clemens' in Chapman Township, probably an uncle and nephew. Michael may have been a son of the older Peter. The Peter of Chapman Twp., in 1790, had one male over 16, and three females in his family.

ISAAC CLYMER, Shoemaker, was assessed in Penn Township for the first time in 1799. The tax list of Selinsgrove in 1802 carried his name, and in 1820 he was listed as a laborer in Selingrove. He came from Philadelphia or Bucks County. An Isaac Clymer served in the Bucks County Militia in May of 1780.

MICHAEL CLEMENS lived in what is now Chapman Township before 1800, and may have been a son of Edward Clemens who lived in that section as early as 1781. Michael's wife was Eva————. Three of their children were baptized at Grubb's church. The dates of their births were: Elizabeth, May 25, 1803; Susanna, January 13, 1805; and Christina. April 16, 1807. John and Juliana Clemens, and George and Susanna Clemens, at a later date. had children baptized at the same church.

LIEUTENANT JOHN COLEMAN probably came from Lancaster Co.,

and was assessed in Penn Township for the first time in 1780. In 1782, and for a number of years thereafter he lived in Mahanoy Township of Northumberland County. In 1792, he was granted a warrant of survey for 130 acres in Dauphin County, part of which touched Mahanoy Township. Before coming to Penn Township, he probably served as a private in Captain Isaac Adams' Company of the Lancaster County Associators in 1776. In May 1780, he was a Lieutenant in command of a party of rangers from Northumberland Co., and in 1782, he was a Lieutenant in the 4th Company, 1st Battalion of the Northumberland County Militia. A John Coleman, aged 84, was granted a pension on May 12, 1820. This man died in Indiana County, Pa., on December 5, 1830. A John Coleman was a private, 6th class, in Captain James Fisher's Company of the Cumberland County Militia in 1780. On Apr. 24, 1785, he was a Lieutenant in the 5th Company, 1st Battalion of the Northumberland County Militia.

DAVID COLLINS was assessed in Beaver Township for the first time in 1789. It is believed that he was a brother of Joseph, who lived in Beaver at the same time, and possibly too, of Moses, who lived in Penn Township from an earlier date. A David Collins served in the Washington County Militia.

JOSEPH COLLINS was listed as a single freeman in Beaver Township for the first time in 1789. It is thought that he was a brother of David. Joseph Collins was listed as one of the "18 months men" in the Northumberland County Militia during the Revolution.

MOSES COLLINS was assessed in Penn Township for the first time in 1780. He owned no real estate at the time. His name does not appear after 1782, and in 1788 with 150 acres of land and personal property in Barree Township, Huntingdon County, Pa. He served as a private in Captain John Moll's Company of the Northumberland County Militia. In 1790, he and wife were the only members of their family.

HENRY CONRAD lived in Northumberland County as early as 1776, and in Penn Township of same, around the year 1780. He was probably a brother of George Conrad. Both served in Captain John Clark's Company in 1776, and Henry was a private in Captain John Moll's Co., at a later date.

LIEUTENANT GEORGE CONRAD was probably a native of Lancaster Co. He was assessed in Penn Township for the first time in 1774. In 1781, and for a number of years thereafter he was taxed with 100 acres and personal property. On September 26, 1776, he enlisted as a private in the 1st Co., 4th Battalion of the Northumberland County Militia (Captain John Clark's Company). On October 8th of the same year he was commissioned First Lieutenant of the 5th Company of the same battalion.

JACOB CONRAD lived in Penn Township in 1790, at that time his family had in it four males over and one under 16, and four females.

JOHN CONRAD was assessed in Penn Township for the first time in 1781, and was designated as a single freeman. It is believed that he was a brother of George and Henry, mentioned above. In 1801, he contributed to a fund for the erection of the First Lutheran church in Selinsgrove, Pa. He served as a Private in Captain Michael Motz's Company from Northumberland Co.

MARTIN COOPER was listed as a single freeman in the city of Lancaster, Pa., from 1772 to 1782. He was a cooper by trade. His name appeared on the Penn Township tax list for the first time in 1799. A Martin Cooper was a private, 8th class, 1st Company, 8th Battalion of the Lancaster County Militia on July 10, 1782. He was a non-resident land-owner in Penn Township as early as 1774.

JOHN COX in the year 1766 had the plot surveyed for himself by William Maclay which George Gabriel seemed to occupy as a squatter. This land was near the old mouth of the Penns Creek and may have included some of the present site of Selinsgrove. There is no evidence that Cox ever actually occupied this land, or lived anywhere in Penn Township.

JOHN CREBS (also Crebbs, Cribs, Crips, Cripps, Krebs, etc) was assessed in Penn Township only in the years 1781 and 1782. He did not own any land at the time. It is believed that he lived in the township at an earlier date. He enlisted in Captain Casper Weitzel's Company at Sunbury, Pa., and was in the battle of Kings Bridge, N. Y., on September 1st., 1777. This organization eventually became a part of the 8th Pennsylvania Regiment, Continental Line, and Crebs appears on the roster of that organization.

JOHN CUMMINGS (also Cummins, Commons, etc.) was born about the year 1760, and died in the year 1829. He came to what is now Snyder County prior to 1800, and lived west of Middleburg. It is supposed that he is buried in the old Swineford cemetery in Middleburg. He married Catherine, daughter of Albrecht Swineford, the pioneer. He served as a private in the 4th Company, 10th Battalion of the Lancaster County Militia.

CHRISTIAN DAUBERMAN (also Doverman, Dowerman, Douberman, Doubermann, Douverman, etc.) was assessed in Penn Township for the first time in 1778, and in 1785 was taxed with 200 acres and personal property. In 1790, he was one of the road supervisors in Penn Township, and in the following years he was appointed one of the viewers to locate a road from the western end of John Adam Fisher's Ferry on the Isle of Que up into Penns Creek Valley. In 1803 he was one of the viewers for a road from Selinsgrove to Freeburg. In 1780, he was one of the first to learn of the massacre of the Stock family by the Indians at Kreamer. He is supposed to have been the father of John and Peter 1765-1839). Christian and Peter are buried in the old cemetery at New Berlin. In May, 1780, Christian was a private in Lieutenant John Coleman's Party of Rangers from Northumberland County. He received depreciation pay for services in the Northumberland County Militia. Tradition has it that the Dauberman family was originally French, but like so many other French protestants, emigrated to the protestant Germany, and after a few generations thehe, came to America. In 1790, his family consisted of three males over 16, and two females.

JOHN DAUBERMAN, carpenter, was assessed in Penn Township for the first time in 1799. It is believed that he was a younger son of Christian and a brother of Peter. John was a member of the Row's (Salem) Lutheran church, prior to 1790. Peter and his wife were also members of this church at the time, and an Elizabeth.

PETER DAUBERMAN, son of Christian Dauberman, was born in 1765 and died in 1839. His wife, Catherine Elizabeth——, was born in 1767 and died in 1854. Both are buried in the old cemetery at New Berlin, and their graves are marked. Prior to 1790, both of them were members of Row's (Salem) Lutheran church, two miles west of Selinsgrove. Peter's brother John, and an Elizabeth Dauberman, probably their sister, were members at the same time. At an early age Peter served in the Revolutionary forces and received depreciation pay for his services

in the Northumberland County Militia. In 1790 his family consisted of one male over and one under 16, and three females. At the time of his death Peter lived in what is now Union Township., Union Co., Pa. A Peter Dauberman (probably his son) was administrator of his estate.

GEORGE DEANER (also Deener, Deiner, etc.) was assessed in Penn Township only in the year 1780. No military record was found for him.

CHRISTOPHER DEININGER lived in Beaver Township in 1790. His family consisted of his wife, self and one son under 16.

JACOB FREDERICK DEININGER (also Dinninger, Dininger, Doninger, Donninger, etc.) was assessed in Penn Township for the first time in 1774. In 1789, he was a resident of Beaver Township. He died in Beaver Township in 1819, and he mentions in his will Christina Mitchell (daughter), Philip Mitchell (grandson), and Jacob Gillen (grandson). Frederick served as a private in Captain William Weirick's Company of Northumberland County.

JACOB DEITZ, blacksmith, was assessed in Penn Township for the first time in 1799. No military record was found for him.

LEONARD DELL was born in Crumru Township, Lancaster Co., Pa., about the year 1750, and died in Penn Township, Northumberland (now Snyder) County, Pa., in 1792. He was assessed in Penn Township for the first time in 1776, and was designated as a single freeman at the time. It is believed that he returned to Lancaster County for a time, because on November 16, he was a private in Captain Peter Decker's Company, Colonel Magaw's 5th Battalion of the Lancaster County Militia or Associators. Leonard Dell's land was sold for taxes to Major Anthony Selin, who in 1792 sold said land to Jacob Bard for 53 pounds. This land lay in what was then Beaver Township.

CHRISTOPHER DERING was born on November 4, 1756, and died in Penn Township on November 22, 1822. It is supposed that he is buried in an unmarked grave in the old Lutheran cemetery in Selinsgrove. He was assessed in Penn Township for the first time in 1783. He served as a private in the 5th Company, 5th Battalion of the Lancaster County Militia.

JOHN DERR was born on August 5, 1753, and died on November 27, 1846. He is buried in the old cemetery at New Berlin, Pa. Owing to the fact that he enlisted in Captain Benjamin Weiser's Company of the Ger-

SNYDER COUNTY PIONEERS

man Regiment, Continental Line, in 1776 and since said company was composed largely of rseidents of what is now Snyder County, it is supposed that he lived in Penn Twp., at the time 1776.

ABRAHAM DEVORE was a native of Northampton County, Pa., and was assessed in Penn Township for the first time in 1785. There is no evidence that he was a landowner at the time. During the Revolution he servedas a ranger, a militiaman, and in the continental line. On May 1, 1782, he was a private, 5th class, in Captain John Long's Company of the 5th Battalion, Northampton Co. Militia. From August 1st to October 9th, 1782, he served in the federal forces. Daniel Devore (1781-1852) probably a son is buried in the Lutheran cemetery at Centerville (Penns Creek Post Office) in Snyder Co. Nicholas may also have been a son. In 1790, his family consisted of one male over and three under 16, and three females.

MICHAEL DIEHLMAN (also Thielman) was a resident of Penn Township prior to 1790. His wife was Christina———. Without doubt they were relatives of Philip, mentioned below. Michael and his wife were also members of the church at Salem. Indications are that they did not remain in the Salem community for a long time.

FRANCIS DEWART was assessed in Penn Township for the first time in 1789. No further data was located.

PHILIP DIEHLMAN (also Dealman, Thielman, Diel, and later used regularly as Deal or Diel) lived in Penn Township prior to 1790, because at that time his name appeared on the roll of members of the Row's (Salem) Lutheran church, west of Selinsgrove. The compiler believes his name was "Philip Diehl" rather than "Philip Diehlman, or Thielman," and that he lived in Longswamp Township, Berks Co., Pa., in 1768,and he received a warrant of survey for 500 acres on land in Northumberland (now Snyder) County.on December 10, 1772. He evidently lived in Berks County during the war and received depreciation pay for services in the Berks County Militia. An Andrew Diehlman lived in Windsor Township of Berks County. John Deal and John Deal, Jr., were members of the church at Salem in 1811.

MICHAEL DIESE (probably meant Dreese) was assessed in Beaver Twp., for the first time in 1789. No further data was obtained.

ANDREW DILLMAN, JUNIOR, was born on October 21, 1751, and

died on May 21, 1823, in Bracken County, Kentucky. Between 1725 and 1730, Andrew Dillman, Sr., and Jacob Dillman, brothers, left Prussia (Germany) for the American Colonies. NOTE: (The compiler believes that the dates of their emigration are wrong, and that it was a later date, probably 1737). Andrew settled in what is now Adams County, Pennsylvania, and Jacob in Franklin County, Virginia. They were of the Dunkard faith. Andrew, Senior, had seven sons, but only three are known to the compiler, and they are, Conrad, George, and Andrew, Jr., subject of this sketch. He was pobably born in what was then York, but now Adams County, Pa. He was listed in Penn Township for the first time in 1776, and designated as a single freeman. In 1785, he was taxed with 100 acres and personal property. About 1794, he and his family moved to Bracken County, Kentucky, via Pittsburgh and the Ohio River, in a flatboat. He had learned the trade of wheelwright, and worked at this occupation for many years. On August 1, 1777, he married Barbara Roush, daughter of George Casper Roush, a pioneer settler in the Freeburg section of Snyder County. On the day of their marriage he returned to the war. Barbara was born in what is now Lebanon County, Pa., on December 17, 1759, and was baptized at the Hill church there. She died in Bracken County, Kentucky, on November 17, 1842. George Casper, father of Barbara, was a Revolutionary soldier, as were her brothers; John Jacob, John, and John George. Casper arrived in America in 1743, from Germany. Andrew Dillman, Jr., and his wife, Barbara Roush, had the following children: first child, born 1778, died in infancy; Eve, born 1779; George, born in March, 1781; John, born 1783, and baptized the same year at the old Zion Lutheran church, about a mile north of Freeburg, Pa.; Susan, born May 29, 1785; Barbara, born, February 2, 1787; Frederick, born on November 14, 1788; Andrew, born on November 7, 1790; Julia, born on October 15, 1791; Catherine, born on Dec 22, 1792; Elizabeth, born on December 18, 1795; Conrad, born on October 29, 1798; and Samuel, born in 1800. Andrew Dillman served under Captain Lewis Farmer in the 2nd Pennsylvania Regiment, Continental Line, and participated in the Battle of Long Island in 1776. On September 9, 1776, he was still a member of the 2nd Pennsylvania Regiment. He also participated in the battles of the Brandywine, Germantown, Monmouth and

Yorktown. He was a pensioner. One record indicates that he was a captain in the Northumberland County Militia after the war. Probably none of his descendants live in this section today. In 1790, his family consisted of one male over and three under 16, and six females. On April 24, 1785, he was an Ensign in the 7th Company, 1st Battalion of the Northumberland County Militia. He also served in Lieut. John Stoy's Company of the 2nd Pa. Regt., in the Revolution.

MICHAEL DILLMAN lived in Penn Township in 1790, and his family consisted of one male over and one under 16, and two females. Michael was probably a brother of Andrew.

FRANCIS DITTO (also Dito, Dido, Diddo, etc.) was a native of York County, Pa. Indications are that he was a resident of Penn Township as early as 1780, but he seems not to have been assessed before 1787, where he was taxed with 300 acres of land and personal property. In 1789, he was a resident of Beaver Township, which two years before had been cut from the western part of Penn. Francis lived near the junction of Swift Run and the North Branch of the Middle Creek, in what is today Beaver Township. He was a farmer, but was more keenly interested in hunting and trapping, and because of the scarcity of game in Pennsylvania, he moved to Pickaway County, in 1812. He married Eleanor, the oldest daughter of the pioneer, John Adam Gift in March, 1782. She was born September 15, 1758, and died in Seneca County, Ohio, in 1858. Their children were: John W. (1785-1853), a soldier in the War of 1812; George, Andrew, Johnson, Catherine, and Mary. John W. died in Seneca County, Ohio, in 1853, and his father died in the same county at an earlier date. Francis, his wife, and most of their children are interred in Seneca County. In May of 1780, Francis was a private in Captain John Snyder's Company, and at an other time he served in Captain Michael Weaver's Company from Northumberland County. It has been stated that he also served in the continental line and that he knew General Washington personally.

Francis Ditto was born at or near York, Pa., in 1756 or 1757. At the age of 20 he enlisted in Lieutenant John Stoy's Company of the 2nd Pennsylvania Regiment, Continental Line. His height was five feet six inches, and he was a weaver at the time of his enlistment. He is buried in an old private cemetery on the McIlheny farm in Eden Township, Seneca, Co.,

Ohio. The date of his death was June 16 or June 25, 1841.

Francis lived at McCollisters Town, York Co., when he enlisted for three years in 1777. He wintered at Valley Forge, fought in the Battle of Monmouth, taken prisoner at Newark, later exchanged. He was discharged Jan. 1, 1781. He had a twin brother named Jacob.

JOHN DITZLER was a single freemen in Bethel Township, Lancaster Co., Pa., in 1779. He was assessed in Penn Township for the first time in 1785, and in that year was taxed with 200 acres and personal property. He probably moved on in a few years, because no other data concerning him was located. He probably served in the Lancaster County Militia.

NICHOLAS DORNMILLER lived in Penn Township around the year 1790. His wife was named Mary. Their daughter Mary Catherine, was baptized at the Old Zion Lutheran church, north of Freeburg in 1791. There is some evidence that the name may have been "Dornmayer" instead of "Dornmiller," but the latter seems to be the one generally used. In 1784, Nicholas was taxed with 150 acres of land and personal property in Pine Grove Township, Berks County, Pa. On August 26, 1776, he was a private in Captain Michael Wolf's Company, stationed at South Amboy, N. J.

GEORGE DOWNER was taxed in what is now Penn Township in 1768. His name does not appear again. On September 3, 1792, a George Downer was granted a warrant of survey for 400 acres in Luzerne County, Pa. No military record was found.

JOHN JACOB DREESE (also Dries, Driess, Tries Treese, Trees, Driese, etc.) was born in Germany about the year 1720, and died in the western part of Snyder County, Pa., in 1794, and is probably buried at Beaver Springs, or Hassingers Old Cemetery. He embarked for America on the British ship "Neptune," John Mason, master, at Rotterdam, Holland, and landed at the port of Philadelphia, where he took the oath of allegiance to the English Government on Oct. 4, 1752. He lived in Berks or Northampton County, or both. He was a blacksmith, and in 1779, he was assessed with 250 acres and personalty in Albany Township, Berks County, Pa. He owned land in Penn Township as early as 1780, but did not become a resident of the district until 1785, and in that year he was taxed with 200 acres and personal property. The same year he was granted a warrant of survey for an additional 100 acres in Northumberland (now

Snyder) County. In 1789, he lived in Beaver Township. In his will, which was recorded at Sunbury, Pa., in 1794, he mentions the following as his children; Jacob Jr., John, Mary Magdalene, Peter, Mary Elizabeth, and Christina. He served in Capt. Nelson's Company, Northampton Co. Militia. Jacob had a brother named John.

JOHN JACOB DREESE, JR., probably came to what is Snyder County with his parents in the year 1785. He was born in Berks or Northampton County, Pa., in 1753, and died in the vicinity of Beavertown in August of 1823. He is buried in the old cemetery at Beaver Springs. Under the name John Trees he served in the Cumberland County Militia. There is some evidence to indicate that he may have preceeded his parents to the southwestern Snyder County section, and while living there, probably as a tenant on some of his father's land, served with the Cumberland County military organization.

JOHN DREESE was a son of John Jacob Dreese, Sr. He was born on August 21, 1752, probably at sea, and died in what is now Snyder County, Pa., in August, 1823. He is buried in the old cemetery at Hassinger's church, west of Middleburg, and his grave is marked "John Tris." He was taxed in Beaver Township for the first time in 1789. Under Pennsylvania Rifleman in 1776. He left no children.

PETER DREESE was a son of John Jacob Dreese, Sr. He was born in Albany Township, Berks County, Pa., about the year 1760. He probably came to what is now Snyder County about the year 1785, and was assessed in Beaver Township for the first time in 1789. In February, 1809, he was one of the executors of his uncle John's estate. He served in Captain Henry Hagenbuck's Company of the 2nd. Battalion, Northampton Co. Militia.

JOHN DREESE, brother of John Jacob, Sr., died in what is now Snyder County, on August 17, 1809. He is buried in the Old Hassinger Cemetery. His wife was named Anna Maria. They had a son John, Jr., and supposedly other children. He may have been the John Trees who served in the Cumberland County militia during the Revolution.

FREDERICK DREONE, surgeon, was assessed in Penn Township for the first time in 1798. No Military record was found for him. His stay in the section must have been short, because later lists do not carry his name.

FREDERICK DRUCKEMILLER (also Druckamiller, Druckemiller, Truckamiller, Truckamiller, etc) was a resident, but not a land owner in the village of Manheim, Lancaster County, Pa., during the early days of the Revolution. He was assessed in Penn Township for the first time in 1780, and in 1785 was taxed with 200 acres and personal property. He lived in the section around Salem, and prior to 1790, he and his wife, Christina, were members of the Lutheran congregation of Row's (Salem) church. He died in Penn Township in 1790, and his will is on record at Sunbury, Pa. It mentions his wife, and the following children: John Frederick, Peter, Mary Elizabeth, Margaret, Christina, Catherine, Magdalena, and Barbara. The last four children were quite young at the time of their father's death. Mary Elizabeth and Margaret were members of the Salem church before 1790. The Frederick of this sketch was the son of Peter Druckmiller, who arrived from Germany in the ship "Beulah" on September 7, 1753. Frederick served in the 5th Company, 7th Battalion of the Lancaster County Militia.

JOHN DRUCKENMILLER was probably a brother of Frederick. He died in Mahantango Township in 1799. The compiler was unable to learn when he first came to Mahantango Township. If he was a brother of Frederick, he no doubt served in the Revolution, probably in Lancaster County. Later evidence seems to indicate that John was a relative of Frederick, mentioned above, but that he was not his brother.

PETER DRUCKENMILLER arrived from Germany in the British Ship "Beulah," and took the oath of allegiance to the British government at the port of entry (Philadelphia) on September 7, 1753. He evidently became a resident of Heidelberg Twp., Lancaster County, Pa. He was assessedin Penn Township for the first time in 1771, having probably arrived in this section with the Herrolds, Meisers, etc. who came at that time. The evidence indicates that he returned to Heidelberg Township, because he was listed there as a resident, but not a landowner, in 1772. His name does not again appear on the Penn Township list until 1780, indicating that he may have remained in Lancaster County during the worst of the indian raids in this section. In 1781, he was taxed with 150 acres and personal property in Penn Township, and in 1789, he was granted a warrant of survey for 339 additional acres in Northumberland, now Snyder County. He died in Penn

Township in 1790, the same year that his son Frederick died. His will is recorded at Sunbury, Pa., and mentions his wife Anna Mary, and their children: Frederick and Elizabeth Stefser (intended probably for Steffen). The compiler believes that Peter served in the Lancaster or Northumberland County Militia, but did not find a record. Peter was born about the year 1722. Later data shows that John Frederick and his sister Elizabeth (Mrs. Andrew Haeffer or Heffer, each inherited 180 acres of land from their father when he died early in 1790. Frederick's half, after his death was sold to Andrew Morr and his sons, and later to Mathias Spotz of Berks County.

LIEUTENANT-COLONEL CHARLES DRUM was assessed with personal property in Strasburg Township Lancaster County, Pa., in 1779. On July 20, 1784, he was granted a warrant for 324 acres in Northumberland (now Snyder) County. A certain tract of land in or near Selinsgrove, was deeded to him and others in 1779. He became a resident of Penn Township in 1792, and lived in Selinsgrove. In 1794, he was taxed with a gristmill and sawmill. On November 25, 1795, he, Simon Snyder and Colonel Peter Hosterman were appointed by the court to locate a road from near Freeburg to Sunbury. In 1800, he was one of a board of viewers to locate a road across the Isle of Que from Selinsgrove to the Susquehanna River. In 1801, he was a subscriber to the fund for the erection of the First Lutheran church of Selinsgrove. On September 19, 1802, he was Penn Township's delegate to the Republican convention, held at Metzger's Hotel at Lewisburg. In 1804 he served on a board of viewers to locate a road from Salem to New Berlin. On January 1, 1806, he was appointed a Justice of the Peace for Penn Township. In April, 1809, he was one of the viewers for the erection of a new bridge over the Middle Creek at Bake Oven Hill, south of Selinsgrove. In April, 1811, he was appointed to a board of viewers to locate a site for a bridge across the Penns Creek, north of Selinsgrove. For years he conducted a tavern at the corner of Front and Pine streets on the Isle of Que, and for several decades that part of Selinsgrove was called Drumtown. Colonel Drum was born in 1748, and died in Selinsgrove, Pa., on October 15, 1811, and is supposed that he is buried in the old Lutheran cemetery at that place. He married Catherine Snyder, sister of Governor Siomn Snyder, and widow of Major Anthony Selin, the founder

of Selinsgrove. Major Selin died in 1792. She had two children with Major Selin; Anthony Charles Selin and Agnes Selin. Catherine Drum, mother of Colonel Drum, died in Selinsgrove in 1799. Catherine Snyder Selin Drum died many years after the death of her husband, one person says in 1862, but the compiler believes this is wrong. Colonel Drum served as a private in Captain John Hubley's Company of the 8th Battalion of the Lancaster Co. Militia, on April 21, 1781. On April 6, 1802, he was commissioned Lieutenant-Colonel of the 77th Regiment of Infantry, Pennsylvania Militia. In 1790, his family consisted of himself and two females. He was one of the petitioners for the formation of Mahantango Township in 1795.

CHARLES DUNKLE was listed on the Penn Township tax list for the first time in 1776, and at that time he was a single freeman. He must have gone to some other section, or returned to the place he came from, because his name does not appear again. No military record was found.

JOHN DUSING, son of Nicholas Dusing, was assessed as a single freeman in Lebanon Township, Lancaster County, Pa., in 1779, and with 250 acres and personal property there in 1782. His name appeared on the Penn Township tax list for the first time in 1793, and his occupation was given as shoemaker. In 1801, he contributed to the fund for the erection of the First Lutheran church of Selinsgrove, and he was still living in Selinsgrove in 1802. On october 17, 1780, he was a private in Captain Balzer Orth's Company of the 2nd Battalion, Lancaster County Militia, then serving in Northampton Co.

NICHOLAS DUSING was born in Germany and embarked for America at Rotterdam, Holland, on the English ship "Halifax," Thomas Coatam, master, and arrived at Philadelphia where he took the oath of allegiance to the British government on October 20, 1754. He probably lived in what is now Lebanon County, and was assessed in Penn Township (now Snyder County) for the first time in 1793. He died in the same year and his will is on record at Sunbury, Pa. The will mentions his wife, Dorothy, and their children; John, and Elizabeth (Mrs. John Hartman). Nicholas was a farmer and lived in or near Selinsgrove, and is probably buried in the old Lutheran cemetery in an unmarked grave. It is believed that he served in the Lancaster County Militia during the Revolution.

PATRICK EAGAN (also Egan,

Egan, etc.) lived in Penn Township around the year of 1780. He was probably a brother of William Egan who lived in the township at the same time. Patrick served as a private in Captain Charles Meyer's Co., from Northumberland County.

BERNARD (or Barnhart) EBERHART was assessed in Penn Township for the first time in 1780, and in 1785 and there after for some years was taxed with 150 acres and personal property. In 1789, he lived in Beaver Township. Frederick and Philip were probably relatives of his. The compiler believes that he was a son or grandson of Frederick Eberhart who came to America in the year 1737. In 1780, Bernard served as a private in Lieutenant Jacob Spees' Company of Rangers from Northumberland County. In 1790, he had six sons under 16 and four daughters.

FREDERICK EBERHART was first assessed in Penn Township in 1778, but it is believed that he returned to Northampton County between the years 1778 and 1783. In 1789, he was living in Beaver Township. He was probably a relative of Bernard and Philip, who lived in Penn Township from 1780. Frederick served in the Northampton County Rangers. There are some indications that there were two Frederick Eberharts, probably father and son. The writer is unable to tell which of these two men is here described. In 1790, he had four sons under 16, and three daughters.

PHILIP EBERHART may have been a son of either Jacob, Joseph or Peter, and in 1785 and 1786, was assessed with 220 acres and personal property in Upper Milford Township, Northampton County, Pa. He was assessed in Penn Township for the first time in 1788. It is believed that he was a relative of Bernard and Frederick Eberhart, who lived in Penn Township, some ten years earlier. In 1789, Philip lived in Beaver Township which formerly was part of Penn. Philip Eberhart was a private in the 2nd Company, 1st Battalion of the Northampton County Militia, on January 1, 1782. A Philip Eberhart arrived from Germany in the English ship "Royal Union," Clement Nicholson, Master, and took the oath of allegiance to the British government at Philadelphia, Pa., on August 15,1750.

JACOB ECKHART was born in Germany about the year 1730, and died in Mahantango Township, Northumberland (now Snyder) County, Pa., in 1809. He embarked for America at Rotterdam, Holland, on the

British ship "Ranier," Henry Browning, master, and arrived at the port of Philadelphia, Pa., where he took the oath of allegiance to the English government on September 26, 1749. Before coming to what is now Snyder County, Jacob lived in Mount Joy Township of Lancaster County. He was assessed in Penn Township for the first time in 1774 and in 1781 was taxed with 50 acres and personal property. When Mahantango Township was formed from the southern part of Penn in 1796, he was assessed there. His will was probated at Sunbury, Pa., on November 13, 1809. It mentions his wife, Christina, and their children; Jacob, Jr., Rosina Meiser, Mary Meiser, Elizabeth Miller, Barbara Eberhart, and Christina Livingood. The ship in which Jacob came to America contained immigrants from Hanau, Darmstadt, Isenberg, and Wurtemberg. On April 20, 1778, a Jacob Eckhart was a private in Captain Thomas Robinsons Company, either in Lancaster or Northumberland County. This may mean Robinson's Rangers. The Jacob who served in this organization may have been Jacob, Jr. His family had one male and two females in 1790.

WILLIAM EDMUNDSON probably came from Philadelphia, or possibly from Northampton County. He was assessed in Beaver Township for the first time in 1791. People of this name lived in Beaver or Spring Township as late as 1890. Several men of this name served in the Revolution.

WILLIAM EGAN (also Egin, Egen, Egeh, etc.) was assessed in Penn Township for the first time in 1780. In 1781, he was assessed with 100 acres and personal property. After 1785, he was assessed as a non-resident owner of 100 acres. It is evident that he moved to some other section. In 1792, he was granted a warrant of survey for 100 acres in Norhumberland County. This indicates that he did not leave the county, but merely moved to some other township. The compiler feels sure that this man served in the military forces, but he did not locate a service for him. It is believed that he was a relative of Patrick Egan, who lived in the township at the same time.

MICHAEL EGOLF (also Eguiph, Egulf, Egolf, etc.) was assessed in Penn Township for the first time in 1771. Later lists do not contain his name, and it is believed that he returned to Lancaster County. A man of his name served in the 8th Company, 1st Battalion of the Lancaster County Militia during the Revolution.

GEORGE ENGLE (also Engel, Angle, etc.) was assessed in Penn Township for the first time in 1799, and his occupation given as weaver. After coming here he lived in what is now Center Township of Snyder County. A George Engle of Northampton County served in the Revolution and applied for a pension on February 4, 1833. His age at that time was 78 years. J. Michael Engle (1787-1875), probably a son, is buried in the old cemetery at Kratzerville in Snyder County, Pa. George was born in Bucks Co., Pa., on Feb. 20, 1754. He came to what is now Snyder County in 1797. In June, 1776, he enlisted, served in the New Jersey campaign and for a time was a prisoner of war. He died in 1838. His wife was Elizabeth ———. Their children were: John, George, Jr., J. Michael, Peter, Solomon, Frederick, Elizabeth, Hannah, and Catherine.

JOHN EPLER was assessed in Penn Township for the first time in 1799, and lived in Middleburg in 1802. His occupation was that of nailmaker. He died in the year of 1806. Peter Epler may have been his son. Three men of the name John Epler served in the Revolution, the compiler is unable to identify the service of this one, if he served.

FREDERICK ESTERLINE was assessed in Penn Township for the first time in 1799. He was a carpenter. In 1814, 1815, and 1816, he was constable of Penn Township. He may have been the son of Jacob Esterly who served in Captain John Clark's Company of Northumberland Co., Associators in 1776. Frederick married Polly (Mary) the daughter of the pioneer, Jacob Gemberling. They had four or five children, when Polly died. The names of only two of these children are known to the writer, one of them being Jacob Esterline of Center Co., and the other Mary Ann Esterline, who married Michael Roush, becoming the great-grand-parents of the compiler. It is said that after the death of his wife, Frederick, gave his younger children to relatives to raise, and that he and his son Jacob moved to Brush or Sugar Valley in Center County, where both died many years ago. Some think that Frederick may have married again, but the compiler has no such information. Mary Ann Esterline was raised in the family of her maternal uncle, George Gemberling, west of Selinsgrove, where she met Michael, the son of John George Roush, a pioneer settler of the Freeburg section. No military record was found for Frederick. In 1786, a Peter and a Michael Enterline lived

in Montgomery Co., Pa. Later data proves that Frederick also had a son named Samuel and one, Frederick, Jr. These sons lived in Center and Clinton counties of Pennsylvania.

JACOB ETTINGER (also Hettinger) lived in Penn or a neighboring township, during the Revolutionary period. In 1780, he served as a private in Ensign Simon Herrold's party of Rangers from Northumberland County. Some Ettingers lived in what is now Adams Township of Snyder County. Henry, supposedly a son, lived in Center Township in 1800.

JOHN GEORGE ETZWEILER, Sr., was born in Germany and embarked for America at Rotterdam, Holland in the British ship "Rosannah," James Reason, Master. He arrived at the port of Philadelphia, Pa., where he took the oath of allegiance to the English government on September 26, 1743. The Herrolds and Hummels of Berks and later Snyder County were fellow passengers with him on the Rosannah. The immigrants on this ship came from Wurtenberg, Durlach and Switzerland. The compiler is not certain that this man ever lived in what is Snyder County, but it seems that he owned land in it. He had a son, John George, Jr., who was killed by the Indians while he was in the service of his country, during the Revolution, and the younger George may have been a tenant on his father's property.

JOHN GEORGE ETZEWILER, Jr., was a son of the man mentioned above. The younger George is supposed to have been a resident of Penn Township from about 1776. In May, 1780, while serving as a private in Captain George Overmire's Company of the Northumberland County Militia in Buffalo Valley, while he and three other men were on patrol duty at "French Jacob" Grossjean's mill were ambushed by the Indians and Etzweiler was killed. He was buried on the farm of Peter Slear in what is now Limestone Township in Union County. He left a widow named Mary. George Etzweiler who was assessed in Penn Township in 1799, was probably their son.

GEORGE ETZWEILER, potter, was assessed in Penn Township for the first time in 1799. The compiler believes he was the son of George, who was killed by the Indians in 1780. He contributed to the fund for the erection of the First Lutheran Church of Selinsgrove in 1801.

LIEUTENANT -COLONEL FREDERICK EVANS, son of George Evans, Jr., was born near the Trappe,

Montgomery County, Pa., in 1765. He was assessed in Penn Township for the first time in 1790. He served on a board of viewers to locate a road between Selinsgrove and Freeburg. In April, 1804, he was foreman of the "Grand Inquest," and later in the same year he was one of a board of viewers to locate a road from Salem to New Berlin. He moved to Lewisburg in 1806. In August, 1807, he was a member of the resolution committee of a war meeting held at Sunbury. About this time he returned to Penn Township, and on June 28, 1808, Philip Morr and he were delegates from Penn Township to the Democratic - Republican convention at Sunbury. He served as county surveyor and in 1810 and 1811 he was a member of the state legislature from Northumberland County. In 1822 he was a member of the Penns Creek Improvement Commission. On June 1, 1792, he was commissioned Lieutenant-Colonel of the 2nd Battalion of the Northumberland County Militia. This battalion consisted of Penn Township men. Thomas Price, a Revolutionary soldier, living in Selinsgrove was a Major in this battalion, and Simon Snyder, later governor of the state, was Captain of the 5th Co. of the said battalion. On February 2, 1 94, he was Lieut.-Colonel of the 3rd Regiment, Northumberland Co. Militia. On July 23, 1812, he was commissioned a Captain in the 2nd Regiment of Artillery in the United States Army, and assisted in the building of Fort McHenry at Baltimore. When it was attacked on September 13, 1814, he was one of its notable defenders. He often described the scenes inside the fort during the battle as having been horrible. One of the British shells weighing 186 pounds, did not explode and after the war he brought it by boat up the Susquehanna and Juniata Rivers, and transported it by wagon to the mill of his brother, Lewis, in Delaware Twp., Juniata Co. The shell was still in existence there in 1886. Colonel Evans' only daughter, Catharine, married the Honorable George Kremer, who was noted for his "Pennsylvania Dutch" speech in the halls of the national congress, when he was a member of it. In his latter years, Colonel Evans lived with the Kremers near Middleburg, in Snyder County, and died there on December 4, 1844. He and his wife, and Kremer and his wife, are buried in the Swineford private cemetery in Middleburg. It is the compilers opinion that Colonel Evans' grave is unmarked. In 1790, his family consisted of one male over and two under 16, two females and two other persons.

JOHN EVANS, was assessed in Penn Twp., for the first time in 1780. In 1786, he was taxed with 100 acres and personal property. Caleb Evans, who died in Penn Township in 1803, may have been his son. Caleb had a brother named Lewis. John Evans served as a private in Captain Charles Meyer's Company of the Northumberland County Rangers or Militia, also in Captain Lowden's Company of Pennsylvania Riflemen.

ADAM EWIG, SR. (also Evig, Evy, Erig, Evey, Ewey, etc.) was born in Germany about the year 1725, and died in Penn Township, Northumberland, now Jackson Township, Snyder County, Pa., in 1802. It is believed that his father was John Ewig. The Ewigs were Palatines, and sailed from London in the British ship "Johnson," David Crockatt, Master. They arrived at the port of Philadelphia, where John took the oath of allegiance to the British government on September 18, 1732. Adam's name was on a list of the boys, under 16 years, on the vessel. Adam's name appeared on the Penn Township tax list of 1768, and at the time he lived on the banks (west) of the Penns Creek, above Schoch's (App's) mill, north of Selinsgrove. In 1781, he was taxed with 200 acres and personal property. In 1801, he contributed to a fund for the erection of the First Lutheran church in Selinsgrove. His will was recorded at Sunbury, Pa., on March 17, 1802. The will mentions these children; George, Adam, Jr., John, Michael, Elizabeth Hehn, Christina (Mrs. John Adams), and Catherine (Mrs. Michael Wartman of Ohio). Simon Ewig, believed to be a descendant, still lives on some of the land once owned by Adam. This farm lies on the highway between Selinsgrove and Kratzerville. It is believed that Christian, Benjamin, and Philip, were brothers or nephews of Adam's.

ADAM EWIG, JR. was a son of Adam, Sr. The younger man was assessed in Buffalo Township, probably just across the creek from his father, for the first time in 1787. Adam, Jr. died in 1821, and his will is recorded at Lewisburg, Pa. Evidently he had no children, and it is possible that he was unmarried, because in his will he mentions his brother, George, and his sisters, Elizabeth Hehn, Christina (Mrs. John Adams), Catherine (Mrs. Michael Wartman of Ohio) and his cousin, Jacob Ewig, son of John Ewig of Cumberland County Pa.

BENJAMIN EWIG was listed on the Penn Township tax list for the first time in 1772. The compiler believes that he was a brother (or pos-

sibly a nephew) of Adam Ewig, Sr. who lived in the township at an earlier date. Later tax lists do not contain his name.

CHRISTIAN EWIG was born in 1759 or 1760, probably in Cumberland County, Pa. It is believed that he was a son of Christian Ewig, who received a warrant of survey for 300 acres of land in Cumberland, now Snyder, County, Pa., on February 27, 1753. It is believed that the Christian of this sketch was a nephew of Adam Ewig, Sr., who lived in Penn Township as early as 1768. Christian was a wheelwright and was living in what is now Snyder County as late as 1820. Christian must have lived in Penn Township prior to 1776, because in April of that year, he enlisted in Captain Casper Weitzel's Company at Sunbury, and served one year and nine months in Colonel Miles' Regiment. Soon there after, he enlisted in Captain James Wilson's Company of the 1st Pennsylvania Regiment, Continental line, and served until the end of the war. In 1790, his family consisted of one male over and one under 16, and four females.

GEORGE EWIG was a son of Adam Ewig, Sr. He was born in what is now either Penn or Jackson Township of Snyder County, Pa., on July 24, 1772, and died on August 25, 1860. His wife, Catherine——, was born on August 19, 1771, and died on October 19, 1857. Both are buried in the old cemetery at Kratzerville. George's father lived along the Penn's Creek, above Schoch's mill as early as 1768. George's brothers and sisters are given in his father's sketch.

JOHN EWIG was a son of Adam Ewig, Sr. He was born about the year 1760. It is believed that he was the "John Erig" who served in Captain John Moll's Company from Northumberland County. He may have been the same John Ewig that lived in Windsor Township of Berks Co., in 1781, and in Maiden Creek Township of the same county in 1784, mentioned in his father's will in 1802.

MICHAEL EWIG was a son of Adam Ewig, Sr. Little is known beyond this fact. He was mentioned in his father's will in 1802.

PHILIP EWIG was probably a brother of Christian Ewig, Sr., and a nephew of Adam, in Penn Township as early as 1774. In the fall of that year he enlisted in Captain John Clark's Company at Sunbury, and served with it for some months. Philip died in 1779, and Adam was administrator of his estate.

JOHN EWING was assessed in Beaver Township for the first time in

1794. A Rev. John Ewing was a non-resident owner of 300 acres of land in Augusta Township in 1785. Several men of this name served in the Revolution.

THOMAS EWING was assessed in Beaver Township for the first time in 1794. The compiler believes that he was a brother of John. A Thomas Ewing of Chester County served in the Revolution. In 1790, his family consisted of three males over and one under 16, four females and one other person.

BENJAMIN FANCY (also Fancey, Fanny, Fannery, etc) was assessed in Penn Township for the first time in 1774. In 1782, he was taxed with 100 acres and personal property. His name disappeared from the tax roll after 1784. He served as a private in Captain John Black's Company, in Captain John Moll's Company, and in Lieutenant John Coleman's Party of Rangers and Militia from Northumberland County.

JOHN FAUST may have been a native of Berks County. It is believed that he lived in Penn Township for a short time. On January 30, 1777, he was a private in Captain Benjamin aWeiser's Company of the German Regiment, Continental Line, stationed at Philadelphia. Captain Weiser's Company was recruited largely from Penn Township.

JOSEPH FEEHRER was born on April 18, 1765, and died on October 5, 1843. His wife, Maria Barbara Ott, was born Dec. 11, 1768, and died on December 1, 1831. Both are buried in the old Lutheran cemetery in Selinsgrove. Joseph was probably a descendant of John Casper Fuhrer, the immigrant. Joseph evidently was born in Lancaster Co. He was assessed in Penn Twp. for the first time in 1799, and his occupation at the time was that of tobacconist. In 1809, Governor Simon Snyder appointed him a justice of the peace for Penn Township, and in 1813, he reappointed him. In 1818, he was one of the auditors of Penn Township, and in 1821 he was elected to the office of county commissioner of Union Co. Union County was formed from part of Northumberland County in 1813). Samuel Feehrer was one of the children of Squire Feehrer, and the late Joseph Feehrer, Mus. D., of Selinsgrove, was his youngest son. Numerous Feehrer descendants live in Snyder and surrounding counties. A Joseph Feehrer served in the 7th Co., 6th Battalion of the Lancaster Co. Militia, in 1777. But since the subject of this sketch was only twelve years old at the time, it is believed that this was his father or uncle. unless the younger Joseph was a drummer

or fifer, in which case he might have served at that early age. Joseph's second wife was Sarah Rupp, and he was 73 years old when his youngest son was born. Joseph's children by his first wife were: Samuel, Catherine Stauffer, Sarah Albert, Polly Long, Rebecca Frank, and Elizabeth Bergstresser.

STEPHEN FEIDLER (also Fiddler, Fidler, etc.) was a resident, but not a land owner, in Heidelberg Township, Lancaster Co., Pa., in 1768, and he was listed as a laborer. His name appeared on the Penn Township tax list for the first time in 1778, but it is believed that he never owned any land in Penn. In 1780, he was assessed in Buffalo Township (now Union Co.) and in 1781, he was taxed with 350 acres and personal property there. In 1787, he was still a resident of Buffalo Township, Center County, and founded the village of Feidler there. Some of his descendants still live in that section. He served as a private in Captain John Beatty's Company of Rangers from Northumberland Co. He asked for tax exemption in 1778.

ADAM FERTIG (also Fertich, Fertick, etc.) probably was a native of Lancaster County. He came to what is now Snyder County prior to 1800. He died in Center Township, and letters of administration were granted to Elizabeth Fertig (possibly his wife) on November 24, 1814. In 1935, several Fertig families were living in Monroe Township, Snyder Co., Pa. Adam's children were: Susan, Elizabeth, Mary, Catherine, Sarah and John.

JACOB FETTER (also Feder, Fedder, Feather, etc.) was assessed as a resident, but not a land owner, in Lancaster Borough in 1771. This may have been Jacob, Sr., and his name appeared there until 1782. Either he, or his son of the same name, came to what is now Snyder County, prior to 1790, because at that time, Jacob Fetter, probably his wife, was a member of the Lutheran church at Row's (Salem) in Penn Township. He died in Penn Township and letters of administration were granted to Philip and Adam Fetter, probably his sons. Jacob may have been a descendant of the Jacob Fetter, immigrant, who arrived in this country about 1730. Some claim that the Fetters of this section came here from Northampton County. Several Jacob Fetters served in the Revolution, one of them in the 8th Battalion of the Lancaster County Militia. A Jacob Fetter married Maria Margaret, daughter of Samuel Weiser, of Mahantango Twp.

JOHN FILMAN, weaver, was assessed in Penn Township for the first

time in 1799. It is believed that he was the man of that name who served in the Chester County Militia during the Revolution.

CHRISTIAN FISHER, second son of John Adam Fisher, Sr., was born in Tulpehocken Township, Berks Co., Pa., on June 21, 1771, and died near Selinsgrove, Pa., on January 26, 1844. It is said that he had three wives, the first, name unknown to the compiler, died soon after marriage and left no issue. His second wife was Hannah, daughter of Captain Casper Snyder, of Northumberland County (Fishers Ferry section). Hannah was born in 1778 and died about 1812. He then married her sister, Elizabeth, widow of——Yocum, Elizabeth was born on April 27, 1779, and died on April 13, 1851. Christian, and his wife Elizabeth, are buried in the old Lutheran cemetery at Selinsgrove, and their graves are marked. It is believed that Hannah is buried there too, but her grave is unmarked. Christian's father, mother, and four or five of his brothers are buried in the same cemetery. Christian was credited with being the first Fisher to live in Penn Township, but this is not true. Nor is it true that he was the drunken roustabout he was pictured by the writer in the Susquehanna and Juniata Valley History. John Jacob Fisher (1720-1803), grandfather of Christian, bought the lower end of the Isle of Que from the Rev. Dr. Henry Melchoir Muhlenberg, and his wife, Mary, daughter of Colonel Conrad Weiser, in 1773. Christian first came to what is now Penn Township with his father, John Adam, in 1774, when he was less than 3 years old. At this time, Captain Benjamin Weiser, and others had lived on the Ise of Que for some years. This explodes the story that Christian was the first white man to live on the Isle of Que. In 1811, Christian and his brother, John George, purchased from their father, John Adam, his holdings on the Isle of Que, each getting about 167 acres In 1814, he built the brick house on the lower farm, this served as both a tavern and dwelling for many years. A grandson of Christian, Michel Oliver Fisher, son of Michael today owns the greater part of Christian's holdings on the Isle of Que. His great-grandson, Frank Fisher, owned part of the same farm until 1935, when he sold it to George W. Rockwell. This land had been in the Fisher family for one hundred and sixty-two years. Christian, his father, and his brother John contributed to the fund for the erection of the First Lutheran church of Selinsgrove, in 1801. In 1811, he was one of a board of viewers to inspect the new bridge built across the Middle Creek, south of Selinsgrove, by Jacob Lechner, contractor. Christian Fisher's only sister Marie Margaret, married "Colonel" John Snyder, a brother, of Christian's second and third wives. Christian's children by his two wives were: John, born 1797, married Anna Zern; George, born 1801, married Rebecca Gemberling and Susan Snyder; Margaret, born 1803, married William Moyer, Elizabeth, married John Motz; Lydia, married Andrew Gutelius; Mary, married Samuel Schoch; Jacob, born in 1808, never married; Daniel, born 1810, married Amelia Laudenslager; Michael, born 1813, married Sarah Hoot; Christian, Jr., born 1816, married Lydia Hendershot; Benjamin, born 1818, married Lydia Snyder, and Jeremiah, born 1819, died before reaching his majority. Christian's descendants are numerous from coast to coast. In Selinsgrove, Professor Geo. E. Fisher, Ph. D., is one of the best known descendants.

JOHN FISHER, a resident of Penn Township, who died in 1792, is believed to have been a kinsman of the Fishers who lived in White Deer Township, prior to the Revolution. He served in Captain William West's Company of Colonel Shea's Battalion at some period during the Revolution. Later evidence indicates that he may have been a descendant of Wilhelm Fischer of Hains Church section, Berks County.

JOHN FISHER, the third son of John Adam Fisher. Sr., and his wife, Margaret Elizabeth Ried, was born in Tulpehocken Township, Berks Co., Pa., on April 28, 1773, and died near Selinsgrove, Pa., on August 19, 1826. He married Catherine, a daughter of Colonel Peter Hosterman. All three are buried in the cemetery of the first Lutheran church in Selinsgrove. John came to the Isle of Que with his parents in 1774. He was assessed in Penn Township for the first time in 1795. He owned land on the north side of the Middle Creek, both east and west of the Bake Oven Hill, some of this land is still in possession of his descendants. In 1801, he contributed to a fund for the erection of the First Lutheran church of Selinsgrove. He was married in 1797. The children of John and his wife were: Margaret, born 1798, married Peter Arnold; John, born 1800, married Lydia Witmer; Elizabeth, married Jonathan Weiand; Amelia, married——Thompson; Peter, born 1809, married Susan Lloyd; Jacob, who died in 1837, had married Fannnie Brobst; Mary, born 1813, married Dr. Henry A. Lechner,

and Jonathan, born 1818, who never married. Frank J. Arnold, district superintendent of schools, Brooklyn, N. Y., is a descendant.

JOHN ADAM FISHER, Junior, was the oldest son of John Adam Fisher, Sr., and his wife, Margaret Elizabeth Reid. He was born in Tulpehocken Township, Berks Co., Pa., on July 13, 1769 and died in Penn Township now Snyder County, Pa., on December 12, 1798. He came to the Isle of Que in Penn Township with his parents in 1774 and was assessed in Penn Township for the first time in 1790. He was married and had one daughter, whose name was Magdalena. She married Elijah Henry, and about 1840 they lived in the state of Iowa. John Adam is buried in the old Lutheran cemetery in Selinsgrove, next to his parents. The name of his wife is unknown to the compiler.

JOHN ADAM FISHER, SENIOR, commonly called Adam, was the oldest son of John Jacob Fisher, and his wife, Mary Elizabeth Frederick. His grandfathers were Sebastian Fisher and John Frederic. He was born in Tulpehocken Township, Berks Co., Pa., on October 7, 1744, and died in what is now Penn Township, Snyder County, Pa., on November 24, 1825. He married Margaret Elizabeth Ried on April 26, 1768. She was born on November 25, 1752, probably in Tulpehocken Township, Berks County, and died in what is now Penn Township of Snyder county, on February 9, 1830. Both are buried in the old Lutheran cemetery in Selinsgrove. In 1767, Adam was listed as a single freeman in Tulpehocken Township. In 1773, his father bought the lower end of the Isle of Que in Penn Township from the Rev. Dr. Henry Melchoir Muhlenberg, and his wife, Mary Mary, daughter of Col. Conrad Weiser and in 1774, Adam and his family came to occupy the land.

In 1784, Adam purchased his father's holdings on the Isle of Que, and in 1787, he purchased at Sheriff's sale the farm of Captain Benjamin Weiser, which joined his on the north. This tract contained 236 acres. From 1779 to 1781, he was one of the road supervisors of Penn Twp., and an overseer of the poor. In 1791, he established a ferry across the Susquehanna River, the eastern end being at the village of Fisher's Ferry, named for him, and the western end at the present home of Michael Oliver and Frank Fisher, on the Isle of Que. This ferry was on the direct route from Berks County and the whole south-eastern section of the state, into the Middle Creek and

Penn's Valleys, which at this time were rapidly filling with settlers from the lower part of the commonwealth. In 1790, his family consisted of four makes over 16, four under, and two females. In 1798, he was taxed with a store and ferry in addition to his large holdings of real-estate and personal property. In 1801, he and his sons Christian and John, contributed heavily to the fund for the erection of the First Lutheran church of Selinsgrove. In 1807, he bought a tract of 144 acres known as "Poland" along the banks of the Middle Creek in the now Penn Township, this later became the property of his son John. In 1811, he divided his holdings on the Isle of Que into two equal parts, selling the upper half to his son John George, and the lower to his son, Christian. At the time of this writing, the lower half is still in the hands of members of the Fisher family, in direct line from the original owner, John Jacob Fisher. The children of John Adam Fisher and his wife were; John Adam, Jr., born 1769, died 1798; Christian (1771-1844), who married Hannah Snyder, and then her sister Elizabeth, widow of——Yocum; John (1773-1826), who married, Catherine, daughter of Colonel Peter Hosterman; Benjamin, born 1775, died in Ohio, unmarried; John George, born 1777, and married, Mary Magdalene, daughter of Captain Francis William Rhoads; Peter, born 1781; Marie Margaret, born 1782, married John Snyder, a brohter of the two wives of her brother, Christian; John Jacob (1786-1846), who married as his second wife, Rebecca Speece; John Michael (1789-1820), who married Catherine Elizabeth Morr; and David, who married Polly Yocum, a daughter of the second wife of his brother, Christian, by her first husband. During the Revolution, Adam received depreciation pay for service in the Berks County Militia, and in 1780, he was a private in Lieutenant Jacob Spees' Company of Rangers from Northumberland County. Indications point to his return to Berks County in 1776 or 1777, and back to Penn Township again in 1778.

JOHN JACOB FISHER was assessed as a non-resident owner of land bly before. He lived in Penn Township for a while, from 1774. He was the father of John Adam Fisher, mentioned above. John Jacob's father was Sebastian, who arrived in New York with the Palatines in 1710, and in 1723, came down the Susquehanna River and settled in the Tulpehocken

Valley in Berks County, Pa. John Jacob was born in the Schoharie Valley of New York, about the year 1720, and died in Tulpehocken Township, Berks County, Pa., in 1803. In the spring of 1743, he and his neighbors were among the founders of the Christ (Tulpehocken) Lutheran church, near Stouchsburg. On December 9, 1743, he married, Mary Elizabeth, daughter of John Frederick. In 1771, the missionary Rev. Frederick A. Muhlenberg states in his diary that he met "old man Fisher" at the home of "J. F.".-, meaning probably John Jacob's son John, who lived about six miles east of the Susquehanna in what is now Jordan Township of Northumberland Co. The compiler believes that on this trip, he examined the Isle of Que land which in 1773, he bought from the missionary's father and mother. John Jacob's will was recorded in Reading in 1803 and mentions the following children; John Adam; John; Christian; Anna Catherine (Mrs. Christian Noecker); Magdalene (Mrs. Jacob Reid), and Anna Elizabeth (Mrs. Adam Creutzer, or Kreitzer.) Jacob and his wife are buried in the cemetery of the church he helped to found, near Stouchsburg. In 1790, according to the U. S. Census, Jacob's family consisted of one male over and one under sixteen, and four females. Jacob served during the Revolution on a relief committee for Tulpehocken Township. Reference to this service is found in the American Archives. (The compiler of this work is a great-great-great-grandson of this pioneer landowner in Penn Township).

JOHN MICHAEL FISHER, was a son of John Adam Fisher. Michael settled on the Isle of Que in 1774. Michael, as he was commonly called, was born in Penn Twp. on August 29, 1789, and died in Washington Township, Union (now Snyder) County, Pa., on July 23, 1820. He married Catherine Elizabeth Morr, daughter of John Philip Morr, and his wife Elizabeth Gemberling, a daughter of pioneer, Jacob Gemberling. She was born on September 1, 1793, and died on April 24, 1856. Both are buried in St. Peters Cemetery in Freeburg. Some time after Michaels death, his widow married John Staley, Sr., and they lived in Selinsgrove. Michael and his wife had four children, one of them, Isaac, died in infancy. An other son, Henry, never married. One of the daughters married George C. Moyer, and the other John A. Hilbish. Christian Fisher (Michael's brother) and Philip Morr (his wife's father) were the administrators of his estate.

PETER FISHER, weaver, son of Michael Fisher and wife Margaret, was born in Ruscomb Manor Township, Berks County, Pa., on September 11, 1763, and died near Selinsgrove, Pa., on September 8, 1852. His wife was Anna Maria Faer, who was born on October 26, 1757, and died near Selinsgrove, Pa., on January 29 1844. Both are buried in the old Lutheran cemetery and their graves are marked. Peter's father, Michael, was born in Germany in 1724, and died in Berks County, Pa., in 1776. Michael served in the French Army from 1744 to 1749, and his French discharge is in the hands of one of his descendants, Howard Fisher of Williamsport, Pa. Michael came to America in either 1752 or 1754, and was made a British citizen at Reading in 1765. Peter was assessed in Penn Township for the first time in 1799¼ In 1814, he was tax collector of Penn Township. Peter lived in the vicinity of Hummels Wharf, and some of his descendants still live there. Peter lived in Ruscomb Township until his removal to what is now Snyder County. In 1790, his family had one male over 16, and four females. The known children of Peter and his wife were: Solomon (1790-1848); Abraham (1792-1873); Sampson (1795-1852); and Hannah, born about 1797. Peter when less than 18 years old, was a private in Captain Sebastin Miller's Company of the Berks County Militia on May 31, 1781. Many of Peter's descendants now live in Snyder and surrounding counties.

CHRISTIAN FORRY (also Forrey, Ferry, Ferree, etc). It seems that there were at least two men of this name in Pennsylvania, prior to 1800. One owned 100 acres and personal property in Colalico Township, Lancaster County, Pa., in 1771. The same, or n other of the same name, was taxed with personal property in Hempfield Township, same county in or one other of the same name, was sessed as a single freeman in Conestoga Township, same county in 1782. The name appeared on the Penn Township tax list for the first time in 1794. In 1796, when Mahantango Township was formed from part of Penn, he was assessed there. The compiler believes that he was a son of the Ferree who bought what is to-day known as Hoover's Island from John Jacob Fisher prior to the Revolution, and that Christian may have at one time been a tenant on it. A Christian Forrey served as a private in Captain Phillip Baker's Company of the Lancaster County Militia in 1782. The 1790 census, indicates that Christian lived in what is now Snyder County in that year, and that his family consisted of one

male over and two under 16, and four females. He died in Mahantango Township before December, 1815.

JACOB FOULKE was probably a son of George Foulke, a German immigrant, who embarked at Rotterdam, Holland in the British ship "Tyger" and landed at Philadelphia, where he took the oath of allegiance to the British government on November 19, 1771. Jacob was assessed in Penn Township for the first time in 1778, and it is thought that he was a non-resident land owner at the time. A Jacob Foulke married Catherine, daughter of Jacob German (now Garman). Garman was an early resident of Penn Township. A Jacob Foulk served in the 4th Battalion of the Philadelphia County Militia during the Revolution.

MICHAEL FOUTZ (also Pfoutz, Fouts, etc.) was listed as a single freeman in Penn Township in 1771, but later lists did not contain his name. The compiler believes that he is the man for whom Pfoutz Valley was named. If this is true, then he possibly lived outside of the present confines of Snyder County, after 1771. He served as a private in Capt. Philip Mathias Company of the Cumberland County Militia, and may also have served in the 1st Pennsylvania Regiment of the Continental Line. It is believed that he married, Hannah, the daughter of Simon Woodrow, who came to Penn Township about 1774. If so, some of his children were Rebecca, Reuben, and Isaac Foutz.

WILLIAM FREDERICK is believed to have come from Philadelphia or Cumberland County. He seems not to have been taxed in Penn Township prior to 1793, but it is believed that he is the same man who served in Captain John Hamilton's Company of the Northumberland County Militia in October, 1777. He may have lived in some other township in the county, before coming to Penn.

ADAM FREIBERGER was assessed as a single freeman in Penn Township for the first time in 1787. He was probably a relative of Ludwig and Frederick, who lived in the township at an earlier date. No military record was found for him.

FREDERICK FREIBERGER lived in Penn Township in 1783, because in that year, Jacob Frederick, son of Frederick and Dorothea Freiberger, was baptized at the old Zion Lutheran church, north of Freeburg. Without doubt he was a relative of Ludwig and Adam who lived in the township at about the same time. Frederick must have removed from the state, or died before 1790, as his name does not appear in the 1790 U. S. Census.

LUDWIG FREIBERG (also Freyberg, Freburg, Froberg, etc.) was assessed in Penn Township for the first time in 1780. It is thought that he was a Jew. In 1787, he was taxed with 80 acres and personal proprety. Ludwig was born in Germany and embarked for America at Rotterdam, Holland, on the British ship "Hero," Ralph Forster, master, and arrived at the port of Philadelphia, where he took the oath of allegiance on October 27, 1764. In 1790, his family consisted of one male over and four under 16 years, and three females. He served in Captain Michael Motz's Company of the Northumberland County Militia, and in Captain John Snyder's Company of Rangers.

DAVID FREY may have been a son of Jacob Fry, Senior, who died in the year 1802. David was assessed in Penn Township for the first time in 1799. He was a shoemaker, and in 1802, he lived in Middleburg. Abraham and John Fry were probably his brothers.

ABRAHAM FRY was a native of Berks County, Pa. He was assessed in Beaver Township for the first time in 1789. He was probably a son of Jacob Fry. An Abraham Fry served in the Berks County Militia during the Revolution.

JACOB FRY was assessed in Beaver Township for the first time in 1799. He died there, and letters of administration were granted to Abraham Fry (probably son) on September 20, 1802. A Jacob Fry served in the Lancaster County Militia.

JOHN FRY (also Frey) lived in Penn Township as early as 1776. In 1781, he was taxed with 100 acres and personal property. On September 26, 1776, he was a private in the 1st Company, 4th Battalion of the Northumberland County Militia. A John Fry served as a private in Lieutenant Frederick Miller's Company of Rangers from Berks County. In 1790, John Fry's family consisted of one male over and four under 16, and two females.

CHRISTIAN FURST may not have lived in Penn Township, but he served with a company recruited there. It is thought that he may have been a resident of Mahanoy Township. He was a private in Captain Benjamin Weiser's company of the German Regiment, Continental Line, serving at Philadelphia, Pa., on January 30, 1777.

CONRAD FURST (Ferst) was assessed as a single freeman in Mahanoy Township, Northumberland county, in 1785. He was probably a brother of Christian, mentioned above. He too, served in Captain Benjamin Weiser's Company at the same time.

FREDERICK GABLE (also Gabel) was a son or grandson of John Frederick Gable, a German immigrant, who came to this country about 1740. Frederick was a farmer in Salisbury Township, Northampton County, Penna., in 1772. In 1785 he lived in the town of Northampton, and in 1788, he was listed as a baker there. He was assessed in Penn Township for the first time in 1793, where he died in 1795. His wife's name was Elizabeth— . On April 23, 1782, he was a private, 3rd class, 3rd Company, 4th Battalion of the Northampton County Militia. It is believed that he was progenitor of all of the name Gable living in this section. It is believed that two of his sons were named Casper, and Daniel.

GEORGE GABRIEL about the year 1754 built the first house on what is now the site of Selinsgrove, and as the ground on which it stood, was later surveyed for others, he was probably a squatter. The Penn's Creek Massacre took place near his home on October 16, 1755, and a few days later French officers and Indians encamped near his house. On the night of October 24, 1755, the Indians set fire to all his buildings, but he and family escaped with their lives, and little else. Gabriel went to Berks County to consult with Conrad Weiser about the messages which he (Gabriel) was to carry to the friendly Indians in the month of November. On June 2, 1756, he entered the service of the Province of Pennsylvania as a guide for the "Augusta Regiment" which was being sent up the river to guard the newly established fort at Sunbury. The regiment arrived at the site of Gabriel's home on July 5, 1756. It is evident that Gabriel rebuilt his buildings, because during this and the following year, Gabriel's settlement was the stopping place for many parties engaged in service against the Indians, and often for the Indians themselves. It was at Gabriel's house that Captain William Patterson and his party found Frederick Stump and John Ironcutter friendly Indians at Middleburg. It was here that Captain Patterson arrested the murderers on January 21, 1768. Gabriel conducted a trading post and frontier tavern. His services to the provincial authorities were numerous, and for this, the fact that he was probably the earliest settler in the section, he should be long remembered. He was assessed in Penn Township in 1768.

His death occurred prior to the Revolution, probably in 1771 or 1772. No one of his name lives in Snyder County today.

MICHAEL GALER (also Gaeler, Galler, etc.) was assessed in Penn Township for the first time in 1798. He operated a saw mill at that time. He died in Center Township and his will was probated at Lewisburg, Pa., on May 23, 1823. His heirs were his sons, Jacob and John. No military record was found for Michael. His daughter married John Krick. The Galer family later lived in the western part of Union County.

JACOB GARMAN (formerly German) was a relative of the Jacob Garman who died in Penn Township in 1787. He may have been a grandson, because the elder Jacob's sons were Christian and John. The younger Jacob lived in Penn Township as early as 1794, because in that year, Mary Eva, daughter of Jacob and Anna Garman was baptized in the old Zion Lutheran Church, north of Freeburg. In 1795, they had a son, Benjamin, baptized there, too.

JACOB GARMAN (the elder) was an early settler in Penn Township. He died in the township in 1787, and his will was recorded at Sunbury, Pa., on June 19, 1787. The witnesses were all residents of Selinsgrove, but it is believed that he lived in what is now Union or Chapman Township. His wife was Anna——. Their children were: Christian, John, Catherine Foulk (probably Mrs. Jacob or Mrs. James Foulke), Rosina Ward, and Regina (Mrs. John Hammersly.) A Jacob Garman was a private, 4th class, 2nd Battalion, Lancaster County Militia in 1781.

HENRY GARMAN was born on November 22, 1763, and died on October 28, 1835, and is buried in the Fremont cemetery. His wife was Elizabeth —————. Henry was assessed in Mahantango Township for the first time in 1796, he had a sawmill in addition to other property. Maria Christina, their daughter, was born on May 29, 1795, and baptized at Grubb's (Botschaft's) church in the same year. In 1805, they had their son, George, baptized at the old Zion Lutheran Church, north of Freeburg. Henry served as a private in the 7th Company, 2nd Battalion of the Lancaster County Militia. Henry Garman's children were: Jacob, John, Maria Christina (Mrs. Dan. Heiser), John Peter, Catherine (Mrs. John Houseworth), George, Adam, Jr., Samuel, Magdalene, and Benjamin.

JOHN GARMAN (also German, Germon, Garmon, etc.) was assessed with 80 acres and personal property in Ralpho Township, Lancaster Co., Pa., from 1771 to 1782. In 1785, he was assessed with 50 acres in Penn Township for the first time, and in 1794 he was granted a warrant of survey for 120 additional acres in Northumberland (now Snyder) Co. This John Garman, or John, son of Jacob, died in Chapman Township in 1822. His will was recorded at Lewisburg, Pa., on May 25th of that year. His heirs were his wife, Margaret, and their children, John and Catherine (Mrs. Michael Kerstetter.) Henry Garman, a brother, was one of the executors. A John Garman was one of the witnesses to the will of John George Herrold, in 1802. In 1790, the family of John Garman consisted of one male over and one under sixteen, and four females. A John Garman served as a private, 3rd class, in the 5th company, 7th Battalion of the Lancaster County Militia during the Revolution. John Garman was a son of Jacob Garman. John married Mary Elizabeth, daughter of the pioneer, John Adam Menges.

PETER GARMAN was born on March 16, 1767 and died in Washington Township, Union (now Snyder) County, Pa., on July 24, 1831. His name appeared on the Penn Township tax list for the first time about the year 1790. In 1796, he was assessed in Mahantango Township. His wife was Mary————. She was born on February 29, 1765, and died on February 13, 1832. Both were buried in the St. Peters cemetary in Freeburg. It is believed that Peter was a relative of John and Jacob, mentioned above.

HENRY GARRETT was probably a native of Lancaster County. His name appeared on the Penn Township tax list for the first time in 1776, and he was a single freemen at the time. As his name does not appear in Penn Township, it is believed that he returned to Lancaster County. A Henry Garrett was a private in Captain McCallens Company of the 1st Battalion, Lancaster County Militia on May 15, 1783.

JOHN CHRISTIAN GAST, SENIOR, was born in Germany on April 23, 1726, and died near Rebersburg, Center County, Pa., about 1805. His wife, Christina Brandt, was born on October 29, 1729, and died near Rebersburg about the year 1803. Both are buried in the Rebersburg cemetery. John Christian and his brother, John Nicholas, embarked at Rotterdam, Holland, for America, in the British ship "Neptune." They arrived at the port of Philadelphia,

where they took an oath of allegiance on October 7, 1755. They sold their services to pay their passage. From 1771 to 1773, they were assessed in Heidelberg Township, Lancaster County, Pa. Some time prior to the Revolution, "Christian" purchased considerable land near the mouth of Middle Creek, in the now Snyder County. He was assessed in Penn Township for the first time in 1774, and in 1781 owned 100 acres and personal property. About 1787, John Nicholas, the son of Christian, bought land in Brush Valley, Center County, Pa., and soon after moved there.

Some years later, "Christian," Sr., sold his buildings in Penn Township to his son, Christian, and moved to Brush Valley, to live with his son, Nicholas. Christian, Jr., soon thereafter sold his land and moved there, too. John Nicholas, the brother of the older Christian, moved to the southern central part of the state, married and had one son, who died without issue. John Christian, Sr. and his wife were the parents of three children; John Christian, Jr., John Nicholas and Catherine, who married a Maurer and moved to Ohio. It is believed that Christian, Sr., and both his sons served in the Revolution. In 1790, the family of Christian Gast, Sr., consisted of one male over and one under 16, and two females.

JOHN CHRISTIAN, GAST, JUNIOR, was a son of Christian Gast, Sr. He was born about 1755, probably in Heidelburg Township in Lancaster County, Pa. He was first assessed in Penn Township about the year 1780. He married Margaret Borer, or Boyer, and about 1790, bought his fathe.s holdings near the mouth of Middle Creek in Penn Township. In 1793, he sold these holdings and moved to Brush Valley, Center County, where his brother Nicholas, and father, had located several years earlier. About 1808, he moved to Blair County, Pa., where he died. Christian and his wife were the parents of the following children: Christian, who married Elizabeth, a daughter of Lieutenant Philip Meyer (Moyer), they moved to Middletown, Ohio; John, married Margaret, a sister of Christian's wife; George, married Susan Lamer; Jacob, William, Samuel, Catherine, who married William Lamer; Mary M., who married John Meyer, son of Lieutenant Philip Meyer, who moved to Iowa; Margaret, and Sarah. Elizabeth, daughter of Christian and his wife, was born on March 20, 1791, and baptized soon thereafter at the Grubb's Lutheran church in the now

Chapman Township. Christian, under the name of Gast, Guest and Gauss, served in Captain John Snyder's Company and Lieutenant Jacob Speese Company of Rangers from Northumberland County.

JOHN NICHOLAS GAST, son of Christian Gast, Sr., was born on April 21, 1760, probably in Heidelberg Township, Lancaster County, Pa., and died near Rebersburg, Center County, Pa., on December 2, 1810. His wife, Catherine Kibe, or (Knipe) was born on November 15, 1771, and died on October 11, 1863. Both are buried at Rebersburg, Pa. He was assessed in Penn Township for the first time about the year 1783. About 1787, he bought some land in Brush Valley, Center County, Pa., and prior to 1790 moved to that section, later to be joined by his parents and brother. Nicholas and his wife had the following children: Adam, George, Henry (lived in Mifflinburg, Pa.,) John (lived in Mifflinburg,) Barbara (who married George Tate, Catherine (who married Daniel Conser, both buried at Rebersburg), Christina (who married the Hon. John Reynolds, was still living at Rebersburg, Pa., in 1889, aged 90 years), Mary (who married Jacob Wolf of Rebersburg), Susan (Mrs. Paul Wolf), and Elizabeth (Mrs. Solomon Crotzer). John Nicholas was a shoe maker and with the earnings of his trade, he bought land in Center County. Nicholas was an Indian scout, and during the Revolution served in Ensign Simon Herrold's Party of Rangers from Northumberland county. The years of birth of some of the above children are known. Christina was born in 1800, Mary in 1802, John 1804, Henry in 1806, and Susan in 1808. Because of Indian savages, he asked for taxexemption in 1778.

GEORGE GAUGLER was assessed in Mahantango Township for the first time in 1796. Letters of administration in his estate were granted on October 23, 1824, His wife may nave been Magdalene. They may have been the parents of Elizabeth born 1815, Christina, born 1817, and Abraham, born in 1820, all baptized at Grubb's church in Chapman Township. G-orge and wife also had these children: John, Sarah, George and Molly.

NICHOLAS GAUGLER, gunsmith, was assessed in Penn Township for the first time in 1799. It is believed that he was a relative of Capt. Michael Gaugler of Frederick Twp., Northampton County, Pa. In 1802, Nicholas was a road supervisor in Penn Township, and in 1804, he was an overseer of the poor. Nicholas was a native of Marlboro Twp., Montgomery Co., Pa. He died in the vicinity of Selinsgrove in 1807 and left a wife, Mary, and seven children: George, Catherine (Mrs. Fred. Sharrett, or Jarrett), Polly, (Mrs. Peter Beistel), Sarah, Elizabeth, William and Margaret. Nicholas was a Revolutionary soldier.

HENRY GEISTWHITE was assessed in Beaver Township in 1790. At that time, his family consisted of one male over and four under 16, and two females.

CASPER GELNET (also Gelnetz and Geinitz, etc.,) was assessed in Mahantango Township for the first time in 1796. It is believed that he was the first of his name in what is now Snyder County. No military record was found for him.

HENRY GETHARD was assessed in Lehigh Township, Northampton County, Pa., in 1785. In 1786 he was taxed in Buffalo Township, of North'd (now Union) County, with personal property only. In 1796, he was assessed in Mahantango Township. He was a cooper. No military record was located.

CHARLES GEMBERLING (also Gamperling, Gamperlane, Kemberling, Gemperling, etc.) was born in Germany, and had a brother Paul and one Jacob. Paul and he embarked for America at Rotterdam, Holland on the English ship "Neptune," commanded by Captain Waire, and landed at the port of Philadelphia, where they took the oath of allegiance to the British government on September 30, 1754. Prior to the Revolution, Charles (or Carl as he was sometimes called) and Paul were land owners in what is now Penn Township of Snyder County. In 1781, Clary Campbell was a tenant on Charles Gemberling's land, and Charles seems to have moved elsewhere, in 1790, Charles lived in Buffalo Township in what is now Union County, and his family consisted of one male over and three under 16, eight females, and two other free persons. Charles once lived in Philadelphia. He died in Harrisburg in 1814 and is buried there. At one time he owned the land on which the village of Salem now stands. For some reason he changed his name to Chamberlin or Chamberling. He was a large land-owner in Penn Twp., and owned a home in Selinsgrove. His children were: John, Catherine (Mrs. John Capp), Mary (Mrs. Conrad Row), Susan (Mrs. Geo. Slotterback), Sarah (Mrs. John Capp), Esther (Mrs. Peter Withington), Anna (Mrs. Christian Glass), Margaret (Mrs. Geo. Elli-

man), Charles, Frances (Mrs. Jacob Albright), and Lydia (Mrs. Fred Kelker).

GEORGE GEMBERLING was a son of Jacob Gemberling, Sr., one of the pioneer settlers in Penn Township. George was born in Lancaster (now Lebanon) County, Pa., on March 6, 1778, and died in Penn Township, Snyder County, on June 3, 1861. His first wife, Anna, was born on July 8, 1776 and died April 29, 1836. His second wife, Barbara S. —was born on March 6, 1778, and died on October 24, 1874. The three are buried in the Row's cemetery in Penn Township. George was a carpenter and farmer, and was assessed in Penn Township for the first time in 1799. George came to what is now Penn Township with his parents in 1785. The children of George and his wives were: Catherine (1807-1883), who married Henry Bickhart (1802-1877); Polly, who married Jacob Bickhart; Lucy, who married a Kinney; Jonathan (1819-1884), who married Sarah— 1819-1893); Daniel (1825-1877), who married Barbara (1827-1898); Henry, George and Sephares.

JACOB GEMBERLING, SENIOR, was born in one of the Palatine Provinces of Germany in 1733 or 1736, and died in what is now Penn Township, Snyder County, Pa., on May , 1824. His wife was Catherine Wolfensberger, who was born in the same section in Germany as her husband. They were married in Germany and their older children were born there. They embarked for America at Rotterdam, Holland, in the British ship "Polly." Robert Porter, master, and arrived at the Port of Philadelphia, where he took the oath of allegiance on August 24, 1765. His brothers, John Charles, and John Paul, had arrived eleven years earlier. In 1771, Jacob was taxed in Heidelberg Township, Lancaster Co., Pa. In 1779 and in 1782, he was listed as a farmer and tavernkeeper in Schaefferstown, now Lebanon Co., Pa. The same year he was listed as the non-resident owner of 300 acres of land in Penn Township, Northumberland (now Snyder) County, Pa. The compiler believes that he bought the holdings, or part of the holdings, of his brothers Charles and Paul, in Penn Township. While some contend that Jacob and his family came to this section in 1772, the tax lists indicate that Jacob was not a resident of Penn Township until 1785, when he was taxed with 300 acres of land and considerable personal property. This land lay about a mile west of Selinsgrove. A. Ira Gemberling, a descendant, is the

present owner of a considerable portion of it. Jacob served as a fence viewer in Penn Township in 1789, and in 1800, he was one of the viewers to locate a road across the Isle of Que from Selinsgrove to the Susquehanna river. In 1801, he contributed to the fund for the erection of the First Luthran and Reformed church of Selinsgrove. He was one of the leading members of the Reformed congregation of this church, and was one of the three Reformeds who served as a building committee with three from the Lutheran congregation. One record states that Jacob was born in 1733, but another record states that he died in May, 1824, aged 88 years, and this would mean that he was born 1736. His wife who died some years earlier at the age of seventy, and brother are buried in unmarked graves in the cemetery of the church which he helped to found. One record states that Jacob had fourteen children, and another states that he had six children when he moved from Lebanon County. The compiler can find only eight, probably the ones that grew to maturity. At some time during the Revolution, Jacob was a private in the 5th Company Captain Nicholas Lutz), of the 3rd Battalion of the Lancaster. Co. Militia. (The compiler is a great-great-great-grandson of this pioneer.) The children of Jacob and his wife were: Elizabeth (1768-1811), wife of John Philip Morr; Jacob, Jr., Philip (1773-1859,) George (1776-1861), Samuel, Sarah (Mrs. Jacob Moyer, Mary (Polly), who married Frederick Esterline, and another daughter who married Joseph Walter, but had no children. In 1790, his family consisted of two males over and two under 16, and three females. Jacob was a non-resident land-owner in Penn Twp., as early as 1774.

JOHN PAUL GEMBERLING was born in Germany, and was a brother of Jacob, Sr., and Charles. His father may also have been named Jacob. With his brother Charles, he embarked for America at Rotterdam, Holland, on the British ship "Neptune," Captain Waire, master, and arrived at the port of Philadelphia, where they took the oath of allegiance to the English government on September 30, 1754. His brother, Jacob, did not come to America until 1765. On March 22, 1774, Paul was granted a warrant of survey for 223 acres of land in Northumberland, now Snyder county, and it is supposed that he immediately became a resident on this land. On the Penn Township tax list of 1782, he was assessed with 150 acres and was designated as a non-resident owner. In the year of 1783, he was taxed as a resident of the town of York in York County. The compiler believes that the descendants of Paul migrated south and west of York, Pennsylvania. He participated in the Revolution by serving as a member of the committee of safety for Penn Township on August 13, 1776. It is believed that he also served in the militia. He may have died before 1790, or moved from the state, because his name does not seem to appear on the U. S. Census for Pennsylvania in that year.

PHILIP GEMBERLING, SENIOR, was the second son of Jacob, Sr., and his wife, Catherine Wolfensberger. He was born in Heidelberg Township, Lancaster (now Lebanon) County, Pa., on July 27, 1773, and died near Selinsgrove, Pa., on October 13, 1859. He came to what is now Penn Township with his parent about the year of 1785. As a young man, he bought about 250 acres from his father's large holdings and lived on them all his life. In 1796, he married Eva Glass, probably a daughter of George Glass. She was born on July 15, 1773, and died on July 13, 1815. They were the parents of five sons and four daughters. His second wife was Judith Fetter, probably a daughter of Jacob. She was born on December 10, 1794, and died August 28, 1862. The issue of this union was six sons and five daughters. Phillip, like his father, was an active member of the Reformed church, and when the new Lutheran and Reformed church was built in Selinsgrove in 1802, was the man who delivered on the ground the first piece of timber for the edifice. Some rivalry having existed as to who would be able to get the first piece there. Phillip was a man of keen business foresight and held various positions of public trust. In 1815, he was one of the viewers for the location of a bridge across the Penn's Creek at Pine street in Selinsgrove. In 1824, and again in 1829, he was a road supervisor in Penn Township. In 1844, he served as an auditor of the Penn Township accounts. In 1794, he became a member of the Reformed church at Kratzerville, then known as Hessler's, and in 1855, when the union of the Lutheran and Reformed church in Selinsgrove was dissolved, he was one of the largest contributors to the fund for the erection of a separate edifice for the Reformed congregation. He and his two wives are buried in the cemetery of the First Lutheran church in Selinsgrove. His parents also rest in the same cemetery. The children

of Philip and his wives were: Philip, John, Jacob, Mary (Mrs. David Hertz), Catherine (Mrs. John Royer and later Mrs. A. Eisenhower), Samuel G., Sarah (Mrs. Michael Neitz), Rebecca (Mrs. Geo. Fisher), Frederick, Esther (Mrs. Fred. Hare), Paul, Amelia, (Mrs. Geo. Ott, Jr.), Benjamin, Lydia (Mrs. John Parks), Caroline (Mrs. Henry Neyer, or Neuer), Joseph V., Reuben, Alfred, and Wm. H.

ANTHONY GIFT, a son of the pioneer, John Adam Gift. He lived in Beaver Township in 1790, and his family consisted of two males over 16, and three females at the time.

JACOB GIFT, was a brother of Anthony, mentioned above. He was born in Weisenburg Township, Northampton County, Pa., about the year 1761. He came to what is now Franklin Township, Snyder County, Pa., with his parents in 1778. When the time came for his father to serve an active period in the militia against the ravages of the Indians, Jacob volunteered to become a substitute for his father. In the spring of 1779, he was serving in the party of Rangers commanded by Lieutenant Jacob Speece at Fort Freeland, near Turbotville. A man by the name of McKnight and his son asked for a guard of four men to protect them while they milked the McKnight cows which were in a pasture outside of the stockade. Four men were sent, but they were attacked and the elder McKnight, and the Rangers, Jacob Gift, Michael Lepley and George Herrold, Jr., were killed and scalped. The younger McKnight and another soldier regained the fort in safety. Jacob's father went to the fort at a later date to secure the body, but because all four men were buried in the same, he was unable to identify it. Thus died another hero.

JOHN ADAM GIFT, commonly called Adam, emigrated to America from Germany about the year 1750. They settled first in Weisenburg Township, Northampton (now Lehigh) County, Pa. In September of 1754, John Adam was granted a warrant for survey of 25 acres of land in that township, and on December 10, 1773, he was granted a warrant for 100 acres more in the said township. He was assessed in Penn Township for the first time in 1778, and lived on the north side of the Middle Creek about three miles west of the present town of Middleburg. The land there was originally granted to Richard Tea, and evidently was sold by him to Gift. The tract contained 250 acres and lies today in what is Franklin Town-

ship, Snyder County. This land was later sold by Adam to his son Anthony Gift. John Adam, in 1793, purchased a tract of 235 acres on the south side of Middle Creek, in Franklin Township. This tract had originally been granted to the Hutr brothers in 1755. The land lays about a half mile west of the village of Paxtonville, and at one time was owned by Jeremiah, the youngest son of Adam, and at a much later date it became the property of the Paxtonville Brick Company and its successors, and an excellent grade of brick has been manufactured from the subsoil of this former Gift farm. John Adam Gift and his wife, Anna Catherine, were the parents of the following children: Jacob (killed by the Indians at Fort Freeland, during the Revolution,) Anthony, Jeremiah, Eleanor (Mrs. Francis Ditto,) Mary, Gertrude and Eva, (who was accidently killed in childhood.) In 1786, John Adam Gift was an inspector of elections in Penn Township, and in 1789, he lived in Beaver Township which was formed from the western part of Penn, this part of Beaver Township later became Franklin Township. Adam Gift and his wife are buried in the old Hassinger cemetery, west of Middleburg, but their tombstones are no longer readable. Adam had two brothers, Peter and Nicholas. Peter was a clock-maker, he settled in the city of Reading and lived there all his life. Nicholas left Weisenberg Township, and settled in Franklin County, Pa. It is believed that Adam Gift served in the Northampton County Militia before he came to what is now Snyder County. On May 21, 1781, and Adam Gift was a private, 5th class, 2nd Company, 1st Battalion of the Cumberland County Militia. In 1790, Adam Gift's family consisted of two males over 16, and three females.

JONATHON GIFT, may have been a relative of Adam, mentioned above. He was a resident of what is now Snyder County before 1800. He died in Center Township, Union (now Snyder) County, Pa., and letters of administration were granted to Jeremiah Gift on August 2, 1827. Andrew and David Gift lived in Center Township in 1800.

ADAM GILBERT. An Adam Gilbert was assessed with 9 acres of land in Douglas Township, Philadelphia County, Pa., in 1769, this assessment continued for some years, and in 1783, he was designated as a cordwainer. It seems that this township later became part of Berks County, and in 1785, he was still assessed in Douglas Township, but now in Berks County. In 1780, the name of Adam Gilbert, Jr., appears on the tax list of Douglas Township, but did not again appear there. In 1784, Adam Gilbert, tailor, was a resident, but not a land owner, in Cole-brookdale Township, Berks County, and the same was true in 1785. In 1790, the Adam who lived in Douglas Township, had a family of one male over and three under 16, and two females. In the same year, an Adam Gilbert lived in Montgomery County, Pa., and his family consisted of two males over 16, and one female. The compiler believes that Adam, Jr., and Adam, the tailor, were the same person, and that he was the man who came to the Freeburg section of Snyder County, just prior to 1800. Adam Gilbert, Sr., was a Captain, and Adam, Jr., a Corporal in the Philadelphia County Militia at some period during the Revolution. Letters of administration in the estate of Adam Gilbert were granted to Adam Gilbert at Lewisburg, Pa., (the then county seat) on February 25, 1820. Henry Gilbert and Isaac Mertz were the sureties. The compiler believes that the Adam Gilbert who died in 1820, was a brother of the Henry Gilbert of Center or Franklin Township, who was a Revolutionary soldier.

HENRY GILBERT may have been a brother of the Adam mentioned above. He was born on December 28, 1758, and died in what is now Center Township, Snyder County, Pa., on August 15, 1840. He came to what is now Snyder County before 1800. His wife was named Elizabeth. Both are buried in the Hassinger Old Cemetery, west of Middleburg. It is believed that he lived in what is now Lebanon County before coming to this section. His will was recorded at Lewisburg, Pa., on August 24, 1840, and mentions the following as his children: George, Henry, Samuel, Mary Magdalene (Mrs. Jacob Bilger, Sr.,) Mrs. Peter Decker, and Elizabeth (Mrs. John Wittes.) His son, Samuel, and son in law, John Wittes, were executors of his will. Henry served in the 4th Company, 2nd Battalion of the Lancaster County Militia in 1782.

LIEUTENANT WILLIAM GILL was listed as a freeman on the tax list of 1768 for Penn Township. He was a native of Bucks County and served as a soldier in a regiment in Forbes' Campaign, and was wounded in the leg in Grants' defeat on September 14, 1758, or in the attack on Bouquet's Camp on the Loyalhanna. After receiving the wound, he started for his home in the eastern part of the state, but his progress was slow and he finally stopped near New Berlin. He remained here, and later married a German woman of that section. The Penn Township tax list of 1781 showed him as the owner of 50 acres, and in 1788, he was taxed with 130 acres and personal property. His property lay in what is now either Beaver or Center Township. William died in Beaver Township about 1820, and left a large number of children. He seems to have been the first of his name to settle in what is now Snyder County, and a number of his descendants still live in the vicinity. He served in the Northumberland County Associators, enlisting in Captain John Clark's Company, at Sunbury, Pa., on September 26, 1776. On October 8th of the same year, he was a Second Lieutenant in the 4th Company, 4th Battalion of the Northumberland County Militia. During the War of 1812, he offered to serve for one of his sons who was drafted, but could not go. His grandson, Jacob Gill, served in Captain Ner Middlesworth's Company in the War of 1812.

MOSES GILLAN (also Gillen, Giellen, etc.) was assessed in Penn Township only in the year 1778, and it is believed that he was merely a transient, or a non-resident landowner. No military record was found for him.

WILLIAM GILLEN may have been a son of Moses, mentioned above. He was taxed in Penn Township for the first time in 1781, and in that year had 130 acres and personal property. In 1787, he had 50 acres and personalty. It is believed that he served in the Revolution.

HENRY GILMAN (also Gillman) was assessed as a laborer in Bethel Township, Berks County, Pa., in 1767. In 1783, a Henry Gilman was assessed in White Deer Township (now Union County), and in 1787 he was assessed with 150 acres in Buffalo Township, same county. There seems to have been a Henry Gilman, Jr. also. A Henry Gilman was assessed in Beaver Township for the first time in 1789. Henry Gilman served as a private in Captain John Forster's Company, and at another time in Captain Joseph Green's Company of the Northumberland County Militia.

CHRISTIAN GILTNER (also Gildner) was assessed as a singlefreeman in Lehigh Township, Northampton County, Pa., in 1786. He was assessed in Penn Township for the first time in 1789. His occupation was that of carpenter. It is believed that he was a relative of Jacob Giltner, who received a grant of land in Penn Township in 1773. A Christian Giltner was a private, 4th class in the 7th Company, 8th Battalion of the Northampton County Militia in 1782.

JACOB GILTNER was a resident of Northumberland County prior to the Revolution. On October 20, 1773, he was granted a warrant of survey for 200 acres of land in Northumberland County, evidently in Penn Township. He was assessed in Penn for the first time in 1774, and from that year until 1784. He became a resident of the township in 1785 and in that year was taxed with 100 acres and personal property. He received additional grants for 150 acres in 1786, and 203 acres in 1797, in Northumberland County. In 1790, his family consisted of one male over, and three under sixteen years, and four females. He received depreciation pay for services in the Northampton County Militia. It is believed that he was a brother of Christian, mentioned above.

SERGEANT GEORGE GLASS (also Gloss, Ghlos, Ghloss, Glahs, Glohs, etc.) was a resident of Elizabeth Township, Lancaster County, Pa., in 1771, 1772 and 1773. His name appeared on the Penn Township tax list for the first time in 1778, and in 1786 he was taxed with 150 acres and personal property. In 1790, his family consisted of one male over and three under sixteen years, and three females. In 1801, he contributed to the fund for the erection of the First Lutheran church of Selinsgrove. He lived in the vicinity of Freeburg and died in the year of 1802. His will was probated at Sunbury, Pa., on November 26, 1802, and mentions his wife, Eva, and the following children: Christian .1768-1852); George, Jr. (1778-1854), John (1783-1811), Salome, who was baptized at the old Zion church, north of Freeburg in 1786, and Barbara, who was baptized in 1788. Eva (1773-1815), wife of Philip Gemberling, Sr., may also have been his daughter. Eva, wife of George Glass, Sr. died in 1817. George Glass, Jr., married Sarah — (1791-1863), and Christian married Anna Gemberling (1777-1847,) and one of their children was Anna Catherine Glass (1798-1863). George served as a private in Capt. Michael Motz's Company, in Captain Charles Meyer's Company, and in Captain John Snyder's Company of the Northumberland County Militia. In 1780, he was a Sergeant in Lieutenant Jacob Bard's Party of Rangers from Northumberland County in service on the frontier. George was born in Germany in 1740 and died in Penn Twp. in 1802. On June

11, 1767, he married Eva Albright (1744-1817).

JOHN GLASS, son of George, mentioned above, was born in 1783, in the then Penn Township, and was baptized at the old Zion Lutheran church, north of Freeburg in the same year. John married Christina —. He died in 1811 and his will was probated at Sunbury, Pa., on January 17, 1811. His wife and two children, Mary and Jacob, were mentioned in the will. The wife was designated as the executrix. John Roush and Fred Roush witnessed the will.

ADAM GOOD (also Guth, Goot, Goote, Gute, etc.), lived in Penn Township prior to 1800. There may have been two men of the same name living in the township at the same time, one dying in 1826, and the other between 1840 and 1845. The Adam who married Mary Magdalene Ulrich of Penn Township in 1799, is believed to have been a son or grandson of Lawrence Guth and his wife, Mary, who emigrated from the Rheinpfalz, Germany, arriving at Philadelphia, Pa., in the British ship "Thistle," where Lawrence took the oath of allegiance to the English government on September 19, 1738. They settled on the Jordan Creek in what is today South Whitehall Township, Lehigh County, Pa. At an earlier date it was Whitehall Township of Northampton County. In 1785, and again in 1788, an Adam Good was taxed with 340 acres of land and personal property in Whitehall Township. Some time prior to 1799, the Adam of this sketch became a resident of what is now Snyder County, where according to the entries in his Bible, he married Mary Magdalene, a daughter of John George Ulrich, a Revolutionary soldier of Penn Township. She was born on October 16, 1778, in what is now Penn Township, and died in or near Selinsgrove, Pa., on October 15, 1858. The Adam Good Bible records the birth of their children as follows: George, November 9, 1800; Magdalene, December 28, 1802; Charles, September 9, 1805; John, April 19, 1807; Daniel, October 26, 1809; Elizabeth (Mrs. John Michael Beaver, Jr.), October 28, 1811; Catherine, December 13, 1813; Susanna, March 20, 1816; Adam, Jr., October 12, 1818, and Amelia, January 1, 1822. George Good, who lived in the same section at the same time, was probably a brother of Adam. Adam and his wife were members of the First Lutheran church of Selinsgrove, and in 1801, he contributed to the fund for the erection of a new church at that place. The will of Adam Good was probated at Lewisburg, Pa., on May 7, 1826, and it is supposed that he and his wife are buried in the cemetery of the old Lutheran church in Selinsgrove. An Adam Good was a private in the Northampton County Rangers during the Revolutionary period, but some think that Adam, the soldier, was the father of the Adam of this sketch.

GEORGE GOOD was born Jan. 2, 1766, probably in what is now South Whitehall Township, Lehigh County, Pa., and died in the vicinity of Troxelville, Snyder County, Pa., June 11, 1835. Around the year 1800, George and family came to what is now Penn Township, Snyder County where he purchased six acres of ground near Salem in 1801 from Jacob Moyer. George's wife was Elizabeth Hammel, Hommel, or Hummel. She was born Jan. 7, 1733 and died June 11, 1811. She is buried in the Salem Cemetery and he at Troxelville. Adam seems to have been a brother of George, and Susanna a sister. The latter married George, son of the pioneer, John Frederick Miller of the Salem section. At least three of the children of George were born in South Whitehall Township, Lehigh County.

MOSES GOODEN was a resident but not a land owner, in Cumberland Valley Township, Bedford County, Pa., in 1784. He was first assessed in Beaver Township in Northumberland County in 1789. No military record was found for him, but it is believed that he served in the Revolution.

HENRY GOTHERS was assessed in Beaver Township for the first time in 1789. Nothing further could be found concerning him.

PETER GOTTSHALL probably lived in what is now Snyder County prior to 1800. He probably came from Lancaster County. He died in what is now Center Township, and his will was probated at Lewisburg, Pa., on November 23, 1826. His wife was Elizabeth —. She and their children; Andrew, Catherine (Mrs. John Hendrix), and Edys, were mentioned in the will. Andrew (son) and Jacob Kessler (a friend) were executors of the will.

JOHN FREDERICK GOY was born on September 12, 1761, and died on November 25, 1825. The name is also given as Gay, Gaw, Ghoy, etc. He was probably a son of Frederick Goy who was a resident but not a landowner in the village of Manheim, Lancaster County, Pa., in 1771. The name of Frederick Goy appeared on the Penn Township tax list for the first time in 1774, and in 1781, and for a number of years thereafter, he was assessed with 50 acres of land and personal property. It is believed that the assessment of 1774 may have been for the older Frederick and that of 1781 and later for the younger one. The elder Frederick may never have lived in the township. He was granted warrants of survey for additional land in Northumberland (now Snyder County) in 1793, and again in 1812. When Mahantango Township was formed from the southern part of Penn in 1796, he was a resident of the new district. His will was probated at Lewisburg, Pa., on December 20, 1828. His wife, Catherine and the following children are mentioned in the will: John, Frederick, Margaret, Catherine, David and Anna. The last two were designated as minors when the will was made at an earlier date. John Frederick's death occurred in what is now Perry Township and it is said he is buried in the Grubb's Cemetery in Chapman Township. He served in Captain Berryhill's Company of the Lancaster County Militia. His wife, Anna Catherine Zeller was born Feb. 4, 1777, and died July 4, 1834. She may have been a daughter of Fred Zeller.

CHRISTIAN GRAYBILL (also Kraybill, Kreybill, Krebihl, Kreybeihl, Grable, Graybeil, etc.) was a son of John Graybill. He was born in Lancaster County, Pa., and died near Richfield, Pa., in 1827, and is buried in the Graybill cemetery near that village. In 1771, he was taxed in Warwick Township, Lancaster County, Pa. On January 3, 1775, he was granted a warrant of survey for 300 acres of land in Northumberland County, now Snyder County, Pa., but his name did not appear on the Penn Township tax list until 1780. In 1787, he was taxed with 100 acres and personal property. It is possible that he did not come to Penn Township as early as his father did. About the year 1800, Christian laid out the village of Richfield, Juniata County, Pa. His will was probated at Lewisburg, Pa., on January 10, 1827, and in it are mentioned his wife, Mary, and the following children: Peter, Jacob, Christian, Jr., Barbara (Mrs. Henry Miller), Sarah (Mrs. Christian Zimmerman), Magdalene (Mrs. Henry Tittle), and Anna (Mrs. Michael Long.) Barbara, Sarah, and Magdalene preceded their father in death. Christian was a minister of the Mennonite faith, and many of the clan still adhere to that belief. Christian had an uncle of the same name. A Christian Graybill was a private, 2nd Class, in Captain John Gingrich's (Gingery's) Company, 9th Battalion of the Lancaster

County Militia. In 1790, Christian's family consisted of one male over and one under sixteen years, and two females.

JACOB GRAYBILL was the second son of John Graybill, Sr. (1735-1806). Jacob was born on May 9, 1761, probably in Donegal Township, Lancaster County, Pa. He came to what is now Snyder County with his parents during or after the Revolution. In 1790, his family consisted of one male under and one over 16 years, and two females. He was a brother of Christian, mentioned above. He died on April 20, 1829, and is buried in the old Graybill cemetery, northeast of Richfield, Pa. It is thought that he was the Jacob Graybill who served in the 2nd Company, 4th Battalion of the Lancaster County Militia in 1782.

JOHN GRAYBILL, SR. was born in Germany on August 18, 1735. His father's name was also John. In 1771, 1772 and 1773, John Graybill, Sr. and John Graybill, Jr., were residents and landowners in Donegal Township, Lancaster County, Pa. In 1772, John, Jr., secured a warrant of survey for a large tract of land in what was then Northumberland, but now Snyder and Juniata Counties. In 1774, he received an additional grant from the provincial authorities of Pennsylvania. About this time he moved to his new holdings in the vicinity of the present village of Richfield, Pa. His name appeared on the Penn Township tax list for the first time in 1776. In 1785, he was assessed with 350 acres of land and personal property. In 1789, he was constable in Penn Township. When Mahantango Township was formed from part of Penn in 1796, John and his sons, Jacob and Christian, were assessed there. The village of Richfield, founded by Christian, about 1800, stands on land once owned by the subject of this sketch. John Graybill, Jr., died in Mahantango Township on February 18, 1806, and is buried in the old Graybill cemetery, about a mile northeast of Richfield, in West Perry Township. His tombstone states "he was the eldest in this vicinity." His will mentions his wife Barbara, and the following children: Christian, Jacob, John, Anna Acker, Mary Knepley, Susan (Mrs. John Snyder), Barbara Shaffer, Magadalene (Mrs. Harman Snyder, Jr.,) and Catherine (Mrs. Peter Sechrist.) A son, Peter, died before his father. The Graybills of Snyder and adjoining counties are descendants of this man. John Graybill, probably a grandson of the subject of this sketch, became a bishop of the Mennonite church at

the age of 21, and retained office until his death in 1838. John Graybill's family in 1790, consisted of one male over 16, and five females. A John Graybill was a private, 7th class, in Captain Abraham Scott's Company, 3rd Battalion of the Lancaster County Militia and the same, or another, in 1779, was a private, 7th class, in Captain Joseph Work's Company, 3rd Battalion of Lancaster County.

JOHN GRAYBILL, SR., was born in Germany about 1710, and was the father of the John, mentioned above. He also had a son Christian, and probably other children. In 1771, 1772 and 1773, he was a resident and large landholder in Donegal Township, Lancaster County, Pa. He may never have lived in Penn Township, but it is believed that at one time he owned some of the land that later belonged to his son, John. Some of the Revolutionary service mentioned above, may have been his, but it seems he was too old to belong to the class mentioned.

EBENEZER GREEN. There were two men of this name on the tax lists of Northumberland County in 1778, and one in Turbot, and the other in White Deer Township. They may have been the same men, who moved from one district to the other during the year. The name remained in White Deer for many years, but Mrs. Bartol states that he lived in Penn Township at one time. Later an Ebenezer Green lived in Washington Township of Northumberland County. One of these men served as a private in Lieutenant Thomas Robinson's Rangers from Northumberland County, during part of the Revolutionary period.

JOHN GREEN was assessed in Penn Township only in the year of 1780. He probably lived in what was Cumberland County after that. No less then four John Greens lived in Pennsylvania during the Revolution. One of them, possibly the above, was a private, 2nd class, in Captain John Jack's Company of the 8th Battalion, Cumberland County Militia, in 1779.

JACOB GRIMM. In 1767 and 1768 a Jacob Grimm was assessed with 50 acres of land and personal property in Bern Township, Berks County, Pa. In 1779, the name of Jacob Grimm, Jr., was given on the tax list of Maxatawney Township, Berks County, for the first time, and in 1787, it first appeared on the tax list of Penn Township. Two years later it was given on the Beaver Township tax list, Beaver Township having been formed from the western end of Penn Township. The

compiler believes that this was the Jacob, Jr., who lived in Berks County. In 1790, his family consisted of one male over and three under sixteen years, and four females. A Jacob Grimm was Captain of the 3rd Battalion of the Northampton County Militia, and another Jacob was a private, 5th class, in the Cumberland County Militia in 1780.

PETER GROGG was assessed in Penn Township for the first time in 1793. He was a sawmill owner and operator. No military record was found for him.

HENRY GRONINGER (also Greninger, Greininger, Groninger, etc.,) is supposed to have lived in what is now Snyder County, or in the border of an adjoining county. In 1819, he was living in what is now Logan Township, Clinton County, Pa. He was born in 1758, and died in Logan Township on September 11, 1833. He served as a private in Captain Benjamin Weiser's Company, German Regiment, Continental Line, stationed at Philadelphia Pa., on January 30, 1777. In 1832, he was a pensioner.

JOSEPH GRONINGER supposedly was a brother of Henry, mentioned above. He lived in what is now Snyder County or in the borders of one adjoining it. On September 26, 1776, he enlisted in Captain John Clark's Company of the Northumberland County Militia at Sunbury, Pa. This organization served three months and eighteen days in the Continental Service. At a later date he served in Captain John Beatty's Company of Northumberland County Rangers.

DANIEL GROSS (also Gros, Grosz, Ghross, Groce, Grose, etc.,) was born on January 20, 1756, and died in Beaver Township on December 5, 1804. He is buried in the old Hassinger cemetery, west of Middleburg. He was taxed in Beaver Township for the first time in 1789. In 1790, his family consisted of one male over and one under 16, and three females. He received depreciation pay for services in the Berks County Militia.

HENRY GROSS, SR. was a native of Berks or Lancaster County. He was assessed in Penn Township for the first time in 1785. In 1787, he was taxed with 300 acres of land and personal property. He lived in that part of Penn Township which became Beaver Township and in 1789 he was assessed there. In 1794, he with Simon Snyder, later Governor of Pennsylvania, and several others, were appointed viewers to locate a road from Selinsgrove westward, toward Lewistown. In 1790, his family consisted of two males over 16, and three females. On September 9, 1776, he was a private in Captain Jasper Yeates' Company of the Lancaster County Associators. He died in Union Twp., Union Co., Pa., and his will was probated at Lewisburg, Pa., Aug. 17, 1842. One of his daughters was Barbara (Mrs. Geo. Kleckner.)

HENRY GROSS, JR., came to what was then Penn Township in 1785. In 1790, he lived in Beaver Township, and his family consisted of one male over and one under 16 years, and one female. He was a son of the man mentioned above.

JOHN GROSS, probably a son of Henry, Sr., was born on September 29, 1764, and died in what is now Snyder County on February 15, 1843. He is buried in the old cemetery at Beaver Springs, Pa. He may not have come to Snyder County until after 1800, because his name does not appear on the Penn or Beaver Township tax lists, or on the U. S. Census of 1790 for what is now Snyder Co. He may have lived in York County at an earlier date. A John Gross received depreciation pay for service in the York County Militia during the Revolution. John and Christian may have been his sons.

HENRY GROSSCOPE (also Grosscup, Grosskopf, Grosscop, etc.) lived in Beaver Township for a time. He may have been a son of Michael, and probably came from Lancaster Co. No additional information was located.

ADAM GROVE lived in what is now Union or Snyder County during the Revolution. It is believed that he came from Cocalico Township, Lancaster County, Pa. He was assessed in Penn Township for the first time in 1790, prior to that he lived in White Deer or Buffalo Township. In 1790, his family consisted of one male over and one under 16 years, two females, and one other person. In 1822, he was still living in what is now Union County, and in that year sold some land to Thomas Nesbit. Adam, and his brothers, Peter, Wendel, and Michael, were relentless Indian fighters, and one of them was in command of a party of Rangers operating against the Indians in the Buffalo Valley in 1779 and 1780. All four of the brothers served in the military forces during the Revolution.

RICHARD GROVE, saddler, was assessed in Penn Township for the first time in either 1779 or 1799. Probably the latter year. He may have been a son of Adam. In 1792, a Richard Grove was granted a warrant of survey for 200 acres of land in Huntingdon County, Pa. The U. S. Census of 1790 for Pennsylvania doesn't contain the name of Richard Grove.

GODFREY GROW (also Groh, Krow, Crow, Groo, Kroo, etc.) was a native of Berks County. He was assessed in Penn Township for the first time in 1774 but it is believed that he was a non-resident landowner at that time. He seems not to have become a resident of the township until 1787, when he was taxed with 400 acres and personal property in the district. It is believed that he was a descendant of Peter Groh, the immigrant. A number of Grows are buried in the cemetery at Liverpool, Perry County, Pa. Galusha A. Grow, was a well known politician in Pennsylvania about fifty years ago. The U. S. Census of 1790, for Pennsylvania, does not list his name under Groh or Grow. It is supposed that he served in the Revolution.

JOHN GRUBB, carpenter, was assessed in Penn Township for the first time in 1799. He was probably a son of Jacob Grubb, who died in Center Township in 1815. Members of the Grubb family lived in Northampton, Lancaster, Montgomery, and other counties in 1790. John Grubb lived in Manor Township, Lancaster County, Pa., in 1782.

JACOB GRUBB died in Center ship, now Snyder County, Pa., in 1815. His wife was named Elizabeth —. Due to the fact that their son John was assessed in Penn Township prior to 1800, it is supposed that Jacob may have lived in the township at the same time. Jacob's children were: Jacob, Jr., John (mentioned above;) Henry, Susan, Catherine and Elizabeth. One of the daughters married John Berger. In 1790, at least six men of the name of Jacob Grub or Grubb lived in Pennsylvania. Susan married John Bishop, Jr. Susan and Henry were minors in 1817.

CHRISTIAN GRUBER. Two men of this name lived in Pennsylvania in Revolutionary days, one of them was assessed with 100 acres of land and personal property in Tulpehocken Township, Berks County, Pa., in 1767 and 1768 The second appears for the first time in Bern Township, same county in 1779. One of these men, probably the latter, came to what is now Snyder County and was assessed in Penn Township for the first time in 1785. At that time he was taxed with 100 acres and personal property. Later information indicates that there was a third Christian Gruber and that he was a native of Lancaster County. The Christian who lived in Penn Township in 1785 was not there in 1790, and it is believed that he is the man who lived in Warwick Township,

Lancaster County at the time of the U. S. Census of 1790. A Christian Gruber received depreciation pay for services in the Berks County Militia, and another of the same name was a private, 6th class, 1st Company, 6th Battalion of the Lancaster County Militia in 1783.

JACOB GUNCKLE (probably Kunckle or Kunkel) was assessed in Mahantángo Township for the first time in 1796. The name seems to have been most common in Northampton County, and he may have come from there. No military record was found.

PETER GUNDY (sometimes given as Van Gundy) was a resident, but not a land-owner in Breaknock Township, Lancaster County, Pa., in 1773. He was assessed in Penn Township for the first time in 1778, but may not have lived there as the tax list of 1761 and 1762, designate him as a non-resident owner of 300 acres of land in 1763, he seems to have been assessed as the owner of 80 acres and personal property in Manheim Township of York County. He was a private, 4th class, 8th Company, 9th Battalion of the Lancaster County Militia in 1782. It is believed that some of his relatives located in what is today Union County.

HUGH GWYNN (also Guinn, Wynn, Winn, etc.) was probably assessed in Penn Township for the first time in 1776 under the name of "Hugh Wing," and it is supposed that he was a non-resident landowner at the time. In 1790, he was assessed with land and personal property. He died in Penn Township, and his will was probated at Sunbury, Pa., on April 28, 1806. The will mentioned his wife, Margaret, and the following children: George, William, Hugh, Jr., Samuel, Margaret, (Mrs. John Tate;) Mary, (Mrs. Jacob Overmire), Daniel, Debrow (Mrs. Archibald Mars), and Thomas. No military record was found, but it is believed that he served in the Revolution. George, one of Hugh Gwynns sons, lived in what later became Hartley Township, of Union County, Pa. George owned the farm which in 1885 was owned by Adam Musser.

VALENTINE GUYER (maybe Geiger) was granted lot No. 285 in the plot of Sunbury, Pa., on August 20, 1774. He was assessed in Penn Township for the first time in 1778, and his name disappeared after merely a non-resident landowner. No military record was found for him.

THOMAS GWYNN was one of the 1782. It is possible that he never lived in Penn Township, but was older sons of Hugh Gwynn, who died in Penn Township in 1806. His sister, Mary, married Jacob, son of Captain George Overmire.

WILLIAM GWYNN, was a son of Hugh Gwynn, Sr. He was assessed in Penn Township prior to 1800. He evidently moved to another locality, because later records do not carry his name.

PETER HACKENBERG, SR., was born in Germany in 1741. His full name was John Peter Hackenberg. He embarked for America at Rotterdam, Holland, in the British ship "Jeneffer," Captain George Kerr, master. He arrived at the port of Philadelphia, where he took the oath of allegiance to the British Government on November 5, 1764. He settled in the southeastern part of the state and in 1790 he lived in Bucks County, and his family consisted of two males over and one under 16 years, and thee females. The exact time of his coming to what is now Snyder County is unknown, but it is supposed to have been about 1795. One of his sons was Peter, Jr., Peter, Sr., died on March 4, 1820, and is buried in St. Peter's Cemetery in Freeburg. He was an Ensign in Col. Baxter's Regiment at the Flying Camp, and in 1778 was a Prisoner of War.

PETER HACKENBERG, JR., was born on June 22, 1773, probably in Bucks County, Pa., and died at Freeburg, Pa., on December 23, 1847. His wife was Hannah—. She was born on January 5, 1772, and died on March 11, 1854. Both are buried in St. Peters Cemetery in Freeburg, Pa. He was assessed in Penn Township for the first time in 1795. In 1813, he was one of the auditors of of Penn Township. On March 26, 1813, he was appointed a Justice of the Peace for Penn Township by Governor Snyder. On June 8, 1836, he was again appointed to the same office. On February 7, 1821, he became Register of Wills and Recorder of Deeds for Union County, and in 1830, he became a member of the Board of Commissioners for Union County. He had a son named Peter, and probably other children. He was an excellent penman, and the records prepared by him are as easily read today as when they were written over a hundred years ago.

JOHN HACKENBERG, carpenter, was assessed in Penn Township for the first time in 1799. It is believed that he was a son of Peter, Sr.

CONRAD HAFFLICH (also given as Hofflich, Hoeflich, Hefleg, Heffling, Haflich, Hayslick, etc.) was listed as a single freeman in Penn Township on the tax list of 1771. It is believed that he came from York County. In 1781, he was assessed with

50 acres and personal property, and in 1785, he was taxed with 150 acres and personalty. He must have moved on, because when Mahantango Township was formed in 1796, his name was not given there, although that is the section in which he lived, but the name of a Jacob Hafflich does. Conrad received depreciation pay for services in the Northumberland County Militia.

JACOB HAFFLICH is believed to have been a brother of Conrad, mentioned above. He was taxed in Penn Township for the first time in 1776, and his status given as a single freeman. When Mahantango Township was formed from part of Penn, in 1796, he was assessed there. He died in Perry Township, and his will was recorded at Lewisburg, Pa., on October 11, 1816. The will mentions his wife, Margaret, and their children, Philip, John (who died before his father;) Christina (Mrs. George Heimbach;) Jacob, Jr., Peggy (Mrs Peter Swartz;) Barbara, (Mrs. Peter Eagler;) Anna Maria, (Mrs. Frederick Roush;) Elizabeth; Catherine (Mrs. Daniel Riblet;) and Magdalena. Jacob served in Captain Michael Motz's Company, and in Captain Michael Weaver's Company of the Northumberland County Militia. It is also believed that he is the man that served in Captain Charles Baltzel's Company of the German Regiment, Continental line.

ANDREW HAFFER (also Hafer, Heffer, Haeffer, Hoeffer, Hoefer, etc.) became a resident of Penn Township prior to 1777. His name appeared on the Penn Township tax list for the first time since 1778. His wife was Elizabeth, daughter of Peter Druckenmiller, who in 1789 bought a tract of 353 acres of land around the present village of Kantz, Pa. He died a year or two later and this land was given to his son, Frederick Druckenmiller, and his daughter, Mrs. Haffer. In 1785, Andrew Haffer was assessed with 100 acres of land and personal property. Andrew Haffer died before 1803, because in this year, Elizabeth Hafer, widow, sold her 153 acre farm which she has inherited from her father, to Christian Kantz, Sr., who had lately moved up from Lebanon County. In 1790, the Haffer family consisted of one male over and three under 16 years, and four females. Christina Eckhart signed the deed when Mrs. Haffer sold the farm, and it is supposed that she may have been a married daughter. They had a son, Andrew, Jr., who was baptized at the old Zion Lutheran Church, north of Freeburg, in 1785. Jacob Haeffer, who was taxed for the first

time in Mahantango Township in 1796, was either a son or other relative. Andrew was a Revolutionary soldier, and on March 4, 1789, he was granted an invalid's pension. In his application he stated "that he had been a Private in Captain Michael Weaver's Company of the Northumberland County Militia, and that on November 20, 1777, he was wounded in the right forearm by which he lost the thumb and forefinger of his right hand." It is presumed that Andrew is buried in the Row's cemetery at Salem in an unmarked grave.

JOHN HAGEMAN (also given as Hagerman, Hugeman, Huguemah; etc.) evidently lived in Penn Township before 1790. He was granted a warrant of survey for 300 acres in Northumberland, now Snyder County, on October 31, 1785. He was born in 1757, and died in what is now Perry Township, Snyder County, in 1840 or 1841. On April 17, 1834, he made application for a pension, which was granted. At the time of his application, he stated that his age was 77 years. In 1790, his family consisted of himself and two females. In 1796, he lived in Mahantango Township. The time and place of his military service is unknown to the compiler.

JOHN HAGER came from either Berks or Bucks County. He was assessed in Penn Township for the first time in 1793, and in that year had a sawmill on the Penns Creek in the vicinity of App's (later known) as Schoch's and then Herman's) mill. His wife was named Elizabeth. He died in Penn Township in 1795. He was a private in Captain Jacob Laidich's Company of the Berks County Militia in 1781. John Hager is supposed to have been a descendent of Henry Hager, widower, and Guda Schram, widow of John Schram, who were married at Antzhausen, Germany, on January 18, 1638. Their third son was Henry Hager, who was baptized on August 27, 1644. He married Anna Catherine, daughter of Jacob Friesenhagen, late Burgomaster of Freudenberg, on December 3, 1678, at Siegen, Germany. Their third son, John Frederick, was baptized on September 28, 1684, and it was he who came to New York in 1710, with the Palatines, and later migrated to Pennsylvania, as did many of the other German immigrants, who landed at New York. It is believed that John Frederick may have been the father of the subject of this sketch.

JOHN FREDERICK HAGER was born on March 19, 1767, and died at or near Selinsgrove, Pa., on April 23,

1815. He is buried in the cemetery
of the First Lutheran church and
his grave is marked. It is believed
that he was a son of John mentioned
above, and a grandson and namesake
of the immigrant also mentioned
above. John Frederick evidently
came to Penn Township with his
parents, and no doubt succeeded his
father in business.

MICHAEL HAHN, SR. (also Hawn,
Hohn, Hoehn, Hain, etc.) was assessed in Penn Township for the first
time in 1772. In 1781, he wsa taxed
with 350 acres of land and personal
property. In 1796, when Mahantango
Township was formed, he lived in
that district and operated a sawmill.
This name may be the same as Hain
today. Michael came from Berks or
York County. A Michael Hahn received depreciation pay for services
in the York County Militia during
the Revolution.

MICHAEL HAHN, JR., was assessed in Penn Township for the first
time in 1785. He was the son of the
man mentioned above. He lived in
Mahantango Township when it was
formed in 1796.

JOHN HAINS (also Hens, Henz,
Haines, etc. Name on tombstone is
Hentz) was born in Germany on July
12, 1735, and died at Freeburg, Snyder County, Pa., on January 3, 1815.
His wife was Regina Schuster. Both
are buried in the St. Peters cemetery in Freeburg. John was a resident of Penn Township as early as
1776. He always lived in the vicinity
of Freeburg. In the U. S. Census of
1790, his family consisted of two
males over and two under 16 years,
and eight females. His will was recorded at Lewisburg, Pa., on February 9, 1815, and it mentions his
wife, Regina, and the following children: John George (1764-1830);
Margaret (Mrs. Peter Frees); Anna
Mary (Mrs. Peter Stroup, Jr., 1772-
1845); Catherine (Mrs. Henry Heimbach); Frederick; Lorentz (Lawrence); Elizabeth (Mrs. John Smith);
John Peter, baptized 1782; Maria
Christina (Mrs. Henry Mertz, 1784-
1862), and Jacob, baptized in 1787.
It is believed that he was the John
Hain who was a private in Captain
John Clark's 1st Company, 4th Battalion of the Northumberland County Militia in 1776.

JOHN GEORGE HAINS, son of
John, mentioned above, was born on
November 16, 1764, and died near
Freeburg, Pa., on September 23, 1830.
He was a millwright. Indications are
that he may have lived in Buffalo
Township for a time after 1785. His
name appeared on the Penn Town-
ship tax list for the first time in
1799. He is buried in the St. Peters

cemetery in Freeburg. A Geo. Haine
served in the Lancaster County Militia during the Revolution.

JOHN HAINES, millwright, was
assessed in Penn Township for the
first time in 1799. A John Haines
lived in Buffalo Township in 1781
and another was a single freeman in
Turbot Township in 1785. The John
of Penn Township is believed to
have been one of these.

PHILIP HAINS (or Hain) seemingly did not live in Penn Township
during the Revolutionary days, but
he did later, at just what time he
became a resident of what is now
Snyder County is unknown. In 1790,
he lived some where in Northumberland County, and his family consisted of one male over, and one under
sixteen years, and one female. He
served as a private under Captain
Stephen Beasley in the Pennsylvania
State Navy on July 1, 1777. He was
born in 1754. On January 25, 1833,
he applied for a pension, giving his
age as 79 years at the time. The pension was granted.

MATHIAS HALL was assessed in
Beaver Township for the first time
in 1789. Indications point to the fact
that he may have lived in Lancaster County in 1790. Nothing further
was found.

JAMES HAMILTON was assessed
in Penn Township for the first
time in 1796. At an earlier date he
was assessed as a non-resident owner
of 300 acres in Turbot Township,
Northumberland County. In 1786, he
was a resident and owner of 145
acres in Bald Eagle Township, same
county. Since there were several
men of this name in Pennsylvania
at the time, part of this record may
be that of another James. Several
men of the name served in the
Revolution, one from Northumberland County. In 1790, the family of
the subject of this sketch consisted
of his wife and himself.

JACOB HAMMERSLY (also Hamerle, Hammersley, Hamerle, etc.)
was born about the year 1736, probably in Lancaster County, Pa. On
May 31, 1760, he enlisted in the military service of the province of Pennsylvania for a period of four years.
His name was on the muster roll of
Colonel James Burd's Detachment
when it garrisoned Fort Augusta at
Sunbury from November 1, 1763 to
June 1, 1764. He was discharged on
May 31, 1764, and no doubt remained in the vicinity for a time
thereafter, because his name was
found on the first tax list ever made
for Penn Township, that of 1768. It
seems that he did not remain for a
long time, and he may have been

the same person who was listed as
a pauper in the city of Lancaster
in 1773. There is no evidence that
he served during the Revolution.
John Hammersly, who married a
daughter of Jacob German (Garman) may have been his son.

JOHN HAMPSHIRE seems to
have been a native of Philadelphia
County, and in 1782, was assessed
in Worcester Township of that
county. He was assessed in Penn
Township for the first time in 1776,
and it is believed that he was a non-
resident landowner, or that his stay
in the township was short and that
he returned to the southeastern part
of the state. The last time his name
appeared in Penn Township was in
1781 and in that year he was taxed
with 50 acres.

FREDERICK HANEY lived in
Penn Township in 1783. He was a
son of the Revolutionary soldier,
Christopher Haney. Frederick serv-
ed in Captain George Overmire's
Company of the Northumberland
County Militia. He moved to Center
County and is buried near Wood-
ward, Pa.

HERONIMUS HANEY (same as
for his brother Frederick, mentioned
above) name given in 1790 census.

THOMAS HARLAN (also Harlen,
Harland, etc.) was a miller and was
assessed in Penn Township for the
first time in 1799. A Thomas Harlan was a freeman in Newlin Twp.,
Chester Co., Pa. In 1779, a Thomas
Harlan was a freeman in Schaefferstown, Lancaster, now Lebanon County, Pa. He died in what is now Snyder County, Pa., in 1813, and it is
supposed that he is buried in the
old Lutheran Cemetery in Selinsgrove. One of his daughters married
Solomon, son of Peter Fisher, a
Revolutionary soldier. No military
record was found for Thomas.

JACOB HARPSTER lived in Penn
Township in 1776. In 1789 he was
assessed in Beaver Township. In the
U. S. Census of 1790, it states that
his family in that year consisted of
one male over and three under 16
years, and three females. In 1776,
he served as a Private in Captain
John Clark's Company, and at a
later date in Captain George Overmire's Company of Rangers, both
from Northumberland County.

BENJAMIN HARRIS was assessed
in Beaver Township in 1790. In 1790,
his family consisted of one male
over and one under 16 years and
three females.

JOHN HARTZ (also Hertz, Harts,
etc.,) weaver, lived in the borough
of Lancaster, Pa., in 1773. He was
assessed in Beaver Township for the

first time in 1789. His name was sometimes given as "Hatz." A John Hatz served in the Lancaster County Militia during the Revolution. In 1790, his family consisted of one male over 16, and one female.

DANIEL HASSINGER was a son of Jacob, Senior. He was born on July 28, 1760, and died on March 1, 1825. His wife, Elizabeth —, was born on January 10, 1790, and died on March 10, 1840. Both are buried in the Hassinger Old Cemetery, west of Middleburg. Daniel was assessed in Penn Township for the first time in 1782, and in that year was designated as a single freeman. In 1787, when Beaver Township was formed, he was assessed there. In April, 1789, he was Tax Assessor for Beaver Township. In the U. S. Census of 1790, it was stated that his family in that year consisted of one male over, and one under 16 years, and three females. No military record was found for him, but it is believed that he served in the Revolution.

FREDERICK HASSINGER was one of the many sons of Jacob Hassinger, Senior. He was assessed in Penn Township for the first time in 1781, and it is supposed that he was born about the year 1758. In 1785, he was taxed with 50 acres of land and personal property. In 1787, he was assessed in the newly formed township of Beaver. In 1794, he was granted a warrant of survey for 400 acres in Northumberland, now Snyder County. Frederick's father was one of the earliest settlers in the Middle Creek Valley, west of Middleburg. It is believed that Frederick is buried in an unmarked grave in the Old Hassinger cemetery, west of Middleburg. Many of his brothers and parents are buried there. He served as a private in Captain William Weirick's Company and in Captain John Black's Company of the Northumberland County Militia, and in May, 1780, in Lieutenant John Coleman's Party of Rangers.

HENRY HASSINGER was assessed as a single freeman in Beaver Townshpi in 1789. It is believed that he is a son of Herman Hassinger. No military record was found for him.

HERMAN HASSINGER was probably a brother of Jacob Hassinger, Sr. He was assessed in Penn Township for the first time in 1778, and in 1781 was taxed with 300 acres of land. In 1785, he was assessed as a non-resident, and it is believed that he became a resident of what is now Union County. In May and June of 1780, he served as a private for 37 days in Lieutenant Jacob Spees' Company of Rangers on the Frontier.

He may have been a son of John, who died in 1797.

JOHN HASSINGER died in what is now Snyder County in 1797. Letters of administration were granted to Catherine Hassinger, probably his wife, in the same year, and a record thereof made at Sunbury, Pa. David Nyhart (Neyhart) and George Adam Hummel were sureties for the administrator. A John Hassinger arrived at Philadelphia, Pa., on the British ship "Judith," James Tait, master, and took the oath of allegiance on September 15, 1748. John Jacob Hassinger, Sr. came in same ship, and the compiler believes they were brothers.

JOHN HASSINGER, was a son of John Jacob Hassinger, Sr. He was born on November 14, 1764, and died on May 12, 1810. His wife was Eva Catherine, daughter of John Bobb and his wife Eleanor Klein, who were also the parents of John Conrad Bobb. Eva was born on November 12, 1769, and died on October 2, 1826. Both are buried in the Old Hassinger Cemetery, west of Middleburg. John was assessed as a single freeman in Beaver Township in 1789. His will is recorded at Sunbury, Pa., and in it he mentions his wife, and a son (unnamed), and other children (names not given.) His brother, George, was executor of the will. No military service was found for him.

JOHN JACOB HASSINGER, SENIOR, (also Hossinger, Hosinger, Hoysinger, Haszinger, etc.) was born in Germany about the year 1730, and died in what is now Franklin Township, Snyder County, Pa., on July 25, 1802. His wife, Elizabeth —, was born on December 6, 1741, and died on September 30, 1826. Both are buried in the Old Hassinger Cemetery, west of Middleburg. Jacob embarked for America at Rotterdam, Holland on the British ship "Judith," James Tait, master, and arrived at the port of Philadelphia, Pa., where he took the oath of allegiance to the English Government on September 15, 1748. The John Hassinger who came on the same ship is believed to have been his brother. On April 19, 1774, he was granted a warrant of Survey for 200 acres of land in Northumberland, now Snyder County, Pa. It is believed that he occupied this land soon after the grant of the warrant. His name appears on the Penn Township tax list for the first time in 1776. In 1781, he was taxed with 250 acres and personal property, and in 1787 with 350 acres, sawmill, and personalty. In 1787, when Beaver Township was formed from the western part of Penn, he was assessed in the new district. In 1794, he or his

son of the same name, was granted a warrant of survey for 400 acres in Northumberland, now Snyder County. In 1790, his family consisted of six males over and one under 16 years, and six females,. His will was recorded at Sunbury, Pa., on August 17, 1802, and mentions his wife, and the following of their children: Abraham, Daniel (1760-1825), Jacob, Jr. (1762-1821), Valentine, George (1773-1855), Frederick, John (1764-1810), Elizabeth, and Philip. No military record was found for Jacob, but several of his sons saw military service during the Revolution.

JOHN JACOB HASSINGER, JR., was a son of John Jacob, Sr. He was born on August 10, 1762, and died on November 1, 1821. His wife, Magdalene —, was born on May 27, 1771, and died on December 22, 1837. Both are buried in the Old Hassinger Cemetery, west of Middleburg, and their graves are marked. In 1790, his family consisted of one male over and one under 16 years, and two females. It is not known when Jacob was first assessed in Penn Township, but in 1790, he lived in Beaver Township. He served as a private in the Continental Line during part of or 10th Pennsylvania Regiment of the all of the Revolutionary period.

HENRY HAUS (probably meant for Haas) was assessed with 100 acres and personal property in Skippack Township, Philadelphia County, Pa. in 1783. He was assessed in Penn Township for the first time in 1798, and at that time was the owner and operator of a sawmill. In 1790, he lived in Montgomery County, formed from Philadelphia County, a few years earlier, and his family consisted of three males over and three under 16 years, and six females. He died in what is now Center Township. in 1827. It is believed that Captain Valentine Haas was his son. It is believed that the subject of this sketch was the Henry Haas who sailed for America from Rotterdam, Holland, in the British ship "Edinburgh," Captain Russell, master, and arrived at the port of Philadelphia, where he took the oath of allegiance to the English government on September 30, 1754. No military record was found for him, but he probably served during the Revolution.

MICHAEL HAWN, SENIOR (probably meant for Hahn, or Hain) was assessed in Penn Township for the first time in 1778. Indications are that he returned to Tulpehocken Township, Berks County, Pa., where in 1790, his family consisted of one male over and one under 16 years, and two females.

MICHAEL HAWN, JUNIOR, was a

son of Michael, Sr. He was assessed in Penn Township for the first time in 1785, and when Mahantango Township was formed in 1796, he was living there. It is believed that he or his father served in the Revolution.

ANDREW HEFFER. See Andrew Haffer above.

· JACOB HEFFER (maybe meant for Haffer or Hafer) was probably a brother of Andrew Haffer who lived in the vicinity of Kantz or Freeburg in the early days of the Revolution. In 1773, Jacob lived in the borough of Lancaster. He was a blacksmith, and was assessed in Mahantango Township for the first time in 1796. In 1790, he was still a resident of Lancaster, and his family consisted of two males over and one under 16 years, and four females. He was a private in Captain Jacob Krug's Company of Colonel Slough's Light Infantry Battalion from Lancaster County on September 9, 1778. This organization served in New Jersey.

DANIEL HEIL was assessed in Beaver Township for the first time in 1789. No military record was found.

PAUL HEIM was assessed in Mahantango Township for the first time in 1796. In 1780, he was assessed with 147 acres and personal property in Brunswick Township, Berks County, Pa. The same was true in 1785. Two Paul Heims lived in Brunswick Township. One was Paul, Sr., whose family in 1790, consisted of three males over and two under 16 years, and one female. The family of Paul, Junior, in the same year, consisted of two males over 16, and six females. It is supposed that this sketch refers to the Paul, Jr. His wife was Catherine, daughter of Christopher Shaffer, Senior. John, who married Margaret Hafflich may have been their son.

PETER HEIM, was probably a son of Paul, Sr., and a brother of Paul, Junior. In 1790, he lived in Brunswick Township, Berks County, and his family consisted of one male over and one under 16, and four females. He must have lvied in Penn Township for a period prior to 1780, because he served as a private in Captain William Weirick's Company of the Northumberland County Militia. Some think he was a son of Paul, Junior.

PETER HEIMBACH was born on December 29, 1738, probably in Germany, and died some where in the vicinity of Grubbs church in Snyder County, Pa., on December 29, 1817. Some think that it may have been at a later date because his will was not filed until 1823. His wife was Mary Barbara —. They are buried in

the old part of the Grubb's Church cemetery in Chapman Township. It is believed that Peter was a son of the Peter Heimbach, who embarked for America in the British ship "Dragon," George Spencer, master, at Rotterdam, Holland, and arrived at the port of Philadelphia, Pa. where he took the oath of allegiance to the English government on September 26, 1749. In 1779 and 1780, a Peter Heimbach was a resident, but not a landowner in Albany Township, Berks County, Pa. In 1784, the same or another of the same name was a carpenter in Windsor Township, same county. The name appeared upon the Penn Township tax list for the first time in 1791, and in 1796, when Mahantango Township was formed from part of Penn, he was assessed there. Peter died in Perry Township. George, who died in the same township in 1828 was probably a son. It is believed that Henry, who married Catherine, daughter of John Hains, and Jacob were also sons. A Peter Heimbach was a private, 8th class, 8th Company, 4th Battalion of the Northampton County Militia during the Revolution.

FREDERICK HEINER (also Hainer, Hehner, Hener, etc.) probably came from York County. He was assessed in Penn Township for the first time in 1781, and in that year was taxed with 150 acres and personal property. His name does not appear after 1785. No military record was found.

HENRY HEISSLER (also Heisler, Heiszler, etc.) was a resident of Penn Township as early as 1792, and maybe before. His wife was Catherine Elizabeth —. They are known to have had at least four children; Suzanna, born March 26, 1792; Mary Margaret, born 1793, Henry, Jr., born July 12, 1795, and Maria, born July 10, 1797. The first and the last two were baptized at Grubb's Church, and the second at the old Zion Church, north of Freeburg. He lived in that part of Penn Township which became Mahantango Township in 1796. No military record was found for him.

CASPER HENDERSHOT was assessed in Penn Township only in the year of 1778. It is supposed that he was a non-resident landowner.

SAMUEL HENDRICKS, SENIOR, was born in Towamencin Township, Philadelphia, now Montgomery County, Pa. He was assessed in Penn Township for the first time in 1794, but some think he came there as early as 1792. The U. S. Census of 1790 states that he lived in Montgomery County in that year, and that

his family consisted of three males over and two under 16 years and two females. One record states that he died in Penn Township in March, 1807, and another seems to indicate that he died in 1810. Samuel, Jr. was one of his sons. It is believed that Jacob was another. Samuel, Senior, owned a farm touching the village of Salem, and it is believed that he is buried in the Row's Cemetery at that place. He served as a private in Captain Benjamin Weaver's Company of the 1st Battalion of the Philadelphia County Militia.

SAMUEL HENDRICKS, JUNIOR, was born in Montgomery County, Pa., probably in Towamencin Township, on July 4, 1779, and died in Penn Township on July 9, 1826. He seems to have inherited his father's farm at Salem, and it was he who gave the one and one-half acres of his farm for the church and cemetery at Salem, known as Row's Church, and he is buried on the ground which he donated. He was assessed in Penn Township for the first time in 1800.

HENRY HERMAN (also Harman, Harmon, Harmin, Herrman, Hermann, Hermon, Hermin, etc.) is believed to have been a native of Hempfield Township, Lancaster County, Pa., where he was assessed in 1779. On September 10, 1773, he was granted a warrant of survey for 50 acres, and on June 25, 1774, another warrant of survey for 90 acres in Northumberland, now Snyder County. If he ever lived in the township, it must have been for a few years around 1781. In 1790, he lived in Strasburg Township of Lancaster County and his family consisted of one male over and two under 16 years, and three females.

JOHN HERMAN was born on March 11, 1761, and died on December 8, 1840. He came from Northampton County or maybe from Lampeter Township, Lancaster County, Pa. It is believed that he was a son of John Herman, who on April 5, 1774, was granted a warrant of survey for 300 acres in Northumberland, now Snyder County, Pa. The compiler is of the opinion that the older John never lived in what is now Snyder County, but that his son became a tenant on the land at an early age, probably about 1780. The John of this sketch is buried in the old part of the Kratzerville Reformed (formerly Lutheran and Reformed Cemetery) at Kratzerville, Pa. He served as a private in Captain William Weirick's Company of the Northumberland Militia. John Herman had two wives, the first one was a Miller. The issue by the first wife follows: Jacob, John, Jr., David, Frederick, Henry, Mrs.

Joseph Berge, Mrs. Isaac Berge, Jonas, Daniel and Philip. The last three sons were not married. The children by the second wife were: Simon, Mrs. Benjamin Brouse, Mrs. Peter Pontius, and Mrs. John Fertig. The compiler has a genealogy of this family.

PHILIP HERMAN was a brother of John, mentioned above. Philip was born in 1763, and died in what is now Jackson Township, Snyder Co., Pa., in 1839. He is buried in the same cemetery as his brother. Philip was a bachelor. He, too, served in the Northumberland County Militia during the Revolution.

SAMUEL HERMAN was assessed in Beaver Township for the first time in 1789. From 1783 to 1786, he was assessed with 300 acres and personal property in Buffalo Township. In 1790, his family consisted of two males over and two under 16 years, and four females. It is believed that he served in the Revolution.

DAVID HERBSTER (also Harpster, Herpster, etc.) was assessed in Beaver Township for the first time in 1789. In 1786, he was taxed with 200 acres and personal property in Buffalo Township. In 1790, his family consisted of two males over 16 years, and two females. He received depreciation pay for services in the Northumberland County Militia.

JOHN FREDERICK HERROLD (also Herold, Heroldt, Herolt, Herhold, Herholdt, Hairhold, Herald, Harhold, Harold, Harrold, etc.) was a son, probably the youngest, of John George Herrold, Sr., and a grandson of George Christopher Herrold, Sr., who arrived at Philadelphia in 1743. The Herrolds were French Huguenots, of noble lineage, who because of their protestant beliefs were compelled to flee to Germany and later came to America. "Frederick" as he was commonly called was born in Heidelberg Township, Lancaster Co., Pa., on September 18, 1765, and a short time later was baptized at the Tulpehocken Lutheran Church, near Stouchsburg, Berks County, Pa. In 1771, Frederick accompanied his parents to what is now Chapman Township, Snyder County, where they were among the first settlers. Frederick was assessed in Penn Township for the first time in 1788, and in 1790, his family consisted of himself and wife. It is believed that her name was Catherine Suffel. She was born on August 24, 1769, and died on October 18, 1866. Her husband died on March 17, 1841. At the death of his father in 1803, Frederick and his brother, Captain Simon, inherited the large properties of their father, which consisted of many hundreds of acres of land, ferries, stills,

sawmill, gristmill, fisheries, etc. Frederick's will is on file at Lewisburg, Pa., and mentions his wife, and their children; "Colonel" John George (who married, Mary, daughter of the Hon. Frederick Steese); John, 1798-1854, (who married Christina Jacob Sechrist); Simon F., 1802-1886; (who married Sarah —; Catherine, 1806-1886, (Mrs. Lewis Kerstetter); Frederick, Jr. (who died in 1829); Maria (Mrs. Daniel Glass); Rebecca (Mrs. William Shaffer); Sarah, 1812-1891, (Mrs. John Holtzapple), and Anna, born April 20, 1819 (Mrs. Levi Rehrer.) Frederick and his wife are buried in the St. John Cemetery at Chapman.

JOHN GEORGE HERROLD, SR., was one of the two known sons of George Christopher Herrold, Sr., who was born in Germany in 1688, and emigrated to America, arriving at Philadelphia on the British ship "Rosannah," Captain James Reason, master, where he and his two sons took the oath of allegiance to the English Government on September 26, 1743. George Christopher, Sr., and his sons settled in Heidelberg Township, Lancaster County, Pa., near Stouchsburg, Berks County, and near Meyerstown, Lebanon County, where he died about October 27, 1749, and is buried in the old cemetery of the Tulpehocken Lutheran Church, near Stouchsburg, Pa. John George seemingly inherited the perental acres, but his brother, George Christopher, Jr., soon after 1750 settled in what is now Bethel Township, Berks County, where he lived until 1770 or 1771, when he moved to Hempfield Township, Westmoreland County, Pa., where he died in 1787. John George Herrold was born in Germany about the year 1725, and died in what is now Union Township, Snyder County, Pa., in October or November of 1803. George's wife was Anna Maria —. The date of her birth and death are unknown. It is supposed that these two are buried in the old, and now almost forgotten cemetery opposite the Lower Herrold School House, south of Port Trevorton, in Union Township, Snyder County. When George's father died in 1749, his wife, Maria Catherine, who was appointed administrator of his estate, and her son, John George, commonly called "George" was one of her sureties, and Colonel Conrad Weiser, the famous Indian Agent and Interpreter was one of the witnesses to the bond. The date of this bond was January 31, 1750, and is on record at Lancaster, Pa. The only appearance of his name on the records of the Tulpe-

hocken (Christ) Lutheran Church, where his father was a member, and is interred, was on October 6, 1765, when "Johann Freiderich Harhold" son of "George Herhold and his wife, Anna Maria was baptized. The sponsors at this baptism were "Frederick Weiser and wife," and it is evident that the child was named for Frederick Weiser, and this leads the compiler to believe that the wife of John George Herrold may have been related to the Weisers. Frederick Weiser's full name was John Frederick, and Frederick Herrold was given the same name. Frederick Weiser was a son of Colonel Conrad Weiser. If the Herrolds and the Weisers were not intermarried, they were at least neighbors and friends. Anna Maria, the oldest daughter of John George and Anna Maria Herrold was born on December 27, 1752, and on Whitsunday 1766, was confirmed as a member of the Tulpehocken Lutheran Church. An A. M. Herrold, believed to have been her mother, was a member of the church some fifteen years earlier. The compiler's immigrant Fisher ancestor was one of the founders of the Tulpehocken Church, in 1743, and donated five acres of land to it. Both the compiler's paternal immigrant ancestors, and his maternal immigrant ancestor were members of this church, and both are buried in it's old cemetery. On August 16, 1751, George Herrold obtained a warrant of survey for 100 acres of land in Lancaster County, probably in Heidelberg Twp. It was surveyed for Andrew Ellick on June 30, 1752, and returned as 219.1 acres, instead of 100. Heidelberg Township at that lay partly in Berks and partly in Lancaster Co., at that time. This land is supposed to have been in Berks County, near the line, or probably partly across the Lancaster County line. One of the neighbors of George Herrold was Henry Meiser, he later became a neighbor again in what is now Snyder County. In fact, it is believed that they moved to the new section at about the same time. On September 5, 1755, George Herrold secured a warrant of survey for 50 acres in Cumb᷏land, now Snyder County. This was surveyed for him on October 26, 1765, and resurveyed for him on December 23, 1785. The tract contained 146.2 acres and the patent shows that it lay on both sides of the Mahantango Creek, mostly in what is now Snyder County. John Martz was an adjoining landowner, on the south. In 1767, George Herrold was one of the signers to a petition made by a large number of Berks County residents, praying for the opening of a road from Reading to Fort Augusta, now Sunbury. This road was built at a later date.

In 1769, the Proprietary Government made the "New Purchase," and when this land, west of the mountains, was officially opened for settlement, it is believed that Herrold and his family moved to what is now Union or Chapman Township in Snyder County. He was assessed in Penn Township for the first time in 1771, when that section of the county was still part of Cumberland County. Prior to that, in 1767 and 1768, he was assessed with 150 acres, and 200 acres and personal property in Heidelberg Township, Berks County. On April 29, 1772, warrants of survey for 15 and 50 acres of land in Northumberland, now Snyder County, were granted to him, and on May 4, 1774, survey warrants for 50, 50 and 100 acres were granted to him in the same section. When these tracts were surveyed, they always ran much above the acreage mentioned in them, and at one time he was the third largest landholder in Penn Township. In 1777, he built the large log house which is still standing on the east side of the Susquehanna Trail at the village of Chapman. The house is now owned by Levi Reichenbach and wife. She was formerly Etta Herrold, a descendant of the builder. In the chimney on the attic of this house is a stone which bears the inscription " G. H. 1777." The house is a large rectangular one and is in a good state of preservation although it is nearly one hundred and sixty years old. On November 28, 1780, he was granted a tavern license, and for a number of years conducted a tavern in the house mentioned. In 1784, he was taxed with a still, in addition to other property. This still was located on the farm in Union Township once owned by the late ex-Sheriff, John S. Wolf. In the spring of 1790, the commission appointed to explore the upper reaches of the Susquehanna River, journeyed northward from Harrisburg and public records state that the commission spent the night at "Herrold's," an indication that the tavern was still in existence at that time. In the same year, according to the 1790 Federal Census, George's family consisted of himself and his wife. In 1796, when Mahantango Township was formed from the southern part of Penn, George was assessed in the new district. A receipted bill in the hands of the compiler shows that the subject of this sketch was selling wheat to parties down the river in the year of 1803. This bill states that

"John Capp of Harrisburg" was the buyer, and "George Herrold" the seller. The price was given in shillings and pence. George Herrold's will was recorded at Sunbury, Pa. in November, 1803, and mentions the following children, his wife having preceded him in death. The children were: Anna Maria, 1752-1820 (wife of Casper Arnold, Sr.;) Captain Simon, born about 1754, died 1827 (married Elizabeth —;) John George, Jr., born about 1756, and killed by the Indians at Fort Freeland in 1779; Susanna (who married a Bother or Potter); Catherine; Elizabeth (who married a Winkelblech,) and John Frederick, 1765-1841, mentioned in the sketch preceeding this one. A George Herrold received depreciation pay for services in the Northumberland County Militia. There are various indications that two men of this name served in the military forces from Northumberland County. The compiler believes that both father and son served in Revolution. John Rehrer, aged 84, of Selinsgrove, Pa., whose mother was a granddaughter of John George Herrold, Sr., told the compiler in the summer of 1934, that his mother told him in childhood that her grandfather was buried in the old pioneer burying plot, opposite the Lower Herrold's School House, about a mile south of Port Trevorton.

JOHN HERSHEY, JR., was assessed in Mahantango for the first time in 1796. His father came to that section about 1793. It is believed that John was born in Cocalico Township, Lancaster County, Pa. No further data was located.

JOHN GEORGE HERROLD, JR., was born about the year 1756, probably in Heidelberg Township, Berks County, Pa., and came to what is now Snyder County with his parents in 1770 or 1771. The Pennsylvania Archives indicate that two "George Herrolds" from Northumberland County served in the Revolution. One of them, believed to have been the subject of this sketch, was a private in Captain Benjamin Weiser's Company of the German Regiment, Continental Line, stationed at Philadelphia, Pa., on January 30, 1777. Linn in his "Annals of the Buffalo Valley" states that in the Indian attack on Fort Freeland, near Turbotville, on April 26, 1779, the following members of the militia (Rangers,) stationed there, were killed; Jacob Gift,— Herrold, and Michael Lepley. An examination of the roster of Captain John Moll's Company, which was stationed there at the time of the attack contains the

names of Jacob Gift, George Herrold, and Michael Lepley, and this leads the compiler to believe that it must have been George Herrold, Jr. who was killed. Later military lists do not contain the name of a George Herrold. George, Jr., must have been unmarried at the time of his death, because his father's will, made in 1802, does not include a George, nor the descendants of a deceased child. It is believed that George, Jr., was buried at the place of his death.

CAPTAIN SIMON HERROLD is believed to have been the oldest son of John George Herrold, Sr. He was born about the year 1754, probably in Heidelberg Township, Berks County, Pa., and came to what is now Snyder County with his parents in the year 1770 or 1771. He died in March, 1827, and is probably buried in an unmarked grave in the St. Johns Cemetery at Chapman. His name appeared on the Penn Township tax list for the first time in 1778. In 1785, he was assessed with 200 acres of land, personal property, a gristmill, and a ferry. On March 25, 1789, he was one of the Road Supervisors of Penn Township. On August 16, 1793, he received two warrants of survey for 100 and 150 acres, respectively, in Northumberland, now Snyder County. On May 2, 1794, he received another warrant, this time for 100 acres. In 1796, when Mahantango Township was formed, he was assessed there. During the year of 1815, he received warrants of survey for nearly 500 acres of land in Northumberland and Union, now Snyder County. Like his father, he was one of the largest landowners in this section. For many years he was an officer of the Lutheran Congregation at Grubb's Church in Chapman Township, in fact, it is believed that he was one of the charter members of the congregation. In 1790, his family consisted of two males over and three under 16 years, and four females. His wife was Elizabeth —. Captain Herrold's will was recorded at Lewisburg, Pa., on March 29, 1827. It mentions the following children: George G., 1785-1847, (who married Elizabeth Gross;) Simon K., 1786-about 1872 (who married Mary Hocker); Philip, 1792-1855, (soldier in the War of 1812, who married Susan C. —; Henry (who married Susan Walborn); Anna Maria, 1778-1862, (who married John Peter Shaffer, 1775-1847), and Elizabeth, 1781-1857 (who married John Witmer, 1778-1853). Simon Herrold gave nearly twenty years of his life to the military affairs of his country. As a young man he was a member of the Northumberland County Militia. In June, 1780, he was an Ensign in command of a party of Rangers on the frontier. Later he was a Lieutenant in Captain Michael Motz's Company of the Northumberland County Militia. On October 23, 1789, he was Captain of the 6th Company, 2nd Battalion, Northumberland County Militia. The same was true in 1790 and 1792. On February 28, 1794, he was Captain of the 2nd Company, 3rd Regiment of the Pennsylvania Militia. Simon was a man of affairs and his counsels were sought on many business, military and political subjects.

JOHN HERSHEY, SR., was assessed with 40 acres of land and personal property in Cocalico Township, Lancaster County, Pa., in 1771. In 1781 he seems to have lived in Manheim Township, York County, where he was taxed with 100 acres of land, personal property, gristmill, and sawmill. In 1783, he had the above property and a hulling mill, and his family consisted of seven persons. He was assessed in Penn Township for the first time in 1793, but it is believed that he was a non-resident landowner before that time. In 1796, when Mahantango Township was formed, he was assessed there. His son, John, Jr., was assessed there for the first time in that year. In 1778, he was a private in Captain John Gingery's (Gingrich's) Company, 9th Battalion of the Lancaster County Militia.

MATHIAS HESS was born in Germany. He sailed for America from Rotterdam, Holland, in the British ship "Billander," Captain Richgate Castle, master, and arrived at the port of Philadelphia, where he took the oath of allegiance to the English government on September 5, 1751. In 1771, he was assessed with 100 acres of land and personal property in East Hanover Township, Lancaster County. His name appeared on the Penn Township tax list for the first time in 1778, and in 1781 he was assessed with 400 acres of land and personal property, but a year later with only 150 acres. In 1783, he moved to Potter Township, which is now within the borders of Center County, where for a number of years he was taxed with 200 acres and personal property. In 1790, his family consisted of two males over and three under 16 years, and three females. No military record was found, but it is believed that he served in the Lancaster or Northumberland County Militia.

JOHN HESSLER was one of three brothers who lived along the Penns Creek, probably in what is now Jackson Township, Snyder County,

Pa. In 1790, his family consisted of one male over and one under 16 years, and four females. In that year he was living in Franklin County, Pa.

The Hessler brothers lived in Penn Township as early as 1776. It is believed that they were sons of Michael Hessler who arrived at Philadelphia in the British ship "Neptune," and took the English oath of allegiance there on October 4th, 1752. Michael embarked at Rotterdam, Holland. The Kratzerville Lutheran and Reformed Church in it's earlier existence was known as Hessler's, an indication that the Hessler brothers had something to do with its founding. John and his two brothers enlisted in Captain John Clark's Company, at Sunbury, in the fall of 1776, and saw active service in some of the early battles of the Revolution.

MICHAEL HESSLER was a brother of John mentioned above, and probably a son of Michael, the immigrant who arrived on the "Neptune" on October 4, 1752. Michael lived along the Penns Creek in what is now either Snyder or Union County as early as 1776. In 1790, his family consisted of himself and wife. Like his brothers, he enlisted in Captain John Clark's Company, at Sunbury, in the fall of 1776, and saw active service in some of the early battles of the Revolution.

WILLIAM HESSLER was a brother of the two mentioned above, John and Michael. It is believed that they were sons of Michael, the immigrant, who arrived in America in 1752. They lived somewhere in the vicinity of Kratzerville, because the first church there was named for them, but the name has since been changed. They lived in the section as early as 1776. In 1790, William's family consisted of one male over and one under 16 years, and four females. Like his brothers, he enlisted in Captain John Clark's Company, at Sunbury, in the fall of 1776, and seems to be living in either Snyder or Union County at present.

MICHAEL HETTRICK lived in Penn Township as early as 1780. It is believed that he was a relative of Adam or Christian Hettrick, or both. He served in Captain William Weirick's Company and in Captain John Moll's Company of the Northumberland County Militia.

MATHIAS HETZEL was assessed in Mahantango Township for the first time in 1796. On March 12, 1795, he was granted a warrant of survey for 250 acres of land in what is now Chapman or Union Townships of Snyder County, and it is evident that

he occupied it soon after the grant. In 1790, several Hetzel families lived in Philadelphia County. No military record was found for Mathias. There were at least six immigrants of the name Hetzel.

JOHN HIGHLAND was assessed in Penn Township for the first time in 1793. In 1790, he lived elsewhere in Northumberland County and his family consisted of one male over and one under 16 years, and two females. No additional data was located.

ADAM HILEMAN was probably a native of Lancaster County. He was assessed in Beaver Township for the first time in 1794. In 1787, he was listed as a single freeman in Augusta Township of Northumberland County. No military record for him was found.

JAMES HOFF, tailor, was assessed in Mahantango Township for the first time in 1796. In 1801, he contributed to a fund for the erection of the First Lutheran Church of Selinsgrove. No military record was located.

STEPHEN HOOK also given as Hock, Huck, etc.) was assessed in Penn Township for the first time in 1780, and in 1785 he was taxed with 100 acres of land and personal property. In 1790, his family consisted of one male over and five under 16 years, and four females. He died in Penn Township and his will was recorded at Sunbury, Pa., on April 27, 1795. The will mentions his wife, Christina, and the following children: Mary, Margaret, Christina, Elizabeth, Conrad, Barbara, Andrew, Henry and Jacob. A Conrad Hook served as a private in Captain Weaver's Company of the Northumberland County Militia. He is supposed to have served as a substitute for his father.

SAMUEL HORN may have been a brother of William Horn, and was probably a native of Cumberland County. In 1780 and 1781, he was assessed as a resident, but not a land owner in Penn Township. In 1782, he was assessed with 200 acres in Bald Eagle Township, and after 1784, with 200 acres and personal property in Penn Township. On July 18, 1779, he enlisted as a private in Captain Gilbert McCay's Company of the Cumberland County Volunteers.

LIEUTENANT CHARLES HORNBERGER (also Henberger, Hernberger, Hunberger, etc) came from either Berks or Northampton County, Pa. In 1780 and 1782, he was listed as a single freeman in Penn Township. In June, 1780, he was a private in Ensign Simon Herrold's Party of Rangers, and at another time he was a Lieutenant in Captain William Weirick's Company of the Northumberland County Militia. In 1778, a Charles Hornberger served as a private in the 8th Company, 2nd Battalion of the Northampton County Militia.

GEORGE HORNER was assessed in Upper Milford Township, Northampton County, Pa., in 1786 and 1787. He and his family came to Penn Township prior to 1790, because their names are recorded on a membership list of Salem (Row's) Lutheran Church made before 1790. Mrs. Horner's baptismal name was Cugipunta. Jacob and John are believed to have been their sons. They, too, were members of the Salem church. Geo. Horner served in the Northampton County Militia during the Revolution.

JACOB HOSTERMAN, SENIOR, is believed to have been a son of Peter Husterman, or Hesterman, who was born in the Palatine section of Germany and sailed from Rotterdam, Holland, for America in the British ship "Snow Fox," Charles Ware, master. He arrived at the port of Philadelphia where he took the English oath of allegiance on October 12, 1738. Peter was born in the year of 1693. Tradition has it that the Hosterman family settled in Lampeter Township, Lancaster County, Pa., soon after their arrival. The first appearance of the name of Jacob, Sr., is in 1771, when he was assessed as a resident, but not a landowner, in Lampeter Township. On August 4, 1773, Jacob, Sr., was granted a warrant of survey for 300 acres of land in Northumberland, now Snyder County, however, it is evident that Jacob lived in what is now Penn Township some time before that date, because on May 25, 1772, shortly after Northumberland County was formed from part of Cumberland County. Jacob, Sr., was appointed road supervisor for Penn Township in the new county.

On February 13, 1777, he was a member of the Committee of Safety for Penn Township, and thus became one of those who helped establish this country. In the same year, his name was found on a petition to the Supreme Executive Council of the State of Pennsylvania, praying that an election be held in Northumberland County. In 1781, he was the owner of 250 acres of land and considerable personal property in Penn Township. His known children were: Colonel Peter (1746-1805), and Jacob, Jr., (1749-1812.) Christian Hosterman may have been a son, and it is believed that there were other children. It is believed that Jacob was born in Germany about the year 1720, and that he died in Northumberland County, before 1800.

JACOB HOSTERMAN, JUNIOR, was a son of Jacob Hosterman, Sr. He was born on Oct. 14, 1749, probably in Lampeter Township, Lancaster County, Pa., and died in Haines Township, Center County, Pa., on February 5, 1812. His wife was Christina—. Both are buried in the cemetery at Wolf's Chapel, east of Aaronsburg, in Center County. Jacob, came to what is now Snyder County with his father and brother, Peter, in 1771 or 1772. That the Hostermans were people of standing is evidenced by the fact that Jacob, Sr. was appointed the first Road Supervisor and his son, Peter, the first Tax Assessor of Penn Township, when the new county of Northumberland was formed in 1772. In 1784, Jacob, Jr., was assessed with 200 acres of land and personal property in Penn Township, and in 1793, he was granted a warrant of survey for an additional 250 acres of land in Northumberland County, this is supposed to have been located in what is now Center County. In 1790, his family consisted of one male over and one under 16 years, and five females. Between 1790 and 1800, he moved to what is now Haines Township, Center County, Pa., and is said to have built the fine old brick colonial house about a fourth of a mile south of the present village of Feidler (named for the pioneer, Stephen Feidler.) The children of Jacob, Jr., and his wife were: John (who married Christina Harper); Elizabeth; Jacob; Magdalene; Barbara; George (who married Catherine Kramer); David, and Anna. Jacob served as a private in Captain Michael Motz's Company of the Northumberland County Militia serving as Rangers on the Frontier. On one occasion he was captured by the Indians and almost starved to death before he could get a chance to escape. Many of this pioneer's descendants live in Center County, today.

LIEUTENANT COLONEL PETER HOSTERMAN was one of the most colorful figures in the military and political annals in Central Pennsylvania, during and after the Revolutionary period. He was a son of the Jacob Hotserman, Sr., and a brother of Jacob, Jr. Peter was born on September 27, 1746, probably in Lampeter Townhsip, Lancaster County, Pa., and died in Selinsgrove, Pa., on January 27, 1805. His wife was Catherine, 1779-1864. Both are buried in the cemetery of the First Lutheran church, which Peter and his father helped to establish. Peter came to what is now Penn Township with his father and brother in 1771

or 1772, and in May of 1772 was appointed a member of a board of viewers to locate a road from opposite Sunbury to the Mahantango Creek, hanna. In the same month, he and three others were granted tavern licenses. On November 23, 1772, when he was only twenty-six years old, he was appointed Tax Assessor for Penn Township, which at that time comprised practically all of the present Snyder County. The settlers were few and far between in those days, there were no roads, many savages still lurked in the forest, but in spite of these drawbacks, he accepted the job. It was necessary for him, personally, to visit once each year, every family in the district, for the purpose of making the assessments, and collecting the taxes due.

On August 25, 1774, he received a grant of lot No. 281 in the townsite of Sunbury, Pa., later he sold the lot to the county and the courthouse now stands on the lot that Peter once owned. In 1777 he was one of the petitioners to the Supreme Executive Council of the state for permission to hold an election in Northumberland County. In November, 1777, he was a candidate for the office of sheriff, but was defeated by Jonathan Lodge. On January 27, 1785, he protested the appointment of Simon Snyder (now Governor of Pennsylvania) to the office of Justice of the Peace for Penn Township. In 1786, he received a warrant of survey for 300 acres of land in Northumberland, now Snyder County. Eventually he became one of the argest land owners in the county. In 1787, he was one of a board of viewers to erect a new township from the western part of Penn, this at first was called Beaver Dam, and later Beaver Township. In November, 1787, he was elected as one of the Commissioners of Northumberland County, and two years later he was re-elected. In 1792, and again in 1794, he received warrants of survey for land in Northumberland County. On March 14, 1796, he was appointed a Justice of the Peace for Penn Township the same year when Mahantango Township was formed from the southern part of Penn, he was assessed as one of the largest non-resident landowners there. In 1801, he was a contributor to the fund for the erection of the First Lutheran Church of Selinsgrove.

He served on many boards of viewers for various public improvements, the last of these was in 1804, vhen he was one of the viewers to ocate a road from Salem to New Berlin. Peter Hosterman and his wife had five children: Jacob, Jonh Peter (who was baptized at the old Zion Lutheran Church, about a mile north of Freeburg in 1785). George, (who served in the war of 1812, and whose widow, Susan, was a pensioner); Catherine, 1779-1864, who married John Fisher, 1773-1826, of Penn Township), and Elizabeth (Mrs. Jonathan Spyker).

The military services of Colonel Hosterman were numerous and varied. On January 30, 1777, he was a private in Captain Benjamin Weiser's Company of the German Regiment, Continental Line, stationed at Philadelphia, Pa. Most of the men of this company were from the eastern section of what is now Snyder County. Late in 1777, or early in 1778, he was appointed a Lieutenant-Colonel in the Northumberland County Militia, and in May of the latter year, he was in command of the militia operating against the Indians in the upper Penns Valley. On May 11, 1778, Col. Hosterman's command, while escorting a party of settlers along the West Branch of the Susquehanna, was attacked by the Indians near the Lycoming Creek, and six men were killed and six missing. On June 10th of the same year the Indians made an attack upon the settlers between the Lycoming and Loyalsock Creeks, and Colonel Hosterman's command was sent there. In July, 1780, while stationed in the Buffalo Valley with his battalion, Indians attacked him at Focht's mill, and in the engagment which followed, both sides lost heavily. On Aug. 18, 1780, Colonel Hosterman joined Colonel M. Smith, commandant of Fort Augusta at Sunbury, in a petition to the Supreme Executive Council of the state, for more arms and men with which to protect the settlers from the attacks and ravages of the Indians. In April, 1785, he was elected Lieutenant-Colonel of the 1st Battalion of the Northumberland County Militia. In 1788, he was a major in the militia of the same county. His connection with the military affairs of his community and country covered a period of more than a dozen years, and he served both in the state and the federal service. He fought the enemies from without, and those from within. His was surely a busy and useful life.

PETER HOUSEL was assessed with 255 acres and personal property in Warwick Township, York County, Pa., in 1779 and 1781. His name appeared on the Penn Township tax list prior to 1790, and in the federal census of 1790, his family consisted of three males over and three under 16 years, and four females. He died in Penn Township in 1797. His wife was named Mary and one of their children may have been named John. No military record was found, but it is believed that he served in the York County Militia.

JACOB HOUSER is believed to have been a son of Mathias, and a brother of John Houser. He was assessed in Penn Township for the first time in 1786, and when Beaver Township was formed he lived there. In 1790, his family consisted of one male over and three under 16 years, and three females. He died in Beaver Township, and his will was recorded at Lewisburg, Pa., on March 21, 1822. He served as a private in Captain Michael Weaver's Company, and in Lieutenant Peter Grove's Party of Rangers from Northumberland County.

JOHN HOUSER (also Howser, Hauser, Hausser, Housser, etc.) was assessed as a single freeman in Earl Township, Lancaster County, Pa., in 1773. He was assessed in Penn Township for the first time in 1781, and at that time was taxed with 130 acres of land and personal property. It is believed that he was a son of Mathias Houser, an immigrant, who arrived in 1751. In 1787, John was assessed with 300 acres and personalty in Penn Township. The Jacob Houser who lived in Beaver Township in 1789, was probably his brother. John may have lived in Penn Township before 1781, because on January 30, 1777, a John Houser was a private in Captain Benjamin Weiser's Company of the German Regiment, Continental Line, staioned at Philadelphia. This Company was recruited from the men of what is now Snyder County in the fall and early winter of 1776. A John Houser served in Captain Alexander Martin's Company of the Lancaster County Militia. The compiler believes they were the same man. In 1790, John's family consisted of one male over and three under 16 years, and four females.

MATTHIAS HOUSER seems to have been a non-resident landowner in Penn Township. In 1771, 1772, and 1773, he lived in Elizabeth Township, Lancaster County, Pa. He was assessed in Penn Township for the first time in 1778, but there is no evidence that he lived in the township. Jacob and John are believed to have been his sons, and that one or both of them may have been tenants on their father's property in what is now Snyder County. Mathias was born in Germany and embarked for America at Rotterdam, Holland, on the British ship "Phoenix," Captain Spurrier, master. He arrived at Philadelphia, where he took the English oath of allegiance on September 25, 1751.

ADAM HOWELL was assessed in Penn Township for the first time in 1788. No further data was available.

JOHN HOWELL was assessed in Penn Township for the first time in 1799. A John Howell lived in Augusta Township, Norhumberland County, in 1787. Several men of this name were in the military service from Pennsylvania, during the Revolution.

HENRY HOYN (probably meant for Hain) was assessed in Beaver Township for the first time in 1799, and one designated as a single freeman. He served as a clerk in the store of Henry Aurand, and it is believed that he was a relative, probably a nephew of Aurand.

GEORGE ADAM HUMMEL was assessed as a tanner, but not a landowner, in Pine Grove Township, Berks County, Pa., in 1779. In 1784 and 1785, he was taxed with 61 acres and personal property in Pine Grove Township. His name appeared on the Penn Township tax list for the first time in 1793, and he lived and died in what is today Middle Creek Township of Snyder County. It is believed that he was a son of George Philip Hummel who came on the ship "Rosannah" in 1743. George Adam was born about the year 1752, and died in 1808. His will was recorded at Sunbury, Pa., on March 7, 1808, and mentions his wife, Magdalene (or Magtaton), and the following children: Henry, Elizabeth, John Jacob (born June 1, 1788, and baptized July 6, 1788, at Christ Lutheran Church, near Stouchsburg, Pa., with Jacob Weiser and wife as sponsors); Anna Maria. Catherine, Susanna, Solomon (1795-1861), whose wife was S u s a n n a—1799-1879); Barbara, Mollie, George Adam, Jr., (1805-1886), who married Sarah—(1806-1883); Benjamin and John.

In 1934, Norman P. Hummel, post-master at Kreamer, Pa., a descendant of this pioneer, stated that his great-grandfather, George Adam, Sr., came to what is now Snyder County in 1793, and that one located in Monroe Township, and the other on Chestnut Ridge. He did not know the names of his ancestors brothers. The compiler believes that George Adam was a cousin, and not a brother of the Hummels who settled in Monroe Township, Snyder County, and Union Township, Union

County. No military record was found for George Adam, but it is believed that he must have served in the Berks County Militia.

GARRET HUGHES lived in Blockley Township, Philadelphia Co., Pa., in 1790, and his family consisted of his wife, self, and daughter. Soon after this date he came to Penn Township and lived near the village of Kantz, where he died intestate in 1797. It is supposed that he was buried in the cemetery of the First Lutheran Church in Selinsgrove. His widow later married George Slotterback. Her name was Susanna. Garrett and Susanna had four children; Lydia (Mrs. Jacob Diffenbach), Charles, Edward and William.

JOHN FREDERICK HUMMEL was the youngest son of John Jacob Hummel, and his wife, Eva Maria De Turk. "Frederick" as he was commonly called was born in Windsor Township, Berks County, Pa., on August 2, 1773, and died near Selinsgrove, Pa., on February 8, 1845. His wife, Elizabeth Becker, daughter of Michael Becker and Elizabeth Beck, was born in Windsor Township, Berks County, Pa., in 1771, and died in what is now Monroe Township, Snyder County, on February 28, 1853. Both are buried in the cemetery of the First Lutheran Church in Selinsgrove. Frederick learned the trade of shoemaker, and was assessed in Penn Township for the first time in 1799, but it is believed that he may have lived in the district a year or two earlier. His brothers, John and John Jacob, and several of his sisters came to what is now Union and Snyder Counties between the years of 1793 and 1799. Frederick became a large landowner in what is now Monroe Township, and many of his descendants still live in the vicinity. On January 11, 1804, Frederick bought 120 acres for 662 pounds, about a mile west of the Susquehanna Trail at the southern boundary of Shamokin Dam Borough. This farm is today owned by his great grandson, George Hummel. Later Frederick bought 30 acres additional to this tract. His son Michael became the owner at his death, then Michael's son, Jeremiah, and then Jeremiah's son George, the present owner. Mrs. John Hartman of the same section was a sister of Frederick. John Jacob Hummel, for many years the proprietor of the "Rising Sun" Inn at Hummels Wharf, was his brother. Frederick served as a road supervisor in Penn Township in the year of 1829.

The children of Frederick and his wife were: Benjamin (1792-1845),

Jacob F. (1793-1873), who married Margaret, daughter of Barnhart Kline, Samuel (1794-1861), who married Catherine —(1789-1840), John (1799-1868), who married Susanna —(1798-1860), Elizabeth (Mrs. John St. Clair), Sarah (Mrs. Henry Sheetz, and Michael (1807-1891), who married Esther Schoch (1807-1877).

JOHN JACOB HUMMEL, was a brother of Frederick, mentioned above. "Jacob" as he was commonly called was one of the older children of John Jacob Hummel and Eva Maria DeTurk, his wife. The elder John Jacob was born in Germany about the year 1725, immigrated to America in 1743, and died in Windsor Township, Berks County, Pa., in 1773. The subject of this sketch was born in Windsor Township, Berks County, Pa., on February 21, 1756, and died in or near Selinsgrove, Pa., on February 22, 1832. His wife was Elizabeth Heffner of Berks County. Both are buried in the cemetery of the First Lutheran Church in Selinsgrove. One authority states that Jacob, and his brothers, John and Frederick, and their sisters Mary, Catherine, Eva Mary, and Mrs. John Hartman came to what is now Monroe Township of Snyder County in 1793. The evidence is that John and Jacob, may have come at that time, but that Frederick, and some of the others came a few years later, probably in 1798 or 1799.

John located near Dry Valley in what is now Union Township, Union County. Jacob, in 1799, was assessed with two stills and a tavern in Penn Township. The tavern was the famous "Rising Sun Inn" and was located near the present day Hummels Wharf, along the Susquehanna Trail. Jacob had learned the trade of gunsmith in his youth, and at one time owned a sawmill. In 1797, he bought 443 acres of land in Monroe Township for 3550 pounds (gold). This tract at an earlier date belonged to the Mannings. In 1807 and 1808, Jacob, was a road supervisor in Penn Township, and again in 1809. In the same year he was one of a board of viewers to locate a bridge across Penn's Creek, north of Selinsgrove. In 1812, he was a viewer for a bridge across the same creek at Pine street in Selinsgrove. From 1819 to 1821, he was again a road supervisor, and in the latter year he was a viewer for a road across the Isle of Que to the Susquehanna River.

Jacob was a member of the Lutheran Church and donated several sums for the erection of the First

Lutheran Church in Selinsgrove in 1801. He was one of the three members from the Lutheran congregation who served on the building committee at that time. His widow was still alive on April 4, 1835. The children of Jacob and his wife were: John, 1778-1853, (who married Catherine Weary, 1785-1883); Captain John Jacob, 1780-1860, (who married Nancy Bower); Benjamin, 1788-1869 (married Catherine Hilbish, 1795-1869); Daniel (married Mary Leonard); Mary (married John Harrison, 1803-1854); Elizabeth (married Jacob Hettrick, and later Daniel Ott, her sister's widower); Hester (married Daniel Ott, 1785-1852, who later married her sister, Elizabeth), and Hannah (married George Gaugler.) John Jacob Hummel served in the Revolution from Berks County, but the compiler does not have the record of his service. The baptismal record of most of the Hummels can be found in Zion (Moslem) Lutheran Church, Richmond Township, Berks County, Pa.

JOHN HURST was assessed in Beaver Township for the first time in 1798. In 1790, his family consisted of himself and his wife.

CHARLES IMHOFF was assessed in Mahantango Township for the first time in 1796, and at the time he was taxed with two legal heirs. His wife's name was Maria. They had at least two children: Jacob and Elizabeth (Mrs. Henry Zeller.) Elizabeth was born on August 31, 1798, and baptized at Grubb's church in Chapman Township was a native of Monroe Township, Lancaster Co., Pa. On February 13, 1801, he bought 60 acres of land in Chapman Township from Casper Arnold, Sr.

FREDERICK ISENHAUER, or EISENHAUER (also Isenhower, Eisenhower, Ironcutter, etc.) was assessed as a single freeman in Penn Township in 1776. His stay in the township was short. He served as a private in the 13th Pennsylvania Regiment, Continental Line, and was killed in action.

JOHN ISENHAUER, or IRONCUTTER, and Frederick Stump, on January 10, 1768, in a drunken brawl, murdered six Indians at the mouth of the Middle Creek in Penn Township. The next days these friends went up the Middle Creek to the present site of Middleburg, and murdered four more offensive Indians. Lieutenant William Blythe reported the murders to the Supreme Executive Council and Captain William Patterson came and arrested the murderers and lodged them in the Carlisle jail. They escaped, and although Governor Penn offered 200 pounds for their recapture, they were never taken.

JOSEPH JACOBS may never have lived in Penn Township, but was one of its largest land owners. His name appeared on the Penn Township tax list for the first time in 1771, and in 1772, he lived in Cocalico Township, Lancaster County, Pa. In 1779 he owned considerable land in Cumberland County, and in 1781, he was assessed as the non-resident owner of 900 acres in Penn Township. In 1782, he was still a resident of Cocalico Township. A Joseph Jacobs served as a Drummer in the 6th Pennsylvania Regiment, Continental Line, and another was a private, 6th Battalion of the Lancaster County Militia.

LIEUTENANT JACOB JARRETT (see Lieutenant Jacob Sharrett) was assessed in Penn Township for the first time in 1776, and his name appeared under various spellings, such as Sharrott, Sharritt, Sharet, etc., but today is universally used as Jarrett. In 1781, he was taxed with 50 acres and personal property, and in 1785, with 200 acres and personalty. In 1787, he was a road supervisor in Penn Township and in the same year he was one of the viewers to form a new township from the western part of Penn.

REV. FREDERICK JASENSKY was the pastor of the Zion (Morr's) Lutheran church, which was located about a mile north of the present village of Freeburg, from 1790 to 1798. His wife's name was Mary Eva—. Two of their children, John Jacob in 1793, and John George in 1795, were baptized at the old church. Evidently he was teacher as well as pastor, and it is believed that he taught one of the first schools in what is now Snyder Co. He was one of those hardy pioneers of the Lutheran faith who did not deem it a hardship to go to the very frontier to minister to his flock.

JAMES JOHNSTON lived in Beaver Township in 1790, and in that year, his family consisted of one male over and one under 16, and one female.

JOHN JOHNSTON was assessed in Beaver Township for the first time in 1791. In 1796, when Mahantango Township was formed from the lower part of Penn, the same, or another of the same name was assessed in the new township. In 1796, he was the owner of a sawmill. Several decades later a John Johnston and his wife had several children baptized at Grubb's church.

in Chapman Township. The evidence seems to indicate that John Johnston lived in Penn Township in 1790, and in that year his family consisted of two males over and one under 16 years and two females.

BENJAMIN JORDAN was assessed in Penn Township for the first time in 1781, but must have lived there at an earlier date. In 1781 and 1782, he was assessed with personal property only, and in 1785 he was assessed with 100 acres and personal property in Potter Township (now within the confines of Center County.) He still lived in Potter Township in 1786. On March 13, 1776, he was an Ensign in the 5th Company, 3rd Battalion of the Northumberland County Militia. At another time he seems to have been a private in Captain Cookson Lon's Company from Northumberland. It is believed that Peter and Philip, who lived in the same section, were relatives of his.

JOHN JORDAN may have been a native of Lancaster County. He was assessed in Mahantango Township for the first time in 1796. A John Jordan served in the Lancaster County Militia during the Revolution.

PETER JORDAN may never have lived in Penn Township, but as early as 1774, he was assessed there. In 1781, and again in 1785, he was listed as the non-resident owner of 150 acres in Penn Township. A Peter Jordan served as a Matross in the 1st Pennsylvania Artillery, and Peter Jordan was listed among the new Levies. He died in West Buffalo Twp. He had two daughters Esther and Margaret.

PHILIP JORDAN was a native of Tulpehocken Township, Berks County, Pa. He was assessed in Penn Township for the first time in 1774 and it is believed that he returned to Berks County during the Great Runaway, because he was assessed with a tannery there in 1779. He seems to have returned to Penn Township about 1783, and followed the same business there. It is believed that he was a relative of the Jordans mentioned above, and may have been the father of all of them. No military record was found for Philip.

CHRISTIAN KANTZ, SENIOR, was born about 1759, probably in Lancaster County, Pa., and died in what is now Penn Township, Snyder County, in 1826. His wife was Anna Margaret, daughter of the immigrant, John Adam Menges (1730-1814.) She was born in the vicinity of Stouchsburg, Pa., probably in what is now Lebanon Coun-

ty, on January 17, 1761. The date of her death is unknown to the compiler, but it is supposed that both are buried in the old cemetery of the First Lutheran Church in Selinsgrove, where they were members. Christian lived in what is now Lebanon County, prior to his coming to what is now Penn Township in 1803. He bought from Elizabeth Haffer, widow, the old Peter Druckemiller farm, which included the present village of Kantz, which was named for Christian. The children of Christian and his wife were: Philip, 1793-1856, (married Catherine Erdley, 1802-1866); Christian, Jr., 1796-1854, (married Polly Ann Stroup, and later Anna Mary Spotts-Grosch); John, 1802-1853, (married Mary Fisher, 1803-1877); Simon, 1805-1873, (married Sarah —, 1806-1895); Catherine (Mrs Joseph Aarens); Margaret (Mrs David Klose), and Mary (Mrs.— Witmer). No military record was found for Christian, but it is believed that he served in the Lancaster County Militia.

HENRY KAUFFMAN lived in Penn Township prior to 1777. He was a private in Captain Benjamin Weiser's Company, German Regiment, Continental Line, stationed at Philadelphia, Pa., on January 30, 1777. It is believed that he was one of the two Henry Kauffmans who lived in Lancaster County, Pa., in 1790.

JACOB KEISER (also Keyser Kiser, Kaiser, Kayser, etc.) was born in Germany and came to America as a young man. He sailed from Rotterdam, Holland, on the British ship "Edinburgh," Captain James Russell, master, and arrived at the port of Philadelphia, where he took the oath of allegiance to the English government on September 16, 1751. Some time after his arrival he settled in Cumberland County. Prior to 1790 he lived in what is now Union Township of Snyder County, in the vicinity of the village of Verdilla. Keiser's Lutheran and Reformed Church was named for him, or his son Jacob. It is supposed that the elder Jacob is buried in the cemetery attached to that church, although his grave may not be marked. The History of the Danville Conference of the Lutheran church states, that old tombstones in the cemetery attached to the church bore dates of as early as 1801, and it is supposed that people were buried there prior to that time. Michael Keiser (1772-1825) and Jacob Keiser (1787-1829) are believed to have been some of the children. Michael married a daughter of Leonard Seebold, a Revolutionary soldier, who came to America in 1750. In 1796, when Mahantango Township was formed from the lower part of Penn, Jacob was assessed there. In the federal census of 1790, it is stated that in that year, his family consisted of one male over and one under 16 years, and four females. On July 27, 1782, he was a private 4th class in the third Company, 3rd Battalion of the Cumberland County Militia. Numerous descendants of his still live in Snyder County.

MARTIN KEISTER was assessed in Penn Township for the first time in 1778, and it is possible that he may have been a non-resident landowner. No military record was found for him.

PETER KEISTER lived in Penn Township in 1781 and 1782. He may have been a son of the man mentioned above. No military record was found, but it was believed that this man served during the Revolution.

MICHAEL KELLER (maybe Keeler) was a freeman in Cocalico Township, Lancaster County, Pa., in 1771, 1772 and 1773. His name appeared on the Penn Township tax list for the first time in 1776, and at that time he may have been a non-resident landowner. In 1790, he lived in Beaver Township, and his family consisted of one male over and four under 16 years, and two females. A Michael Keller served in the 6th Company, 2nd Battalion of the Berks County Militia. The same man, or another of the same name, served as a private in Captain Charles Gobin's Company, 6th Battalion of the Berks County Militia in the service of the Continental Congress on August 10, 1780.

JOHN KELLEY, carpenter, was assessed in Penn Township for the first time in 1799. No further data was found for him. A John Kelley from Northampton County served in the Revolution.

PETER KEMERER was assessed with 40 acres and personal property in Warwick Twp., Lancaster Co., Pa., from 1772 to 1782. He was assessed in Penn Township for the first time in 1780, but it is evident that at the time he was a non-resident landowner. It is supposed that he came to live in Penn Township in 1785, and in 1786 he was taxed 100 acres and personalty. It is believed that he was a relative of the man mentioned above. Some think the assessment lists were wrong and that the name should have been Kremer. The Federal

Census of 1790, stated that this man's family consisted of himself and wife and that year. The compiler believes that this man served in the Lancaster County Militia.

JAMES KENNEDY was a resident of Penn Township for a short time. He served as a private in Captain Charles Meyer's Company of the Northumberland County Militia.

JOHN KEPLER (aslo Keppler, Kebler, etc.) may have been a native of Northampton County, Pa. His name appeared on the Penn Township tax list for the first time in 1776, but it is believed that he was a non-resident landowner at that date. In 1779, he was taxed with 100 acres and personal property in Greenwood Township (now Juniata County.) On July 9, 1776, he was a private in Captain John Arendt's Company of the Northampton County Associators at the Flying Camp. He also seems to have served in the German Regiment of the Continental Line.

ANTIONE KERBACH may have been a native of York County. He was assessed in Beaver Township for the first time in 1789, and died there in 1792. He served as a private in Colonel Hazen's Regiment "Congress' Own" during the Revolution.

GEORGE KERN embarked for America in the British ship "Fane" at Rotterdam, Holland. William Hyndman was master of the ship. He arrived at Philadelphia, Pa., where he took the oath of allegiance to the English Government on October 17, 1747. He settled in Northampton County, and in 1790 was assessed in Heidelberg Township of that County, and his family consisted of himself and four females. It is believed that he was the father of Mathias Kern, who came to what is now Snyder County about 1789. George seems to have followed him to the new locality and died in Penn Township, Northumberland (now Snyder) County, in 1793. His wife was named Barbara.

HENRY KERN, SENIOR, was the oldest son of John Yost Kern and his wife, Eva Maria Weiss. He was born in Germany on November 17, 1769, and came to America with his parents two years later. He died at the home of his brother Peter in Thompson Township, Seneca County, Ohio, on March 21, 1835. He married Catherine, a niece of Michael Lepley, who was killed by the Indians at Fort Freeland in 1779. She died some years after her husband. Their children were: Henry, Jr., Elizabeth, (Mrs. John Swinehart); Catherine (unmarried);

Mary (married Enoch Dick and died in Seneca County, Ohio); Susan (married George Fender and died in same county); Margaret (married George Fall, and died in Marshall County, Indiana); Barbara (married Henry Etzler, and died at Beavertown, Pa.,) in 1885; Leah (married Martin Fogle, died at Beavertown). Henry was assessed in Beaver Township for the first time in 1791. In 1806, he bought his father's farm which lay near Beavertown. This farm he sold to his son, Henry, Jr., in 1832.

JOHN ADAM KERN was the third son of John Yost Kern and his wife, Eva Maria Weiss. He was born in what is now Franklin Township, Snyder County, Pa., on April 27, 1772, and died near Troxelville, in the same county, on June 22, 1842. His wife, Maria—, was born on June 12, 1781, and died on February 4, 1834. Both are buried in the Lutheran and Reformed cemetery at Troxelville. John Adam Kern was assessed in Beaver Township for the first time about 1795, and in 1799, was designated as a single freeman. He owned and operated a large farm in what is now Adams Township of Snyder County, Pa.

At a much later date this farm was divided and owned by Harrison Moyer and Daniel A. Kern. John Adam and his wife were the parents of four children: Jacob (1804-1858), who married Sarah Weirick; John S. (1802-1865), who married Catherine E. Tittle (1814-1900), and died at Rennsalaer, Jasper County, Indiana; Daniel S. (1809-1883), who married Sarah Jane Parker, and died at Hanna, LaPorte County, Indiana; and Susan, who married William Frederick and died without issue at Beavertown, Pa.

JOHN YOST KERN (commonly called "Yost" or "Jost") was born in Freisbach, Germany, in 1746, and died in what is now Franklin Township, Snyder County, Pa., in the year 1815. In Germany, he married Eva Maria Weiss, who was born on November 17, 1749, and died in what is now Franklin Township, Snyder County, Pa., on March 21, 1835. They embarked for America at Rotterdam, Holland, and, in the British Ship "Betsy", Captain John Osmond, master, and arrived at the port of Philadelphia, Pa., where he took the oath of allegiance to the English government on October 13, 1766, and settled in the eastern section of the state for a few years. On June 24, 1772, he was granted a warrant of survey for 200 acres in the Middle

Creek Valley, west of Middleburg, in the now Snyder County, and it is presumed that he occupied this land soon after securing the warrant. He was granted 260 acres more in the year 1788 and 1789. His first grant adjoined the lands of John George Esslinger (maybe Ettinger), Leonard Diehl, Jacob Walter and other pioneers. In 1908, the original grant was owned by Hopner Mitchell and Robert Rearick. When he first settled in the valley, the Indians were still plentiful and the rifle was carried to the fields with the hoe. The Kerns had six sons and three daughters. The oldest, Henry, was born on November 17, 1769, and died at the home of his brother, Peter, in Seneca County, Ohio, on March 31, 1835. His wife was Catherine Lepley. (2). John, born about 1771, and died in 1823. He married Catherine Royer, who died about the same time. (3). John Adam (see sketch above). (4). Peter was born in what is now Franklin Township, Snyder County, Pa., on February 22, 1776, and died in Thompson Township, Seneca County, Ohio, on June 12, 1855. His wife was Christina Lepley, who was either a sister or daughter of Michael Lepley, a Revolutionary soldier, who was killed by the Indians in their attack on Fort Freeland, near Turbotville, Pa., on April 26, 1779. Christina was born in New Jersey on September 4, 1775, and died in Seneca County, Ohio, on March 3, 1857. (5). George Jacob (commonly called Jacob) was born in what is now Franklin Township, Snyder County, Pa., on April 22, 1784, and died in Thompson Township, Seneca County, Ohio, on June 21, 1853. His wife was, Elizabeth, daughter of George Schoch, she was born in what is now Snyder County, Pa., on October 17, 1787, and died in Thompson Township, Seneca County, Ohio, on October 22, 1856. (6). Phillip, was born in what is now Franklin Township, Snyder County, Pa., and lived and died in Beaver Township of the same county. (7). Anna Mary, married John Walter. (8). Louisa, married Jacob Bubb or Bobb. (9). Christina, married Jacob Walter and lived at Selinsgrove, Pa. John Yost Kern bought a farm from John Swift at the present site of Beavertown, in 1790. This farm in 1885, was owned by a grandson, Henry Kern (son of Henry.) A sister of John Yost Kern, a Mrs. Miller, came to America from Germany in 1823. Her nephew, Henry Kern, went to Germany to accompany her across. All of her wealth was invested in clocks and Bibles, all of

which she brought with her, and later sold them at a considerable profit in this country. John Yost Kern, and his wife, are buried in the Old Hassinger Cemetery, west of Middleburg, Pa., in unmarked graves. Many of their descendants live in Snyder and surrounding counties. The Federal Census of 1790, stated that the Kern family consisted in that year of three males over 16, four under that age, and four females, the compiler was unable to find a military record for Yost, and it is believed that he served during the Revolution. Credit for much of the data in this sketch is due to the late Aaron Kern Gift of Middleburg, Pa.

NATHAN KERN, SENIOR, was assessed in Upper Milford Township, Northampton County, Pa., in 1772. It is believed that he was a son of George and Barbara Kern. The former died in Penn Township in 1793. In 1787, Mathias was assessed with 100 acres and personal property in Upper Milford Township. He became a resident of what is now Snyder County about the year 1789, and the Federal Census of 1790, stated that his family at that time consisted of one male, over, and one under 16 years, and three females. On May 14, 1778, he was a private, 1st Company, 2nd Battalion of the Northampton County Militia. From October 5th to November 22, 1781, he was a private in Captain Adam Gerfass' Company from the same county.

MATHIAS KERN, JUNIOR, was a son of Mathias Kern, Sr., who came to what is now Snyder County from Upper Milford Township, Northampton County, Pa., about 1789. Mathias, Junior, is supposed to have come with his parents at that time. In the federal census of 1790, Mathias, Jr., lived in Beaver Township, and his family consisted of himself and his wife. His father, in the same year lived in Penn Township.

PETER KERN was the fourth son of John Yost Kern and his wife, Eva Maria Weiss. Peter was born in what is now Franklin Township, Snyder County, Pa., on February 22, 1776, and died in Thompson Township, Seneca County, Ohio, on June 12, 1855. His wife was Christina Lepley, a sister or daughter of Michael Lepley, a Revolutionary soldier who was killed by the Indians in their attack on Fort Freeland in April, 1779 .She was born in New Jersey on September 4, 1775, and died in the same county as her husband, on March 3, 1857. Peter was assessed in Beaver Township

for the first time in 1799, and in that year was designated as a single freeman. He owned a farm in what is now Adams Township of Snyder County, Pa., and followed the trade of wagon builder. He also built wooden plows with metal covered jointers and shares, and wooden framed harrows and also other farm implements. It is not known when he moved to Seneca County, Ohio, but is supposed to have gone there after his older brothers settled in that section. The children of Peter Kern and his wife were: Michael (1802-1847); Mary (1803-1884), who married Samuel Romig; Peter, Junior (1807-1857), and Anthony (1813-1886).

ADAM KERSTETTER (also Karstetter, Carstetter, Kastetter, Casteter, Castetor, etc.,) is believed to have lived in Penn Township for a short while around the year 1776. In 1783, he was assessed in Mahonoy Township of Northumberland County. H elived in the same county in 1790, and the federal census of that period states that his family consisted of one male over and one under 16 years, and four females. On January 30, 1777, he was a private in Captain Benjamin Weiser's Company, German Regiment, Continental Line, stationed at Philadelphia, Pa.

JOHN KERSTETTER (commonly called "Big John") was a resident, but not a land owner in Mahonoy Township, Northumberland County, Pa., in 1787. He was assessed in Penn Township for the first time in 1795, and the next year when Mahantango Township was forced, he was assessed there. A John Kerstetter, Jr., was assessed in Mahantango Township for the first time in 1796. A John Kerstetter served as a private in Captain William Weirick's Company, also in Captain John Moll's Company of the Northumberland County Militia. In 1790, Big John's family consisted of one male over and two males under 16 years, and four females.

JOHN GEORGE KERSTETTER was commonly called "George." He was born in 1756, he died in Snyder County, Pa., about 1840. His wife's first name was Elizabeth, and it is believed her surname was Foltz. George was assessed in Penn Township for the first time in 1785, and in that year he was taxed with 200 acres and personal property. When Mahantango Township was formed in 1796, he lived there. In 1820, he lived in Washington, and in 1821, it is said he lived in what is now Perry Township of Snyder County. In addition to being a farmer, he was also a blacksmith. The following children of George and his wife were baptized at the Grubb's Lutheran Church in Chapman Township: Catharine, born March 8, 1792; Salomonis, born February 5, 1794; Maria Magdalene, born October 31, 1806; and Jacob, born December 10, 1814. On July 29, 1776 George enlisted in Captain Daniel Burhcardt's Company of the German Regiment, Continental Line, and served in the battles of Brandywine, New Brunswick, Trenton, Germantown, and took part in Sullivan's Expedition. He was discharged at Northumberland, Pa., in 1779.

LEONARD KERSTETTER, SENIOR, was assessed in Mahanoy Township of Northumberland Co., in 1778. Leonard, Junior, was assessed in the same township for the first time in 1782. One of these men was assessed in Penn Township only in the year 1780. Both were assessed regularly in Mahanoy Township from 1782 on. It is believed that Leonard, Senior, was the son of Sebastian, Senior, who died in Penn Township in 1787. In 1790, his family consisted of one male over and one under 16 years, and three females. No military record was found for him, but it is believed that he served in the Revolution.

LEONARD KERSTETTER, JUNIOR, was assessed in Mahanoy Township from 1782 on. It seems that he lived in Penn Township in the year 1780. In 1790, his family consisted of one male over and five under 16 years, and one female. Leonard was a private in Captain Benjamin Weiser's Company of the German Regiment, Continental Line stationed at Philadelphia, Pa., on January 30, 1777. It is believed that Leonard, Junior, was a grandson of Sebastian, Sr., who died in Penn Township in 1787.

MARTIN KERSTETTER was the oldest son of Sebastian Kerstetter, Senior, who died in Penn Township in 1787. Martin was assessed in Penn Township for the first time in 1776, but owing to his service in the army for some years his name does not appear again until 1781, when he was assessed as a single freeman. In 1782, he was assessed with 300 acres and personal property in Penn Township. In 1796, when Mahantango Township was formed he was taxed there. There were two Martins died in Penn Township in Snyder County at the same time. They were sons of brothers (Michael and Sebastain, Sr.) One of the Matrins died in Penn Township in

1798, and the other died in Beaver Township in 1815. In 1788, Martin and Assilonia Kerstetter had their son Peter baptized at the Old Zion Lutheran Church, north of Freeburg. It is believed that there were other children. Martin served as a private in Captain Casper Weitzel's Company of the Pennsylvania Rifle Regiment, and on August 27, 1776, was reported missing after the battle of Long Island. Later he seems to have served as a Private in Captain John Moll's Company of the Northumberland County Militia. In 1790, the family consisted of one male over and two under 16 years, and two females.

MARTIN KERSTETTER (son of Michael, and a first cousin of the Martin mentioned above) lived in Penn Township at the same time as his cousin of the same name—thus causing confusion to the compiler. This Martin died in Beaver Township, and his will was probated at Lewisburg, Pa., on September 5, 1815. The will mentions his wife (Elizabeth) and two sons (Simon and Tobias.) Other children were referred to, but their names are not mentioned. This Martin seems to have been a private in Captain Benjamin Weiser's Company of the German Regiment, Continental Line, and was stationed at Philadelphia, Pa., on January 30, 1777.

MICHAEL KERSTETTER was a brother of Sebastian Kerstetter, Senior. Michael was assessed in Penn Township for the first time in 1771, but seems not to have lived there until later. He was the father of one of the two Martin Kerstetters who lived in Penn Township at the same time. His brother, Sebastian, Senior, was father of the other. Michael also seems to have been the father of John George and John, mentioned above. Michael seems not to have served in the Revolution, but all three of his supposed sons did.

PETER KERSTETTER was a son of Sebasian, Sr. He lived in what is now Snyder County prior to 1800, because Peter and his wife, Susanna, had their daughter Maria Elizabeth, who was born on September 11, 1794, baptized at the Grubb's Lutheran Church in the now Chapman Township in that year

SEBASTIAN KERSTETTER, SENIOR, was a brother of Michael Kerstetter, and was commonly called "Bastain" or "Bostain." He was assessed in Penn Township for the first time in 1771. In 1785, he was assessed with 300 acres and personal property. The Kerstetters lived in

the southern part of what is now Snyder County. Sebastian died in Penn Township, and his will was recorded at Sunbury, Pa., on March 20, 1787. It mentions his wife (Mary) and their children: Martin (oldest son), Leonard (probably Leonard, Senior,) Peter, Sebastian, Junior; Frances; Catherine and Margaret.

GEORGE KESSLER was a resident, but not a land owner in Winsdor Township, Berks County, Pa., in 1779. The next year he was assessed as a tanner there, and in 1784, he was assessed with 60 acres of land and personal property, and his occupation designated as tanner. He was assessed in Penn Township for the first time in 1798, and still designated as a tanner. The federal census of 1790 states that his family at that time consisted of one male over and six under 16 years, and three females, and at that time he was still living in Winsdor Township. George was born in 1746, and died in Penn Township on February 21, 1813, and is buried in the cemetery at Salem (Row's) Lutheran Church in Penn Township. In 1811, he was one of the elders of the Salem Church. John was one of his sons. He served as a private in Captain Joseph McClellan's Company of Colonel Stewart's Light Infantry Regiment, the 9th Pennsylvania Regiment, Continental Line) in August, 1780. Many of his descendants still live in Snyder County. George Kessler's children were: George, Jr., Michael, William, Mary Laudenslager, Susanna, John, Jacob, Peter, Daniel, Catherine Laudenslager, Jonathan, Barbara, Elizabeth, and Magadalena.

DANIEL KETTLEMAN was assessed in Penn Township only in the year of 1780 The federal census of 1790, does not list his name. No military record was found for him.

JACOB KINDIG (sometimes given as Kendig) was probably a son of Jacob Kendig, Senior, who died in Manor Township, Lancaster County, Pa., about 1770. Indications are that the Jacob of this sketch was a descendant of Martin Kendig who sailed from Rotterdam, Holland, in the British ship "Molly" and took the oath of allegiance at Philadelphia, Pa., on September 30, 1727. In 1782, Jacob was assessed with 80 acres and personal property in Manor Township, and 300 acres in Buffalo Township, Northumberland County. This land lay north of Penns Creek in what is today Monroe Township of Snyder County. He was assessed in Penn Township for the first time in 1788, and in 1789, he and others petitioned that what is now Monroe Township. but then part of Buffalo Township, be annexed to Penn Township. This was done the same year. In 1789, he was one of the road supervisors of Penn Township. In 1797, he was one of the viewers to locate a road from Selinsgrove to Freeburg. In 1801, he donated to a fund for the erection of the First Lutheran Church of Selinsgrove, Pa. In 1804, he was one of the viewers to locate a road from Salem to New Berlin. In 1809, he lived along the Penns Creek, north of Seli:.sgrove, and in 1811, he was one of a board of viewers, appointed to fix a site for a bridge across the Penns Creek, near his home. He married the widow of "Black" John Snyder, a brother of Governor Simon Snyder. John lost his life by being thrown from a fractious horse in Penn Township in 1787 In 1790, Jacob Kindig's family consisted of two males over, and two under 16 years, and two females. In 1782, Jacob was a private 5th class, 2nd Company, 4th Battalion of the Lancaster County Militia. In May, 1783, a Jacob Kindig, was a private 3rd class, 7th Company, 9th Battalion of the militia of the same county.

U. S. census of that year his family consisted of himself and wife.

JACOB KINNEY (also Kinny, Ginny, Guinny, Gunies, etc.,) was assessed in Penn Township for the first time in 1700. Prior to 1787, he seems not to have owned any real estate. One record states that he lived on John Aurand's farm at Turtle Creek in Buffalo Township, above Winfield. In 1790, his family consisted of noe male over and three under 16 years and three females. Jacob served his country well during the Revolution. In 1775, he was a private in Captain John Clark's Company of the Northumberland County Associators. He also served as a private in Captain Michael Weaver's Company and Captain John Moll's Company of the Northumberland County Militia. and in 1780, he was a member of Ensign Simon Herrold's party of Rangers in service against the Indians on the Frontier.

MICHAEL KISK (also Kark) was assessed in Lack Township, Cumberland County, Pa., in 1776 His name appeared on the Penn Township tax list for the first time in 1781, but there is no evidence that He lived somewhere in Northumberland County at the time of the federal census of 1790, and his family consisted of one male ovrr and three under 16 years, and four females.

The records seem to indicate that he served in the 5th Comvany, 3rd Battalion of the Lancaster County Militia at some time during the Revolutionary period. He may have served in the Cumberland County Militia also.

THOMAS KITCH (also Ketch) is supposed to have lived in Penn or an adjoining township. At least he served as a private in Captain John Moll's Company of the Northumberland County Militia. In 1790, he lived in Dauphin County, Pa., and his family consisted of one male over and one under 16 years and three females.

GEORGE KLINE was assessed with land and personal property in Heidelberg Township, Lancaster County, Pa., in 1771 and 1772. His name appeared on the Penn Township tax list for the first time in 1776, but he evidently was a nonresident landowner at the time, for the years of 1781 and 1782, he was assessed as a non-resident landowner in Penn Township. In 1789, the tax list of Beaver Township carried the name of George Kline, but whether as non-resident land owner or not, the compiler is unable to tell. In 1781, a George Kline was a private, 6th class, 5th Company, 2nd Battalion of the Lancaster County Militia.

JACOB KLINE, SENIOR, was a resident but not a land owner in Heidelberg Township, Lancaster County, Pa., in 1772 and 1773. His name appeared on the Penn Township tax list for first time in 1776 but the indications are that he was a nonresident land owner at the time. In 1782, he was assessed with 300 acres and personal property in Penn Township. The federal census of 1790, states that at that time his family consisted of one male over and one under 16 years and three females. Several men of this name served in the Revolution, but the compiler could not distinguish them.

JACOB KLINE, JUNIOR, seems to have been a son of the above man. In 1790, his family consisted of one male over and one under 16 years and two females.

ERNEST KLOSE (also Close, Kloese, Kloss, Closs, Close, Klose, etc.) was born in Germany ¦n 1738 and died at Selinsgrove (now Snyder County), Penna., in 1805. He married Catherine Suter, who died at the age of 67 years. Both are buried in the old Lutheran Cemetery at Selinsgrove, but their graves are unmarked. Ernest was the son of Melchoir (sometimes called Leonard, probably because his full name may have been Leonard Melchoir Klose),

It is said that Melchoir was born in 1708, and at the time of his immigration to America, he lived at Esling Allrum, Wittenberg, Germany. He married Margaret (Margretha) ——. They embarked for America at Rotterdam, Holland, in the spring of 1738, on the British ship "Glasgow", Captain Walter Sterling, master, and arrived at the port of Philadelphia, where he took the English oath of allegiance on September 9, 1738. A daughter was born to Melchoir and his wife in 1741, and it is supposed that they had other children. Ernest, son of Melchoir, was a shoemaker, and lived ed in Weisenberg Township, Northampton County, Pa., in 1772. From 1785 to 1788, he was assessed with 250 acres of land and personal property in that township. In 1790, under the name of "Arnst Close" he was listed in the Federal cen'sug in Weisenberg Township, and his family consisted of two males over sixteen years, one under that age, and two females. Henry and Jacob lived in the same township at the same time. Jacob was probably his son, and Henry his brother. Ernest had a son named Jacob. Ernest came to what is now Penn Township about the year 1793, and owned a farm of 300 acres along the Middle Creek, just above the village of Kantz. The old log barn and house, owned by the late Calvin Seebold of Kantz, were the buildings of the Klose farm. The compiler remembers these as a boy, and believes that pictures of them are still in existence among members of the Seebold family. The children of Ernest and his wife were: Aaeon, Pacob, Abraham, Eugeeon, Jacob, Abraham, Elizabeth (who married Peter, Michael, or Henry Bobst , or Pobst), Esther (who married——— Henker), Catherine (who married——— Fenstermacher), and Daniel (who married Margaret Richards). Daniel lived in Penn Township at one time. In 1778, Ernest Klose was listed as a private in the 8th Company, 6th Battalion of the Northampton County Militia.

DANIEL KOCH (also Cogh, Coch, etc.) was granted warrants of survey totaling 150 acres in Northumberland (now Snyder) County, on May 25, 1774. On June 19, 1792, he was granted a warrant for an additional 100 acres. In 1781, he was taxed with 80 acres and personal property in Penn Township. In 1790, a Daniel Cogh was assessed in Allen Township, Northampton County, but if the subject of this sketch still lived in what is now Snyder County, his name was so perverted that the compiler did not locate it. In 1776, Daniel served as a private in Captain John Clarks Company of the Northumberland County Associators.

ANDREW KOHLER (also Koehler, Koller, and probably Keller, etc.) was assessed in Manchester Township, York County, Pa., in 1779 and 1780. He was assessed in Penn Township for the first time in 1781, and in 1782, his name seems to have been changed to Keller. He was assessed with 100 acres of land and personal property. Michael and Mary Catherine Kohler, probaly children of Andrew, were members of Salem (Row's) Lutheran Church, prior to 1790. Tax lists after 1790 do not seem to carry the name of Kohler in Penn Township. This might be accounted for by the fact that it was changed to Keller. No military record was found but it is believed that he served.

PAUL KOPPENBERGER (also Coppenberger, Cappenberger, Capenberger, Knippenberger, Knoppenberger, etc.,) was assessed in Penn Township for the first time in 1778. In 1781, he was taxed with 50 acres of land and personal property. No military record was found for Paul, but it is believed that he was the father of Charles Cappenberger who served as a private in Captain John Snyder's Company of the Northumberland County Militia. Paul and Charles are believed to have been descendants of Frederick Christian Koppenberger who came to this country from Germany in the British ship "Royal Union" in the year 1750.

ANDREW KLINE (also Klein, Cline, Clein, etc.,) was born in Germany and sailed for America from Rotterdam, Holland in the British ship "Brothers" or "St. Michael" and took the English oath of allegiance at Philadelphia, Pa., the port of entry, on September 16, 1751, or September 10, 1753. The compiler is not sure which of these two men the subject of this sketch was. In 1771, Andrew was a landowner in Heidelberg Township, Lancaster County, Pa. On May 29, 1772, he was granted a warrant of survey for 100 acres in Northumberland (now Snyder) County. He seems to have been assessed in Penn Township for the first time in 1776, but the indications are that he became a resident of Penn in 1773 or 1774. In 1781, he was assessed with 100 acres and personal property. He lived in that section of the county which became Beaver Township in 1787. In 1790, his family consisted of himself and

wife. It is believed that he was a relative Christopher Sr. George, and Jacob, who lived in the same section at that time. He served as a private in Captain John Moll's Company, in Captain Michael Weaver's Company of the Northumberland County Militia, and in Lieutenant John Coleman's Party of Rangers on the Frontier.

LIEUTENANT BARNHART KLINE (commonly known as "Barny, "Berny" or "Barnhardt") was born on December 16, 1756, probably in Upper Milford Township, Northampton County, Pa., and died near what is now Kratzerville, Pa., on August 3, 1837. His wife, Margaret ———, was born on February 6, 1761, and died on December 20, 1850. Both are buried in the old Lutheran and Reformed cemetery in Kratzerville, and their graves are marked. The federal census of 1790, states that he lived in Towamensink, Township, Northampton County, in that year, and his family consisted of one male over and three under 16 years, and four females. John and Frederick, who lived in the same township at that time, were probably his brothers. He settled in what is now Jackson, but then Penn Township, Snyder County, some time before 1800. It is believed that he was a son, or grandson, of the Bernhart Kline, who sailed for America from Rotterdam, Holland in the British ship "Lydia," landed at Philadelphia, and took the English oath of allegiance there on September 29, 1741. On January 4, 1786, he was granted a warrant of survey for 25 acres in Northampton County, and his name appeared on the Upper Milford Township tax lists of 1785, and 1786. The known and supposed children of Barnhart and his wife were: Barnhart, Jr., (who settled near Clyde or Bellevue, Ohio); Margaret, 1792-1871 , (who married Squire Jacob F. Hummel); Fanny, January 22, 1798-January 25, 1888 (who married Jonas Sassaman, Sr., and lived in what is now Jackson Township of Snyder County); and Henry, August 26, 1880-September 17, 1883 (who lived in Jackson Township). It is supposed that there were other children, but the compiler was unable to locate their names. Most of the above people are interred in the Kratzerville Cemetery. The Revolutionary service of this pioneer was long and varied. In 1775, he was a private in Captain Abraham Miller's Company.

On May 14, 1778, he was a Second Lieutenant of the 3rd Company, 4th Battalion of the Nor-

thampton County Militia. On September 28th, 1782, Captain Peter Roods (probably Rhoads) certified that Barbard Kline was on Frontier Duty seven days during the month of March, 1782. The wife of the compiler of this work is a great-great granddaughter of the subject of this sketch, and has the unique distinction of being a great-granddaughter of one of his daughters on her maternal side, and a great-granddaughter of her sister on her paternal side.

CHRISTOPHER (S T O P H E L) KLINE, SENIOR, was taxed in Penn Township for the first time in 1776. It is thought that he came from Berks or Lancaster County. He seems not to have lived in Penn Township until about 1783. In 1785, he was assessed with 75 acres and personal property. He lived in that section, which after 1787, became Beaver Township. The federal census states that in 1790, his family consisted of one male over and three under 16 years, and three females. A Christopher Junior, lived in the same section in 1790. One of these two men died in Beaver Township and his will was recorded at Lewisburg, Pa., on September 18, 1823. The will mentions his wife, Catherine, and the following children: Michael, John, Peter, Barbara (married to ——— Krick), and Catherine (Mrs. Jeremiah Gift). Andrew, George and Jacob Kline seem to have been relatives of Christopher, Sr. A Stophel (Christopher) Kline was a private, 4th Class, 4th Company, 3rd Battalion of the Lancaster County Militia in 1781, and in the 4th Company, 6th Battalion of the same county in 1783. A Stophel Clein (probably meant for Klein, or Kline) was a private in Captain William Weirick's Company, Northumberland County, Militia. at some time during the Revolution.

CHRISTOPHER KLINE, JUNIOR, according to the federal census of 1790, lived in Beaver Township, and in that year his family consisted of one male over and three under 16 years, and three females. Part of the data in the sketch above may refer to the younger man.

DAVID KLINE was assessed in Penn Township only in the year of 1778, and may never have lived in the Township. In 1771, and for a number of years thereafter he lived in Lebanon Township, now Lebanon County) Lancaster County, Pa. In 1782, he was a private, 6th class, 2nd Company, 2nd Battalion of the Lancaster County Militia. In the federal census of 1790, two David

Klines were listed, both lived in Berks County, one of them in Tulpehocken Township.

MICHAEL KRAIL (also Krahl, Kraihl, Kralll, etc.) embarked for America at Rotterdam. Holland, in the British ship "Phoenix," Captain John Spurrier, master, and arrived at Philadelphia, where he took the English oath of allegiance on October 1, 1754. He was assessed in Penn Township for the first time in 1776. He may have been a non-resident land owner. Several men of the name Crail lived in Allegheny County in 1790. No military record was found for Michael.

HUGH KRAIN (also Crane, Krane, Crain, Krahn, etc.) was assessed in Penn Township only in the year 1776. It is evident that he was a non-resident land owner, or a transient single freeman. No military record was found for him.

BENJAMIN KRATZER, shoemaker, was probably a native of Northampton County, Pa., and was assessed in Penn Township for the first time in 1799. It is believed that he was a brother of Philip Kratzer (1763-1843), a Revolutionary soldier. Benjamin and Philip seem to have been the first of the family name to live in what is now Snyder County, and the village of Kratzerville was named for one of them. The names was sometimes spelled Cratzer, Crotzer, or Krotzer. The children of Benjamin pere probably Henry (born 1788), John (born 1790) Jacob (born 1796,) Daniel (born 1798), and Philip. In 1778, Benjamin was a private in the 4th Company, 4th Battalion of the Northampton County Militia. He is buried at Kratzerville, Pa.

PHILIP KRATZER, supposed brother of Benjamin, was born about 1763, probably in Northampton Co. Pa., and died on November 5, 1843. It is supposed that he came to Penn Township at about the same time as Benjamin. He is buried in the old Lutheran and Reformed cemetery at Kratzerville, Pa. In 1782, he was a private in Captain Jesse Jones' Company of the Northampton County Militia.

HENRY KREEGER (also Kreger, Kreager, Kregar, etc.) was assessed in Penn Township only in the year of 1776, but as the tax list of that date does not make a distinction between resident and nonresident landowners, the compiler does not know if he lived in the district, or not. No military record was found.

ISAAC KREIDER, carpenter, was a native of either Northampton or Lancaster County. He was assessed in Penn Township for the first time

in 1799. His wife was Catherine, daughter of Leonard Boyer. Leonard died in Penn Township in 1826.

DANIEL KREMER (also Kramer, Cramer, Cremer, Creamer, Kreamer, etc.) was listed as a single freeman in Penn Township in 1776, but it is believed that he left during the Indian uprisings, because in 1780, he was assessed as a resident, but not a landowner in Heidelberg Township, Berks County, Pa. The following year, he was listed as a nonresident landowner in Penn Township. In 1784 or 1785, he again moved to the township and was assessed with 400 acres and personal property. No military record was found but it is believed that he served in Berks County.

PETER KREMER was assessed in Penn Township for the first time in 1776. Indications are that he was a nonresident landowner, and that his actual residence was in Conestoga Township, Lancaster County. The compiler believes that he was a relative of Daniel, mentioned above. No military record was found for him, but this is not to be construed that he did not serve in the Revolution.

JACOB KRICK, SENIOR, (also Crick, Krik, Kreek, Creeck, Creek, etc.) was a blacksmith, and a resident, but not a landowner in Crumru Township, Berks County, Pa., in 1767 and 1768. His name appeared in the Penn Township tax list for the first time in 1778. From 1781 to 1787, he was taxed with 200 acres of land and personal property. In 1789, he was assessed in Beaver township, which had been erected from the western part of Penn in 1787. The federal census of 1790 states that at that time his family consisted of two males over and two under 16 years, and six females. He died in Beaver Township in 1823, and his will was recorded at Lewisburg, Pa. The will mentions his wife, Catherine, and these children: Jacob, Jr., John, George, Adam, Catherine, (Mrs. George Stock), Elizabeth (Mrs. Michael Maurer), Mary (Mrs. Jacob Klose)) Barbara, (Mrs. Michael Moyer), Polly (Mrs. Jacob Hassinger, Jr.) Margaret (Mrs. George Sharatz, or possibly Jarrett, Judy (widow of Henry Mowrer or Maurer), Susanna (Mrs. Michael Kline), Eva (Mrs. John Fite), and Rebecca (Mrs. John Kline). Jacob served as a private in Captain Michael Motz's Company of the Northumberland County Militia.

JOHN KRICK was a son of Jacob Krick, Senior (mentioned above). John was assessed in Beaver Town-

ship for the first time in 1790. In the same year the federal census recorded his family as consisting of himself and wife.

PHILIP KRICK is supposed to have been a brother of Jacob Krick, Senior. Philip was assessed in Penn Township for the first time in 1778. In 1781 and 1782, he was taxed with personal property only. In 1781, he was constable of Penn Township. After 1782, his name does not again appear on the Penn Township list, and it is supposed that he moved to what is now Juniata County, because the federal census of 1790, states that he lived in the eastern part of Cumberland County in that year. Juniata County was formerly part of Cumberland County. Philip's family in 1790, consisted of two males over and 4 under 15 years and five females. The compiler believes that he is the same Philip Krick who was a Captain in Colonel Joseph Heister's Battalion of the Berks County Militia in May, 1777. Philip also served as a private in Captain John Moll's Company of the Northumberland County Militia.

JACOB KUHN, weaver, was assessed as a single freeman in Conestoga Township, Lancaster County, Pa., in 1782. He was assessed in Penn Township for the first time in 1799. No military record was found for him.

PETER KUSTER (also Kister, Kester, Coster, Koster, Custer, etc.) was assessed in Penn Township for the first time in 1781, and in that year was taxed with 100 acres of land and personal property. A Peter Kuster, Jr., was granted a warrant for survey for 200 acres of land in Northumberland (now Snyder) County, on November 1, 1784. The Kusters lived in what is today Penn Township, not far from the village of Pawlings Station, and the old stone house erected by the pioneer or one of his sons. still stands. It is believed that Peterr was a son of Hermanus Kuster, who died in Perkiomen Township, Philadelphia County, Pa., in February of 1760. Hermanus was the son of Paulus Kuster, who was born near Crefield, Germany, about the year 1640, and came to America soon after William Penn. Paulus and his son, John, were naturalized in Philadelphia in the year 1691 and Paulus' will was recorded in Philadelphia, Pa., on February 23, 1708. Peter served as a Private in Captain Charles Meyer's Company, in Captain John Forster's Company and in Captain Michael Weaver's Company. A Peter Kester was a private in the 6th Pennsylvania Regiment, Continental Line. He died on

July 23, 1833, and was aged 77 years at the time.

JACOB LABEL was assessed in Penn Township only in the year 1778. No military record found.

GEORGE LANDIS was assessed in Penn Township for the first time in 1794. In 1780, he was taxed with 92 acres and personal property in Colebrookdale Township, Berks Co., Pa. In 1790, his family consisted of one male over 16 years, and two females. No military record was found but it is believed that he served during the Revolution.

JOHN GEORGE LAUDENSLAGER is supposed to have been born in Northampton County, Pa. He was one of the earliest settlers in Penn Township, because in 1773 he was an overseer of the poor in the township. His wife was Catherine ———. They were members of the Salem (Row's) Lutheran Church prior to 1790. In 1781, and for a number of years thereafter he was assessed with 150 acres and personal property. He and his wife are supposed to have died in the Salem cemetery. Valentine was a son. John George was probably a son of John, or John Peter, who came to America in 1749. "George" served as a private in Captain John Moll's Company, and at another time in Captain John Black's Company of the Northumberland County Militia.

VALENTINE LAUDENSLAGER (sometimes called "Velty" or "Felty" Laudenslager) was a son of John George Laudenslager, mentioned above. The name has had various spellings such as Lautenslager, Lautaslager, Laudalager, Laudsleger, Loudasleger, etc. Valentine was probably born about the year 1756, and died in Penn Township in 1806. He lived in the vicinity of Selinsgrove, and was assessed for the first time in 1778. In 1785, he was assessed with 100 acres of land and personal property. In 1790, his family consisted of one male over and four under 16 years, and three females. From 1790 to 1792, he was one of the fence viewers of Penn Township. In 1798, he was assessed with a store and grist mill in Selinsgrove. In 1801, he contributed to the fund for the erection of the First Lutheran and Reformed Church of Selinsgrove. In 1805 and 1806, he was an overseer of the poor in Penn Township. Two of his sons were George and Henry. He served as a private in Captain John Snyder's Company of the Northumberland County Militia. In May, 1775, he married Magdalene, daughter of George Kochendoerfer of Tulpehocken Township, Berks County, Pa.

JOHN ADAM LEBER (also Lebar, Lever, Leaver, Liever, etc.) was born in Germany, and sailed for America from Rotterdam, Holland, in the British ship "Union," Captain Andrew Bryson, master, and arrived at the port of Philadelphia, where he took the English oath of allegiance on September 30, 1774. He was assessed in Penn Township for the first time in 1776, and in 1781, he was assessed with 100 acres of land and personal property. The federal census of 1790 states that he lived in the district, and that his family at the time consisted of one male oer and four under 16 years, and two females. An Adam Leaver served in Captain Brumbach's Company of the Chester County Militia. JOHN LEBER was either a son or brother of the man mentioned above. He was assessed in Beaver Township for the first time in 1789. Some Lebers lived in York County, Pa.

JACOB LECHNER was born in Berks County, Pa., on July 25, 1774, and died in Selinsgrove, Pa., on October 9, 1815. His wife was Mary Snyder, a sister of Governor Simon Snyder, whose father was Anthony Snyder of Lancaster County. Jacob was probably a son of George Lechner, who owned a grist mill and saw mill in Tulpehocken Township, Berks County, Pa., in 1767. George may have been the son of Christopher Lechner, who constructed the Reed's Lutheran Church, east of Stouchsburg, in what is now Berks County, Pa., in 1727. George married a daughter of Leonard Ried (Rieth), Junior, a son of Leonard, Senior, who came down from the Schoharie Valley in New York, in 1723. Jacob came to what is now Penn Township prior to the year 1800. He was a contractor, builder, surveyor, conveyancer, and on many occasions his services were sought as a viewer for various public projects and improvements. In 1804 he was one of the viewers to lay out a road from Salem to New Berlin, andabout the same time he surveyed the premises of the Salem (Row's) Church in Penn Township. In 1811, he built a bridge across the Middle Creek at Bake Oven Hill; this is now part of the Susquehanna Trail. At one time he served as a viewer for the removal of the obstructions in the Penns Creek. A post office was established in Selinsgrove in 1808, and he was the first postmaster. In 1801, he contributed to the fund for the erection of the First Lutheran and Reformed Church of Selinsgrove. He and his wife are both buried in the old

cemetery of this church. His wife survived him. They had two children, William Michael and Dr. Henry Augustus. The latter was a well known Selinsgrove physician, and married Mary, the daughter of John Fisher, and granddaughter of the pioneer, John Adam Fisher. Mrs. Edward A. Phillips, wife of the well known Selinsgrove and Milton dentist, is a descendant of Jacob Lechner.

EDWARD LEE (also Lea, Leigh, etc.) was listed as a free man in what is now Snyder County as early as 1768. It is believed that he is the same man to whom a warrant of survey for 50 acres was granted in Cumberland (now Snyder) County on February 7, 1755. A man of the same name received a grant for 30 acres in Lancaster County in 1772. Edward served as a private in Robinson's Rangers on the Frontier and received depreciation pay for services in the Northumberland County Militia. He may have been a relative of Major John Lee, who was killed by the Indians at Winfield, about 1780.

MAJOR JOHN LEE was listed as one of the residents in what is now Snyder County in the year 1768. Some time later he became a resident of Buffalo Township, and lived on the present site of the village of Winfield. In 1781, he was assessed with 250 acres of land and considerable personal property in Buffalo Township, and seemingly was one of the richest men at that time in that section. In August, 1782, the Indians attacked his home, killed him, took his wife captive and later killed her, and captured their son, Thomas. He is buried near the site of his old home, not far from the ruins of the old iron furnace at Winfield. A John Lee, probably his son, was a resident of Chillisquaque Township, just across the river (Susquehanna) from Winfield, in 1787. The older John, served with the rank of Major or in the Northumberland County Militia, during the early days of the Revolution.

ADAM LEFFLER (also Lefler, Loeffler, Lefler, etc.) lived in Penn Township in 1778, or before. In 1790, his family consisted of two males over and three under 16 years, and four females. In 1810, he lived in Walker Township, Center County, Pa. He served as a private in Captain Benjamin Weiser's Company, German Regiment, Continental Line, at Philadelphia, Pa., on January 30, 1777.

WILLIAM LEHR (also Leer, Lear, Lahr, etc.) was assessed in Beaver Township for the first time in 1789.

No further data was available.

JOHN LEITER (also Leider, Liter, etc.) may have come from Lancaster County. He was assessed in Mahhantango Township for the first time in 1796. He died in what is now Chapman Township, Snyder County, and his will was recorded at Lewisburg, Pa., on July 28, 1828. The will mentions the following children: Elizabeth, Barbara, Abraham, John, Jr., Mary, Mattie, Ann, and Jacob.

LEONARD LEMLEY was assessed in Penn Township only in 1774. It is believed that he moved to Washington County, Pa. No further data was available to the compiler.

SERGEANT JACOB LEPLEY was assessed in Penn Township for the first time in 1778, and in 1781 was assessed with 150 acres of land and personal property. In 1794, he was granted a warrant of survey for an additional 25 acres. In 1787, he was one of the board of viewers appointed to fix the boundries of a new township to be created from the western part of Penn. The new township was called Beaver and he lived within its precincts. Jacob seems to have been the brother of Michael Lepley who was killed by the Indians at Fort Freeland on April 26, 1779. Jacob died in what is now Center Township, and his will was recorded at Lewisburg, Pa., on July 29, 1815. It mentions his wife, Catherine, and the following children: Jacob, Jr.,Henry, Anthony, Margaret Kern, Michael, John, Catherine Kern, Elizabeth, Adam, Christian, and Mary (Mrs. Henry Kern, Sr.). In 1790, Jacob's family consisted of one male over and seven under 16 years, and five females. Jacob served as a Sergeant in Lieutenant Jacob Spees' Company of Northumberland County Rangers in their operations against the Indians in 1780. Some think Jacob was a son of the Michael who was killed by the Indians in 1779, but the compiler thinks he was a brother.

MICHAEL LEPLEY (also Lipley, Lapley, Leply, etc.) was born in 1738, probably in Bucks County, Pa., and was killed by the Indians at Fort Freeland, near Turbotville, Northumberland County, Pa., while in the service of his country, on April 26, 1779. On December 30, 1772, he was granted a warrant of survey of 50 acres in Northumberland (now Snyder) County. His name appeared on the Penn Township tax list for the first time in 1776, but it is evident that he lived in the township at an earlier date. He served during the Revolution in Captain John Moll's Company of

the Northumberland County Militia and in Lieutenant Jacob Spees' Company of Rangers from the same county. The Pennsylvania Archives state "Mary Anne Lepley," widow of the late Michael Lepley, states that the said Michael was a Private in a Company of the Northumberland County Militia, stationed at Freeland's Fort, under the command of Lieutenant Jacob Speece, and that on April 26, 1779, that he and five others were ordered upon an escort from the said fort, and while on the march, a short way from the fort, they were attacked by the Indians and that he was killed and scalped. Age at the time of his death 41 years." An increase of pension was granted to his widow and family. Other soldiers killed at the same time were Jacob Gift (son of John Adam Gift) and John George Herrold, Jr. (son of John George Herrold, Sr.).

JACOB LEVY lived in Penn Township in 1789. It is believed that he was a brother of Aaron Levy, the founder of Aaronsburg in Center County. The Levys were Jews. Jacob was one of the petitioners to make what is now Monroe Township of Snyder County, a part of Penn Township. Until 1789, it was part of Buffalo Township.

HENRY LEWIS, probably a son of John Lewis, lived in Beaver Township in 1789. His family at that time consisted of one male over 16 years and four females.

JOHN LEWIS was granted a warrant of survey for 100 acres of land in Northumberland (now Snyder) County, on December 28, 1774, and he was assessed in Penn Township for the first time in 1776. His name seems to disappear from the records for some years. The compiler believed he is the same man that received a warrant of survey for 400 acres in the same county on March 15, 1794. He served in the Northumberland County Militia and his name on one record was given as "John Levis," Henry Lewis and Thomas Lewis, who lived in Beaver Township in 1790 are believed to have been his sons.

THOMAS LEWIS is supposed to have been a son of John Lewis, mentioned above. He lived in Beaver Township in 1790, and his family consisted of five males and one female at that time.

ANDREW LINTERS lived in Beaver Township and his family consisted of one male over and one under 16 years. and one female, in 1790.

SERGEANT ANDREW LIST (also Least, Leist, etc.) was assess-

ed in Penn Township for the first time in 1776, and at that time he was designated as a single freeman. This situation continued for some years. An Andrew List, mason. was assessed in Penn Township in 1799. The federal census of 1790 states that his family at that time consisted of one male over and five under 16 years, two females, and one other person. He served as a private in Captain John Moll's Co., in Captain Michael Motz's Company, and as a Sergeant in Lieutenant Jacob Spees' Company, and in Lieutenant Jacob Bard's Party of the Northumberland County Militia and Rangers. David List may have been his brother, or as some think, his father. In 1785, Andrew was a Captain in the Militia.

ADAM LIST is supposed to have been a son of David List (given below). He lived in Penn Township during the Revolutionary period. He was a private in Captain John Black's Company of Northumberland County.

DAVID LIST, SENIOR was assessed in Penn Twp., for the first time in 1774. In 1781, and again in 1787, he was assessed with 50 acres and personal property. In 1802, he lived in Middleburg, Pa. It is supposed that he was the father of Adam and Andrew, mentioned above.

JOHN LIVELY was assessed in Penn Township only in the year of 1774. It is believed that he was a non resident landowner. Peter, mentioned below, may have been his son. A John Lively was a private in Captain Hambright's Troop of Horse in the service of the Province of Pennsylvania, in camp at Raystown, Pa., on July 11, 1758.

PETER LIVELY was assessed in Penn Township only in the year of 1776.He may have been a non resident landowner, and it is supposed that he was the son of John, mentioned above.

LIEUTENANT JOHN FEIGHT (or Veit or Feit) LIVINGOOD- also LIVINGOOD, Libengood, Leben-good, Lieberguth, etc.) may have been a son of Jacob Livingood, Sr., who died in Penn Township in 1794. Feight was assessed in Penn Township for the first time in 1776. In 1781, he was assessed with 400 acres of land and personal property. In May and June of 1780, he was a private in Lieutenant Jacob Spees' Company of Rangers, at an other time he was a Liutenant in Captain John Snyder's Company. He also served as a private in Captain Micael Motz's Company, all of which were organizations of the Northumberland County Militia. George was his son.

GEORGE LIVINGOOD was granted a warrant of survey for 100 acres of land in Northumberland (now Snyder- County on April 8, 1774. He was asesssed in Penn Township for the first time in 1776, It is said that he died in Penn Township in February. 1781. He was a son of John Viet Livingood. George served as a private in Captain John Moll's Company of the Northumberland County Militia. On November 16, 1773, he married Anna Maria, daughter of Henry Werner, Tulpehocken Township. Their children were: Jacob, John, and George.

JACOB LIVINGOOD, SENIOR, was assessed with 100 acres of land and personal property in Douglass Township, Berks County, Pa., in 1767 and 1766. About 1773, he came to what is now the southern section of Snyder County, and was assessed there for the first time about 1776. From 1781 to 1787, he was taxed with 100 acres and personal property. Jacob, Senior, died in Penn Township in 1794. Jacob, Jr., Feight, John and Peter, may all have been his sons, if not sons, relatives. One or more men of the name of Jacob Livingood served in the Northumberland County Militia. It is possible that Jacob, Sr., as well as his son, Jacob, Jr., served in the forces from Northumberland County. Letters of administration in his estate were granted to Peter Livingood (probably a son) on November 18, 1794. John Cummings and Deitrick Stonebraker were sureties for the administrator. His children were: Peter, Elizabeth Crawford, Rebecca Bachman, Jacob, Jr., Catherine, Polly, and Esther.

JACOB LIVINGOOD, JUNIOR, was assessed in Penn Township before 1790. In 1796, when Mahantango Township was formed from the lower part of Penn 'he was assessed with 100 acres of land, personal property, and a sawmill. In 1790, his family consisted of one male over and three under 16 years, and four females. Jacob died in what is now Chapman Township of Snyder County, in 1822. He served as a private in Captain Michael Weaver's Company of the Northumberland County Militia, and in Lieutenant Jacob Spees Company of Rangers on the Frontier, Christian Livingood may have been one of his sons.

JOHN LIVINGOOD is supposed to have been a son of Jacob Livingood, Sr. He lived in Penn Township as early as 1776. In 1790, his family consisted of one male over and

three under 16 years, and three females. In 1796, when Mahantango Township was formed from the lower part of Penn, he was assessed there. On January 30, 1777, he was a private in Captain Benjamin Weiser's Company of the German Regiment, Continental Line, stationed at Philadelphia, Pa.

CHRISTIAN LONG was assessed in Penn Township for the first time in 1776, There are some indications that he was a non resident landowner. Before the Revolution a Christian Long lived in Carnarvon Township, Berks County, and one in Bethel Township of Lancaster Co. John Long, possibly a son seems to have been a tenant on Christian's land from 1872. A Christian Long wasa private, 2nd class, in the 1st Company, 2nd Battalion of the Lancaster County Militia at some period during the Revolution.

PETER LONG, shoemaker was assessed in Penn Township for the first time in 1799. He was born on July 8, 1765, and died in what is now Monroe Township, Snyder Co., Pa., on August 22, 1852. He is buried in the Shriener's Church cemetery in that township. He served either in the New Levies or the York County Militia during the latter part of the Revolution.

PETER LONG is supposed to have lived in what is now Snyder County before 1800. He died at Freeburg, Pa., and his will was recorded at Sunbury, Pa., on March 12, 1803. The will mentions his wife, Catherine, and their children; Elizabeth, Peter, Jr., Hannah, and Catherine. One of the military records attributed to the Peter Long, above, may have belonged to this man. There is a possibility that he was the father of the Peter mentioned above.

JACOB LONG was a resident of Penn Township of a neighboring community as early as 1776. He was born on April 20, 1762, and died in or near Selinsgrove, Pa., on June 28, 1840. He is buried in the old Lutheran Cemetery in Selinsgrove. Although he was quite young, it is supposed that he was the Jacob Long that served in Captain John Clark's Company, 4th Battalion of the Northumberland County Militia.

HENRY LOUTHER was a resident of Beaver Township as early os 1789. In 1790, his family consisted of one male over and three under 16 years, and seven females.

MICHAEL LOWER (also Lauer, etc.) was assessed with 200 acres and personal property in Penn Township in 1782. It is believed that

he came from Philadelphia County, and that he was the father of Peter Lower, who later lived in what is now Snyder County.

PETER LOWER may have been the son of Michael Lower. He seems to have been assessed in Penn Township as early as 1776, but there seems to be no evidence of his living there as early as that date, or that he lived in the Township at all. A Peter Lower lived in Philadelphia County, town of Germantown, in 1790. This man also served in the Philadelphia County Militia during the Revolution.

GEORGE LOWREY (also Lowry, Lowery, Lowrie, etc.) was assessed in Penn Township for the first time in 1776. The evidence indicates that he was a non resident landowner and that he really lived in Cumberland County. In March, 1778, he was a private, 7th class, in Captain William Findley's Company, 8th Battalion of the Cumberland County Militia.

JACOB LUKE lived in Beaver Township prior to 1789. In 1790, his family consisted of one male over and three under 16 years, and five females.

PETER MADDOX (also Mattox, Maddocks, Maddex, etc.) lived in Penn township in 1790 and his family consisted of one male over 16, and two females. It is believed that he was the father of Jacob and Richard Maddox who lived in Beaver Township at about the same time.

JACOB MADDOX lived in Beaver Township in 1790, and his family consisted of one male over and one under 16 years, and four females. He served as a Private in Captain Church's Company of the 5th Pennsylvania Regiment, Continental Line. It is believed that he was son of Peter.

RICHARD MADDOX was assessed in Penn Township for the first time in 1781, and in that year was taxed with 150 acres and personal property. Richard lived in Penn Township in 1790, and his family consisted of one male over and one under 16 years, and four females. In 1776, he served as a private in Captain Cookson Long's Company, 2nd Battalion of the Northumberland County Militia.

ELISHA MANNING was assessed in Beaver Township for the first time in 1789. He was designated as a single freeman. He may have been a son of Nathan, Sr. In 1789, his name was on a petition asking for the election of a justice of the peace for Beaver Township.

JOHN MANNING was assessed

with 100 acres and personal property in Manor Township, Lancaster County, Pa., from 1771 to 1779. The next year he was assessed in Penn Township for the first time, and was taxed with personal property only. It is believed that he lived in what is now Beaver Township. On September 11, 1776, he was a private in Captain Joseph Wright's Company. Colonel Slough's Battalion of the Lancaster County Militia.

NATHAN MANNING, SENIOR, was assessed in Beaver Township for the first time in 1789. In the same year he signed a petition requesting that a justice of the peace be elected for that district. In 1790, his family consisted of one male over 16, and one female.

NATHAN MANNING, JUNIOR, was assessed in Beaver Township for the first time in 1789. He was designated as a single freeman at the time.

CAPTAIN RICHARD MANNING was a native of Lancaster County, Pa., and on September 13, 1773, he received a warrant of survey for 300 acres of land in Northumberland (now Snyder) County. This land lay in what is now Monroe Township, and about twenty years later was bought by the Hummel family when they came from Berks County. Richard was assessed in Penn Township for the first time in 1774, but it is believed that he did not occupy his new holdings until 1777 or 1778. He remained a resident of Penn Township until 1785, when he moved to Lycoming Township (now Lycoming County) of Northumberland County. On March 13, 1776, he was Captain of a company in the 4th Battalion of the Lancaster County Militia. In Northumberland County he served in the companies of Captain William Weirick and Captain Michael Weaver of the Northumberland County Militia. In 1799, he seems to have lived in Beaver Township.

SIMON MANNING, SENIOR, was assessed in Penn Township only in the year of 1778, and the evidence indicates that he was a non resident landowner.

SIMON MANNING, JUNIOR, was assessed in Penn Township only in the year of 1778. He too, seems to have been a nonresident landowner.

GEORGE MARKLE (also Merckle, Merkley, Markley, etc.) was assessed in Penn Township for the first time in 1780, and he was designated as a single freeman. Indications are that he lived in the township at least four years earlier. It is believed that he was a son of

Simon Markle, who died in the township in 1789. From 1784, he was assessed with 200 acres of land and personal property. In 1790, his family consisted of one male over and two under 16 years, and three females. He served as a pirvate in Captain Michael Weaver's Company of the Northumberland County Militia, and was Second Sergeant in Captain Benjamin Weiser's Company of the German Regiment, Continental Line, stationed at Philadelphia, Pa., on January 30, 1777.

PETER MARKLE (or Markley) was a son of Simon, and brother of George, mentioned above. He was assessed in Penn Township for the first time in 1776. He died in 1791. His wife was named Elizabeth. In 1785, he was assessed with 100 acres of land and personal property. In 1790, his family consisted of two males over and one under 16 years, and six females. No military record was found for him, but the compiler believes that he served in Northumberland County.

SIMON MARKLE (or Markley) was assessed in Penn Townhip for the first time in 1776. He died in the township in 1789. It is believed that George and Peter were his sons. No military record for him was found.

WILLIAM MARES (or Maris) was assessed in Penn Township only in the year of 1778. It is believed that he was a non resident landowner in Penn and that he really lived in Cumberland County. In 1780, he was a private, 7th class, 4th Company, 6th Battlaion of the Cumberland County Militia. In 1790 he lived in Harrisburg with his wife and a daughter.

DR. FREDERICK MARTIN was assessed in Penn Township for the first time in 1776, and may have been a non resident landowner. Before the Revolution he lived in Upper Milford Township, Northampton County, Pa. He was a farmer and a physician. In 1790, he lived in Upper Milford Township and his family consisted of two males over and three under 16 years, and five females. Jacob was one of his sons. He was Surgeon of the 1st Battalion of the Northampton County Militia during part of the Revolution.

JACOB MARTIN was a son of Dr. Frederick Martin of Upper Milford Township, Northampton County, Pa. Dr.Martin was a land owner in Penn Township as early as 1776. Jacob became a tenant on his father's land some time before the formation of Mahantango Township from the lower part of Penn, in 1796.

DANIEL MATTIG (maybe Maddox) was assessed in Penn Township only in the year of 1780. No military data was found for him.

HENRY MAURER lived in what is now Snyder County prior to 1800. Center Township. He was married to Judy, daughter of Jacob Krick.

JOHN MAURER (also Mowrer, Mowrey, Maury, Maurey, etc.) was assessed in Penn Township for the first time in 1799. He was a tailor.

LAWRENCE MAURER was born in Germany about 1734. He embarked for America on the British ship "Mary and Sarah," Captain Thomas Broderick, Master, at Rotterdam, Holland, and arrived at the port of English oath of allegiance on October 26, 1754. In 1768, he lived in Heidelberg Township, Berks County, Pa. His name appeared on the Penn Township tax list for the first time in 1776. It is supposed that he was the father of Peter Maurer. No military record was located.

MICHAEL MAURER, SENIOR, was assessed in Penn Township for the first time in 1778. In 1767, a man of this name lived in Albany Township of Berks County, and another in Alsace Township, same County. One, or both of these men came to what is now Snyder County. A Michael Maurer (presumably the older) was assessed with 300 acres of land and personal property in Penn Township in 1781, and thereafter for a number of years. Michael the Sr., and Michael, Jr., were taxed in Beaver Township in 1789. In 1790, Michael, Senior's, family consisted of one male over and one under 16 years, and two females. A Michael Maurer, aged 24 years, sailed from Rotterdam, Holland, on the British ship "Glasgow," arriving at Philadelphia, where he took the oath of allegiance on September 9, 1738. The compiler believes that this may have been the father of the Michael of this sketch.

MICHAEL MAURER, JUNIOR, was a son of he man mentioned above. He was probably born in Berks County. Pa., about the year 1762, and died in Beaver Township (now Snyder County) in 1824. He seems to have been assessed in Beaver Township for the first time in 1789, but no doubt lived in what is now Snyder County for at least ten years before. In 1790, his family consisted of one male over, one under 16 years, and seven females. His wife was Elizabeth, daughter of Jacob Krick. Henry, married to Judy Krick, Elizabeth's sister, was probably a brother of Michael. In

1780, Michael served as a private in Lieutenant John Coleman's Party of Rangers from Northumberland County. A Michael Maurer served in Captain Jacob Rohrer's Company of the Berks County Rangers.

PETER MAURER was born about 1755, probably in Berks County, Pa., and is supposed to have been a son of Lawrence Maurer. Indications are that he became a tenant on his father's land in what is now Snyder County in 1776 In 1781, he was assessed with 100 acres and personal property, but in 1787, he was taxed with 450 acres and personalty. His wife was Catherine ———, and one of their children was named John. This child was baptized at the old Zion Lutheran Church, north of Freeburg, in 1786. In 1790, his family consisted of one male over and two under 16 years, and five females. He served in the militia and ranger companies of Lieutenant Jacob Speese. Captain Michael Weaver, and Captain Charles Meyer, of Northumberland County. On November 15, 1832, a Peter Maurer, aged 76, was living in Lancaster Co., Pa., and was granted a pension by the federal government.

HENRY MAWHORTER was a son of Thomas, a tanner, of Northampton County, Pa. In 1786, Henry was assessed in the town of Northampton County, Pa., but he owned no land at that time. He came to what is now Selinsgrove about the year 1788, and from 1790 to 1792, was a fence viewer for Penn Township. In 1801, he contributed to the fund for the erection of the First Lutheran and Reformed church of Selinsgrove. Henry was an innkeeper. He died in Selinsgrove in 1817, leaving a wife and children. His father, Thomas, was a Revolutionary soldier.

ROBERT McATEER was assessed in Penn Township only in the year of 1778. No additional data available. Name may have been Robert Mateer. He served in the Cumberland County Militia. He died in Ohio.

LIEUTENANT EDWARD McCABE was a resident of Penn Township as early as 1776, but his name did not appear on the tax list until 1778, and remained until 1782. In the latter year he was taxed with 50 acres and personal property. On October 16, 1776, he was commissioned a Second Lieutenant in the 12th Pennsylvania Regiment of the Continental Line. On March 28, 1777, he was promoted to First Lieutenant. He resigned his commission on December 20, 1777. He sold his land to Anthony Selin.

SAMUEL McCLINTOCK was assessed in Penn Township for the first time in 1795. The following year when Mahantango Township was formed from the southern part of Penn, he was assessed there. He died in the town of Northumberland, and his will was probated in Sunbury, Pa., on August 17, 1812. The will mentions his wife, Hannah, and the following children: Jean, Andrew, and James.

EDWARD McCONNELL was assessed in what is now Snyder County in 1771, but owing to indefinite lines at the time he probably lived in Greenwood Township, Cumberland County. In 1785, he was granted a warrant of survey for additional land there. He served in the Cumberland County Militia during the Revolutionary period.

JOHN McCORMICK was listed as a freeman in Penn Township in 1768. In 1783, he was listed as a resident of Potter Township, and in 1785, he was assessed with 50 acres of land and personality there. Potter Township lay in the section now included in Center County. It is believed that in 1790, he lived in what is now Huntingdon County. He received depreciation pay for services in the Northumberland County Militia.

JAMES McDONALD must have lived within Penn Township for a short time. He was a private in Captain Charles Meyer's Company of the Northumberland County Militia.

JOHN McDONALD, probably a brother of James, lived in the township for a time and served in the same organization during part of the Revolution. Indications seem to point that they either came from, or moved to York County.

WILLIAM McKEAN was granted a warrant of survey for land in Northumberland (now Snyder) County in 1772, and he was assessed in Penn Township for the first time in 1776, but it is believed that he was a nonresident landowner, and that his home was in Mount Joy Township, Lancaster County, Pa., where he was assessed from 1770. In 1781, he was a private, 8th class, 6th Company, 7th Battalion of the Lancaster County Militia. On July 23, 1819, a William McKean, Jr., applied for a federal pension from the state of New Jersey, stating that he had served in the Pennsylvania Line. He died in 1824.

ABRAHAM McKINNEY was a resident of Augusta Township, Northumberland County, Pa., in 1787. He was assessed in Penn Township for the first time in 1793. In 1790,

his family consisted of one male over and one under 16 years, and three females. No military data found.

JOHN McQUEEN lived in Lancaster County, Pa., in 1770. He was assessed in Penn Township for the first time in 1776. It is supposed that he was a nonresident landowner. He served as a private in the 4th Pennsylvania Regiment, Continental line.

WILLIAM (Billy) McTAGET was assessed in Penn Township only in the year of 1780. No military data was found for him.

ANDREW MEEK was assessed in Beaver Township for the first time in 1789. In 1790, his family consisted of one male over and two under 16 years and three females.

PETER MEEK, probably a brother of Andrew, was assessed in Beaver Township for the first time in 1789. No military data was found for him.

THOMAS MEESE (also Mease, Mees, Meas, etc.) was assessed in Penn Township for the first time in 1776, and the evidence indicates that he was a nonresident landowner and that his home was in Lancaster County. It is believed that he was a descendant of Philip Mease who sailed from Rotterdam, Holland in the British ship "St. Mark," Captain Wilson, master, and took the oath of allegiance at Philadelphia, on September 26, 1741. Thomas was granted a warrant of survey for two tracts totalling 70 acres, in Northumberland (now Snyder) Co. on Feb. 15, 1775. In 1782, Thomas was a private, 8th class, 8th Company, 2nd Battalion of the Lancaster County Militia. William, mentioned below, was probably his son.

WILLIAM MEESE was assessed in Penn Township for the first time in 1780 or 1781. It is believed that he was a son of Thomas Meese of Lancaster County, and that he was a tenant on the land granted to Thomas in what is now Snyder county in 1775. William was overseer of the poor for Penn Township on March 25, 1781. No military record was found for him.

SIMON MEIKEL (also Meichel, Michael, etc.) was a resident, but not a landowner, in Elizabeth Township, Lancaster County, Pa., in 1771 and 1772. He was assessed in Penn Township for the first time in 1781, and in that year was taxed with 50 acres and personal property. His name was missing after 1785. No military data was located for him.

ADAM MEISER lived in what is now Snyder County as early as 1780,

In 1790, his family consisted of one male over and two under 16 years, and two females. In 1796, he was assessed in Mahantango Township. He served as a private in Captain Michael Motz's Company of the Northumberland County Militia.

GEORGE MEISER (also MISER, Misor, Myser, Mysor, etc.) was a son of Henry Meiser, Sr. He was a joiner. He was assessed as a single freeman in Mahantango Township for the first time in 1796.

HENRY MEISER, SR., was of German Palatinate descent, and is believed to have been a son of Michael Meiser to whom a warrant of survey for a large tract of land was granted in 1734. The Meisers were among the Palatines who landed at New York, lived there some years, and about 1730, came down the Susquehanna River from the Schoharie Valley of New York, ascended the Swatara Creek to near the present town of Hummelstown, now in Dauphin County, but in earlier days, part of Lancaster County. Henry lived neighbor to John George Herrold, Sr., in Heidelberg Township, Lancaster County, both of them later became some of the earliest settlers in what is today Chapman Township of Snyder Co. On April 19, 1763, Henry Meiser was granted a warrant of survey for 200 acres of land in Cumberland (now Snyder) County. On June 29, 1773, he was granted a warrant for an additional 100 acres in the same locality. His name appeared on the Penn Township tax list for the first time in 1772, but it is believed that he lived there a year or two earlier. His holdings were near the present village of Aline, and he came there with all his personal effects and family in a two horse wagon. He built a bark hut and on three different occasions was forced to move away because of the unfriendliness of the Indians. On one occasion he placed his children in a chaffbag (bedtick), put them on the back of a horse and went down the river to the present village of New Buffalo, to escape from the ravages of the Indians. A temporary fort for the protection and refuge of the settlers had been erected there. On one occasion the Indians took the baking bread from an outdoor oven, and at another time, during the absence of Mr. Meiser, an angry Indian appeared at the cabin. Mrs. Meiser gave him things to eat, but he went away in a sullen mood. When Mr. Meiser returned to the cabin, he took up the trail of the Indian, a fight ensued and the Indian lost his life. Meiser

was a great hunter and had a deer lick in a swamp near his home, and it is said that his larder seldom lacked venison. One day a pair of panthers passed near their cabin and he followed them, killing one. That night the other returned to the cabin seeking it's mate, and he shot it through a port hole in the cabin wall. In 1775, he was a road supervisor for Penn Township. He lived in that section of Penn Township, which became Mahantango Township in 1796. In that year he was assessed with land, personal property, and a sawmill. His was one of the first sawmills in the section. The village of Meiserville was named for this pioneer. His son Michael, built an oilmill near the site of this village. Henry died in Mahantango Township, and his will was probated in Sunbury, Pa., on August 7, 1801. His wife was Anna Maria ———, and she must have died before him, because her name is not given in the will, but the names of these children are: Mary Elizabeth, Catherine, Barbara, John, Michael, Philip, George, Frederick, and Andrew. Andrew was one of the first children baptized at the old Zion Lutheran Church, north of Freeburg, in 1781. It is believed that John Meiser, Senior, was his brother. Henry Meiser, Jr., was assessed in Mahantango Township in 1796, but it is believed that he was a son of John, Senior, Henry, Jr., was not mentioned in Henry, Sr.'s will, and because of this it is believed that he was John's son, or died before Henry, Sr. Henry, Senior. served in the organization of Captain John Snyder, Captain John Moll, and Lieutenant Jacob Bard of the Northumberland County Militia and Rangers.

HENRY MEISER, JUNIOR, was a son of Henry, Senior, or of his brother, John, Senior. If he was a son of Henry, Sr., he must have died before him, because he was not mentioned in the older man's will. Henry, Jr., was assessed in Penn Township in 1790, and his family at the time consisted of one male over and five under 16 years, and two females. When Mahantango Township was formed in 1796, he was assessed there. His wife's name was Margaret, and three of their children (John, born Nov. 19, 1795; Henry, Sept. 7, 1796, and Anna Maria, September 25, 1798) were baptized at Grubb's (Botschafts) Lutheran Church in what is now Chapman Township, prior to 1800. Part of the military record mentioned under Henry, senior, above, may

have belonged to this man.

JACOB MEISER may have been a son of John Meiser, Senior. He served in Captain Michael Motz's Company of the Northumberland County Militia.

JOHN MEISER, SENIOR, was assessed in Penn Township for the first time in 1776. It is believed that he was a son of Michael Meiser, and a brother of Henry Meiser, Senior. In 1778, he was a road supervisor in Penn Township. In 1781, he was assessed with 100 acres of land and personal property. Three John Meisers lived in Penn Township at the same time. They were John, Senior, John, Junior, his son, and John, son of Henry, Senior. John, Senior, died in Penn Township, and his will was probated at Sunbury, Pa., on November 19, 1795. It mentions these children of his; John, Junior; George; Margaret (Mrs. Peter Stoke), she had two daughters and died before her father; Barbara (Mrs. George Coystewile, who died before her father, and whose children were Elizabeth, Margaret, Barbara, and George Coystewile). John had three sons and four daughters. The third son may have been Adam Meiser. In 1790, John's family consisted of himself and two females. A John Weiser served in each of the following organizations; Captain Benjamin Weiser's Company, German Regiment, Continental Line; Captain Michael Motz's Company; Captain John Snyders Company, Captain Michael Weaver's Company, Ensign Simon Herrold's Party, and Lieutenant Jacob Spees' County Militia and Rangers.

JOHN MEISER, JUNIOR, was a son of John Meiser, Senior. He was assessed in Penn Township for the first time in 1782, and in that year he was taxed with 100 acres and personal property. In 1790, his family consisted of one male over and two under 16 years, and three females. When Mahantango Township was formed from the lower part of Penn in 1796, his name did not appear on the tax list there, which indicates that he may have removed from that section. The compil . feels certain this man served in the Revolution, and that some of the services mentioned above belonged to him.

MICHAEL MEISER. A Michael Meiser was granted a large tract of land in Lancaster County in 1734. It is believed that this Michael was the father of Henry, Senior, and John, Senior. The Michael of this sketch was a son of Henry, Senior. Michael's name appeared on the Penn Township tax list for the first time in 1776. After 1782, it seems 'to disappear, but in 1796, when Mahantango Township was formed he was assessed there. In 1782, he was taxed with 50 acres of land and personal property. He died in Perry Township of Snyder Conty in 1827. No military record was found for him.

PHILIP MEISER was a son of Henry, Senior. He was assessed in Mahantango Township for the first time in 1796, but he lived there at an earlier date, because he and his wife had one of their children baptized at Grubb's Church, in what is now Chapman Tow ship in 1794.

CONRAD MEISINGER (maybe Messinger) lived in Penn Township for a short time during the Revolutionary period. He served as a private in Captain Black's Company of the Northumberland County Militia.

JOHN ADAM MENGES was born in Germany on September 2, 1730, and died near Freeburg, Snyder County, Pa., on May 6, 1814. He is buried in the cemetery of the old Zion Lutheran Church, about a mile north of Freeburg. His wife was Anna Margaret ————. He embarked for America at Rotterdam, Holland, in the British ship "Mary and Sarah" and arrived at the port of Philadelphia where he took the oath of allegiance to the English government on October 26, 1754. In 1771, he was assessed in Lebanon Township (now Lebanon County) of Lancaster County with 50 acres of land and personal property. In 1782, he was assessed with 78 acres and personality in the same township. In 1793 or 1794, he moved to what is now Washington Township of Snyder County, but was then Penn Township of Northumberland County. He was assessed in Penn Township for the first time in 1794, and in addition to land and personal property, he was assessed with a saw mill and grist mill. These properties lay about half way between the present villages of Kantz and Freeburg. Andrew Morr moved into the same vicinity in the year 1770 or 1771, and erected a gristmill and sawmill. Some of the Morrs moved to Center County about the same time that Menges moved to what is now Snyder County and some think that Menges bought the Morr holdings. The compiler thinks otherwise. In 1795, it was proposed to build a road from Menges' mill to Selinsgrove. This was eventually done, and the road now is part of the Selinsgrove-Mifflin highway. In 1799, Adam was one of the road supervisors of Penn Township. Adam and his family were members of the Lutheran church. They had eight children, some of them moved to the middle

west and several of the descendants of them rose to high political favor in Indiana and Ohio. The names of their children (not in the order of their birth) were: George, John, Peter, Margaret, born January 17, 1761 (married Christian Kantz, Senior, 1758-1826), Jacob, born 1775, died 1847 (married Catherine, 1791-1869), Mary Elizabeth, born February 29, 1765, died February 13, 1832 (married Peter Garman, March 16, 1767, died July 24, 1831), Catherine (married Michael Miller), and Mary (married the Rev. Dr. John Peter Shindel, Sr., noted Lutheran divine). Adam Menges' will was probated at Lewisburg, Pa., on January 6, 1815. Some think that Adam served in the Revolution under the name of "Adam Mingo" but the genealogist of the Penna. State Library states that his Revolutionary service consisted of giving large amounts of wheat and forage for the use of the American Army (Pennsylvania Archives, 5th series, vol. 7, page 1149). Anna Margaret Menges wife of Christian Kantz, 3rd child of Adam Menges and wife, was baptized at the Tulpehocken (Christ) Lutheran Church, near Stouchsburg, Pa., in 1761, soon after her birth. Her sponsors were Peter Menges and wife. Mary Elizabeth, born January 18, 1759, was baptized at same church, and her sponsors were John Peter Laudenslager and Mary Elizabeth Menges (probably an aunt). Their daughter Anna Maria (Mary) was born on September 2, 1768. She was baptized at the same church and her sponsors were John Peter Menges and wife (probably an uncle and aunt of the child.)

SIMON MENICH (also Mennich, Minnich, Minnick, Minnig, Mennig, etc.) was born in Germany and embarked for America in the British ship "Brotherhood." Captain John Thompson, master. He arrived at the port of Philadelphia, Pa., where he took the English oath of allegiance on November 3, 1750. He came to Penn Township before 1773, and in that year was one of the constables of that township. It is believed that he returned to Lancaster County during the Indian uprisings. In 1779, he was a private, 4th Class, 8th Company, 6th Battalion of the Lancaster County Militia.

BALTZER MENICH lived in what is now Snyder County prior to 1770, but seems to have remained only a short time. Indications are that he was a relative of Simon.

CHARLES MENSCH was a non-resident landowner and seems to have been taxed only in the year of

1776.

LIEUTENANT N I C H O L A S MERTZ (also Merts, Martz, etc.) was born on August 8th, 1748, and died on February 22, 1801, probably in Franklin Township, or what is today Franklin Township. He is buried in a private cemetery on the Wittenmeyer farm in that township. He was a native of Hereford Township, Berks County, Pa., and came to Penn Township about 1789. In 1790, his family consisted of one male over and five under 16 years, and five females. In 1781, he was Second Lieutenant of the 1st Company, 2nd Battalion of the Berks County Militia.

LIEUTENANT PHILIP MERTZ is supposed to have been a brother of Nicholas Mertz, mentioned above. It is supposed that he was born in Germany, and that he was the Philip Mertz, who embarked for America on the British ship "Edinburgh" at Rotterdam, Holland, and arrived at the port of Philadelphia, where he took the oath of allegiance to the English government on October 15, 1749. He lived in Richmond Township from 1768 to 1784, also in Maxatawney Township for a while, both in Berks County. In Richmond Township he was taxed with 100 acres and personal property. He came to Penn Township in 1785, and in 1787 was taxed with 140 acres of land and personality. In 1793, he was a viewer for the location of a road from Selinsgrove toward Lewistown. In 1795, he was one of the viewers appointed to fix the boundaries of the newly created Township of Mahantango. In 1787, Gertrude, daughter of Philip and Anna Eva Mertz, was baptized at the old Zion Lutheran Church, north of Freeburg. In 1789, their daughter Anna Mary was baptized there. Philip died in Penn Township. and his will was probated at Sunbury, Pa., on January 14, 1804. His will mentions his wife, Anna Eva, and their eleven children: Peter, 1774-1845 (whose wife was Catherine ————, 1776 - 1852); Henry, 1781-1857, (whose wife was Maria C. Hains, 1784-1852); Abraham; Catherine (Mrs. John Weyand, or Weiand); Susanna, (Mrs. Peter Reeves); Eva (Mrs. Nicholas Arbogast); Elizabeth (Mrs. Adam Holtzapple) Margaret; Gertrude, born 1787 (Mrs. Ludwig or Lewis Arbogast); Anna Mary, born 1789, and Sarah. The last four mentioned were unmarried at the time of their father's death. On May 17, 1777, Philip was First Lieutenant of the 1st Company, 2nd Battalion of the Berks County Militia.

DANIEL MESHALL (probably meant for Mitchell)) was assessed as a single freeman in Penn Township only in the year of 1776. No military data was found concerning him.

ALEXANDER MEYER also Myer, now Moyer) was assessed in Penn Township only in the year of 1776. No further data available.

CHARLES MEYER (supposedly Charles Meyer, Senior, now Moyer) lived in Penn as early as 1778. It is believed that he is the same Charles Meyer that lived in East Hanover Township, Lancaster County, Pa., in 1771. In 1781, he was taxed with 200 acres, personal property, and a still. In 1787, he was granted a warrant of survey fo 200 additional acres in Northumberland (now Snyder) County. In 1778, he was an overseer of the poor in Penn Township. He died in Penn Township, and his will was probated at Sunbury, Pa., on March 11, 1800. His will mentions his wife, Christiana, and two children: Jacob and Mary (Mrs.— Skyler). There were other children, but the names were not given in the will. In 1790, his family consisted of two males over 16 years, and four females. It is believed that he served in the Revolutionary forces, and one of the records given below may have been his. Christina, his wife, died in Penn Township and her will was recorded at Sunbury, Pa., on Aug. 28, 1805. It mentions these children: Charles, Jacob 5-19-1789-1-7-1853) whose wife was Sarah ——— (4-20-1802 - 6-1-1851, Fred, Martin, Anna, Maria (Mrs. Peter Richter) and Catherine, Mrs. John Haas.

CAPTAIN CHARLES MEYER (now Moyer) is supposed to have been a son of Charles Meyer, Senior, mentioned above, he probably came to the township with his parents about the year 1778. He died in Penn Township in 1811. In 1780, he was a private in Lieutenant Jacob Spees' Party of Rangers, his name also appears among the New Levies, and at another time he was Captain of a company of Rangers or Militia from Northumberland County.

FREDERICK MEYER (now Moyer) lived in Penn Township in 1791. He was one of the signers of the petition for the formation of Mahantango Township.

JOHN GEORGE MEYER (now Moyer.) He was a son of John Jacob Meyer, Senior, was born near Mill Creek, Lebanon County, Pa., on June 3. 1757, and died near Freeburg. Snyder County, Pa., on September 5, 1813. The cause of his death was tuberculosis, which was caused by a cherry seed lodging in his lungs. His first wife was Elizabeth, daughter of John Buchtel (who lived near the present village of McKees Half Falls). She was born on September 4, 1762, and died on September 4, 1801. His second wife was Mary Brosius. The issue of the first marriage was seven children, and of the second, three. "George" as he was commonly called came to what is now Washington Township, Snyder County, with his parents in 1768, and at the death of his father became the owner of the parental farm, west of Freeburg. The children of George and his wives were: George (who married Catherine, daughter of Christopher Moyer, and moved to Ohio); Elizabeth (Mrs. Frederick Richter); Julia (never married); Susan (married Jacob Hess and lived east of Tylersville, Sugar Valley, Clinton County, Pa.,) Mary (married David Batdorf and lived in Freeburg, Pa.); Barbara (married Jacob Hains and their daughter, Catherine, married Joseph son of the pioneer, John George Woodling); Margaret (married George Weaver of Penns Valley, Center County, Pa. Major Jared Fisher was her son in law); Lydia (married Benjamin Hess of Penns Valley and moved to a western state); Christina (married John Weaver and lived near Pine Grove Mills, Center County, Pa., and David, (who married Anna Salters.) In 1790, George's family consisted of one male over 16 years and four females. George served as private in Captain Benjamin Weiser's Company, German Regiment, Continental Line, at Philadelphia, Pa., on January 30, 1777. Later he served as a Private in Captain Charles Meyer's Company of the Northumberland County Militia. The compiler has a rather complete genealogy of some of the descendants of this pioneer.

LIEUTENANT COLONEL HENRY MEYER (name not changed to Moyer) was a son of John Jacob Meyer, Sr He was born at Mill Creek, now Lebanon County, Pa., on October 15. 1764, and died in or near what is now Rebersburg, Center County, Pa., on May 17, 1820. He is buried in one of the cemeteries at Rebersburg His first wife was Mary, daughter of Jacob Steese, of what is now Snyder Co. She was a sister of the Hon. Frederick Steese, the noted millbuilder of the Middlecreek and Penns Valley. She died in 1801, of what is believed to have been yellow fever. She is buried at Rebersburg. Colonel Moyer moved to Brush Valley, now Center County in the year 1797. About 1805, he married Margaret, the daughter of Judge John Adam Harper of Center County. She was born on June 30, 1787, and died on February 27, 1871. She is buried in the Lutheran and Reformed Cemetery at Rebersburg. Colonel Meyer was a large man, at least six feet tall, and weighed over 200 pounds. He was a millwright by trade, but in his latter years he engaged in farming. Some of the older mills in the Penns, Brush and Sugar Valleys of Center County were built by him. It is evident that he learned his trade from his famed brother-in-law, Hon. Frederick Steese, who built several scores of gristmills. Colonel Meyer was a great reader both in German and English texts. He was a Democrat and a member of the Reformed Church. At the age of sixteen years he enlisted in Captain John Snyder's Company of Northumberland County Rangers and served against the Indians during the Revolutionary period. On February 28, 1794, he was commissioned Major of the 1st Battalion, 3rd Regiment of the Northumberland County Militia, and on January 4, 1802, he was commissioned Lieutenant Colonel of the 131st Regiment, 1st Brigade, 10th Division, of the Pennsylvania State Militia. He served as a Justice of the Peace from 1814. His children were Henry, 1795-1881, (he married Hannah, daughter of Nicholas Bierly); Jacob, 1797-1873, (unmarried); Benjamin, died 1824 (married Mary, daughter of Melchoir Poorman); William, 1804-1824 (unmarried); John, born 1806 (married Mary Catherine, daughter of Daniel Poorman and later Susan Confer); Reuben, born 1808 (married Mary, daughter of George Corman); Judith, born 1811 married Philip Walker, and lived at Clintonville, Clinton County, Pa.); Susan, 1813-1883 (married Griffin Rote, 1810-1879, they lived near Salona, Clinton County, Pa.); Dr. Jonathan 1816-1880 (married Elizabeth, daughter of Melchoir Poorman), and Abigail, 1819-1849 (unmarried). The compiler·has a rather complete genealogy of this family.

JOHN MEYERS, shoemaker, was assessed in Penn Township for the first time in 1799. He was a son of Stephen Meyer, who was assessed as a cordwainer in Whitehall Township, Northampton County, Pa., in 1788. In 1801, he contribut-

ed to the fund for the erection of
the First Lutheran Church of Selinsgrove.

JOHN MEYER now Moyer), weaver lived in Beaver Township in 1789.
It is believed that this was the
John who died in 1792 and is buried in the old part of the Hassinger Cemetery, west of Middleburg,
Pa. His wife, Susan—— died in
1793, and is buried in the same
cemetery. Private, 1st Company,
2nd Battalion of the Lancaster
County Militia.

JOHN MEYER, probably a son
of the John Meyer (Moyer) who
died in 1792. This man died in
Beaver Township in 1827, and may
have been one of the Moyer family of what is now Adams Township.

JOHN MEYER (now Moyer) was
born in what is now Berks County,
Pa., on May 27, 1771, and died in
what is now Penn Township, Snyder County, on September 17, 1865.
His wife was Anna Margaret, daughter of the pioneer, Frederick Miller, of what is now Penn Township.
She was born on April 17, 1771, and
died in Penn Township on January
5, 1847. Both are buried in the old
cemetery at the Salem (Row's)
Church, near their home. They were
married in 1794. John was a farmer
and shoemaker, and he cleared
most of the farm he tilled. His land
adjoined that of his father-in-law,
from whom he purchased 36 acres
more. Later he bought 28 acres
from the church lands. The writer
thinks that John Moyer was a relative of Charles Meyer who died in
Penn Township in 1792, and of Captain Charles Meyer. who died there
in 1811. In 1811, John was a member of the council of the Salem
(Row's) Lutheran and Reformed
Church. A descendant states that
John was not of the same clan
of Meyers as those which settled at Freeburg. John Meyer and
his wife had four children; Elizabeth, a twin, born June 2, 1798,
died April 15, 1877 (she married
John Gemberling of Selinsgrove);
Catherine, a twin sister of Elizabeth,
born June 2, 1798 (she also married
a John Gemberling, probably a cousin of her sister's husband); Samuel,
born August 4, 1800, died April 22,
1865; William, born November 15,
1801, died January 4, 1876 (on Mar.
21, 1825, he married Margaret, daughter of Christian Fisher, and
granddaughter of the pioneer, John
Adam Fisher. She was born on December 24, 1803, and died December
26, 1886). Descendants of this pioneer still in Penn Township and surrounding sections. The compiler has
a geneology of this family.

JACOB MEYER (now Moyer),
tailer, was a son of Stephen Meyer,
mentioned above under John Meyer,
shoemaker. He was probably born in
Whitehall Township, Northampton
County, Pa. He was assessed in
Penn Township for the first time in
1799.

SERGEANT JOHN JACOB MEY-
ER, SENIOR, (now Moyer) is believed to have been a son of the immigrant, Henry Meyer, who settled
at Mill Creek, Lebanon County, Pa.
Some think his father might have
been John Meyer. The evidence
seems to indicate that the Meyers
came down from the state of New
York, and that they were among
the Palatines which landed at New
York harbor in 1710. The subject of
this sketch was born about 1735,
probably at Mill Creek, Lebanon
County, Pa., but then a part of Lancaster or Berks County. A Henry
Moyer and his wife, and
their three children lived in the
New Queensbury Camp in the colony of New York, in 1712. "Jacob"
as he was commonly called was one
of the first settlers in what is today
the Freeburg section of Snyder
County, he came there about the
year 1768, and settled about a mile
west of the present village, others
who settled there about the same
time were Peter Straub, Andrew
Morr, and Casper Roush. Indians
lived near where Jacob settled and
his younger children often played
with the Indian children. Later
when the Indian upraisings came,
Jacob moved his family back to
Mill Creek for a time. Some think
they returned several times. Jacob
kept a sort of tavern and Colonel
Samuel Miles several times stopped
at his home on his journeys back
and forth between Philadelphia and
his large land holdings in Center
County. Jacob is supposed to have
had two wives, Susan Zartman and
Susan Ream, the latter was a daughter of Peter Ream of Dauphin
County, Pa. The house which Jacob
built was still standing in 1934. In
1781, Jacob, Sr., was assessed with
100 acre and personal property. In
1787, he was one of the fence viewers for Penn Township, and in 1789,
he or his son of the same name,
was constable of the same township. In 1790, his family consisted
of six males over 16 years, and one
female. Jacob died in Penn Township in 1808, and is buried in one
of the cemeteries in or near Freeburg. Jacob and his older sons served in the Revolution. Jacob served
as a private in Captain Charles
Meyer's Company, and as a Sergeant in Lieutenant Jacob Spees'

Company of the Northumberland
County Militia. The children of Jacob were: Catherine (who married
John Meyer, probably a relative,
and moved to Center County); Barbara (married Captain Michael
Motz, and moved to Center County,
see Michael Motz sketch); Lieutenant Philip Meyer (married Margaret, daughter of Andrew Morr, Jr.,
see their sketches elsewhere); John
Jacob, Jr. married Julia Morr, sister
of Margaret, who married Jacob's
brother Philip); John George (see
sketch above); Henry (see sketch
above); Michael (see sketch below);
Christopher,. The compiler has an
almost complete geneology of this
man.

JOHN JACOB MEYER, son of the
above, was born about the year 1760
near Mill Creek, Lebanon County,
Pa., and died in 1813, on the Pine
Creek, near Jersey Shore, Pa. His
wife was Julia, daughter of Andrew
Morr, Jr., and a sister to Margaret
Morr, who married Jacob's brother
Philip. His wife, Julia Morr, was
born on July 18, 1770, and died on
November 8, 1824. Jacob and his
wife are buried in the Pine Creek
Cemetery, near Jersey Shore. The
children of Jacob were; Catherine
(married George Meyer, her father's
cousin. She is buried at Aaronsburg,
Pa); Jacob (married Barbara Wise
and later Martha Clark, he lived at
Jersey Shore, Pa.); George (married Mary Snyder and lived at Jersey Shore); Mary (married John
Fessler and lived at Newberry, Pa.);
Barbara (married her cousin Henry,
son of Michael Motz); Lydia (married Thomas Weaver and later Michael Zeigler, and lived at Aaronsburg, Pa.); Philip (married Abbie
Snyder, and lived near Jersey
Shore); Elizabeth (married Thomas
Harper, and lived near Woodward,
Pa.); Samuel (married Kate Nep-
ley and lived at Jersey Shore); John
(never married); Christina (married John Ginder, or Ginter, and lived in the Lykens Va ley of Pennsylvania); and Julia, who married
Benjamin F. Lamb, and moved to
Illinois. In 1787, Jacob was assessed with 150 acres of land and personal property in Penn Township.
In 1790, his family consisted of one
male over 16 years and two females. In 1787, Jacob and his wife
had their daughter Catherine baptized at the old Zion Lutheran
Church, north of Freeburg. Jacob,
Jr., and his father served in Captain Charles Meyer's Company, and
he and his brothers, George and
Philip served in Captain Michael
Motz's Company of the Northumberland County Militia. On May

13, 1780, he was a private in Captain John Snyder's Company of Rangers.

LIEUTENANT PHILIP MEYER (not changed to Moyer) was a son of John Jacob Meyer, Senior. He was born near Mill Creek, Lebanon County, Pa., on November 14, 1755. His wife was Maragaret, daughter of Andrew Morr. Jr., and a sister of Julia Morr, who married Philip's brother, Jacob. He was assessed in Penn Township for the first time in 1778. In 1790, his family consisted of one male over 16 and four under that age, and three females. His wife was born Aug. 20, 1759, and died on March 12, 1829. Both are buried in the Lutheran Cemetery at Rebersburg, Penna. Three of the children of Philip and his wife were baptized at the old Zion Lutheran Church, north of Freeburg. They were: Anna Barbara, 1782, John George, 1784, and John Jacob, 1788. Philip was a robust and strong man, although not very tall. Philip lived in what is now Snyder County from 1768 (when he was thirteen years old) until about 1802, when he moved to the Brush Valley in Center County, where he bought a tract of land near the village of Wolf's Store. His brother, Henry, had settled there some five years earlier, and his brother, Michael, came some years later. Philip was a kind and generous man and well thought of. For many years he held the office of road supervisor in Miles Township. In 1815, when the road was built over the mountain from Wolfe Store to Penns Valley, he was one of the men in charge. He was a member of the Reformed Church. Many of the descendants of this man moved to the west and can be found in Ohio, Indiana, and Iowa, in numbers. Many of them intermarried with the same Morr family from which his wife came. The children of Philip and his wife were eleven in number; Philip, Jr., 1780-1858 (married Elizabeth Meyer and moved to Kentucky about the year 1801. He had a second wife); George, 1784-1842, (married Rosena Kreamer and moved to Marion County, Ohio, in 1832) John Jacob, born 1788 (married Mary Stein and lived at Hamburg. Clinton County, Pa., from where they moved to Wayne, now Ashland County, Ohio); Henry (married Barbara Foreman 1795-1885, they lived in Brush Valley, Center County, then moved to Ohio); John, 1794-1872, (married Mary N , daughter of Christian Gast, they lived in Brush Valley,

Center County, and in 1833 moved to Marion County, Ohio, and in 1851, from there to Scott County, Iowa); Benjamin (lived in Brush Valley, moved to Ohio, married Margaret, daughter of John Wolfart); Samuel, 1805-1884, (married Esther, sister of the Hon. John Reynolds. His second wife was Susan J. Russell. They moved to Ohio, and from there to near Garvin, Iowa); Barbara, (Mrs. John Motz). Elizabeth, born 1792, (married Christian, son of Christian Gast, 1790-1858. He was the founder of Middletown, Ohio); Margaret (married John, son of the older and brother of the younger Christian Gast. They lived west of Rebersburg, Center County, Pa., then moved to Frankstown, Blair County, Pa., and from there, in 1832, to Prospect, Ohio), and Catherine (married Daniel, brother of Abraham Kramer. They moved from Center County to Uniontown, Ohio). Philip Meyer was First Corporal of Captain Benjamin Weiser's Company, German Regiment, Continental Line, stationed at Philadelphia on January 30, 1777. At another time he was a private in Captain Michael Motz's Company, Captain Michael Weaver's Company, and Lieutenant in Captain Charles Meyer's Company of the Northumberland County Militia.

JACOB MICHAEL, may have been a son of George Michael who was buried at Selinsgrove. Jacob was assessed in Penn Township for the first time in 1786 and in that year was taxed with 50 acres and personal property. When Beaver Township was formed in 1787, he was assessed there. In 1790, his family consisted of himself and wife. A Jacob Michael was Chaplain of the 1st Battalion Berks County Militia, in 1777, but this seems to have been an older man.

JOHN MIDDLESWORTH was born in 1745, probably in the state of New Jersey, and died in what is now Beaver Township, Snyder County, Pa., on May 14. 1815. He is buried in the old cemetery at Beaver Springs, Pa. It is said that he came to what is now Snyder County in 1792. Some of the Middlesworth family lived in Berks County in 1790. It has been said that John served in the Revolution with the New Jersey troops, or with Pennsylvania troops which fought there.

ADAM MILLER was assessed in Penn Township for the first time in 1781. In 1754, he was taxed with 270 acres and personal prop-

erty. His name does not appear after the latter year. Men of his name from Northampton, York, and Bedford Counties, served in the Revolution.

BENJAMIN MILLER lived in Penn Township in 1790, and his family consisted of one male over and two under 16 years. and one female.

CHRISTIAN MILLER may have been a native of Berks County. Pa. He was born in 1754, and died in Gregg Township, Center County, Pa., in 1824. He is buried in Heckmans Cemetery, near Center Hall, Pa. He lived in Penn Township from 1776 to 1784, when he moved to Center County. In Penn Township he was assessed with 50 acres and personal prrperty. It is believed that he is the man who served as a private in the 3rd Pennsylvania Regiment,, Continental Line. A Christian Miller served as a private in Captain Jacob Meyer's Company, 6th Battalion, Berks County Militia in 1782.

CONRAD MILLER was assessed in Penn Township from 1776 to 1778. In 1790, he lived elsewhere in Northumberland County, and his family consisted of one male over and two under 16 years, and three females. He probably served in the Northumberland County Militia, and in 1820 was a Pensioner.

DAVID MILLER was a resident of Penn Township prior to 1777, but the date of his first assessment is unknown. In February, 1777, he was a member of the Committee of Safety from Penn Township, and at another time he served as a private in Captain John Moll's Company and Lieutenant Jacob Spee's Company of Rangers from Northumberland County.

DEWALT (or DEWALD) MILLER seems to have been a native of Berks County and a carpenter by trade. He was assessed in Penn Township for the first time in 1774. From 1779 to 1781 he was listed as a resident of the city of Reading, and at the same time was listed as a nonresident landowner in Penn Township. In 1785, he was assessed with 250 acres of land, personal property, and a saw mill in Penn Township. He probably died in 1785 or 1786, because in the latter year "Widow Miller" was taxed with this property. In 1776, he was Color Bearer of the 4th Battalion of the Northumberland County Militia. This battalion was commanded by Colonel Philip Cole. Dewalt Miller also served in Captain Sheffer's (Shaffer's) Company of the 1st Battalion, Berks

County Militia.

GEORGE MILLER was a son of John Frederick Miller, a pioneer in Salem section of what is now Penn Township of Snyder County. George was born April 18, 1773, probably in Berks County, Pa., and died near the village of Salem in Penn Township on May 1, 1836. His wife was Susanna, a sister or daughter of George Good, who lived in the same section. She was born on January 1, 1774 and died on July 26, 1806. He married a second time and that his second wife was Magdaline Deshler, who was born on June 21, 1779, and died July 18, 1826. All three are buried in the old part of the Salem (Row's) Cemetery in Penn Township. George was a farmer and operated his father's farm after his death. The children of George and his first wife were: John (1799-1877); Mary Magdalene, born 1801, (married John Kline); Elizabeth (1803-1869), she was deaf and dumb and never married; Catherine, born 1805, married Jacob Schoch. George's children by his second wife, Mary Magdalene Deshler, were: George D. (1806-1884) who married Mary Kessler (1813-1861), Jacob (1811-1866), married Catherine Klose (1812-1894); Daniel (1813-1882), who lived near Dreisbach's Church in what is now Union County, Pa.; Sarah, born 1814, who married John Swengle; Hannah, born 1816, married Michael Swengle and died at Princeon, Illinois; and Frederick, born 1817, who died in young manhood, unmarried. George served as an officer of the Salem Lutheran and Reformed Church.

GEORGE MILLER was born in 1761 and died in what is now Snyder County, Pa., in 1844. He lived in Penn Township as early as 1774. His wife was Catherine Markle. In 1840, he applied for a pension and in his application he stated that he was nearly eighty years old. It is said that he took his brother's place in Captain Henry Wright's Company in 1777, and that in 1778 he was a teamster in the Revolutionary Army.

HENRY MILLER was assessed in Penn Township for the first time in 1776. On September 1, 1776, he was a private in Captain Casper Weitzel's Company in the Continental Service at King's Bridge, New York. He lived at Aaronsburg, Center County, Pa., from 1789 to 1810. He was a pensioner in 1825.

JOHN MILLER was assessed in Beaver Township in 1799. No military data for him was found.

JOHN FREDERICK MILLER, commonly called "Frederick," was the son of John Daniel Miller and his wife, Ottilia Catherine Rummel who came to America with their family in the British ship "Patience" sailing from Rotterdam, Holland, and arriving at the port of Philadelphia, Pa., where John Daniel took the English oath of allegiance on August 11, 1750. They settled either in Berks or Northampton County. Frederick was born in the village of Freymerdsheim, Germany, on November 22, 1738, and the next day baptized by the Rev. John Ludwig Gulick, pastor of the Evangelical Lutheran Church of that village. He was the second of the six children of his parents born in Germany, and was twelve years old when he arrived in America. He as assessed in Penn Township for the first time in 1776, but it is believed that he did not actually become a resident of the township until 1782 or 1783. In the latter year, he was assessed with 50 acres and personal property. The warrant of survey of the bought was granted to Martin Treaster of Buffalo Township in 1776. He sold it to Colonel Peter Hosterman on April 3, 1778, and Hosterman to Frederick Miller on October 5, 1788, and from that day to this the land has been in the hands of the Miller family, first owned by Frederick, then his son George, grandson, George D., great grandson, Hon. Charles, and now by the children of Charles, the great great grandchildren of the original owner. Frederick's wife was Eva Maria Albright, she was born on July 25, 1740, and died on September 14, 1822. Frederick died on July 14, 1821. Both are buried in the cemetery at Salem in Penn Township. In 1785, Frederick was one of the road supervisors of Penn Township. One cannot help but admire the forsight of this pioneer, who built his massive stone house over a never failing spring, both house and spring are in use today, and are located on the south side of the Middleburg- Selinsgrove Highway, about two miles west of the village of Salem. In 1790 Frederick's family consisted of two males over and one under 16 years, and four females. Frederick Miller and his wife were married in 1763, and they had four children who grew to maturity, they were: Mary Magdalene, (1764-1832), who married John George Benfer, (1745-1818), and may have been his second wife; Catherine (Mrs. Henry Bollender); Anna Margaret (1771-1847), who married John Moyer

of the same section, he was born in 1771 and died in 1865; and George (1773-1836), who married Susanna Good (1774-1806), and Mary Magdalene Deshier (1779-1826). Frederick served in Captain Henry Storuch's Company, 6th Battalion of the Berks County Militia, and in Captain Michael Motzs Company of the Northumberland County Militia or Rangers. Former District Attorney of Snyder County, William K. Miller, is one of the occupants of the old Miller farm today, and his brother Frank is the actual operator of it.

SIGISMUND MILLER was assessed in Penn Township for the first time in 1778. In 1781, he was assessed with 134 acres of land and personal property. In 1787, he was granted a warrant of survey for 150 acres additional, and in 1792, for 200 acres more. In 1790, his family consisted of one male over and four under 16 years, and five females. No military record was found for him, but it is believed that he served in the Revolution.

JOHN MITCHELL was assessed in Beaver Township prior to 1789. In 1790, his family consisted of one male over and two under 16 years, and one female.

BALTZER MITTERLING lived in Penn Township soon after the Revolution, and in 1790, his family consisted of one male over and one under 16 years, and two females. In 1796, when Mahantango Township was formed from the lower part of Penn, he was assessed there.

CHARLES MONEY is supposed to have been a résident of Penn Township for a short time. He served as a private in Captain John Moll's Company of the Northumberland County Militia.

ARTHUR MOODY, on May 25, 1757, enlisted as a bateauman (boatman) in the brigade raised by the Province of Pennsylvania. It was the duty of these men to transport the military supplies up the Susquehanna River and other streams to the forces on the frontier. A mutiny occurred at the tavern of George Gabriel, somewhere near the present site of the town of Selinsgrove, when they were transporting supplies from Fort Halifax to Fort Augusta, at Sunbury. It is supposed that at the time of his discharge, some years later, he settled nearby, at least, as f'nd his name on the tax list for what is now Snyder County as early as 1768. Nothing was found that would indicate that he remained there for any length of tiime, or that he served in the Revolution.

ROBERT MOODY (Moodie) was assessed in Penn Township in 1771, and on July 4, 1772, was granted a warrant of survey for 60 acres in Northumberland County, formed that year. In 1778, he was assessed as a resident of Turbot Township in the saee county, and in 1781, he was taxed with 550 acres and personal property in that township. For a few years during the Revolution a Robert Moody was assessed in Augusta Township of Northumberland County. A Robert Moody died in Northumberland County in 1785. One of these men was Lieutenant Colonel of the 2nd Battalion, Northumberland County Militia, at some period during the Revolution.

GEORGE MOOK was born on December 25, 1764, and died on December 30, 1843. He is buried in the St. John Church Cemetery, West Beaver Township, Snyder County. His will is recorded at Lewisburg, Pa. In 1786, he was assessed with 50 acres and personal property in Buffalo Township, and in 1789, in Beaver Township. In 1790, his family consisted of one male over and one under 16 years, and three females. He received depreciation pay for services in the Northumberland County Militia.

CASPER MOON, SENIOR. (This name may be at the present day Mohn), was assessed in Penn Township for the first time in 1774. The name did not appear after 1783. In 1782, he was assessed with 150 acres and personal property. No military record was found for him.

CASPER MOON, JUNIOR, was assessed in Penn Township for the first time in 1776. His name appeared for the last time in 1784. He may have been a tenant on his father's farm. A Jasper (maybe a mistake for "Casper") Moon served in Captain Robert Patterson's Company of the Bucks County Militia.

JAMES MOON was assesser in Penn Township only in the year of 1780. He was a native of Bucks County and was born in the year 1738. He served as a private in the 1st Pennsylvania Regiment, Continental Line, and became a pensioner on February 10, 1819. He lived in Fayette County, Pennsylvania, at that time.

JOHN MOON was asssessed in Penn Township for the first time in 1778, but the evidence seems to indicate that he lived there at an earlier date. For a few years his name seems to disappear from the tax list, but in 1785, he was assessed with 300 acres of land, a gristmill, and personal propery. In 1779, a John Moon was assessed in Cumru Township, Berks County, and it is believed that he may have returned there during the Indian uprisings. He served as a private in Captain John Moll's Company, and in Lieutenant John Black's Party of the Northumberland County Militia and Rangers..

NATHANIEL MOON was assessed in Beaver Township for the first time in 1789. In 1790, his family consisted of one male over and one under 16 years, and three females. He served as a private in Captain Joseph McClellan's Company, 9th Pennsylvania Regiment, Continental Line.

THOMAS MOON was assessed in Penn Township from 1780 to 1782. but it is believed that he lived in the township before the first date. He served as a private in Captain John Moll's Company of the Northumberland County Militia.

WILLIAM MOON may have been a brother of Casper Moon, Sr. He was assessed in Penn Township for the first time in 1774. Then his name seems to disappear until 1781 1782. In 1790, a William Moon lived in Bucks County, Pa., and his family consisted of three males over and two under 16 years, and four females. In 1779, he was a private 7th Class, Captain John Jack's Company, 8th Battalion of the Cumberland County Militia.

ANDREW MORR, SENIOR, was born in Germany, probably about the year 1700. He embarked for America at Rotterdam, Holland, in the British ship "Brothers," Captain William Muir, master, and arrived at the port of Philadelphia, Pa., where he took the English oath of allegiance on September 16, 1751. John Michael Morr, who came on the same ship, may have been his son. Others, who later settled in what is now Union or Snyder Counties, were on the same ship. It is believed that Andrew Morr, Junior, was the oldest son of this immigrant, came over in 1749. An Andrew Morr was granted a warrant of survey for 200 acres in Lancaster County, on November 17, 1742, but the compiler believes that this was some other Andrew. The Andrew of this sketch s so seems to have lived in Lancaster County, probably in that section which is now Lebanon County. On March 18, 1769, Andrew bought a tract of land from a man named Ort in what is now Washington Township, Snyder County, east of the village of Freeburg, and it is supposed that he moved there soon after the purchase, because in 1770 he, Peter Straub, and Casper Roush made application for a tract of land for a church and school. This land was granted in 1774, and the location was about a mile north of the tract having about 40 acres in it. A Lutheran Church was built there about 1780, and used until about 1808. He was first assessed in Penn Township in 1770. He must have died in 1771, or early in 1772, because in that year the Penn Township tax list did not contain his name, but had "Widow of Andrew Morr' instead.

ANDREW MORR, JUNIOR, was a son of Andrew Morr, Senior. He was born on April 30, 1727, supposedly in Germany, and died in what is now Washington Township, Snyder County, and his will was probated at Sunbury, Pa., on May 18, 1801. It is supposed that he came to America before his parents, and that he was the Andrew Morr, who sailed from Rotterdam, Hollond in the British ship "Dragon," Captain Daniel Nichols, master. He arrived at the Port of Philadelphia where he took the English oath of allegiance on October 17, 1749. His father seems to have come two years later. In 1758, Andreas (Andrew) Morr lived in what is now Shaeffertown, Lebanon County, but was then Heidelberg Township of Lancaster County. His wife was Catherine Elizabeth ———, and she was born on April 17, 1732. On September 3, 1766, he made application for a warrant of survey for 40 acres adjoining the land of George Bumbach (died Penn Township in 1780) and Charles Brunk, on the Middle Creek, in what is now Washington Township. Andrew and his father and their families came to the new land in 1770 or 1771. In 1772, "Widow of Andrew Morr" was assessed in Penn Township, but as Andrew evidently became the owner of his father's holdings, we do not find his name on the Penn tax list until 1776. In November of that year he was elected assessor of Penn Township, and on February 13, 1777 he was a member of the Committee of Safety for Penn Township, and thus became one of those who helped to establish our present country. In 1780, he was constable of Penn Township. In 1781, he was assessed with 400 acres of land, a sawmill, gristmill, and personal property. In 1787, he was one of the viewers for the formation of Beaver Township. In 1790, he was again a constable for Penn Township. The next year he was a viewer to establish a road from John Adam Fisher's ferry on the Isle of Que, below Selinsgrove, up the Penns Creek Valley. In 1796, he was appointed a viewer to help fix the boundry lines of Mahantango Township. In 1801, he lived in the village of Freeburg. The Lutheran Church, north of Freeburg, was sometimes known as Morr's Church, because Andrew and his fahter had much to do with the founding and support of it. In 1794, Andrew and his wife gave the church a fine silver communion set, which was inscribed with their names. This set is still in existence, altho no longer in use. In addition to other property, Andrew owned an oil mill and a distillery. He dealt extensively in real estate, and at one time was one of the largest realty owners of this section. His wife, Catherine Elizabeth, died about 1795, and he married the widow Dewald. Andrew and his two wives are buried in the cemetery of old Zion or Morr's Church. Only the grave of his second wife is marked. In order that we may know all that is known of the second Mrs. Morr, her tombstone inscription is given "Here rests Anna Maria, a born Renninger, she was born on July 12, 1747. She was the wife of Christopher Beisel, Peter Dewald and Andrew Moore. While married to Christopher Beisel she was the mother of twelve children. She died April 25, 1817, aged 69 years, 9 months and 14 days." The children of Andrew Morr and his first wife were: Christina, 1757-1793, (married John George Roush, a Revolutionary soldier. He was the great-great-father of the compiler; Anna Margaret, 1759-1829, (married Lieutenant Meyer, a Revolutionary soldier, they are buried in the Lutheran and Reformed Cemetery in Rebersburg, Pa.); John George, 1761-1817, (he, too, was a Revolutionary soldier. He married Catherine Dieffenbach. George lived in Center County, but died near Freeburg, while visiting friends, and is buried there); Philip, 1766-1826, (he married Elizabeth, daughter of Jacob Gemberling, the pioneer. After the death of his first wife, he married Mrs. Mary Ebly, a widow, of Sunbury, Pa.); Magdalene, 1763-1800, (she married Adam Bollender, Jr., a Revolutionary soldier, who died in 1801;) Catherine Elizabeth born 1768 (she married Michael Weaver, maybe a son of Captain Michael Weaver, and it is supposed that they moved to Canton, Ohio); Julia, 1770-1824, (married John Jacob Meyer, Jr., a Revolutionary soldier. They moved to Pine Creek Township, Clinton County, Pa., and are buried in the Pine Creek Cemetery about two miles west of

Jersey Shore); and Anna Barbara, 1772-1804, (married the Hon. Frederick Steese, and became the great-great- great- grandparents of the compiler.)

JAMES MORR (maybe Moor or Moore) lived in Penn Township in 1791. It is believed that he was a son of John Morr, who died in Penn Township in that year, and a brother to Thomas L. Morr. James lived in Center County.

JOHN MORR (maybe Moore) died in Penn Township in 1791. Letters of administration were granted to James Morr, supposedly his son.

JOHN GEORGE MORR was a son of Andrew Morr, Jr. He was born on August 3, 1761, probably in what is now Schaefferstown, Lebanon County, Pa., and died near what is today Freeburg, Snyder County, Pa., on October 18, 1817, while visiting relatives and friends. He is buried in one of the Freeburg cemeteries. At the time of his death his family was living in Center County, about a mile north of the village of Coburn. "George" as he was commonly called was assessed in Penn Township for the first time in 1783, with personal property only. In 1787, he was taxed with 100 acres and personal property. In 1792 he moved to Haines Twp., Center Co. Pa., and in 1794, he moved back to what is now Washington Township, Snyder County. In 1808, he again moved to Haines Township, and it was there that his family lived when he died, while on a visit to his kin at Freeburg. The children of George Morr were: George, 1784-1867 (who married the daughter of Jacob and Susan (Wittenmeyer) Roush. George died near Wooster, Ohio); John Philip, 1787-1835, (he married Sarah Beisel, or Beistel. They moved to Moorland, Wayne County, Ohio, where both died); John, 1789-1845 (he married Hannah Sunday, and in 1828 they moved to Ashland County, Ohio; he is buried in the Pleasant Valley Cemetery, near Ashland); Mary Magdalene, 1792-1860, she (married Valentine Mogle. They moved to Ohio, and both are buried at McComb, Hancock County, Ohio); Andrew, 1794-1857, (he married Elizabeth Stover and they moved to Perry Township, Ashland County, Ohio, where both died); Benjamin, 1795-1870, (he married Catherine Kerstetter, they died and are buried in Ashland County, Ohio); Michael, 1796-1877, (he married Christina Stover. They lived and died in Perry Township, Ashland County, Ohio); John Adam, 1798-1880, (he

married Sarah Harter, and both are buried at Millheim, Pa.); Daniel, 1802-1867, (married Eva Swartz of Center County and they moved to Ashland County, Ohio, where both died); Elizabeth, 1804-1876, (married Jacob Albright, and they are buried at Wooster, Ohio); Peter, 1806-1877, (married Elizabeth Wise. He died at Auburn Junction, Indiana); and Samuel, 1809-1882, married Mary M. Knouse, and they died in DeKalb County, Indiana). George Morr served as a drummer boy in the Revolution and was engaged in the Battle of Brandywine. Later he served in the companies of Captain John Moll and Captain Charles Meyer of the Northumberland County Militia. (The compiler has a complete genealogy of this man and his father.)

JOHN PHILIP MORR was a son of Andrew Morr, Jr. He was born on January 1, 1766, probably in Schaefferstown, Lebanon County, Pa., and died in what is now Washington Township, Snyder County, Pa., on April 13, 1826. His first wife was Elizabeth, daughter of the pioneer, Jacob Gemberling. She was born on July 13, 1768, and died on August 11, 1811. She and some of her infant children are buried in the Old Zion Cemetery, north of Freeburg. His second wife was Mrs. Mary Ebley, a widow of Sunbury, Pa. After Philip's death, she married Jacob Kline. Philip was assessed in Penn Township for the first time in 1790. Philip was a large real estate owner, but through the dishonesty of others, he lost much of it. He was a farmer and storekeeper, and in 1813, Governor Simon Snyder appointed him one of the commissioners of the newly founded county of Union. The children of Philip were: Philip, 1788-1824, (married Elizabeth Lotz, and both are buried in St. Peters Cemetery in Freeburg); Catherine, 1793-1856, (married John Michael Fisher, and after his death, John Stahley, she and first husband are buried in St. Peters Cemetery at Freeburg); Michael, 1791-1794; Elizabeth, 1795-1796; Anna Mary, 1797-1871, (married Aaron N. Missimer, and both are buried in the cemetery at Jersey Shore, Pa.); Lydia, 1800-1801; and John Jacob 1803-1858, (married Maria Naugle, and both are buried in one of the Freeburg Cemeteries). (The compiler has a genealogy of this family).

JACOB MORTON was assessed in Penn Township only in the year of 1780. No further data found.

GEORGE P. MOTZ (also Moatz, Mootz, Mots, etc.), was born on June 26, 1743, probably in Berks

County, Pa., and died in what is now Washington Township, Snyder County, Pa., on February 6, 1806. His wife, Maria ————, was born on June 25, 1755, and died in Washington Township, on January 26, 1816. Both are buried in St. Peters Cemetery in Freeburg, Pa. He was a brother to John and Captain Michael. He and his brothers were assessed in Penn Township for the first time in 1774 and in 1787, he was taxed with 200 acres of land and personal property. In 1790, George's family consisted of one male over and one under 16 years, and six females. They had one son and five daughters, some of these are mentioned in his will which was probated at Sunbury, Pa., on February 22, 1806. The known children of this family were; John, 1781-1847, who married Barbara, daughter of Lieutenant Philip Meyer, both are buried at Freeburg. Another daughter was Mrs. Lawrence Haines. The two youngest daughters of George Motz were Susan and Barbara, these two, were baptized at the old Zion Lutheran Church, north of Freeburg, in 1786 and 1789, respectively. In 1801, George contributed to the fund for the erection of the First Lutheran Church of Selinsgrove, Pa. No military record was found for George, but it is believed that he served at some period during the Revolution.

JOHN MOTZ was born in 1758, or before, probably in Berks County, Pa. He died at Woodward, Center County, Pa., in 1802. His wife was Mary, daughter of Peter Witdier, who died in Penn Township in 1793. She was born in Lancaster County, Pa., on October 9, 1767, and died near Woodward, Pa., on March 13, 1839. It is supposed that John came to Penn Township about the time that his brothers did, at least he was assessed in Penn Township in 1776, which would indicate that he was born before 1758. In 1785, he was taxed with 100 acres of land, personal property, and an oil mill. In 1790, his family consisted of himself and two females. In 1791, or 1792, he moved to what is now Center County, Pa., and it is said that he was the first settler on what is now the site of the village of Woodward. His brother Captain Michael Motz moved to that section too. John was a man of considerable educational attainments, and a sculptor. He and the pioneer, John Buchtel, were close friends, nd met together to discuss astronomy, philosophy, nd mathematics. They ordered books on these subjects from Germany. The

children of John Motz and his wife were; John, Jr., who married Elizabeth, granddaughter of the pioneer and Revolutionary soldier, John Adam Fisher, she was born in 1801, and died in 1882. Both are buried at St. Paul's church, near Woodward. Pa. 2 Elizabeth married George Weaver, and they lived in Venango County, Pa., 3. Jacob, married Elizabeth Hess, and they are buried at St. Pauls, mentioned above. 4. George, married Rachel Harper, and moved to the state of Indiana. 5. James, married Rebecca Mark, and lived at Woodwa...!, Pa. 6. Sarah, married Daniel Barnes and moved to the state of Indiana. 7. Susan, who never married. 8. John Motz, maybe not the same, served in the York County Militia during part of the Revolution.

CAPTAIN MICHAEL MOTZ was mer, Senior, a Revolutionary soldier, born in the year 1745, probably in Berks County, Pa., and died in Haines Township, Center County, Pa., in 18:0. His wife was Barbara, daughter of the pioneer and Revolutionary soldier, John Jacob Meyer (Moyer), Senior. Captain Motz and his wife are buried in St. Paul's Lutheran Cemetery, about two miles west of the village of Woodward, Pa. He came to what is now Snyder County with his brothers George and John. and was assessed in Penn Township for the first time in 1774. In 1785, he was assessed with 170 acres of land and personal property. In 1790, his family consisted of one male over and one under 16 years, and seven females. Some time around the year 1790, Michael and his brother John, moved to the east end of the Penns Valley in what is now Haines Township, Center County, Pa. Michael and his wife had one son and six daughters, four of the daughters married four brothers of the name of Wise. Elizabeth, the fifth daughter of Michael and his wife was born in 1783 and in the same year baptized at the old Zion Lutheran Church, north of Freeburg, Pa. The children of Michael and Barbara (Moyer) Motz were; 1. Eva, born 1772, married John Wise and lived in Penns Valley, Center County. 2. Susanna, born 1774, married Geo. Wise. 3. Barbara was born 1775, married Martin Wise. 4. Catherine (Nov. 11, 1781-Feb. 12, 1836), married John Harper. 5. Elizabeth, born 1783, married Jacob Hess. 6. Margaret, born 1785, married Conrad Wise. 7. Henry (Feb. 15, 1788-Jan. 31, 1847), married his cousin, Barbara Meyer (Moyer), daughter John Jacob Meyer, Jr., of Jersey Shore, Pa. Mi-

chael Motz served as a private in Captain Michael Weaver's Company, and later was himself a captain of a company of the Northumberland County Militia.

LIEUTENANT JOHN PHILIP MERTZ, commonly called Philip, was the son of the immigrant, John Henry Mertz, who took the oath of allegiance at Philadelphia, Pa., on Sept. 26, 1737. John Henry Mertz seems to have been the son of John Mertz, Stockhausen, Wurtemberg, about 40 miles northeast of Coblenz, Germany. John Henry settled in Rockland Township, Berks County, Pa., where he married Anna Maria, tht daughter of Jacob Rossman and his wife, Anna Magdalene Scheuer, or Scheur. John Henry donated the land in Rockland Township on which the Mertz church stands today. John Philip, subject of this sketch, was born in Rockland Township on October 14, 1738, and grew up in Berks County, Pa. He seems to have lived in Richmond Township, Berks County from 1768 to 1784, and was assessed there with 100 acres of land and personal property. He, or another of the same name, lived in Maxatawney for a short period between these years. He was assessed in Penn Township, Northumberland County, now Washingtown Township, Snyder County, for the first time in 1785, and in 1787 was listed as owning 140 acres of land, and considerable personal property. In 1793, he was one of the viewers appointed to locate a road from Selinsgrove toward Lewistown. In 1795, he was one of the viewers appointed to fix the boundries of the newly created township of Mahant.ny. In 1787, Gertrude, da..ghter of Philip and Anna Mertz, was baptize.. at the old Zion Lutheran Church, north of Freeburg and their daughter, Anna Mary, was baptized there in 1789. Philip died in what is now Washington Township, in December of 1803, and his will was probated at Sunbury, Pa., January 14, 1804. The will was dated Dec. 19, 1803. The witnesses to the will were Christopher Moyer, Pete.' Hilbish, and George Motz. Philip's son, Peter, and his son-in-law, Nicholas Arbogast were the executors. The will mentions Anna Eva, his wife, and their eleven children, the last four were unmarried at thtir father's death. The names of the children follow: Peter, 1774-1845, married Catherine ————— 1776-1856, Henry, 1781-1857, whose wife was Maria Christina, 1784-1862, daughter of John Hains; Abraham; Catherine, Mrs. John Weyand, or Weiand; Susanna, Mrs. Peter Reeves; Eva, Mrs. Nicholas Arbogast; Elizabeth, Mrs. Adam Holtzapple; Margaret; Gertrude, Mrs. Ludwig, or Lewis Arbogast; Anna Mary, and Sarah. On May 17, 1777, was first lieutenant of the 1st Company, 2nd Battalion of the Berks County Militia.

GEORGE MOYER (also Meyer) was a resident of Penn Township before 1800. It is said that he is buried in an unmarked grave in the Salem Church Cemetery in Center Township. He served in Captain Michael Motz's Company of the Northumberland County Militia, and in Captain John Black's Company of Rangers from the same county.

HENRY MOYER (also Meyer) was assessed in Beaver Township for the first time in 1791. At that time he was operating a grist and sawmill. It is believed that his full name was Daniel Henry Moyer, sometimes written Mayer, and that his brothers were, John, the Tanner, and Michael, and that they were the sons of Jacob, who lived in an eastern county.

JOHN MOYER (also Mayer), the tanner, is supposed to have lived in what is now Snyder County prior to 1800.

ANTHONY MULL (in earlier days the name was written Moll) was a farmer in Macungie Township, Northampton County, Pa., in 1772. On December 2, 1774, he was granted a warrant of survey for 100 acres in Northumberland (now Snyder) Co. He was taxed in Penn Township for the first time in 1774, and his name seems to have disappeared after 1782. It is believed that he was the father, or a brother of Captain John Moll (Mull). Anthony served as a private in Captain John Moll's Company of the Northumberland County Militia.

CAPTAIN JOHN MULL (also MOLL) is believed to have been a relative of Anthony Mull or Moll, who lived in Macungie Township, Northampton County in 1772, and in 1774 was assessed in what is now Snyder County. It is not known when Captain Mull, or Moll, first came to the section that is now Snyder County, but it must have been some time prior to 1780. In 1790, he seems to have been living in Cumberland County, in either Hopewell, Newton, Toboyne, or West Pennsboro Township, and his family consisted of one male over and three under 16 years, and three females. He served as a Captain of a Company of the Militia or Rangers from Northumberland County.

JOHN MUMMA (also Mummah, Mummaw, etc.) was probably a native of Lancaster County. He was assessed in Beaver Township for the first time in 1789. Mummas live in western Snyder and eastern Mifflin Counties at this time. In 1790, his family consisted of one male over and two under 16 years, and four females. A John Mumma served in the Lancaster County Militia during the Revolution.

ALEXANDER MURRAY (also Murry, Murrey, etc.) was granted a warrant of survey for 100 acres in Cumberland County on July 1, 1762, and a warrant for 100 acres in Northumberland (now Snyder) County on October 27, 1772. He may have never lived in the township at all, and merely have been a non resident landowner. In 1782, he was assessed as a resident of Toboyne Township, Cumberland County. In the same year he was assessed as a nonresident owner of 300 acres in Penn Township. He was a lawyer or justice of the peace and seems to have died before 1790. His son, Alexander, Junior, was assessed in Toboyne Township in 1790, and his family consisted of one male over, and six under 16 years, and three females. Alexander, Sr., was a private, 7th class, Capt. John Buchanan's Company, 7th Battalion of the Cumberland County Militia.

ZACHRIAH MUSSINA was assessed in Beaver Township for the first time in 1799. He was a single freeman at the time. Some Mussinas live in Union County today.

JOHN MYST (maybe Moist) was assessed as a single freeman in Penn Twp., only in the year of 1776. No military or other records concerning him was located.

HENRY NEES (also Neese, Nies, Nease, Niess, Knees, Knies, etc.) was a nephew of William Nees, who was one of the earliest settlers in Penn Township. He was a resident of Penn Township before the Revolution, because in 1776, he was a private in Captain John Clark's Company of the Northumberland County Associators.

PETER NEES was a nephew of William Nees, and a brother of Henry, mentioned above. He, too, was a resident of Penn Township before the Revolution, and he, too, served in Captain John Clark's Company, while it was in the continental service. He died of wounds at Piscataway, New Jersey, on February 1, 1777. He left a wife, Mary, and three children. In her application for a pension, she stated as follows: "Peter Nees in December, 1776, was a private in Captain John Clark's Company of the Northumberland County Militia, commanded by Colonel (later General) James Potter. While on a tour of duty at Piscataway, New Jersey, he was mortally wounded in January of 1777, by a musket ball, by reason of which and for lack of attention, he died before his return from the tour." The pension was granted.

PETER NEES, son of William Ness, was born in the year of 1763. and died somewhere in Center County, Pa., in 1852. He is buried in Heckmans Cemetery near Penn Hall in Center County. His wife was named Christina. Peter and Christina had their daughter, Susanna, baptized at the old Zion Lutheran Church, north of Freeburg, in 1791. It is believed that Peter's wife was a daughter of Mathias Hess. On May 13, 1780, Peter was a private in Captain John Snyder's Company of the Northumberland County Militia. As early as 1789, Peter was a landowner in Haines Township, Center County, but it is believed that he did not move there until after 1791.

WILLIAM NEES was on the tax list of Penn Township for 1771. He was a German sailor, and one of the earliest settlers in the Township. He was still living in 1787, when he was taxed with 200 acres of land and personal property. It is believed that he had other children than the Peter, mentioned above. If he served in the Revolution, the compiler did not find his service record.

JACOB NEFF was a resident and landowner in Strasburg Township, Lancaster County, Pa., in 1771. On March 16, 1776, he was granted a warrant of survey for 300 acres of land in Northumberland (now Snyder) County. There is no conclusive evidence that he lived in the township, and if he did it was for a short period only, after which he returned to Lancaster County. In 1781, he was a Private in Captain William Smith's Company, and in 1782, a private, 6th class, in the 5th Company, 1st battalion, of the Lancaster County Militia.

JACOB NEITZ (also Nitz, Nits, Knitz, Nitts, Knights, etc.,) SENIOR, seems to have lived in Penn Township, before 1780. No military record of this man was found.

JACOB NEITZ, JUNIOR was assessed for the first time in Mahantango Township in 1796. He was a single freeman at that time. The Neitz family is still resident of Union Township.

JOHN NEITZ is supposed to have lived in Berks or Lancaster County, and seems to have only been a nonresident landowner. At one time he was assessed with 130 acres of land in Penn Township. It is supposed that some of his sons were tenants on his land.

. LUDWIG (LEWIS) NEITZ was born in Germany. He sailed for America on the British ship "Nancy," Captain John Ewing, master, from the port of Rotterdam, Holland. He arrived at the port of Philadelphia, where he took the English oath of allegiance on September 27, 1752. In 1757 and 1768, he was a resident, but not a landowner in Longswamp Township, Berks County, Pa. His name appeared on the Penn Township tax list for the first time in 1778. In 1787, he was taxed with 70 acres and personal property. In 1789, he was granted a warrant of survey for an additional 100 acres. It is believed that he was the father of some of the other Neitzs who lived in what is now Snyder County. No military record was located for Lewis. In 1790, his family consisted of three males over 16 years of age.

MATHIAS NEITZ lived in Penn Township as early as 1780. He served as a private in the companies of Captain Michael Motz and John Snyder of the Northumberland County Militia.

SERGEANT PHILIP NEITZ was a resident of Penn Township in 1780 or bfore. In 1796, when Mahantango Township was formed, he was assessed there. In 1790, his family consisted of one male over and three under 16 years, and two females. He was born in the year 1752, and was still living in 1833. On January 30, 1777, he was a private in Captain Benjamin Weiser's Company, German Regiment, Continental Line, stationed at Philadelphia, Pa. He was a Sergeant in Captain John Snyder's Company of the Northumberland County Militia, he also served as a private in Ensign Simon Herrold's party and Lieutenant Jacob Bard's Party of Rangers from Northumberland County. He was a pensioner on February 7, 1833. It is supposed that he was a relative of the other Neitzes of the section now known as Union, Washington, and Chapman Township. The compiler believes he was a son of Ludwig.

1774, but he may have been merely PETER NEIMAN (probably Newman), fiddler, was assessed in Penn Township for the first time in 1799. A Peter Neiman, shoemaker, was assessed in Douglass Township, Berks County, Pa., in 1768. No military record was found for one of the name.

JOHN NELSON, tailor, was as- sessed in Penn Township for the first time in 1799. Several men of this name served in the Revolution from Pennsylvania.

HENRY NERHOOD (also Nearhood, Nerhut, Nerhoot, Nearhoot, etc.) was a resident of Albany Township, Berks County, Pa,. in 1767, and was assessed there with 100 acres of land and personal property. He was assessed in Penn Township for the first time in 1785, and in 1787, he was taxed with 50 acres and personality. In 1789, he was assessed in Beaver Township, where he died. In 1790, his family consisted of two males over and two under 16 years, and three females. His will was probated at Sunbury, Pa., on October 17, 1803, and mentions his wife and the following children; Jacob, Adam, Michael, Catherine, and Mary Magdalene. Adam became an early resident of what is now Chapman Township. No military record was found for Henry, but it is believed that he served in Berks County.

FRANCIS NEWCOMER was granted a warrant of survey for 176 acres in Lancaster County, Pa., in 1750, and at that time Cumberland county was still a part of Lancaster county. Until 1772, the lower part of what is now Snyder county was part of Cumberland. The name of Francis appeared on the Penn Township tax list for the first time in 1776, but he may have been merely a nonresident landowner. No military record can be found for him.

PETER NEWCOMER was probably a son of Francis Newcomer, mentioned above. He was assessed in Penn Township for the first time in 1778, and may have been a tenant on his father's land. In 1788 he was assessed with 150 acres and personal property, and in 1789, he lived in Beaver Township. In 1790, his family consisted of one male over and one under 16 years, and five females. He served as a private in the companies of Captain John Black and Lieutenant John Coleman of the Northumberland County Militia, or Rangers.

JACOB NEWMAN, SENIOR, was assessed with 150 acres and personal property in Douglas Township, Philadelphia County in 1769. His name appeared on the Penn Township tax list for the first time in 1774. In 1787 he was taxed with 200 acres and personal property. In 1790, his family consisted of one male over and one under 16 years, and three females. He died in Penn Township and his will was probated at Sunbury, Pa., on December 21, 1791. The will mentions the following children: Michael (oldest son); Weygant (usually spelled Wiant); Gertrude, Eva, Ann, Susanna (Mrs. Jacob Thomas); and John, (the youngest). It is believed that he had a son or nephew of the name of Jacob. Jacob Newman, and Jacob Newman, Jr., served as privates in Capt. John Snyder's Company of the Northumberland County Militia on May 13, 1780.

JACOB NEWMAN (also Neuman, Neumann, Newmann, Neiman, Neyman, etc.) JUNIOR, was either a son or other relative of Jacob Newman, Senior. He lived in Penn Township during part of the Revolutionary period, and seems to have been assessed for the first time about the year 1788. In 1790, his family consisted of two males over 16 years, and one under that age, and three females. Jacob, Junior, served in the companies of Captain John Snyder and Captain Michael Weaver of the Northumberland County Militia. The pension records states that Jacob Newman, who served in the Pennsylvania Militia, in 1833, lived in Jackson County, Tennessee, and that at the time he was 72 years old. At another place it states that Jacob Newman; who served as a private and a sergeant in the Pennsylvania Militia, in 1833, lived in Knox County, Tennessee, and that his age at the time was 85 years. One of these men seems to have been the Jacob, who lived in what is now Snyder County of Pennsylvania.

JOHN NEWMAN was the youngest son of Jacob Newman, Senior. He lived in Mahantango Township and died there in 1812. He was probably to o young to serve in the Revolution.

MICHAEL NEWMAN was the oldest son of Jacob Newman, Senior. He came to what is now Snyder County with his parents before the Revolution, and was probably assessed in Penn Township for the first time in 1783. On January 30, 1777, he was a private in Captain Benjamin Weiser's Company, German Regiment, Continental Line, stationed at Philadelphia, Pa. He was mentioned in his father's will in 1791.

RICHARD NEWMAN may have been a relative of Jacob Newman, Senior. He served as a private in Captain Casper Weitzel's Company from Northumberland County. This Company was organized at Sunbury, Penna.

WIANT .also spelled Waygant, Weygand, Weiant, Wyant, etc.,) NEWMAN was probably the second son of Jacob Newman, Senior. It is supposed that he was born about the year 1766. He was assessed in Penn Township for the first time in 1788, and in 1796, when Mahantango Township was formed he was assessed there as the owner of a sawmill, land and personal property. No military record was found for him.

DAVID NIHART (also Nyhart, Neihart, Neihart, etc.,) was assessed in Penn Township for the first time in 1793. He died in Buffalo Township, Union County, Pa., in 1824. No military record was found for him.

JOHN NORTH /as an early resident of Penn Township, and it is believed that he lived in the vicinity of Freeburg. He served in the Northumberland County Militia in the organizations of Captain Michael Motz, Captain Charles Meyer, and Lieutenant Jacob Spees. In 1790, he lived in what was then Cumberland, now Juniata County, Pa.

JOHN NOTESTINE was a native of Northampton County, Pa. He was assessed in Penn Township for the first time in 1788. In 1790, his family consisted of one male over and one under 16 years and three females. In 1792, he was granted a warrant of survey for 50 acres in Northumberland (now Snyder) County. In 1782, he was a private in Captain William Meyer's Company, 6th Battalion of the Northampton County Militia.

NICHOLAS NYER (also Nier, Neyer, etc.,) was assessed in Beaver Township for the first time in 1789. He was the owner of a gristmill. No military record was found for him.

ASA OATLEY (also Otley, Oatley, Oattly, etc.,) may have been a son of Edward Oatly, who was assessed in Penn Township as early as 1778. Asa was assessed in Beaver Township for the first time in 1789, and in the same year he was one of the petitioners for the holding of an election to elect a justice of the peace for Beaver Township. No military record was found for him.

EDWARD OATLY was assessed in Penn Township for the first time in 1778. In 1784, he was taxed with 50 acres and personal property. In 1789, he was a resident of Beaver Township in 1790, his family consisted of one male over 16 years, and two females. It is believed that he was the father of Joshua, George and Asa.

GEORGE OATLEY (Otly in the military records) seems to have been a son of Edward. In May, 1780, he was a private in Lieutenant John Coleman's Party of Northumberland County Rangers.

JOSHUA OATLEY seems to have been a son of Edward. He served as a private in Captain John Black's Company of the Northumberland County Militia.

ANDREW OBERDORF (also Ov-

erdorf, Overdorff, Oberdorff, etc.,) was born in Germany. He sailed for America from Rotterdam, Holland, in the British ship "Hope" Captain George Johnson, master. He arrived at the port of Philadelphia where he took the oath of allegiance on October 1, 1773. He was assessed in Penn Township for the first time in 1791, and lived in Selinsgrove, where he operated a gristmill. In the same year he sold his mill to Major Anthony Selin. The mill later was known as Schnure's mill and was in operation until about 1920. Andrew served as a private in the 6th Pennsylvania Regiment of the Continental Line, but was discharged for physical disability. Henry and Herman may have been sons of Andrew.

HENRY OBERDORF, mason, was assessed in Penn Township for tht first time in 1799. It is believed that he was a son of Andrew, mentioned above. No military data was found for Henry.

HERMAN OBERDORF may have been a son of Andrew Oberdorf. He was assessed in Beaver Township and died there. His will was recorded at Lewisburg, Pa., on November 22, 1823. His wife was named Rosina, and his children were: George, Rebecca, Mathias, Polly (Mrs. George Becker or Baker), Sallie (Mrs. John Treaster), Catherine (Mrs. Christian Knouse), and Lydia (Mrs. Booth).

PATRICK O'BRIEN was born in Ireland in 1730. On May 18, 1758, he enlisted in the service of the Province of Pennsylvana, in Captain Montgomery's Company. Occupation at time of enlistment—laborer. In 1767, i.e seems to have lived in East Wheatfield Township, Chester County, Pa. His name appeared on the Penn Township tax list only in the year of 1776, and he may have been a nonresident landowner.

JOSEPH OGDEN was assessed in Penn Township only in the year 1780, but it is believed that he lived there at an earlier date. He served as a private in Captain William Weirick's Company, 4th Battalon of the Northumberland County Militia.

JOHN OLDT (also Old, Alt, Aldt, Ault, etc.,) was a son of John George Oldt who was born in Germany and embarked for America on the British ship "Chance," Captain Charles Smith, master, at Rotterdam, Holland. He arrived at the port of Philadelphia, where he took the English oath of allegiance on September 23, 1766. John George Oldt was born in 1745 and died in Berks County, Pa., in 1795. John

Oldt was born in Berks County, Pa., on December 15, 1771, and died in what is now Union County, Pa., in 1854. His first wife, Susanna Kren (or Crane), was born on June 10, 1776, and died on February 13, 1815. His second wife, Susan Beaver, born 1792 and died 1852. The three are buried in the old cemetery at New Berlin. John Oldt came to Buffalo Township prior to 1800, and while he may not have lived within the present confines of Snyder County, it seems he was a landowner there. His death occurred in Union Township, Union County, and his will was probated at Lewisburg, Pa., May 2, 1854. His children were: John, Junior; Simon; David; Benjamin; Daniel; Michael; Reuben; Charles; Catherine (Mrs. Joseph Swarm, who died before 1852, and left Daniel, Lucy Ann, Dianna and Sarah Swarm); Elizabeth (Mrs. Samuel Beaver); Susanna (Mrs. Daniel Swartzlander); Rebecca (Mrs. Charles Benfer); Sarah (Mrs. Joseph Lepley); Lydia (Mrs. Elias Hoy); Rachael J. (Mrs. Fred Steese), and Barbara Ann. John was the great-great-grandfather of the compiler's wife.

JOHN OSWALD, tailor, was a single freeman in Lynn Township, Northampton County, Pa., in 1788. He was assessed in Penn Township for the first time in 1799. A John Oswald from Lancaster County served in the Revoluton, but he must have been a different man.

JOHN GEORGE OTT was born on June 24, 1745, probably in Northampton County, Pa., and died near Selinsgrove, Snyder County, Pa., February 13, 1814. His wife, M. Catherine —— was born on July 13, 1745, and died on February 27, 1827. Both are buried in the old Lutheran Cemetery in Selinsgrove. George was listed as a farmer in Salisbury Township, Northampton County, Pa., in 1772. In 1788, he was taxed with 200 acres of land and personal property in that township. He was assessed in Penn Township for the first time in 1794. In 1801 he contributed to the fund for the erection of the First Lutheran Church in Selinsgrove. In 1803, he was one of the road supervisors of the township, and in 1810, he was an overseer of the poor. The children of George Ott and his wife were: Daniel; Frederick; Barbara (Mrs. Joseph Feehrer); Susanna. 1770-1845. (Mrs. Michael Beaver); Catherine (Mrs. Jacob Jorrett, or Jarrett); Hannah (Mrs. John Leyman. or Lehman); Christina (Mrs. Nicholas Pontius); Elizabeth (Mrs. Jacob Steininger), and Maria (Mrs. Jacob Tries, or Dreese). During the early part of the Revolution he served as a private, 3rd Class, 7th Company 1st Battalion of the Northampton County Militia. This company was commanded by Captain Francis William Rhoads, who became a resident of Penn Township in 1787. A number of the men who served under him, followed him to what is now Snyder County. During the later part of the Revolution he was a private in the 7th Company, 3rd Battalion, same County (Northampton.) He was a great-great-great-grandfather of the compiler's wife. S. William Ott and J. G. Ott, living in Selinsgrove in 1935, are descendants of this pioneer. George was a rich man, each of his children received $2246.44, additional data; Dainel was born in 1784; died 1852; Catherine, 1772-1847; married Jacob Jarrett who served in the War of 1812; Frederick, moved to Lycoming Co., Pa.; Hannah married John Lehman or Lyman and moved to Starke Co., Ohio; Christina (Mrs. Pontius) moved to same county; Maria, 1782-1856, married Peter or Jacob Dreese. and later Michael Schoch. Daniel Ott, famous buffalo hunter, was a grandson of George Ott.

CAPTAIN GEORGE OVERMIRE, SENIOR, was born in Germany, and sailed for America from Rotterdam, Holland, in the British ship "Brothers," Captain William Muir, master. He arrived at Philadelphia, where he took the English oath of allegiance on September 16, 1751. He settled in some part of Buffalo Township in the vicinity of New Berlin before the Revolution, and as part of Buffalo Township later became part of Penn Township, he may have lived within the present confines of the county, or owned land in it. He died in 1805 and his will was probated at Sunbury, Pa., on November 29th of that year. The will mentions his wife, Barbara, and their thirteen children: George, Jr., Peter, Phillip, John, David, Jacob, Catherine, Margaret (who died before 1797), Elizabeth, Eva, Esther, Magdalena, and Barbara. In October 1776, he was Captain of the 6th Company, 4th Battalion of Northumberland County Associators. In February of 1777, he was a member of the Committee on Safety for Buffalo Township. His sons, George and Peter, served under him in 1776. The name may have been given in some records as Obermire or Obermyer.

ABRAHAM PAGE (also Paige), was assessed in Penn Township for the first time in 1794. At that time he was listed as a distiller. No military data was found for him. Several families of the name of Paige lived in Chapman and Perry Townships around the year 1900.

MURDOCK PATTERSON was assessed in Beaver Township for the first time in 1793. In 1780, he was a private in the Colonel's Company, 1st Pennsylvania Regiment, Continental Line.

ROBERT PATTERSON was assessed in Mahantango Township for the first time in 1796. At least three Pennsylvania men of this name served in the Revolution.

JOSEPH PAWLING, JUNIOR, (also Palling, Pauling, etc.,) was assessed in Skippack Township Philadelphia County, Pa., as a single freeman from 1781 to 1783. His father, whose name is also supposed to have been Joseph, came from England prior to the Revolution. The Joseph of this sketch was born on August 28, 1753, and died in what is now Penn Township, Snyder County, Pa., on October 23, 1840. He was twice married, but the name of his first wife is unknown to the compiler. His second wife, Mary Shannon, was born on March 20, 1766, and died in the same township as her husband, on March 8, 1839. Both are buried in the Salem (Rowe's) Lutheran and Reformed Church Cemetery in Penn Township. Joseph was first assessed in Penn township in 1794, when he bought some 300 acres of land about three miles west of Selins grove. He contributed to the fund for the erection of the First Luth eran Church in Selinsgrove in 1801. In 1803, he was one of the viewers for a road between Selinsgrove and Freeburg, and in 1804, for a road between Salem and New Berlin. In 1813, he was one of the auditors for Penn Twp. He had one son with his first wife, his name was John. John went west and his descendants live in Kentucky and elsewhere. With his second wife he had four sons and four daughters. The oldest of these sons was Samuel, who was born on February 9, 1794, and died on November 23, 1874. Samuel married Elizabeth, daughter of John Woodling (also an early settler in Penn Township). Samuel and Elizabeth were the parents of eleven children: Harriet (Mrs. David Schoch), Maria (second wife of David Schoch), Susan (Mrs. Jacob Hilbish), Levi, (who married Margaret Weaver), John (who married Barbara Gemberling), Jane (who married Lewis Gemberling), Samuel B., (who married Leah Huffman, and later Sarah J. Marshall), Rebecca (Mrs. James Biehl), Angeline (Mrs. Benjamin Ulrich), Charles W., (who married Lydia C. Long), and Lewis

E., who married Amanda Schoch) Joseph served as a private in Captain Casper Dull's Company, 1st Battalion, Philadelphia County Militia, in 1778.

NICHOLAS PEEP lived in Penn Township for a short time. He was a private in Captain John Black's Company of the Northumberland County Militia.

GEORGE PEIFER (also Pfifer, Pfeifer, etc.) was probably a native of Northampton County Pa. He came to Penn Township before the Revolution. He served as a private in Captain Benjamin Weiser's Company, German Regiment, Continental Line, in service at Philadelphia, Pa., on January 30, 1777.

ANHONY PERKINS lived in Beaver Township in 1790, and his famly consisted of one male under, and one over 16 years and two females. No further data is available.

JACOB PETERS was assessed in Beaver Township for the first time in 1789. It is believed that he was the Jacob Peters who served as a matross in the Pennsylvania Artillery Regiment, Continental Army.

MICHAEL PETERS was assessed in Penn Township only in the year 1780. He may have been a nonresident landowner. A Michael Peters was First Lieutenant of the 7th Company, 3rd Battalion, Lancaster County Militia, in 1777. The same, or another Michael Peters, was a pensioner in York County, Pa., on May 16, 1818, and his age at the time was 83 years.

GEORGE PFILE (also Pfeil, Pfeill, File, etc.) was a son of Jacob Pfile. He had a brother named Henry. George died in Penn Township in 1791. His wife was named Frenie. It is believed that George was a Revolutionary soldier.

HENRY PFILE was a son of Jacob and a brother of George, mentioned above. He had a sister, Betsy. Henry lived on the south side of the Middle Creek and operated a grist mill. He was assessed in Penn Township for the first time in 1793. On May 3, 1792, he was granted a warrant of survey for 10 acres of land in Northumberland (now Snyder) County. In 1796, when Mahantango Township was formed, he was assessed there.

JACOB PFILE seems to have become a resident of Penn Township about 1788. His will was probated at Sunbury, Pa., on September 5, 1795, and it mentions the following children: Betsy, George and Henry.

BENJAMIN PHILLIPS, Senior, was assessed in Penn Township for the first time in 1778. In 1786, he was taxed with 50 acres and personal property. In 1789, he lived in Beaver Township. In 1790, his family consisted of two males over and one under 16 years and one female. In 1789, he was one of the petitioners praying for the election of a justice of the peace for Beaver Township. He served as a private in Captain William Weirick's Company of the Northumberland County Militia.

BENJAMIN PHILLIPS, Junior, was a son of the above. He was assessed in Beaver Township for the first time in 1789, and was designated as a single freeman.

JACOB POE was assessed in Beaver Township for the first time in 1789. In 1790, his family consisted of one male over and three under 16 years, and one female.

JOHN PONTIUS was assessed in Buffalo Township in 1778, but he lived there before. He was assessed in Penn Township for the first time in 1785, and in 1787, was taxed with 100 acres and personal property. He was a descendant of the well known French Huguenot family of that name. He served as a private in Captain Peter Grubb's Company, Colonel Miles' Pennsylvania Rifle Regiment, Continental Line, on April 28, 1776. In October of the same year he was in a military hospital.

PETER PONTIUS lived in Penn Township in 1785, and is believed to have been a native of Berks County, Pa. In 1787, he was assessed with 100 acres and personal property. In 1779, a Peter Pontius, single freeman, lived in Bethel Township, Berks County, and in the same year, a Peter Pontius, tailor, was assessed in Robeson Township, same county. One of these men served in Captain John Lesher's Company, Colonel Patton's Battalion of the Berks County Militia. The Peter of this sketch died in what was then Center Township of Union (now Snyder) County, Pa., on March 17, 1835.

FRANCIS PORTZLINE (also Portsline) was born in France in 1762, and died in what is now Perry Township, Snyder County, Pa., in 1858, aged 96 years. He is buried in the Portzline Cemetery in that township in an unmarked grave. His father was the principal of a select school in France, and gave his son a good education, particularly in the languages, and the son was able to speak well, French, German, and English. In 1777, at the age of fifteen, he came to America landing at Baltimore. Later he came north to York, Pa., where he married a German girl of the name

of ————— Heiges, and soon thereafter, he came to what is now Perry Township, Snyder county. Francis taught one of the first schools in Perry township (about 1800), and continued for many years. It was a subscription school. Francis was an artist with brush, pen, and quill, and the compiler has seen at least a dozen of baptismal and marriage certificates designed, drawn, and painted by hand. Each one bears the signature of "Francis Portsline" somewhere upon it. All of these certificates were highly colored in red, yellow, green, brown, black, and blue, and all of them were of exceptional workmanship. All of them bore dates prior to 1800 which indicates that he came to what is now Snyder County before that time. These certificates have numerous bits of scripture and poetry entwined among the birds, flowers, leaves and branches, which adorned them. Two known sons of this pioneer were George and Frank. George was living in 1885, aged about 85 years at the time. Eli Portzline, a grandson of Francis, taught school all his life in Snyder County, and was still living when the writer began his teaching career in the Snyder County rural schools. A. Bahner Portzline, of Selinsgrove, is a descandant of this pioneer. It is believed that Francis served in the American Army during the Revolution, but the compiler was unable to locate his record.

MAJOR-GENERAL JAMES POTTER was born in Tyrone, Ireland, in 1729, and died in Franklin County, Pennsylvania, in 1789. He is buried at Brown's Mills in Franklin County. His father, John Potter, was the first sheriff of Cumberland County, Pa. In 1758, he and William Blythe (one of the earliest settlers of Penn Township) were lieutenants in Colonel John Armstrong's Battalion of Pennsylvania Foot in the service of the Province during the French and Indian War. He married Elizabeth Cathcart, a sister of Mrs. George Latimer of Philadelphia. His first wife died, leaving him a son and a daughter. Later he married a widow, Mary Chambers, a sister of Captain William Patterson. At the beginning of the Revolution he resided in White Deer Township, just north of the village of New Columbia, on what was later known as the Ard farm. It is supposed that because of the Indian uprisings he moved south into the Middle Creek Valley, and in 1781 and 1782, he was assessed with 200 acres of land, 2 slaves, and personal property in Penn Town-

ship. Tradition states that his oldest son, John, died in Penn Township. In 1786, General Potter was again living in White Deer Township. His oldest daughter married Captain James Poe. His daughter, Mary, married George Riddle, who died March 14, 1796, and is buried in the Presbyterian cemetery at Northumberland. Their daughter, Mary Riddle, married W. H. Patterson, and her sister, Eliza Riddle, married Dr. Joseph B. Ard, late owner of the General Potter farm in White Deer Township. Martha married ————— Gregg. James, one of the younger children of the General, married Mary, daughter of Judge Brown of Mifflin County. (The children of James Potter and Mary Brown were; General James Potter, III, Attorney William Potter of Bellefonte; Mary, wife of Dr. W. I. Wilson of Potter's Mills, John Potter, Martha, wife of Abraham Valentine, Peggy, wife of Dr. Charles Coburn of Aaronsburg, and Attorney George L. Potter of Danville). Governor Andrew Gregg Curtin was a great- grandson of the first General James Potter. At the outbreak of the Revolution, General Potter was respectively Major and Lieutenant-Colonel of the 2nd Battalion of the Northumberland County Association.

On April 5, 1777, he was commissioned a Brigadier-General in the Pennsylvania Militia. In 1781, he was a Member of the Pennsylvania Supreme Executive Council, and later Vice President of the State of Pennsylvania. In 1782, he was commissioned a Major-General in the Pennsylvania Militia, Potter Township, and Potter's Mills, in Center County, were named for him. The Rev. Wilson Potter Ard, noted Lutheran pastor, Denver, Colorado, is a descendant of this pioneer.

JOSEPH PRICE may have been a brother of Lieutenant-Colonel Thomas Price. He lived in Penn Township before 1730. He served as a private in the companies of Captain Michael Weaver and Captain John Black of the Northumberland County Militia.

LIEUTENANT- COLONEL THOMAS PRICE lived in what is now Snyder County before the Revolution. He was a Sergeant in Captain Casper Weitzel's Company in federal service at King's Bridge, N. Y., on September 1, 1776. At another time he and Joseph Price served in the 2nd Company (Captain Michael Weaver's), 4th Battalion of the Northumberland County Militia. On June 1, 1792, he lived in Selinsgrove and was Major of the 2nd Battalion of the Northumberland County Militia. In November, 1798, he was Lieutenant-Colonel of the 2nd Regiment of the Northumberland County Militia. On November 4, 1798, he wrote a letter to the Hon. Samuel Maclay, Member of Congress, protesting against the manner of elections in the militia. His friends knew him as "Sergeant Tommy," and in his later life he lived on Water Street, in Selinsgrove, Pa.

DEWALL PUFF may have been a son of Valentine Puff, immigrant, aged 30, who came to America on the British ship "Lydia" and took the oath of allegiance at Philadelphia on September 29, 1749. Dewall was assessed in Penn Township for the first time in 1776. He may have been a non resident landowner. Philip Puff, probably a son of Dewall, died in what is now Snyder County in 1817. No military record was located for Dewall.

PHILIP PUFF is believed to have been a son of Dewall Puff. Philip seems to have come to Mahantango Township, prior to 1800, and died there. His will was probated at Lewisburg, Pa., on July 5, 1817. It mentions his wife, Mary, and their children; John, Catherine, Susanna, Mary, Elizabeth, and Anna. John Puff was a well known school teacher in what is now Perry Township about 1830. In 1790, Philip lived in Montgomery County, Pa., and his family consisted of one male over and three under 16 years, and four females. It is believed that he served in the Revolution. Mary was born on August 8, 1788, and died on February 26, 1861. She was the wife of Casper Arnold, Jr. (1787-1859). Both are buried in the Grubbs Church Cemetery.

GEORGE PYLE may have been a son of Peter Pyle, mentioned below. It is believed that the Pyles came from Berks County, Pa. George was assessed in Penn Township for the first time, but it is believed that he did not live in the township until 1784. In this year he was assessed with 300 acres of land and personal property. He received depreciation pay for services in the Berks County Militia.

PETER PYLE was assessed in Penn Township only in the year of 1776 and it is supposed that he was a non resident landowner at the time. Twenty years later, in 1796, the same or another Peter Pyle was assessed in Mahantango township. Peter may have been the father of George, mentioned above. No military record was found for Peter.

JOHN RAFTER lived in Beaver Township in 1790, and his family consisted of one male over and two under 16 years, and two females.

NICHOLAS RAM (also Rem, etc.) was a native of Lancaster County, Pa. He was assessed in Penn Township for the first time in 1793. His name was also written as Rahm and Rehm. In 1801, he contributed to the fund for the erection of the First Lutheran Church of Selinsgrove. He once lived in Buffalo Township. His death occurred in 1828. He was a private in the 3rd Pennsylvania Regiment of the Continental Line, having been transferred from the 12th Pennsylvania. He was wounded in the service and honorably discharged in 1781.

JOHN REAM seems to have been a non resident landowner in Penn Township. He was assessed in the township for the first time in 1776. In 1771, he was a resident, but not a landowner in Donegal Township, Lancaster County. On August 26, 1772, he was granted a warrant of survey for 100 acres in Northumberland (now Snyder) County, and on August 17, 1774, he was granted Lot No. 264 in the town of Sunbury. In 1773, and again in 1779, he was assessed with 300 acres and a mill in Cocalico Township of Lancaster County. On September 6, 1777, a John Ream was a Lieutenant in the 3rd Company, 10th Battalion of the Lancaster County Militia. In 1790, a John Ream lived somewhere in Northumberland County, and one somewhere in Lancaster County, and the above data may in part belong to each of the two men.

JOHN REBER was first assessed in Penn Township in 1772, continuing until 1778. It seems that in 1779, he returned to Windsor Township, Berks County, where he was assessed as single, and followed the occupation of weaver. In 1796, a John Reber was again assessed in what is now Snyder County, this time in Mahantango Township. Two men of this name, one from Berks County, and one from Northampton County, served in the Revolution.

CAPTAIN CASPER REED (also Ried, Rieth, Riet, etc.) was assessed as a' resident, but not a landowner in Heidelberg Township, Berks County, Pa., in 1767. The following year he was assessed as a resident of what is now Snyder County, and he lived along the Susquehanna River on the present site of the village of Port Trevorton, where he had a frontier inn. It is

supposed that he was a son, or grandson, of John Casper Ried who came down the Susquehanna River from New York State with the Palatines in 1723, and settled in Tulpehocken Township, Berks County. Rev. Frederick A. C. Muhlenberg, the noted Lutheran missionary of that period, states in his diary that he stopped at his inn. Captain Reed did not leave his property during the Indian uprisings, as many of his neighbors did, but his home seems to have been the embarking place for those who desired to go further down the river. In 1772, Casper Reed, Peter Hosterman, and George Wolf were granted tavern licenses in Penn Township. Reed was located at Port Trevorton, Hosterman at Selinsgrove, and Wolf near Hummel's Wharf. On November 23, 1772, Casper Reed was sworn in as one of the commissioners of Northumberland County. This and his large land holdings would seem to indicate that he was a man of considerable wealth and standing in the frontier community. In 1781 he was assessed with 200 acres of land, a sawmill, and considerable personal property. On April 10, 1794, he was granted a warrant of survey for 400 acres in Bedford County, and on June 20th of the same year 94 additional acres in Northumberland (now Snyder) County. Captain Reed died in Mahantango Township, now Union Township, Snyder County, in the summer of 1802. His wife's name was Anna, the will mentions her and their children: Frederick, Hannah (Mrs. Christopher Witmer), Mary (Mrs. Jacob Witmer), and Eva (Mrs. Simon Rohrabach). Eva died before 1798, and left the following children: Hannah, Catherine, Elizabeth, John, and David Rohrabach. The compiler believed that Captain Reed is buried in the old pioneer cemetery, opposite the Lower Herrold's School House, south of Port Trevorton. On May 1, 1778, he was Captain of the 1st Company 3rd Battalion of the Northumberland County Militia. In 1790, his family consisted of two males over 16 years, and two females.

FREDERICK REED (or Ried) was the only son of Captain Casper Reed. He was born in Tulpehocken Township, Berks County, Pa. About 1768, his father located at Port Trevorton and soon thereafter started a tavern there. It is supposed that Frederick came with his parents. He had three sisters (see father's sketch). On May 17, 1772, Frederick married Barbara, daughte of John Wurtz (Wertz) of Tulpehocken Township. No military record was found for Frederick, but it is believed that he served in the Revolution. About the year 1785, Frederick moved to the state of Virginia, where he died. His will was probated on October 1827. It is supposed that he was born about the year 1748, and his wife about the same time. One of their daughters was Catherine Barbara, who married John Peter Anspach in Virginia. John Peter came to America in 1788, lived in Pennsylvania until 1791 or 1792, when he moved to Virginia. There are many of the descendants of this couple living in the south.

JOHN REED was probably a brother or nephew of Captain Casper Reed. He was assessed in Penn Township for the first time in 1776. In 1782, he was assessed with 100 acres and personal property, then for some years he was assessed as a non resident landowner. Tradition has it that he lived in Upper Bald Eagle Township during this time. In 1796, when Mahantango Township was formed, he was a resident there. One record states that he died in 1827. Two John Reeds lived in Northumberland County during the Revolution, one of them was granted a warrant of survey for 920 acres in 1774. The John Reed of this sketch was a private in Captain John Moll's Company and in Lieutenant John Coleman's Party of Rangers and Militia from Northumberland County. In May, 1778, a John Reed was an ensign in the Northumberland Militia.

ADAM REGER (also Regar, Reaber, Regor, etc.,) was born in Germany on October 11, 1749, and died on March 17, 1826 near what is now Beaver Springs, Snyder County, Pa. He is buried by the side of his wife in the cemetery there. He was assessed in Penn Township for the first time in 1776, and in 1786, was assessed with 200 acres of land and personalty. In 1789, he was taxed as a resident in Beaver Township. In 1806, he laid out the village of Beaver Springs, which at first was known as "Adamsburg," from the first name of the founder. In 1790, his family consisted of one male over and one under 16 years, and seven females. His will was probated at Lewisburg, Pa., on April 15, 1826, and mentions his wife, Charlotte, and their children: Catherine, Margaret (whose first husband was Peter Wagner, with whom she had one son—Absalom P. Wagner. Her second husband was John Lechner), John, Mary, Rachael, Susanna,

Barbara, Eve, Adam, Jr., Elizabeth and Magdalene. The last two preceded their father in death. One of his daughters was married to Thomas Youngman of Mifflinburg. It is believed that Adam was a son of Michael Reger, and a brother of Elias and John, who lived in the same section. Adam served as a private in the companies of Captain Michael Weaver and Captain John County Militia.

ELIAS REGER is supposed to have been a son of Michael Reger. His name appeared on the Penn Township tax list for the first time in 1780, and the next year he was taxed with 50 acres and personal property. In 1789, he lived in Beaver Township, and the next year his family consisted of one male over and two under 16 years, and two females. On June 21, 1793, he was granted a warrant of survey for 400 acres in Northumberland (now Snyder) County. He was a cooper, and in 1820 was living in what is now Snyder County. He was 77 years old at that time, which would indicate that he was born in 1743. In May, 1775, he enlisted in Captain George Nagle's Company, Colonel Thompson's First Rifle Regiment. He participated in the siege of Boston on Long Island in June, 1776.

JOHN REGER is supposed to have been a son of Michael Reger, and a brotehr of Adam and Elias, metnioned above. He was assessed in Penn Township for the first time in 1778, and in 1786, he was taxed with 150 acres and personal property. In 1793, he was granted a warrant of survey for 25 additional acres. He served as a private in the companies of Captain John Black, Captain John Moll, Captain John Snyder of the Northumberland County Militia, and in the party of Lieutenant Jacob Spees of the Northumberland County Rangers. This last service was in May, 1780.

MICHAEL REGER (or Regar) was assessed in Penn Township for the first time in 1768, and his name remained on the list until 1780 or 1781. In 1788, he was assessed in Dublin Township, Huntington County, Pa. It is believed that he was the father of Adam, John, and Elias, mentioned above. A Michael Reger was a private, 6th Class, Captain Daniel Clapsaddle's Company, 1st Battalion, Cumberland County Militia.

GEORGE REICHENBACH is believed to have been a son of John Reichenbach, Sr. He seems to have been assessed in Penn Township for

the first time about the year 1781. He served as a private in Captain Michael Weaver's Company, 4th Battalion of the Northumberland County Militia.

JACOB REICHENBACH (also Reichenbaugh, Rigabach, Richenbach, Rikenbach, etc.) was a son of John Reichenbach, Senior, and a brother of George and John, Junior. He was assessed in Penn Township for the first time in 1783, and in 1785, was designated as a single freeman. In 1787, he was taxed with 100 acres and personal property, and in 1796, when Mahantango Township was formed, he was assessed there. In 1790, his family consisted of one male over and one under 16 years, and two females. His wife was named Elizabeth Steffen and she was a daughter of John Adam Steffen, an early resident of the Grubb's Church section. Their son, Jacob, was born on January 19, 1792, and baptized soon thereafter at Grubb's Church. In 1801, he contributed to the fund for the erection of the First Lutheran Church of Selinsgrove, Pa. In May, 1780, Jacob served as a private in Captain John Snyder's Company of the Northumberland County Militia.

JOHN REICHENBACH, SENIOR, was one of the earliest settlers in what is now Snyder County. When the first tax list of that section was prepared in 1768, John, Junior, already lived in what is now Chapman Township. John Reichenbach came from Germany and took the oath of allegiance at Philadelphia on September 29, 1733. His wife was named Catherine, and they brought three daughters with them: (Catherine, aged 8½ years, Maria Barbara, 5 years, and Anna Maria, 2 years). The John of this sketch was granted a warrant of survey for 100 acres in Lancaster County, Pa., on August 29, 1754. In 1778(John, Senior, was assessed with 100 acres and personal property. He and his three sons served in the Northumberland County Militia during the Revolutionary period.

LIEUTENANT JOHN REICHENBACH, JUNIOR, was the son of John, Senior. The younger man is supposed to have been born in Lancaster County, Pa., about 1745. He and his father were assessed in what is now Snyder County in 1768. In 1778, he was assessed with 100 acres and personalty, and in 1787, with 200 acres and personal property. In 1790, his family consisted of one male over and two under 16 years, and two females. In 1796, when Mahantango Township was formed, he was taxed there. He died in that township and his will was probated at Sunbury, Pa., on September 24, 1810. The will mentions his wife, Mary, and two children; John, and Mary, who married a Boyer (probably Jacob). The Reichenbachs are buried in the Grubbs Church Cemetery. John, Junior, served as a Lieutenant in the companies of Captain John Black and Captain Michael Motz of the Northumberland County Militia.

ADAM REIGSLDERFER, was assessed in Beaver Township for the first time in 1789. The next year his family consisted of one male over and one under 16 years, and three females.

GEORGE REINARD (also Reinerd, Rinard, etc.) was assessed in Mahantango Township for the first time in 1796. He may have been the same man who lived in Chestnut Hill Township, Northampton County, Pa., from 1772 to 1778, or the one who lived in Upper Milford Township, same county, in 1785, and for a few years more in Salisbury Township, said county. A George Reinerd received depreciation pay for service in the Northampton County Militia during the Revolution.

DANIEL REISCH (also Reish, Risch, etc.) was a resident, but not a landowner in Macungie Township, Northampton County, in 1785 and 1786. In 1788, he was taxed with ½ acre and personal property. His name appeared on the Penn Township tax list for the first time in 1794, and he was assessed as a sawmill owner and operator. He seems to have been the first of his name to settle in the county. From September 22 to November 22, 1781, he served in Capt. Adam Serfass' Company of the Northampton County Militia.

JOSEPH REYNOLDS was listed as a freeman in what is now Snyder County in 1768. Some years later he lived in Washington Township of Northumberland County. He served in the Northumberland County Militia at some period during the Revolution.

HENRY RICHART (Richard) was assessed in Penn Township only in the year of 1776. It is evident that he was the "Hendry Richarts" who was a private, 1st Class, in Captain Alex Peebles' Company, 1st Battalion of the Cumberland County Militia, in 1782.

LIEUTENANT CHRISTIAN RICHTER (also Rigter, Righter, Reichter, Ricter, Rictor, (etc.) seems to have been a son of Christian Richter of Northampton County. Pa. The Christian of this sketch, was as-

sessed in what is now Snyder County for the first time in 1776. In 1786, he was assessed with 100 acres of land and personal property. In 1792 he was granted a warrant of survey for an additional 100 acres. In 1790, his family consisted of one male over and five under 16 years, and four females. Christian and his son, John, were assessed in Mahantango Township in 1796. He died in the year of 1827 and is buried in an unmarked grave in the | Grubb's Church Cemetery. He served in Captain John Snyder's Company and was a Lieutenant in Captain Michael Weaver's Company of the Northumberland County Militia. His children were: John, Peter, Godfrey, George, Frederick, Catherine (Mrs. Leonard Kerstetter), and Mary (Mrs. John Milchard).

CHRISTIAN RICHTER, SENIOR, lived in Northampton County, Pa., and the evidence seems to indicate that some time after the Revolution, he came to what is now Snyder County, to live with his son. He died in Mahantango Township in 1797. In 1780, he was a private. 8th Class, in Captain Jacob Balliett's Compan. 2nd Battalion of Northampton County Militia. The evidence indicates that he was the father of Lieutenant Christian Richter.

JOHN RICHTER was assessed in was a private in Captain Adam Serfass Company of the Northampton County Militia.

JACOB REPASS (also Repasz, Rebass, etc.) was assessed with 100 acres of land in Penn Township in 1781 and 1782. He was born in Germany and sailed for America from Rotterdam. Germany, in the British ship "Minerva," Captain Thomas Arnot, master. He arrived at the port of Philadelphia where he took the English oath of allegiance on December 12, 1768. No military data was located for this man. He was a Reformed minister and was one of the first pastors of the Reformed congregation at Grubb's Church.

SOLOMON REPASS seems to have been a son of Jacob. He was assessed in Mahantango Township before 1800. He married Anna Riblett. Three of their children were baptized at Grubb's Church early in the nineteenth century. They were born as follows: William, March 16, 1811; Daniel, April 13, 1819; David, August 8, 1815.

PETER RICHER was probably a son of Christian Richter, Senior, and a brother of Lieutenant Christian Richter. His wife, Anna Maria Meyer, was born on July 11, 1773,

and died on August 26, 1825. She is buried in the cemetery of the First Lutheran Church of Selinsgrove. She seems to have been his first wife. Peter was born on February 21, 1778, and died May 25, 1846, and is buried in the cemetery of Trinity Lutheran Church, which he helped to found, a short time before his death. Elizabeth, wife of a Peter Richter, who died n 1896, aged 67 years, was either his second wife, or a daughter-in-law, Peter was one of the auditors of Penn Township in 1814. In 1821, he was appointed as one of the commissioners to improve the navigation of Penns Creek. In December of the next year, he asked for a board of viewers to report on the commission's work. On April 2, 1832, the Pennsylvania State Legislature passed an act granting him the right to use the towing path of the Pennsylvania Canal on the Isle of Que, at Selinsgrove along his store, under certain restrictions from the Canal Commissioners. In 1843, he was again an auditor of Penn Township. His wife was a daughter of Charles Meyer (or Moyer) who died in Penn Township in 1800, and his wife Christiana, who died in the same township in 1805. Peter's second wife was Elizabeth Holstein, and one of their children was Mrs. Calvin B. North, of Selinsgrove, Pa.

JOHN RICKERT seems to have been a native of Northampton County. His name appeared on the Penn Township tax list for the first time in 1776 when he was lister as a single freeman. A John Rickert, maybe his father, was a private, 8th Class, Captain George Nolff's Company, 7th Battalion of the Northampton County Militia in May, 1782.

JOHN YOST, (or Jost) RIDDLE (also Riddell, Ridel, Ridle, Rith, etc.) was born in the year 1735, and on April 3, 1756, was a private in Captain Joseph Shippen's Company in the Pennsylvania Regiment of Foot, in service of the Province of Pennsylvania, on that date stationed at Fort Augusta (now Sunbury, Pa.) It is believed that after his discharge he settled somewhere in the vicinity of Sunbury. His name appeared on the Penn Township tax list for the first time in 1776. In the same year he was a private in Captain John Clark's Company of the Northumberland County Associators. John Riddle was a non resident landowner in Penn Township in 1787. A Yost Riddle took the otah of allegiance at Philadelphia, Pa., on September 26, 1749, but if the date of his birth, as given above, is correct, he would not have been old enough to be required to take the oath. The Yost who took the oath came from Rotterdam, Holland, on the British ship "Ranier," Captain Henry Browning, master.

HENRY RINE was a son of George Rine. He was born in 1747, and died in Mahantango Township, Union (now Snyder) County, Pa., in 1814. He became a tenant on his father's land in what is now Chapman Township, Snyder County, in 1768. In 1781, he was taxed with 100 acres and personal property. In 1790, his family consisted of one male over and one under 16 years, and seven females. In 1796, when Mahantango Township was formed, he was assessed there with realty, personalty, and two stills. Henry's will was probated at Lewisburg, Pa., on June 3, 1814, and mentions his wife, Christina, and the following children: John, Margaret Neyman (Newman), Ann Elizabeth Shetterly, Christina Coleman (believed to have been the wife of Lieutenant John Coleman), Barbara Coleman (who died before her father, and left a son, Henry Coleman), and Magdalena (Mrs. Frederick Meiser). Mrs. Meiser wa the mother of Maria, born in 1816, and Frederick, Junior, born in 1829. Henry had several wives. Henry and his wives and John and some of his descendants are buried in the Rine and Sechrist Private cemetery in Chapman Township. In 1883, John M. Rine, a descendant, placed a fine monument over their graves. It is believed that Henry Rine served in the military forces during the Revolution.

ROBERT RITCHIE (also Ritchy, Ritchey, etc.) was assessed in Penn Township for the first time in 1780, and in the following year he was taxed with 100 acres and personal property. His name does not appear on the Penn Township tax list after 1781, but in 1794, he was granted a warrant of survey for 300 acres of land elsewhere in Northumbreland County. Several men of his name lived in Pennsylvania during the Revolution, but it is believed that he was the Robert Ritchie who served in Captain John Lowden's Company on Long Island in 1776. This company was recruited at Sunbury, Pa., On September 29, 1818, a Robert Ritchie was a pensioner, aged 75 years. This man died on August 17, 1825.

JOHN RITTER may have been a brother of Simon Ritter, who came to Penn Township from Maytown, Lancaster County, in 1794, or he may have come from the Ritter families living in either Berks or Lancaster County. John was born on March 15, 1743, and died in Beaver Township, now Snyder County, Pa., on April 18, 1816. He is buried in the St. John Church Cemetery, in Black Oak Ridge, West Beaver Township. It is believed that he came to what is now Snyder County prior to 1800. He served in Captain John Rutherford's Company of the Lancaster County Militia in 1779, in the expedition which marched to Fort Bedford.

SIMON RITTER was a son of the Widow Ritter, who lived in Maytown, Lancaster County, Pa., in 1790. It is believed that his father was also named Simon. The older Simon was assessed in Donegal Township, Lancaster County, in 1773. The Simon of this sketch was born on February 15, 1763, probably in Lancaster County, and died in what is now Penn Township, Snyder County, on March 8, 1848. His wife was Anna Elizabeth, daughter of Michael Albright. She was born on February 23, 1760, and died in Penn Township on January 20, 1832. Both are buried in the cemetery of the Salem (Row's) Church in Penn Township. In 1790, Simon lived in Maytown, Lancaster Township, and had one son and one daughter, both under 16 years of age. He was assessed in what is now Penn Township for the first time in 1794. He owned the farm adjoining Joseph Pawling, southwest of the village of Salem. In addition to farming he also operated a still in 1794. In 1811, he was one of the overseers of the poor for Penn Township. His mother, and some younger brothers and sisters seem to have lived in Maytown in 1790. The children of Simon and his wife were; Michael, 1789-1860, (married Catherine Sechrist), Frances, 1791-1869, (never married), Henry K., 1792-1875, (1st wife, Elizabeth Kessler, 2nd wife, Anna Webb), Elizabeth, 1794-1872, (Mrs. Israel Luck), Nancy Ritter, 1796-1873, (Mrs. George Gemberling), Samuel, 1798-1885, (married ——— Kuster), Susan, 1799——— (Mrs. Isaac Luck), Peter, (1803-1872) and John, 1806-1872). It is believed that Simon served in the Lancatser County Militia during the Revolution.

JOHN ROBERTS (maybe Rodgers) was assessed in Penn Township from 1776 to 1778. He may have been a nonresident landowner. A John Roberts served in the New Levies.

JOHN RODGERS (or Rogers) may have been a native of Lancas-

ter County. He was assessed in Penn Township for the first time in 1780. It is believed that he was a brother of Michael. He served in Captain Michael Motz's Company of the Northumberland County Militia.

MICHAEL RODGERS (or Rogers) seems to have been a brother of John, mentioned above. They lived in Penn Township for a short time. Michael also served in Captain Michael Motz's Company of the Northumberland County Militia.

JOSEPH ROMICH (now Romig) was assessed in Beaver Township for the first time in 1794. He may have served in the Revolution. In 1790, he lived in Macungie Township, Northampton County, and his family consisted of three males over and three under 16 years, and three females. Jacob Romich who lived there at the same time may have been a brother.

JOHN RONE (or Rhone) is supposed to have come from Northampton County. In 1790, he lived in Bedford County and his family consisted of one male over and one under 16 years, and four females. His stay in what is now Snyder County is supposed to have been only for a year or two. He served as a private in Captain Michael Motz's Company of the Northumberland County Militia.

GEORGE ROOK (maybe Ruch) lived in Penn or a neighboring township. He served as a private in Captain John Moll's Company of the Northumberland County Militia.

ELLIS RIGHT (also Richt, Recht, Wright, etc.) was assessed in Penn Township for the first time in 1776. He was assessed as a nonresident landowner of 500 acres in 1781. The evidence seems to indicate that he never lived in the township at all.

GEORGE RINE (also Rein, Rhein, Rhine, Rhyne, Rhyn, etc.) was a native of Lancaster County. He was assessed in Penn Township for the first time in 1768, but it is said that his son, Henry lived on his land in what is now Snyder County at that time, and that George did not come to the section until after the Revolution. The Rines settled around the village of McKees Half Falls in what is now Chapman Township, Snyder County. It is believed that this George Rine is the man who sailed from Rotterdam, Holland in the British ship "Peggy," Captain James Abercombie, master. He arrived at the port of Philadelphia, where he took the English oath of allegiance on October 16, 1754. A George Rine was a private in the 1st Company, 5th Battalion, Lancaster County Militia on June 15, 1780. George B. Rine. of Sunbury, Pa., and Bert Rine of RFD, Port Trevorton, Pa., living in 1935, are descendants of this pioneer.

SIMON RORABAUGH (also Rorabach, Rhorabach, Rohrbaugh, Rohrabaugh, etc.) may have come from Berks County. He was assessed in Penn Township for the first time in 1778. In 1782, and thereafter, he was assessed with personal property only. His wife was Eva, daughter of Captain Casper Reed. She died before 1798 and left the following children who were mentioned in their grandfather's will made in that year (1798); Hannah, Catherine, Elizabeth, John, and David. Simon lived in what is now Union or Chapman Township, his father-in-law, Casper Reed, lived on the present site of Port Trevorton. Philip Rorabaugh who died in the year 1837, aged 86, may have been a brother.

PHILIP RORABAUGH was born in 1751, and died on February 3, 1837. He is buried in the German Cemetery in Lewisburg, Pa. It is supposed that he was a relative, maybe brother of Simon Rorabaugh, who lived in what is now Chapman or Union Township of Snyder County. Philip seemingly lived in the same section at one time. He served in Captain Slaymaker's Company of Colonel Bull's Regiment, during the Revolution. In 1794, he was with the troops which were sent to western Pennsylvania to quell the Whiskey Insurrection, and in 1814, he served for three months in Captain John Bergstresser's Company at Marcus Hook, Pa., in service of the federal government in the War of 1812.

JACOB ROTE was first assessed in Beaver Township in 1799. It is believed that he was a brother of John, mentioned below.

JOHN ROTE was assessed in Beaver Township for the first time in 1799.

CAPTAIN FRANZ WILHEM ROTH (translated Francis William Rhoads was born on February 1, 1746, probably in Salisbury Township, Northampton County, Pa. Little is known of his early life. In 1773, he was a farmer in Salisbury Township, and 1786, he was taxed in the same township with 460 acres of land, and personal property. The same was true the next year. In the fall of 1786, or the spring of 1787, he moved to what is now Selinsgrove, Snyder County, Pa., where in 1787, he was assessed with 200 acres and personal property. He lived in a house on the same site of that of the late Hen-

ry E. Philips on North Market street, in Selinsgrove. He was considered a man of excellent judgment, this is deduced from the number of times he was appointed to boards of viewers for roads, bridges, etc. In 1791, he was one of the viewers for extending the "Reading Road" from the western end of John Adam Fisher's ferry on the Isle of Que on up the Penns Valley to what is now Center County. On August 24, 1795, he was one of the viewers for a road from Selinsgrove to Freeburg. The same year he was one of the road supervisors of Penn Township. In 1798, he, or his son of the same name, ran a store and a tavern, and a ferry across the Penns Creek, just north of the town of Selinsgrove. On December 2, 1799, he bought the northeast corner of Market and Pine streets in Selinsgrove from John Kern. The same land in 1935 was owned by the Snyder County Trust Company and John Snyder In 1800, he was one of the viewers appointed to change the present Susquehanna Trail between Selinsgrove and the Middle Creek. In 1801, he contributed to the fund for the erection of the First Lutheran Church of Selinsgrove, and served as a member of the building committee. In April, 1810, he was again one of the road supervisors of Penn Township. His death occurred on March 25, 1811, just five weeks after the death of his oldest son and namesake. Hannah ——, wife of the subject of this sketch, was born on December 1, 1745, and died at Selinsgrove, Pa., on April 17, 1843. Both are buried in the old Lutheran Cemetery in Selinsgrove. Their children were: Francis William, Junior, 1768-1811, Daniel, Peter, Jacob (who married Catherine ——), Henry, died in 1807, Susanna (Mrs. George Roth, or Rhoads) and Mary Magdalene (Mrs. John George Fisher). During the greater part of the Revolution Rhoads served as Captain of the 7th Company, 1st Battalion of the Northampton County Militia. A number of the men who served under him in Northampton County, later followed him to what is now Snyder County, one of these was John George, Ott. Captain Rhoads owned the land in Selinsgrove where the railway station now stands and beyond to Broad Street.

ENSIGN FRANCIS WILLIAM RHOADS (or Roth), JUNIOR, was the oldest son of Captain Rhoads and his wife. He was born in Salisbury Township, Northampton County, Pa., on April 15, 1768, and died

at Selinsgrove, Snyder County, Pa., on February 20, 1811, just five weeks before his father. His wife, Elizabeth ——, was born on June 9, 1770, and died at Selinsgrove, on September 8, 1848. Both are buried in the old Lutheran cemetery in that town. Ensign Rhoads came to what is now Selinsgrove with his parents in 1786 or 1787, and was assessed in Penn Township for the first time in 1793. He was one of the contributors for the erection of the First Lutheran Church in Selinsgrove. He assisted his father in his various enterprises, and like his father, he was interested in things military. On February 28, 1794, he was Ensign of the 7th Company, 3rd Regiment of the Northumberland County Militia. The same was true on May 22, 1798.

JACOB RHOADS seems to have been the father of Captain Francis William Rhoads. He died in Penn Township, and letters of administration were granted to Jacob Gable (possibly a son-in-law) on August -8, 1804.

HENRY RHOADS was a son of Captain Rhoads. He was born in Salisbury Township, Northampton County. He died in Selinsgrove, and letters of administration were granted to his brothers, Francis W., and Jacob, on June 16, 1807.

GEORGE CASPER ROUSH (also Raush, Rausch, Rousch, Rauch, etc.) was born in Germany, in 1721, and died near what is now Freeburg, Snyder County, Pa., in 1815. He is buried in the old Zion Lutheran Cemetery, about a mile north of Freeburg, in an unmarked grave. He helped to found the church to which the cemetery was attached. "Casper," as he was commonly called, sailed for America from Rotterdam. Holland, in the British ship "Robert and Alice," Captain Martley Cusack, master, and arrived at Philadelphia, where he took the English oath of allegiance on September 24, 1742. His wife, Anna Maria ——,) is also buried in the old Zion Cemetery. In 1749, Casper was a landowner in Lancaster (now Lebanon) County, Pa. Some of his older children, including John George, were baptized at the Hill Church (probably Lutheran) in that county. About the year 1770, Casper and other families moved into the section around Freeburg, and in that year, he, Andrew Morr, Sr., and Peter Straub, made application to the proprietors of the state for some land on which to build a church and school. In 1774, 42 acres were granted to them, about a mile north of Freeburg, and about 1780, they began a church and school there. The church was never completely finished, but was used for about 25 years. In 1787, he was assessed with 100 acres of land and personal property. In 1790, his family consisted of one male over and one under 16 years, and two females. The children of Casper and his wife were, John Martin, born 1743; Elizabeth, 1745; Anna Magdalene, 1747; Sophia, 1748; John Jacob, 1751-1819 (he married Barbara ————; John George, 1753-1823, (he married Christine daughter of Andrew Morr, Jr., and later as a second wife, Barbara Potter); John, 1757, and Barbara, 1759-1842 (who married Andrew Dillman on August 1, 1777). Casper and his sons John George, John Jacob, and John, and his son-in-law, Andrew Dillman were Revolutionary soldiers. Probably some of his other sons-in-law served. Casper received depreciation pay for services in the Northumberland County Militia. His actual service seems to have been in Captain Michael Weaver's Company. This pioneer was the great-great-great-grandfather of the compiler.

JOHN GEORGE ROUSH was the sixth child of George Casper Roush and his wife, Anna Maria. "George" as he was commonly called, was born in what is today Lebanon County, Pa., on August 2, 1753, and died near what is today Freeburg, Pa., in 1822 or 1823, and is buried in an unmarked grave in the old Zion Lutheran Cemetery, about a mile north of Freeburg. His father is buried there, too. His first wife was Christina, the oldest daughter of Andrew Morr, Jr., who came to the Freeburg section about 1770. She was born on August 4, 1757, probably at Schaefferstown, Lebanon County, Pa., and died near Freeburg, on June 7, 1793. She was the first of the Morr family to be buried in the cemetery of the church (Morr's or Zion Lutheran) which her ancestors helped to found. Her grave is unmarked. George came to what is now Washington Township, Snyder County, with his parents in 1770, or before. He was assessed in Penn Township for the first time in 1776, and in 1787, was taxed with 300 acres of land and personalty. In 1790, his family consisted of one male over and six under 16 years, and two females. In 1801, he contributed to the fund for the erection of the First Lutheran Church at Selinsgrove. John Philip, John Martin, and John Michael, sons of George and his first wife, Christina, were baptized at the old Zion Lutheran Church in 1783, 1787, and

1789, respectively. The children of George and his first wife were, Margaret (Mrs. George Shellenberger, or Snellenberger, who moved to Ohio); (Andrew who moved to Lucas County, Ohio); George (moved to Lucas County, Ohio); John (who moved to White House, Lucas County, Ohio, in 1846.) His first wife was Catherine Bickel, and his second, Mrs. Salome Reddick, nee Salome Glass, of Freeburg, Pa. John died in 1867 and is buried at Waterville, Ohio); John Philip (was born in 1783 and died in 1844, his wife Maria Verigant was born in 1782 and died in 1858); Catherine was born Sept. 29, 1791, and died on January 15, 1869 (she married Jacob Menges, 1775-1847, and both are buried at Freeburg, Pa.) Barbara Potter, the second wife of George Roush, may have been a relative of General James Potter. The children by the second wife were; Jacob, 1796-1880, (married Salome Housworth, 1802-1882); David, 1799-1877, (married Sarah Zellers, 1806-1876); Simon, 1801-1884, (married Yydia————, 1805-1887); Julia Ann, 1805-1887, (married Jacob Bertch); Elizabeth 1805-1829, (was first wife of Simon Kantz, 1805-1873); Rebecca, 1808-1889, (Mrs. William F. Charles), and Michael, 1812-1864, (married Mary Ann Esterline, 1814-1888, a granddaughter of the pioneer, Jacob Gemberling). George served as a private in the companies of Captain Michael Motz and Captain Michael Weaver of the Northumberland County Militia and in the Party of Rangers commanded by Lieutenant Jacob Speece.

JACOB ROUSH was assessed in Beeaver Township for the first time. The compiler does not know his family connection.

JACOB ROUSH, JUNIOR, was assessed in Mahantango Township for the first time in 1796. Te compiler believes that he was of the Freeburg Roush family, but does not know his connection.

JOHN JACOB ROUSH was the fifth child of George Casper Roush and his wife, Anna Maria. He was born in what is now Lebanon County, Pa., on July 22, 1751, and probably baptized at the Hill Lutheran Church there. He died near what is now Freeburg, Snyder County, Pa., on December 3, 1819. His wife was named Barbara————, and he may have had a second wife named Susan————. He is buried in St. Peter's Cemetery in Freeburg. He was assessed in Penn Township for the first time in 1778, and in 1787 was taxed with 300 acres of land and personal property.

In 1796, he was granted a warrant of survey for an additional 60 acres. In 1801, he contributed to the fund for the erection of the First Lutheran Church of Selinsgrove, Penna. In 1806 he was on e of the road supervisors of Penn Township. The following children of Jacob and Barbara Roush were baptized at the old Zion Lutheran Church, north of Freeburg: Eva Barbara in 1783; Catherine Elizabeth in 1784; Mary Elizabeth 1784; and David J., in 1799 (this David is not to be confused with his cousin David, son of John Geo. Roush, who was born the same year). Mary and Hannah, daughters of Jacob and Susanna Roush were baptized at the same church in 1807 but this may have been another Jacob Roush. Jacob was a member of the building committee of the old Zion Lutheran Church, erected north of Freeburg, in 1780. He served in the companies of Captain Michael Motz and Captain Charles Meyer of the Northumberland County Militia. It is believed that he was the Jacob Roush, who served as a private in the 3rd Pennsylvania Regiment, Continental Line, from January 1, 1777, to 1781. His brother-in-law, Andrew Dillman, servved with the Continentals. His father and brothers John and John George also served. Jacob's son. David was born in 1799. His wife was Anna ————, who was born on April 11, 1802, and died November 1, 1864. Both are buried in the United Brethren Cemetery in Freeburg.

JOHN ROUSH was the seventh child. and youngest son. of George Casper Roush and his wife, Anna Maria. John was born in what is now Lebanon County, Pa., in 1757, and came to what is now Snyder County with his parents about the year 1770. His name appeared on the Penn Township tax list for the first time in 1778. and in 1787 he was taxed with 150 acres of land and personal property. In 1802, he owned a tan yard in Freeburg. A John Roush and his wife. Barbara, had a son, John, baptized at the old Zion Lutheran Church, north of Freeburg in 1804. The same, or and other John Roush and his wife, Catherine, had the following children baptized at the same church; Anna Mary in 1805, and Eva and Catherine in 1808. John received depreciation pay for services in the Nothumberland County Militia. It is believed that he also served in the 3rd Pennsylvania Regiment. Continental Line.

JOHN ROUSH died in Penn Township in 1792. George Casper Roush was the executor of his estate. It is believed that he was a brother of Casper's. However, it might have been his son of that name.

FREDERICK ROW, mason, was assessed in Penn Township for the first time in 1799. He was one of the Rows of the Salem section of Penn Township.

GEORGE ROW, SENIOR, (also Raw, Rau, Rowe, Rhow, etc.) was born in Germany in 1723, and killed in the service of his country in the Buffalo Valley, now Union County, Pa., in 1780. He embarked for America at Rotterdam, Holland, on the British ship "Phoenix," Captain Waire, master, and arrived at Philadelphia, where he took the English oath of allegiance on September 30, 1754. On May 18, 1774, he was granted a warrant of survey for 50 acres of land in Northumberland (now Snyder) County. He was assessed in Penn Township for the first time in 1776. It is believed that he became a resident on his land soon after the granting of the warrant, and lived there until his death. This tract lay back (probably north) of the present Salem Church. His wife was named Mary Magdalene ————. George, Junior, and John, both Revolutionary soldiers, were their sons. George, Sr., served as a private in Captain Michael Weaver's Company of the Northumberland County Militia, and may also have served in Lieut. Jacob Spees' party of Rangers. His widow's application for pension follows: "George Row, Senior, enlisted in a Battalion of the Northumberland County Militia, commanded by Colonel Peter Hosterman. He was stationed at Foutz (Focht's) Mill in the Buffalo Valley in July. 1780, was wounded by the Indians in defence of this place; a musket or rifle ball pierced his breast. and he died within five hours after he was wounded. His widow, Mary Magdalene Row, is much in need of a pension." The pension was granted. The Widow Row, was a member of the Lutheran congregation at Row's (Salem about the year 1790. George Row was one of the first persons buried in the Row's (Salem) Cemetery, and his grave is marked.

GEORGE ROW, JUNIOR, was born about the year 1751. He was a son of George Row, Senior, and his wife, Mary Magdalene. He was assessed in Penn Township for the first time in 1776, and in 1781, was taxed with 200 acres of land and personal property. In 1790, his family consisted of one male over and seven under 16 years, and six fe-

males. The Rows lived, and still live, in the Middle Creek Valley, in the vicinity of the villages of Salem and Kreamer. He served as a private in Captain Michael Motz's Company of the Northumberland County Militia. In May, 1780, he was a private in Lieutenant Jacob Bard's Party of Northumberland County Rangers in service on the Frontier. It is supposed that he is buried in the Salem Cemetery, in an unmarked grave.

ENSIGN JOHN ROW was born about the year 1749, probably in Germany. He was the son of George Row, Senior, and his wife, Mary Magdalene. In 1772, he was a resident, but not a landowner in Stumptown, Lancaster County, Pa. On September 22. 1773, he was granted a warrant of survey for 100 acres of land in Northumberland (now Snyder) County, and soon thereafter, he became a resident of Penn Township. He was assessed in Penn Township for the first time in 1776, and in 1787, he was taxed with 200 acres of land and personal property. In 1790, his family consisted of three males over 16 years and three females. In 1801, he lived in what is now Haines Township, Center County. On August 17, 1833, a John Row, believed to be the same, made application for a pension from Hart County, Kentucky. He stated that he served in the Pennsylvania Militia and that he was 84 years old at the time of the application. The subject of this sketch served as a private in the companies of Lieutenant Jacob Spees and Captain William Weirick of the Northumberland County Militia. He also served as an Ensign in Lieutenant Simon Herrold's party of Northumberland County Rangers.

LUDWIG (Lewis) ROW may also have been a son of George Row, Senior. He was assessed in Penn Township for the first time in 1780. He served in Captain John Clark's Company when it was in the Continntal service in 1776, and later he served as a private in the 2nd Company, 4th Battalion, and 4th Company, 4th Battalion, of the Northumberland County Militia.

MARTIN ROW, SENIOR, was assessed in Penn Township for the first time in 1776. His death was a tragic one. He went to a mill. a short distance from his home, and while his grist was ground he stood in the doorway of the mill. An arrow shot by an ambushed Indian pierced his body and he died soon afterwards. It is said that he is buried in the Salem cemetery.

MARTIN ROW, JUNIOR, evidently was a son of Martin, Senior. The younger man was assessed in Penn Township for the first time in 1780, and in that year was taxed with 80 acres and personal property. In 1790, his family consisted of one male over and three under 16 years, and four females. On February 25, 1793, he was granted a warrant of survey for 400 acres in Northumberland (now Snyder) County. It is believed that he is the "M. Row—1805" who is buried in the Row's (Salem) Cemetery. He served as a private in the 2nd Company, 4th Battalion of the Northumberland County Militia.

CHRISTIAN ROYER was assessed in Beaver Township for the first time in 1789. This family consisted of one male over 16 years, and two females. It is supposed that he was the son of John Michael Royer, who came in the British ship "Patience" in 1749.

SEBASTIAN ROYER was the fourth son of Christian Royer, Senior. Sebastian was born in Berwick Twp., Lancaster Co., Pa., on June 21, 1758, and died in what is now Franklin Township, Snyder County, Pa., in 1828. He married Mary Elziabeth Weber (Weaver) and moved to Rehrersburg, Berks County, Pa., and about 1785, to near Royer's Bridge in what is now Franklin Township, Snyder County. In that year he was assessed with 150 acres and personal property in Penn Township. The actual size of his farm was 170 acres, and was located at what is now known as Royer's Bridge which was named for him. This farm is today owned by Kemer C. Walter. When Beaver Township was formed, he was assessed there. Part of Beaver later became Franklin Township. Sebastian's will was probated at Lewisburg, Pa., on January 28, 1829. It mentions his wife and their children: John, 1796-1837 (he married Elizabeth, daughter of Philip Gemberling of Selinsgrove); Samuel C., 1803-1872, (married Anna Kramer), Catherine E., (1787-1865), (Mrs. John Gramley, Rebersburg, Pa.); Jacob (died before his father); Margaret (Mrs. George Dreese, Sr.), son of John Haines (of Freeburg). After the death of Sebastian, his widow married George Aurand, grandfather of the Rev. Frederick Aurand. Sebastian served in Captain Michael Wolf's Company of the Berks County Militia in 1781.

STEPHEN ROYER was assessed in Beaver Township for the first time in 1789. It is believed that he was a brother of Sebastian.

GEORGE RUPP, carpenter, was probably a native of Northampton County. He was assessed in Penn Township for the first time in 1799. In 1801, he contributed to the fund for the erection of the First Lutheran Church of Selinsgrove, and evidently was one of the men who built it.

DANIEL RUSH was the oldest son of John Rush, a Quaker, who was one of the earliest settlers in the vicinity of Globe Mills. Daniel was assessed in Penn Township for the first time in 1786, and was designated as a single freeman.

JOHN RUSH was a Quaker, and an early settler in what is now Snyder County. At one time he owned about 600 acres, south of the Middle Creek, in the vicinity of Globe Mills. One of the tracts owned by him was known as "Rushfield," and another as "Hickory Bottom." His son Daniel followed him in ownership of the property. Peter Gottshall owned the farm east of the Rush lands, and Melchoir Yoder that to the west. The cemetery at Globe Mills was donated by the Rush family and originally known by their name. John's will was probated at Sunbury, Pa., on February 4, 1796. His wife must have preceded him in death, as she is not mentioned in the will. The children of John were; Daniel, Catherine (Mrs. Samuel Meyer, or Moyer), Peter, Jacob, Elizabeth, and Salome (Mrs. John Shellenberger). Because of their faith, it is supposed that the Rush men did not bear arms in the Revolution.

JOHN RYHART, (or Rihart, Reyhart, etc.) was assessed in Penn Township for the first time in 1780. In 1782, he was taxed with 50 acres of land and personal property. This is the last year in which his name appears on the tax records. No military data was found for him.

STEPHEN SADDLER was assessed in Mahantango Township for the first time in 1796. No additional data was located.

ADAM SANTZINGER (also Zansinger, Zantzinger, Zinsinger, etc.) was granted a warrant of survey for 200 acres in Northumberland (now Snyder) County on Oct. 3, 1774. In 1787, he was assessed as a non resident owner of 300 acres in Penn Township. In 1782, he was a resident of Northern Liberties Township, Philadelphia County. No military record was found for him.

MICHAEL SCHANER, (also Schoener), lived in Penn Township in 1784, and in this year, he and his wife, Christina, had their daughter, Anna Mary, baptized in Old Zion Lutheran Church, north of Freeburg.

JACOB SCHIEB lived in Penn Township in 1782. He and his wife, Mary Elizabeth, had their daughter Mary Christina, baptized at the old Zion Lutheran Church, north of Freeburg, in that year.

JOHN SCHNEE was born on May 15, 1758, probably in Lancaster County, Pa., and died in what is now Perry Township, Snyder County, on November 25, 1826. He owned the land whereon the Fremont Lutheran Church now stands. He also owned the ground now used as the cemetery attached to that Church. He and his four sons were prominent members and heavy donors to the Schnee's or Fremont Lutheran congregation. John is buried in the cemetery which he once owned. His sons were named Henry, Joseph, Phillip, and George. Joseph was a well known surveyor and conveyancer. John served as a private in the 4th Company, 7th Battalion of the Lancaster County Militia. The exact date of his coming to what is now Snyder County is unknown to the compiler, but the indications are that it was before 1800.

JOHN CHRISTIAN SCHNURE was a son of John George Schnure and his wife, Anna Catherine Mennor. John Christian was born in Dudenhopen, Hesse Cassel, Germany, on July 2, 1763. He came to America in 1781 and after working three years in Berks County to pay for his passage, he came to what is now Middle Creek Township, Snyder County, Pa., where he met and married Elizabeth Pontius. She was born on February 19, 1776, and died in Hartley Township, Union County, Pa., on September 17, 1852. Christian died on July 27, 1827. Their children were; Catherine (Mrs. Tobias Miller of Venango County, Pa.); Henry (whose descendants live in Indiana and Michigan; Elizabeth (Mrs. Charles Miller, whose descendants live in Union and Center Counties); Christian, Jr. (whose descendants live in Center and Union Counties); Michael (who lived in Union County); Mary (never married); George (whose descendants lived in Snyder County); Levi (descendants live in Ohio, and Margaret (Mrs. Robert Lucas, who lived in Union County).

GEORGE SCHOCH (also Shoch, Schuck, Schock, Shock, Shuck, etc.) was a brother of Jacob and Mathias Schoch. He was assessed in Penn Township for the first time in 1776. He and his brothers were born in Germany. In 1781, he was taxed with 50 acres of land and personal property. When Beaver Township was formed he was assessed there. In 1790, his family consisted of one male over and four under 16 years, and one female. He served as a private in Captain John Clark's Company of Northumberland County Associators in 1776. A George Schuck died in Penn Township in 1826, but this may have been a different man.

JACOB SCHOCH was born in 1737, supposedly in Germany. He was a relative, probably a brother of George and Mathias Schoch. He served in the French and Indian War, having on May 13, 1759, enlisted in Captain Richardson's Company, 3rd Battalion, Regiment of Foot, in the service of the Province of Pennsylvania. It is supposed that he came to what is now Snyder County at about the same time as the other Schochs. He was assessed in Penn Township for the first time in 1778, and in 1781, he was assessed with 300 acres of land and personal property. In 1802, he lived in the village of Freeburg. He served as a private in the 2nd and at another time in the 4th Company of the 4th Battalion of the Northumberland County Militia during the Revolution.

JOHN SCHOCH was a son of Mathias Schoch. On November 2, 1772, he was granted a warrant of survey for 200 acres in Northumberland (now Snyder) County, and on December 18, 1774, one for 200 acres in the same section. He was assessed in Penn Township for the first time in 1776. In 1787, he was taxed with 300 acres. John's wife was named Catherine, and in 1795, they had their son, John, baptized at the old Zion Lutheran Church, north of Freeburg. Prior to 1790, John and his wife were members of the Row's (Salem) Lutheran congregation. John was born on September 15, 1761, probably in Heidelberg Township, Berks County, Pa., and was killed by a falling tree in Center County, Pa., on February 11, 1799. He moved to what is now Center County about the year 1796. He is buried in Heckman's Cemetery, near Penn Hall in Center County. On September 26, 1778, when only a little over fifteen years of age, he enlisted as a private in Captain John Clark's Company of the Northumberland County Associators. He also served in the companies of Captain Michael Motz and Captain Michael Weaver of the Northumberland County Militia, and in the Ranger Party of Lieutenant Jacob Spees of the same county. Thus he served in all branches of the time—the rangers, the militia, and the continentals. Some of this data seems to refer to another John, maybe an uncle of Mathias' John.

HENRY SASSAMAN (also Sasseman, Sosseman, Sossaman, and originally Sassamanhausen) was born about the year 1745, probably in Maxatawney Township, Berks County, Pa., and died in what is now Monroe Twp., Snyder Co., Pa., during the summer or fall of 1794, and is buried in a family plot on the farm which he once owned. This farm is located near the Kratzerville mill and is now owned by Carey Snyder of Winfield, Pa. Until a few years ago the family burial plot was easily noticeable on the farm. Henry was assessed as a non resident land owner in Buffalo (now Union) Township for the first time in 1786. The same was true in 1787, but some time between 1787 and 1794, he became a resident on the land where he died, and is buried. His wife was named Catherine, and she was living as late as Oct. 16, 1816. It is presumed that she was also buried on the farm. Their children were; Mary (Mrs. William Reichley); Jacob, who married Mary Ann ———; Henry, Jr.; Peter, who married Mary ———; John, who married Catherine ———; Sarah; Catherine (Mrs. Samuel Morrison); and Jonas (3-24-1793—9-3-1878), who married Fanny Kline (1-22-1798—1-25-1882). Fanny was the daughter of Barnhart Kline, a Revolutionary soldier. It is believed that Henry Sassaman was a son of Yost Henry Sassaman (Sassamanhausen in earlier days), who died in Maxatawney Twp., Berks Co., Pa. in 1767, and whose will was probated at Reading, Pa., Nov. 11, 1767. Yost Henry Sassamanhausen was granted a warrant of survey for land in Philadelphia County (Berks was then part of Philadelphia County) on August 13, 1734, and various other parcels from time to time in various places. On March 4, 1761, he was granted a warrant of survey for 120 acres in Berks County, presumably in Maxatawney Township of that county. Yost Henry was a farmer and a blacksmith. He seems to have had two wives, Katherine and Betronella. Katherine was still living in 1750. Yost Henry's will mentions his wife, Betronella, and the following children; Henry (presumably the Henry who came to Snyder County); George, Jacob, Andrew, Elizabeth, Julia Ann, Ca-

therine, Dorothea, Sophia and Gertrude. The will does not say with whom the daughters were intermarried. Two Henry Sassamans lived in Pennsylvania during the Revolutionary War, one in Maxatawney Twp., Berks County, and the other in Frederick Twp., Philadelphia County, this section later became Frederick Township of Montgomery County. The Henry of that section was a tax collector for his township in 1780. In 1778, Henry Sassaman was a private, 8th Class in the 6th Company, 4th Battalion of the Philadelphia County Militia. The same was true in 1786. The compiler's wife is a great-great-granddaughter of the Henry who came to what is now Snyder County. The Henry of this sketch served in Capt. Crouse's Company of the Berks County Militia during part or all of the Revolutionary period.

MATHIAS SCHOCH, was born father's land, which he eventually on December 16, 1738, in Germany. One record states that he came to America in 1749, but the compiler doubts this. He died in what is now Penn Township, Snyder County, Pa., on May 12, 1812. He was twice married. His first wife, Maria Margaret ......, died in 1785. His second wife, Catherine ———, was born in 1754, and died in 1832. All three are buried in the Row's (Salem) Cemetery in Penn Township. It is believed that Mathias' father was named Michael, and that he was the Michael who came to America in the British ship "Speedwell" and took the oath of allegiance at Philadelphia on September 25, 1749. Mathias Schoch secured a warrant of survey for 200 acres of land in Cumberland (now Snyder) County, Pa., on June 4, 1762. On Aug. 9, 1773, he secured a warrant of survey for 50 acres in Northumberland (now Snyder) County, and it is believed that he soon afterward became a resident of what is now Snyder County. His brothers George and Jacob, seem to have come at about the same time, also two sisters of theirs. In 1790, his family consisted of three males over and two under 16 years, and five females. In 1795, he signed the petition for the formation of Mahantango Township. In 1779, he was one of the road supervisors of Penn Township, and again in 1787. In 1789, he was one of the overseers of the poor of the same township. The children of Mathias and his first wife were; John, Henry, Michael, Jacob, Peter, and Catherine, and by his second

wife; George, Daniel, and Rebecca. Jacob was the father of George, Michael, Jacob, Jr., Sem, Abram, John, David, Benjamin, Catherine (wife of George A. Snyder, probably a son of the Governor, Simon Snyder), Susan (wife of Rev. J. G. Anspach), Elizabeth (wife of Colonel Philip Gross), and Mary (Mrs. Beatty Cook). Michael, son of Mathias was the father of George W. Schoch of Mifflinburg, Pa. Michael, the second son of Jacob, married Rosanna Klose. This Michael was born on May 15, 1799. He and Rosanna had seven children; Emanuel (born Aug. 2, 1822, died Nov. 23, 1889). Emanuel married Susanna, daughter of John Kline, and they had two children; Hon. G. Alfred Schoch (1843-1917), and Amanda D., who married the late Lewis E. Pawling of Selinsgrove. The Pawlings had four children, two of whom are living in Selinsgrove today (1935); Attorney Emanuel E. Pawling, and Alice, widow of the late Charles Grant Hendricks. John A. (1808-1863) was a son of Jacob, and grandson of Mathias. He married Lydia Houtz and they had the following children; Franklin J. (married Catherine Leisering), Anna M. (married John Smith and lived at Platte River. Nebraska), Davd A. (married Harriet Wagner and lived at Orangeville, Illinois), Catherine M., Ada (Mrs. Samuel Kempher), John H., (died in infancy), John Calvin (married Margaret Hassinger, and lived at Middleburg, Pa.,) Ammon Z. (married Margaret Appleman, and was living at Bloomsburg, Pa., in 1935), Silas H. (1850-1872), Ira Christian (married Mary E. Schnure, and after her death ——— Richter, and lived in Selinsgrove, and H. Harvey (married Emma C. Schnure, who with her son Marion S., and daughter, Agnes S., were living in Selinsgrove in 1935). The following children of Mathias Schoch and his second wife, Catherine, were baptized at the old Zion Lutheran Church, north of Freeburg; Mary in 1788, John George, 1789, and Margaret, 1791. He served in the Company of Lieutenant Jacob Spees of the Northumberland County Militia.

PHILIP SCHOCH was a relative of George, Jacob, and Mathias Schoch, probably a brother. He came to what is now Snyder County prior to the Revolution. He served in the companies of Captain Michael Motz, Captain Michael Weaver, and Captain Charles Meyer (Moyer) of the Northumberland County Militia, and in the parties of Ensign Simon Herrold and Lieutenant Jacob Spees' (Speece) of the Northumberland County Rangers.

JOHN SCHRECKENGAST (also Schreckengost. etc.) was born in Germany. and embarked for America at Rotterdam, Holland, in the British ship "Polly," Captain Robert Porter, master. He arrived at Philadelphia where he took the English oath of allegiance on October 13, 1764. He lived in Penn Township for a short period during the Revolution and served as a private in Captain John Moll's (Mull's) Company of the Northumberland County Militia.

ENSIGN SIMON SCOUTEN was assessed in Penn Township for the first time in 1772. Later he lived in Greenwood Township of Cumberland County, which then lay just across the narrow Mahantango Creek. This section is today part of Juniata County. In 1781, he was taxed with 50 acres of land and personal property in Greenwood Township. On May 1, 1780, he was a private, 3rd Class, 2nd Company, 7th Battalion of the Cumberland County Militia. From September. 12th to November 11, 1782, he was Ensign of Captain George Hay's Company of Cumberland County Rangers doing scout duty on the Frontier.

CHRISTIAN SECHRIST, SENIOR, (also Segrist, Seagrist, Seegrist, Secrist, Secrest, Seachrist, etc.) was the son of Jacob Sechrist, who on July 26, 1767, bought a tract of land from Thomas McKee, or what had at one time been owned by him, south of the Mahantango Creek. This later became known as "Sechrist's Meadows." Thomas McKee, the Indian Trader, had lived at what is now McKee's Half Falls as early as 1744, and soon after the land office of Cumberland County was opened, he on March 5, 1755, was granted a warrant of survey for a large tract of land on both sides of the Mahantango Creek. The tract purchased by Jacob Sechrist seems to have included some on the north side of the creek, also. Christian, some time after 1770, became a tenant on the land purchased. As early as 1774, Christian was one of the road supervisof Penn Township. In 1776, Christian was tax collector for the township, and probably was the successor to the inimitable Colonel Peter Hosterman, who held the office from 1772. In 1781, Christian was assessed with 150 acres of land, personal property, and a sawmill. In 1784, he was taxed with the same and 250 acres of land. In 1796,

when Mahantango Township was formed from the southern part of Penn he was assessed there. In this year he was also taxed with a still. The Sechrists came from either Berks or Lancaster County. In 1790, Christian's family consisted of two males over and three under 16 years, and three females. He died in what is now Chapman Township in 1797, and his wife, Nancy, and their son Christian, Jr., and Michael Laver (or Lauver), probably a son-in-law, were the administrators of his estate. Indications are that he is buried in the Rine and Sechrist Private Cemetery in Chapman Township. No military record was found for him, but the compiler believes that he served during the Revolution.

CHRISTIAN SECHRIST, JUNIOR, was a son of Christian. Senior, mentioned above, and his wife, Nancy. He was one of the admnistrators of his father's estate in 1797. In 1805, he owned land adjoining that of John George Herrold on the south, in what is now Chapman Township. In 1814, he was one of the viewers for a bridge across the Mahantango Creek, near where the present one on the Susquehanna Trail is located. It is believed that he is interred in the Rine and Sechrist Private Cemetery in Chapman Township. Henry Sechrist (1789-1859) was probably his brother, and John (1814-1857) may have been his son.

MAJOR ANTHONY SELIN, founder of the town of Selinsgrove, Snyder County, Pa., was born in the country of Switzerland, and died in what is now Selinsgrove in 1792. Little is known of his early life, but when in January, 1776, it was decided by the Continental Congress to raise two regiments among the Canadians, Anthony Selin was proposed for one of the officerships, because of his military training and experience in the armies of Europe. It seems, however, that this proposal was never carried out, and that instead, he was commissioned as a Captain in Baron Von Ottendorf's Corps, by Congress, on December 10, 1776. Von Ottendorf's Corps of Dragoons was being formed at this time at Great Plains, New York, and was directly under the command of Baron Washington, himself. In May, 1778, an Independent Corps was formed by Washington at Valley Forge, and Captain Selin was given command of it. Captain Selin and his command participated in General Sullivan's Expedition against the Indians in February, 1779. and later he was given command of the pion-

eer corps in the van of the expedition. In the spring of 1780, he was still in the service, and was stationed. at Wyoming, Pa. On January 1, 1781, Captain Selin petitioned the Continental Congress for a command in Colonel Hazen's Regiment. Evidently his request was granted, and later service brought him the rank of Brevet-Major in the Continental Army. He resigned his commission on January 1, 1783, having had one of the longest and most varied military careers of any one at the time living in the Susquehanna Valley. Major Selin was a member of the Society of the Cincinnati, and his certificate, written in the field, is still in possession of one of his descendants in Selinsgrove. In 1788, Major Selin was commissioned Lieutenant-Colonel of the 5th Battalion of the Northumberland County Militia, and altho he held a higher rank in the militia, he is best remembered by the rank he held in the Continental Line (Regular Army). Major Selin married a sister of Simon Snyder, later Governor of Pennsylvania.

Snyder and Selin were partners in various business enterprises. Major Selin and Catherine Snyder had two children; Anthony Charles Selin. born June 19, 1786, and Agnes Selin, later the wife of James K. Davis, Sr. Anthony Charles Selin was an officer in the War of 1812, and died in Selinsgrove, Pa., on November 3, 1823. His wife, Mary C. —— died at the home of her son-in-law, Robert Swineford, in Selinsgrove, on November 3, 1868. All of the Selins are buried in the Trinity Lutheran Cemetery in Selinsgrove. On November 12, 1790, Major Selin bought the estate of his brotherin-law, John Snyder, who had died from a fall, in 1787. This tract contained most of the land on which Selinsgrove is now built. Finding the plat as laid out by Snyder, unsuited, he resurveyed it, and gave it the name of "Selin's Grove." He was one of the few men of the section who served through the entire period of the war, and is believed to have been the only one of the immediate section who was a member of the Society of the Cincinnati. Anthony C. and his sister were granted much land because of their father's outstanding service in the Revolution.

FREDERICK SENSILL was a shopkeeper and resident of the City of Reading, Pa. He was a real estate owner there in 1767 and 1768, and at later dates. On September 6, 1773, he was granted a warrant of survey for 100 acres in Northumberland (now Snyder) County, and for a number of years thereafter he was assessed as a non resident land owner in the township. In 1782, he was assessed with 300 acres. Frederick Sensill, single, was a resident of Alsace Township, Berks County, Pa., in 1785, and may have been a son of the Frederick of Reading.

HENRY SHADLE (also Shadel, Sch..del, Schadle, Schoedel, etc.) was born in Wurtemberg, Germany, on October 22, 1752, and according to the Berks County History, was a son of John Shadle, who sailed from Rotterdam, Holland, with his family in the British ship "Brothers," Captain William Muir, master, and ..rrived at the port of Philadelphia, where he took the oath of allegiance on September 30, 1754. John, the father of Henry, was born in 1721, and was 33 years old when he came to America. The Shadles settled in Richmond Township, Berks County, Pa. In 1784, Henry was assessed with 21 acres and personal property in Richmond Township. He came to what is now Perry Township, Snyder County, in 1795, and built a gristmill and sawmill near the present village of Fremont (Mt. Pleasant Mills.) His wife was Maria Ohlinger, who was born in France on February 2, 1752, and died in Perry Township, now Snyder County, Pa., on May 31, 1832. Henry died in Perry Township on January 21, 1822, and both are buried in the cemetery at Grubb's Lutheran Church in Chapman Township and their graves are marked. In 1790, Henry's family consisted of one male over, and four under 16 years, and five females. The children of Henry and his wife were: John. Samuel, Solomon, Abraham, Mary, Elizabeth, Susan, Esther, and Hannah, Of the sons. only Samuel, who was born on March 3, 1784, remained in what is now Snyder County. The others migrated to the vicinity of Mansfield, Ohio. Samuel was an officer in the War of 1812, and after the war served as a captain in the militia. Henry, his father, served as a teamster in Washington's Army, and is said to have had very retentive memory, and many years afterwards was able to recall incidents that happened during his army experiences. Two Henry Shadles served in the Revolution, and it is supposed that they were cousins, one of them seemingly being the son of Urban Shadle. an immigrant. Both Henrys seem to have served in the Berks County Militia. Squire J. Albert Shadle, a great-grandson of Henry, lives at Mt. Pleasant Mills today (1935) and is aged about 80 years.

ANDREW SHAFFER was assessed in what is now Penn Township for the first time in 1768. In 1782, he was taxed with 200 acres and personal property. About 1790, Andrew and Catherine Elizabeth Shaffer were members of the Row's (Salem) Lutheran Church. Frederick Shaffer, probably a son, was also a member of the same church at the same time. Andrew Shaffer and Andrew Hafer lived in the same section at the same time and sometimes confusion has arisen concerning them. Andrew Shaffer died in Penn Township and his will was probated at Lewisburg, Pa., on July 2, 1816. It mentions his wife, Catherine L'izabeth, and their two children; John, and Catherine (Mrs. Thomas Bickle). Andrew Shaffer, born November 20, 1759, and died June 16, 1816. He is buried in the Salem Cemetery. The Bickles and Shaffers lived neighbors and this may account for Catherine Shaffer having married Thomas Bickle. Two Andrew Shaffers served in the Revolution from Pennsylvania, but the compiler was unable to distinguish them. One of them served in the 9th Pennsylvania Regiment, and both were pensioners. Andrew's family consisted of two males ..nd five females in 1790, one male under 16. John Shaffer (1789-1860) is buried at Salem.

ANDREW SHAFFER was assessed as a single freeman in Mahantango Township for the first time in 1796. Maybe he was the son of Christopher, Senior, who died in 1793.

CHRISTIAN (possibly Christopher) SHAFFER lived in 'enn Township in 1776. If he was a son of Christopher, Senior, the name should be "Christopher" because he had a son named for himself. This man was a private in Captain Benjamin Weiser's Company, German Regiment, Continental Line, stationed at Philadelphia, Pa., on January 30, 1777.

CHRISTOPHER SHAFFER (also Shaeffer, Schaeffer, Schafer. etc.) seems to have been born in Wurtemberg, Germany, about the year 1721, and died in what is now probably Chapman Township Snyder County, Pa. His will was probated at Sunbury. Pa., on October 5, 1793. The will mentions his wife, Maria Eva Rosina, and the following children: Christopher, Jr., Catherine (Mrs. Paul Hime). Barbara, (Mrs. Abraahm Markley), Elizabeth (Mrs. Philip Foulkrod), John, Philip, Andrew, Rosina, Daniel, Magdalena, Anna Maria, and Ja-

cob. Christopher, Jr., and Simon Snyder (later Governor of Pennsylvania) were executors of his will. It is believed Christopher, Sr., was the Christopher who embarked at Rotterdam. Holland on the British ship "Chesterfield." Captain Thomas Coatam, master, arrived at Philadelphia, where he took the oath of allegiance to the English government on September 2, 1749.

GEORGE SHAFFER was assessed in Penn Township only in the year of 1780. He may have been the George Shaffer who died in Penn Township. Letters of administration in his estate were granted to Catherine Shaffer, probably his widow, on October 14, 1795. Henry Treisbach (Driesbach) and John Graybill were suretes on her bond. It is believed that he was the George Shaffer who was a private, 2nd class, in Captain Michael Holdeborn's Company, 2nd Battalion, Lancaster County Militia in May, 1781.

JOHN SHAFFER seems to have been the son of Christopher Shaffer. Senior. John was assessed in Mahantango Township for the first time in 1796. He married Anna Maria Reichenbach, and they had at least one daughter, named Sarah, who was born on September 9, 1791, and baptized at Grubb's Church. He died in Mahantango Township and letters of administration in his estate were granted to Christopher, his brother, at Sunbury, Pa., on August 31, 1812. He served in the companies of Captain John Black, Captain Michael Weaver, and Captain William Werlick of the Northumberland County Militia. He seems to have been the man who enlisted in Captain Casper Weitzel's Company for continental service at Sunbury, Pa., on September 1, 1776.

JOHN PETER SHAFFER, JUNIOR, son of John Peter Shaffer, commonly called Peter, John Peter, Junior, was born in what is now Chapman Township, Snyder County, Pa., June 15, 1775, and died in the same section, May 21, 1847. He married Anna Maria, daughter of Captain Simon Herrold. She was born in what is now Union or Chapman Township of Snyder County, Pa., on Dec. 15, 1778, and died Nov. 2, 1862. They were consistent and regular members of the Lutheran congregation of Grubb's Church, are buried in the cemetery there, and their graves are marked. John Peter, was a farmer, and was assessed in Mahantango Township for the first time about the year 1798. His will was probated at Lewisburg, Pa., on June 11, 1847, and mentions his wife, and the following children in the order of their birth: George H.; Sarah (Mrs. Jacob Bear); Elizabeth (Mrs. Frederick Wendt, Jr.); Philip, Catherine (Mrs. John Steffen); Peter; Anna Maria (Mrs. George Steffen); John; Barbara (Mrs. Peter Bertch) and Jacob (born Oct. 10, 1818).

MICHAEL SHAFFER lived in what is now Chapman or Perry Township before 1790. In the U. S. Census of 1790, his family consisted of one male over, and one under 16 years, a..d five females. In 1796, he was assessed land. personal property, and a sawmill in Mahantango Township. He married Salome, who it is believed was a daughter of John Reichenbach, Sr. Jonn was an early resident of that section. Michael died in Perry Township. His will was made on April 19, 1821, and probated at Lewisburg, Pa., on May 15, 1821. The will mentions his wife, Salome, and the following children: Anna Maria (Mrs. John Troup). who died before her father: Catherine (Mrs. Peter Troup); Elizabeth (Mrs. Jacob Reichenbach); Susan (Mrs. Solomon Gamby); Sarah (Mrs. George Gamby); Margaret and Christina. Maria, Elizabeth, and Sarah were baptized at Grubb's Church. The dates of their births were: May 21, 1790, April 23, 1792, and Feb. 1, 1799. respectively. Michael served in the companies of Captain William Weirick, Captain Charles Meyer, and Captain John Snyder of the Northumberland County Militia during the Revolutionary period.

SECOND LIEUTENANT JOHN ADAM SHAFFER lived in Penn Township in 1776, and in Miles Township, now Center County, Pa., about 1790. He was born on October 31, 1752, and died in Center County on January 14, 1840. He is buried in Madisonburg in that county. He was Second Lieutenant of Captain Benjamin Weiser's company, German Regiment, Continental Line, and was stationed at Philadelphia, Pa., on January 30, 1777.

LUDWIG (LEWIS) SHAFFER from 1776 to 1781, when his name from 1776 to 1761, when his name disappeared. In the latter year he was taxed with 50 acres of land and personal property. He served as a private in the 4th Company, 4th Battalion of the Northumberland County Militia, under Captain William Weirick.

NICHOLAS SHAFFER lived in Penn Township as early as 1776. In 1797, he lived in Miles Township, Center County. He served as a private in Captain Benjamin Weiser's Company, German Reigiment,

Continental Line, and on January 30, 1777, was stationed at Philadelphia, Pa. It is believed that he was a brother of Second Lieutenant John Adam Shaffer of that company.

PETER SHAFFER. One record states that he settled at the mouth of Mahantango Creek as early as 1765. (The compiler doubts this.) His name appeared on the Penn Township tax list for the first time in 1776. In 1781, he was assessed with 100 acres and personal property. In 1796. when Mahantango Township was formed, he was assessed there. He died in what is now Perry Township, Snyder County. and his will was probated at Lewisburg, Pa., on September 17, 1819. It mentions his wife, Eve, and the following children: John George, John Peter\ 1775-1847, who married Anna Maria. daughter of Captain Simon Herrold, and they had a son Jacob, who was born Oct. 10, 1818, according to the Grubb's Church Baptismal Record), Henry, Jacob, Sarah. Susanna, Elizabeth, Barbara, and Samuel. His wife and Adam Nerhood (maybe a son-in-law) were the executors of the will. Peter served as a private in the companies of Captain Michael Weaver and Captain John Black of the Northumberland County Militia. In 1790, his family consisted of one male over and three under 16 years and five females.

WILLIAM SHAW was assessed in Penn Township only in the year of 1781. In 1778, he was assessed in Buffalo Township, and in 1786, he was assessed with 400 acres, gristmill, and personal property in Turbot Township, Northumberland County. It is believed that he died in 1811. Several men of this name served in the Revolution. One of them was a Sergeant in the 11th Pennsylvania Regiment. and the other received depreciation pay for services in the Cumberland County Militia.

CHRISTOPHER SHAWVER, JUNIOR, (also Shawber, Shauver, etc.) was assessed in Penn Township for the first time in 1793. No military record was found for him.

ANDREW SHEARER. blacksmith, was assessed in Penn Township for the first time in 1799. An Andrew Shearer served as a private in Captain Paxton's Company of the Bedford County Militia.

MATHIAS SHEARER lived in Penn Township in 1780. The date of his first assessment there is unknown to the compiler, He served as a private in Captain Michael

Motz's Company of the Northumberland County Militia.

JACOB SHEASLEY (also Sheessley, Sheasley, Shissley, Shessly, etc.) was assessed with real and personal property |in Upper Paxton Township, Lancaster County, Pa.. in 1782. He was assessed in Penn Township for the first time in 1785, and in 1786 he was taxed with 150 acres and personalty. No military record was found for him.

GEORGE SHERRARD (probably meant for George Jarrett) was assessed as a single freeman in Beaver Township for the first time in 1789. He may have been a son of Jacob Jarrett, who lived in that section at that time.

ABRAHAM SHESSARE lived in Penn or an adjoining township during part of the Revolutionary period. He served as a private in Captain William Weirick's Company of the Northumberland County Militia.

ANDREW SHETTERLY (also Shetterley, Shetterle, Shatterly, Shatterle, etc.) was assessed in Penn Township as early as 1776, but at the time was a nonresident landowner. He lived in the township for the first time in 1782. John, probably a son, may have lived in the district before that time. In 1784, Andrew was assessed with 200 acres and personal property, and in 1796, when Mahantango Township was formed he was taxed there. Andrew and his wife, Anna Maria. were among the early members of the Grubb's Lutheran Church in what is now Chapman Township. and they stood as sponsors for more children there than any other couple. The last occasion of this kind was on July 3, 1831, when they were sponsors for Andrew Washington, son of Samuel and Elizabeth Ketterman. John, George, David, and Henry, were sons of other relatives of Andrew. In 1790, Andrew's family consisted of one male over and one under 16 years, and two females. It is believed that Andrew was a son of Jacob Shetterly, who embarked for America at Rotterdam, Holland, in the British ship "Anderson," Captain Hugh Campbell, Master. arrived at Philadelphia, and took the English oath of allegiance there on August 25th, 1751. No military record was found for Andrew, but it is believed that he served during the Revolution.

DAVID SHETTERLY lived in what is now Chapman or Perry Township before 1800. He may have been a son of Andrew, mentioned above. He died in 1802.

GEORGE SHETTERLY lived in what is now Chapman or Perry

Township before 1800. He may have been a son of Andrew.

HENRY SHETTERLY seems to have been a son of Andrew and his wife. He was born in Berks County, Pa., and was assessed in Mahantango Township for the first time in 1796, but may have been assessed in Penn Township before. Henry was born on May 6, 1761, and died in what is now Perry Township of Snyder County on January 6, 1835. His wife, Veronica————, was born on August 12, 1770, and died on August 21, 1844. Both are buried in the Portzline Cemetery in Perry Township, and their graves are marked. Their known children, who were baptized at Grubb's Lutheran Chmurch were: Barbara, born March 12, 1791; Maria Magdalene, May 8, 1794; and Andrew. born on May 22, 1796, and died on May 12, 1873. No military record was found for Henry.

JOHN SHETTERLY may have been a son of Andrew and Anna Maria Shetterly. He was probably born about the year 1760, and was assessed in Penn Township for the first time in 1781. In 1786, he was taxed with 150 acres of land and personal property. In 1796, when Mahantango Township was formed, he lived there and was assessed with the same and a sawmill in addition. No military record was found for him.

LAWRENCE SHELLENBERGER (also Shallenberger, Shellenbarger, Shelenberger, etc.) was a native of Greenwich Township, Berks County, Pa. He was assessed in Penn Township for the first time in 1776, but was listed as a nonresident landowner for many years. He came to what is now Snyder County in 1787. and in that year was taxed with 20 acres of land and personal property. He received depreciation pay for services in the Berks County Militia. He probably lived in what is today West Perry Township. It is believed that a son of his married a daughter of John Rush a Quaker, of what is now Globe Mills.

JOHN SHERRICK also Sherick, Sharrick. but is today probably the name SHIRK) was a native of Lancaster County. Pa., as early as 1776, he was a non-resident landowner in Penn Township. He moved to the township in 1784, and in 1787, was taxed with 50 acres of land, a still and personal property. His wife was named Catherine, and they had children, but the compiler did not find their names. His will was probated at Sunbury, Pa., on July 15, 1794. His neighbors, Christian Sechrist and Michael Albright. were executors of the will. He served as a private, 4th Class, 4th Company,

4th Battalion. Lancaster County Militia. It is believed that he was the ancestor of the Shirks of Snyder and adjoining counties.

SQUIRE THOMAS SHIPTON was born on April 22, 1753, and died on February 24. 1827. His wife Hannah, was born on October 21, 1753, and died on May 7, 1812. It is thought that he had a second wife named Nancy. The Shiptons are buried in the Hassinger Old Cemetery, west of Middleburg, Snyder County, Pa. Thomas was a resident, but not a landowner in Huntington Township, York County, Pa., from 1779 to 1781. The next two years, he was a resident of Warrington Township, same county. He was assessed in Penn Township for the first time in 1785, and two years later was assessed with 100 acres of land, a still and personal property. In 1790, his family consisted of one male over and two under 16 years, and two females. In 1794. he was assessed in Beaver Township. He was appointed a justice of the peace and served nearly thirty years. His justice and integrity were highly respected. He died in what is now Center Township. (formed from part of Beaver) and his will was probated at Lewisburg, Pa., on February 26, 1827. His will mentions his second wife, Nancy, and his children: Ann, Elizabeth, Henry, William, and John. John was born on March 22, 1789, and died on December 25, 1866. John's wife, Elizabeth, was born on January 17, 1801, and died on May 14, 1885. Both are buried in the Beavertown cemetery. It is believed that Thomas served in the York County Militia.

CONRAD SHIVELY lived in Penn Township in 1795. He was one of the petitioners for the formation of Mahantango Township.

PETER SHOEMAKER (also Schuhmaker, Schoemacher, etc,) was a resident, but not a landowner, in Warwick Township, Lancaster County, Pa., in 1772. He was assessed in Penn Township for the first time in 1780, but the indications are that he did not come there to live until 1784, at which time he was assessed with 50 acres and personal property. In 1790, his family consisted of himself and four females. He died, and letters of administration in his estate were granted to his wife, Catherine, on February 3, 1791, at Sunbury, Pa. Several Peter Shoemakers served during the Revolution, but this man's service seems to have been as a private, 7th Class, 4th Company, 3rd Battalion, Lancaster County Militia, in 1781.

SIMON SHOEMAKER was probably a son of Peter and Catherine

Shoemaker, mentioned above. He was assessed in Penn Township for the first time in 1792. Simon and his wife, Laura, had their son, Simon Junior, born September 10, 1791, baptized at Grubb's Lutheran Church some time during 1792.

CHRISTOPHER SHOTZBERGER, SENIOR, (also Shatzberger, Shotsberger. Shottzberger, etc.) lived in Penn Township before 1790. In that year his family consisted of himself, wife, and one daughter. His wife was Catherine, daughter of the pioneer, John Arbogast. In 1795, Christopher and Catherine had their son, Christopher, Junior, baptized at that date at Old Zion Lutheran Church, north of Freeburg. One of their sons seems to have been Jonathan (Sept. 26, 1793-Feb. 4, 1859), who married Catherine (April 3, 1794-Aug. 29, 1874). Jonathan and his wife are buried in the Keiser Cemetery in Union Township. No military record was found for Christopher, Sr.

ADAM SHOWER (also Shover. Shaurer, Sharrer, etc.) was assessed in Mahantango Township in 1796. He died in Center Township and his will was probated at Sunbury, Pa., on December 7, 1805. The will mentions his wife, Elizabeth, and these children of theirs: Adam, Jr., Anna Mary, John, Magdalene, Elizabeth, Jacob and Frederick. Adam, Sr., still lived in Mahantango Township in 1801. Michael. who lived in the coun ty from an earlier date seems to have been his brother.

MICHAEL SHOWER was probaly a native of Berks County. Michael Shower, weaver, was assessed in Greenwich Township, Berks County, Pa., in 1779. A man of the same name was assessed in Penn Township for the first time in 1780, and the compiler believes that they were the same man. In 1781, he was taxed with 80 acres of land, personal property, a gristmill and a sawmill. In 1790, his family consisted of one male over and four under 16 years and three females. In 1796, when Mahantango Township was formed he was assessed there. He was still living in Mahantango Township in 1801. Michael served as a private in Captain John Snyder's Company of the Northumberland County Militia.

PHILIP SCHREIBER (also Schreib ', etc.) was assessed in Mahantango Township in 1796. In 1780, he lived in Penn or an adjoining township, probably in Greenwood Township. Cumberland County. In 1780, he served in Captain John Snyder's Company of the Northumberland County Militia.

JOHN SHREINER lived in what

is today Monroe Township, in the vicinity of Schreiner's Church, which was named for him or one of his descendants. He lived there as early as 1789, because in that year he was one of the petitioners asking that the lower part of Buffalo Township (now known as Monroe Township) be annexed to Penn Township. The compiler believes that he is buried in the Schriner Cemetery.

JOHN SHULTZ (also Schultz) probably came from Lancaster County. He was assessed in Beaver Township for the first time in 1789. In 1790, his family consisted of one male over and one under 15 years, and two females. Several men of this name served during the Revolution.

JAMES SILVERWOOD was assessed in Augusta Township, Northumberland County, for the first time in 1778. In 1786, he was taxed with 150 acres and personal property. In 1790, his family consisted of one male over and two under 16 years, two females and two other persons, one slave. He was assessed in Penn Township for the first time in 1793, and was still living in Selinsgrove in 1802. One of the larger islands in the Susquehanna River south of Selinsgrove was named for him. He was commonly called "Jimmie." No military record was found for him.

JOSEPH SIMON was a resident of the borough of Lancaster in 1773. From 1776 to 1783, he was a nonresident landowner of 200 acres in Penn Township. Indications are that he never lived in the district.

DUNCAN SINCLAIR (also St. Clair) was a single freeman in Hanover Township, Lancaster County, Pa., in 1779. He was assessed in Penn Township for the first time in 1785, and in 1787, he was taxed with 40 acres of land and personal property. On June 6, 1776, he was a private in Captain James Roger's Company, Green's Rifle Battalion of the Lancaster County Associators, and on August 31st of the same year he was a member of Captain Wm. Brown's Company of the same battalion.

NEAL (or NEIL) SINCLAIR may have been a native of Cumberland County. In 1787, he was listed as a single freeman in Chillisquaque Township, Northumberland County. He was assessed in Penn Township for the first time in 1798. He was a ranger in the Revolution, and another record states that he was a private in Captain Robert Samuel's Company, Cumberland County Militia, in active service from April to June, 1782. Some Sinclars lived in Monroe Township up to a generation or two ago.

ADAM SMITH seems to have lived in Penn Township for a short time, but later in Beaver Township where he died. Letters of administration were granted to his son, Adam, and Ner Middlesworth at Lewisburg, Pa., on July 26, 1827. It is stated that he is buried in the Dreisbach's Cemetery, Union County. The known children of Adam were: John (lived in Beaver Township), George, Michael, Mrs. Michael Maize, and Mrs. Stephen Touchman. Adam was a teamster during the Revolution.

DAVID SMITH lived in Buffalo Township, Northumberland County, in 1778. He was assessed in Penn Township for the first time in 1785, and in that year was taxed with 250 acres and personal property. In 1790, his family consisted of one male over and one under 16 years, and two females. In 1796, when Mahantongo Township was formed, he was assessed in the new district. He had an oil mill in addition to large real estate holdings there at that time. He died in Mahantongo Township and his will was probated at Sunbury, Pa., on September 26, 1801. The will will mentions his wife, Rebecca, and their children: Joseph, David Jr., Jacob, Abraham, Daniel, Solomon, Elizabeth, and Barbara. His wife, and Michael Albright, a neighbor, were executors of the will. Smith's school house in Chapman Township is located near the former holdings of this pioneer. David served as a private in Captain Patrick Watson's Company of the Northumberland County Militia.

JOHN SMITH was a native of Lancaster County, Pa. He came to Penn Township in 1774, and purchased the Hopewell tract of 206 acres on the south side of the Middle Creek. He built a cabin, dug a well, planted an orchard; then, because of the ravages of the Indians, he returned to his old home in Lancaster County. Nine years later he returned, found his cabin and well in fair shape, the orchard in bloom. In 1787, he was assessed with 300 acres and personal property in Penn Township, and his will was probated at Lewisburg, Pa., on December 15, 1823. His children were: John (who probably married Elizabeth, daughter of John Hains, a pioneer, of the Freeburg section), Martin, Henry, Michael, George, Mary (Mrs. Joseph Miller, and Elizabeth Mrs. John Weller.) On May 8, 1782, he was a private, 8th Class. 6th Company, 1st Battalion, Lancaster County Militia. (A John Smith, noncommissioned officer in the 11th

Pennsylvania Regiment, was wounded at Sunbury, Pa., on July 4, 1780.

NICHOLAS SMITH was a landowner in Colebrookdale Twp., Berks County, Pa., in the year 1767. From 1776 to 1782, he was assessed as the ed at Sunbury, Pa., on July 4, 1790.) nonresident owner of 30 acres in Penn Township. Indications are that he never lived in Snyder County. He seems to have lived in Washington County, Pa., in 1819. He served as a private in Captain John Lesher's Company of the Berks County Militia on August 26, 1776.

PETER SMITH was an early resident of Penn Township. Little is known concerning him. He served in the companies of Captain John Snyder and Ensign Simon Herrold of the Northumberland County Rangers in the summer of 1780.

STEPHEN SMITH was assessed in Penn Township for the first time in 1778. It is believed that he came from Philadelphia County. In 1787, he was taxed with 100 acres and personal property. In 1784, he and his wife, Mary Elizabeth, had their son, John Peter, baptized at the old Zion Lutheran Church, north of Freeburg. He served as a private in Captain John Moll's (Mull's) Company of the Northumberland County Militia, and in May, 1780, in Lieut John Coleman's Party of the Northumberland County Rangers. In 1790, his family consisted of one male over and three under 16 years, and four females.

ABRAHAM SNAVELY (also Snavely, Snabley, Snebly, Snevely, etc.) was assessed as a nonresident land owner in Penn Township for the first time in 1776. In 1787, he was still a nonresident and was taxed with 100 acres of land only. It is believed that he lived in Lancaster County. An Ebraim (possibly Abram or Abraham) Sneavley was a private 8th Class, Captain Samuel Henry's Company of the Lancaster County Militia.

ANTHONY SNELLENBERGER (maybe Shellenberger) lived in Penn Township in 1790, and his family consisted of three males over 16 years, and one female.

ABRAHAM SNYDER (also Snider, Sneider, Schneider, Schneyder, etc.) was a native of Tulpehocken Township, Berks County, Pa. It is believed he came to Penn Township before 1790. He died in Penn Township and his will was probated at Sunbury, Pa., on July 17, 1793. His children were: Jacob, Abraham, Jr., John (probably Captain John), George, Thomas (probably Ensign Thomas), and Maria.

ANTHONY SNYDER was the father of Simon Snyder, the third Governor of the State of Pennsylvania. He was born in Germany about 1710, and emigrated to this country about 1740. He died in Lancaster, Pa., in April, 1774. In 1771, he was listed as a resident in the village of Manheim Lancaster County. Before the Revolution he secured a large tract in what is now Snyder (named for Governor Snyder) County, and this land remained in his name, or that of a son of the same name for a number of years. The children of Anthony known to the compiler were: Simon (the Governor), John (who died at Selinsgrove 1787), Catherine (wife of Major Anthony Selin), and another daughter who married Jacob Lechner (the first postmaster at Selinsgrove). He and his wife were the parents of Dr. Henry A. Lechner, a well-known physician in Selinsgrove a hundred years ago.

CAPTAIN CASPER SNYDER was assessed as a freeman in Penn Township in 1771, and from 1774 on was a resident of Augusta Township, Northumberland Co., Pa. He was born on May 2, 1745, and died, Sept. 3. 1821. He is buried in the Cemetery at Fishers Ferry, Pa., and his grave is marked. In the U. S. Census of 1790, he is listed as "Jasper Sneider," and his family consisted of one male over 16, and four under 16 years, and five females. Casper settled along the Hallowing Run and in 1798 built the famous brick Blue Ball Tavern, which is still standing today. His wife was Elizabeth Farst (probably the same as Fuerst, Furst, or Ferster, today). She was born Feb. 5, 1754 and died Aug. 12, 1823, and is buried in the same cemetery as her husband. It is believed that she was a sister of Peter Ferster, who was connected with Himmel's Church. Neither Casper or his wife are believed to have been immigrants. It is supposed that Agnes Snyder, wife of John George Furst, of the Himmel Church section was Casper's sister. Casper's daughter, Maria, was baptized at the Himmel Church on Aug. 4. 1782. The children of Captain Snyder and wife were: Colonel John Snyder, born Nov. 29, 1776, died, April 29, 1851. John married, Marie Margaret, only daughter of the pioneer, John Adam Fisher of the Isle of Que. Hannah, born 1778, died 1812, was the wife of Christian Fisher. Elizabeth born Apr. 27, 1779 died Apr. 13, 1851 was the second wife|of Christian Fisher.

Thomas, born Dec. 6, 1781, died Apr. 13, 1828, was a soldier in the war of 1812. He married Catherine Kehl. Mary, born Jan. 24, 1783, died March 7, 1856, married Isaac Updegraf. George, born, Sept. 3, 1785. died, Feb. 19, 1812, Peter, born, April 21, 1788, died Feb .19. 1886. His wife was Joanna Shipman. Catherine, born, Feb. 13, 1790. died, Oct. 17, 1854. She married William Silverwood. Sarah, born, Nov. 22, 1790, or 1791, died Feb. 23, 1863. Her husband was John Hendershott. Casper, Jr., born about 1794, died in youth. Lydia, born, Aug. 24, 1797, died, June 19. 1863. She married Samuel Aucmuthy, Jr. Casper Snyder served as a private in Robinson's Rangers. In 1782, he was a Lieutenant in the 6th Company, 1st Battalion of the Northumberland County Militia, and after the war he was Captain of a militia company.

FIRST LIEUTENANT CHRISTOPHER (STOPHEL) SNYDER was listed as a single freeman in Penn Township only in the year of 1776. It is said that he died in Bald Eagle Township in 1811. On January 30, 1777, he was First Lieutenant in Captain Benjamin Weiser's Company, German Regiment, Continental Line, stationed at Philadelphia.

GEORGE SNYDER was a son of Abraham Snyder, who died in Penn Township in 1793. He served as a private in Captain John Black's Company of the Northumberland County Militia.

GEORGE SNYDER. shoemaker, was assessed in Penn Township for the first time in 1799. In 1796, he lived in Mahantango Township. It believed that he was a son of John Snyder, Senior, who died in Mahantango Township in 1805.

GEORGE SNYDER, innkeeper, was assessed in Penn Township for the first time in 1799. He may have been a son of Governor Simon Snyder.

HARMAN SNYDER, SENIOR, was listed on the Penn Township tax list for the year 1771. In 1773, he was one of the road supervisors of the township. He lived in the vicinity of the present village of Richfield and his land holdings were large. In 1796, when Mahantango Township was formed, he and his son, Harman. Junior, were assessed there.

HARMAN SNYDER, JUNIOR, was a son of Harman. Senior. He was assessed in Penn Township before 1790, and in Mahantango Township in 1796. In 1790, his family consisted of one male over and one under 16 years, and three females. He married Magdalena,

daughter of the pioneer, John Graybill, Junior.

JACOB SNYDER was a son of Abraham Snyder, Senior. He was probably born in Tulpehocken Township, Berks County, Pa. He came to Penn Twp., before the Revolution. He was a private in Captain Benjamin Weiser's Company, German Regiment, Continental Line. stationed at Philadelphia, Pa., on January 30th, 1777. It is believed that Captain John and Ensign Thomas were his brothers.

JOHN SNYDER was assessed in Penn Township for the first time in 1789. Maybe son of Capt. John.

"BLACK" JOHN SNYDER was a son of Anthony Snyder. mentioned above, and a brother of Gov. S. Snyder. He was born in Lancaster Co., Pa., and came to what is now Selinsgrove, about 1780, probably as a tenant or the owner of the land his father had owned. His brother Simon came to the same section in 1784. In 1781, John was taxed with 50 acres and personal property. On July 26, 1785, he bought the upper end of the Isle of Que at Sheriff's sale. In 1787, he was taxed with 250 acres and personal property. The town of Selinsgrove is built on part of land once owned by John Snyder. John was born on November 15. 1785, and died in May, 1787, by being thrown from the back of a riding horse. He was a fancier of race horses. Some time after his death his widow married Jacob Kindig, or Kendig, a resident of Penn Township. John served as a private in Captain John Gregory's Company of Lancaster County Rangers, or was adjutant of the 3rd Battalion of the Lancaster County Militia.

JOHN SNYDER, SENIOR, came to what is now Snyder County, before or during the Revolution, and lived in what is now Chapman or Union Township. In 1790, his family consisted of one male over and two under 16 years, and two females. In 1796, when Mahantango Township was formed, he was taxed there. His wife was named Susanna. John died in Mahantango Township and his will was probated at Sunbury, Pa., on June 29, 1805. The will mentions these children: John, Jr. George, Jacob, Margaret, Stahley Elizabeth Kerstetter, and Christian. It is believed that Elizabeth was the wife of John George Kerstetter. He received depreciation pay for services in the Northumberland County Militia, and may have been the John Snyder, private, who was pensioned on September 4, 1790.

CAPTAIN JOHN SNYDER, son of John Snyder, Senior, mentioned

above, was born in 1750, and died on February 21, 1839. He is buried in the old Graybill Cemetery, near Richfield, Pa. He came to what is now Snyder County, before or during the Revolution. In 1790, his family consisted of one male over and two under 16 years, and three females. About 1780, he served as a Captain of a Company of the Northumberland County Militia, or Rangers.

SIMON SNYDER, son of Henry, was assessed in Penn Township for the first time in 1790. It is believed that his father was a Revolutionary soldier.

SIMON SNYDER, JUNIOR, was either a son or nephew of Governor Simon Snyder. He was an innkeeper, and was assessed in Penn Township for the first time in 1795, but indications are that he lived there at an earlier date, because in 1795, he signed a petition praying for the formation of Mahantango Township.

GOVERNOR SIMON SNYDER was a son of Anthony Snyder, who came to this country from Germany about 1740, and died at Lancaster, Pa., in April, 1774. Simon was born on November 5, 1759, probably at or near Manheim in Lancaster County, Pa., and died at Selinsgrove, now Snyder County (named for him), on November 9, 1819. Shortly after the death of his father he went to York to learn the tanning trade and currying business. He remained there until 1784, when he moved to what is now the town of Selinsgrove. During his apprenticeship he studied continuously and attended a night school taught by an old Quaker. At an early age he began the study of law. When he came to Selinsgrove in July, 1784, he entered into partnership with his brother-in-law, Major Anthony Selin in the milling and store business, and also acted as a public scrivener. Shortly thereafter he was appointed a justice of the peace and served for twelve years. In 1789, he was a member of the convention which framed the first constitution for the State of Pennsylvania, and in 1797, he was elected a member of the State Legislature. He was re-elected in 1802, and in 1804, and was Speaker of the House from 1802 to 1805. In 1806, he was again elected to the Legislature and was again elected Speaker. He was candidate for the Governorship in 1805, but was defeated. He was a candidate in 1808 and was elected. He was elected again in 1811, and in 1814, and

was the only man who ever served three terms in the Governor's Chair in the State of Pennsylvania. After the expiration of his third term, he returned to Selinsgrove, but shortly thereafter he was elected a state senator. Governor Snyder is buried in the Cemetery of the First Lutheran Church (which he helped to found), and the State of Pennsylvania has erected a fine monument to his memory there. The state also created an endowment fund, the income of which is used to keep his grave and the monument always in presentable condition. Governor Snyder was married three times. His first wife was Elizabeth Michael of Lancaster, Pa., with whom he had two children; Amelia (wife of Dr. Phineas Jenks), and the Hon. John Snyder, a soldier in the War of 1812. His second wife was Catherine, daughter of Colonel Frederick Antes, Northumberland, Pa. The date of their marriage was June 12, 1796. The children of this union were; Major Henry W. Snyder (Paymaster, United States Army); George A. Snyder, and Antes Snyder, a noted engineer and graduate of the United States Military Academy. His third wife was a widow, Mary Slough Scott, Harrisburg, Pa. The Governor's brother, John, died in Selinsgrove in 1787, and his sister, Catherine, wife of Major Anthony Selin, and another sister, Mrs. Jacob Lechner, lived there. Governor Snyder was a private in Captain Rudolph Spengler's Company of the York County Associators in 1776. In 1789, he was Captain of a company in the 5th Battalion of the Northumberland County Militia, and in 1794, he was a Major in the 3rd Regiment of the militia of the said county.

ENSIGN THOMAS SNYDER was assessed in Penn Township for the first time in 1780. At that time he was designated as a single freeman, and he so remained for several years. He was a son of Abraham Snyder, Senior, who died in Penn Township in 1793. He served as an Ensign in the 9th Pennsylvania Regiment. Continental Line.

PETER SNYDER was assessed in Beaver Township for the first time in 1789. He died in Center Township, formerly part of Beaver Township) and letters of administration were granted to Sarah Marshall, Anthony Romig, and Christopher Seebold on March 5, 1828. Several men of this name served in the Revolution.

DAVID SOLT (also Soult, Sault,

etc.,) was born on March 18, 1752, probably in Northampton County, Pa. He was assessed in Penn Township for the first time in 1793, and lived near New Berlin. He died in that section and letters of administration were granted to his son, Jacob, on October 13, 1824. His known children were; John, Jacob, Philip, George, and Michael. He applied for a pension, and his application he stated that he enlisted in Captain Warner's Company, 5th Pennsylvania Regiment, Continental Line, in 1775, and that he served in it for more than a year. He then enlisted in Captain Marion Lamar's Company, and that he served in Canada with the 1st Pennsylvania Regiment in 1776. He re-enlisted and served in the 2nd Pennsylvania Regiment, and was discharged by General Wayne, after the revolt at Trenton, N. J.

DAVID SPADE (also Spaide, Spate, Spaht, etc.) seems to have been a son of Jacob Spade. He was assessed in Penn Township for the first time in 1788. In 1802, he lived in Middleburg as did George Spade. probably his brother.

JACOB SPADE was a resident but not a landowner in Middletown, Lancaster (now Dauphin) County, Pa., from 1771 to 1773. Soon thereafter, he became a resident of what is now Penn Township and his name appeared on the Penn Township tax list for the first time in 1776. In 1787, he was taxed with 100 acres of land and personal property. In 1790, his family consisted of three males over and one under 16 years, and two females. In 1804, he was one of the overseers of the poor in Penn Township. David and George are believed to have been his sons. He served as a private in Captain John Black's Company of the Northumberland County Militia, and in May, 1780, in Lieutenant Jacob Bard's Party of Rangers on the Frontier.

ADAM SPANGLE (also Spengle, Spengel, Spangel, etc.) was probably the present name of Spangler) was assessed in Penn Township only in the year 1778. Changing county and township lines may have caused him to be assessed in Greenwood Township. Cumberland County in 1779 and 1780. It is believed that he was the father of Zachrias Spangle, mentioned below. On May 1, 1780, Adam was a private, 5th Class, 2nd Company, 7th Battalion of the Cumberland County Militia.

ZACHRIAS SPANGLE is believed to have been a son of Adam, mentioned above. He was assessed in Penn Township for the first time in 1778, and the next year in Greenwood Township, Cumberland County, and again in Penn Township in 1782. In this year he was taxed with 50 acres and personalty. In 1785, he was granted a warrant of survey for 150 acres somewhere in Northumberland County, but his name then seems to disappear. In 1800 and again in 1814, a Zachriah and Mary (Polly) Spangle had children baptized at Grubb's Lutheran Church in what is now Chapman Township. The Zachrias of this sketch served as a private in Captain John Murray's Company of the —th Pennsylvania Regiment in 1777. On Jan. 30, 1777, he was a private in Captain Benjamin Weiser's Company of the German Regiment, Continental Line, stationed at Philadelphia.

JAMES SPEAKMAN (also Spekeman, Speikman, etc.) was assessed in Penn Township for the first time in 1785, and in that year he was taxed with 100 acres and personal property.

HARMAN SPEECE (also Spees, Spies, Spiess, Speiss, etc.) was assessed as a freeman in Lebanon Township, Lancaster County, Pa., in 1782. On October 26, 1792, Philip Moor (probably Morr, and he were granted warrants of survey for 1200 acres in Northumberland Co. On December 12th of the same year he was granted a warrant for 400 acres more, and on the same day, Abraham Bollender and he were granted a warrant for another 400 acres. During the Revolution he served as a private, 2nd Class, 2nd Company, 2nd Battalion of the Lancaster County Militia. He lived in Penn Township in 1790, and his family consisted of one male over and one under 16 years, and two females. In 1796, Herman was living in Mahantango Township. It is believed that his daughter, Rebecca, (1799-1862) married John Jacob Fisher, great-grandfather of the compiler.

LIEUTENANT JACOB SPEECE was listed as a laborer in Bethel Township, Berks County, Pa., in 1767, and the next year with 4 acres and personal property in the same district. His name appeared on the Penn Township tax list for the first time in 1776. In 1781, he was taxed with 50 acres and personal property. The compiler could not find a record of this man after 1781. One party states that he lived in White Deer Township, if so, it must have been after 1782. A Daniel Spees died in that township in 1824. Jacob enlisted as a private in Captain John Clark's Company at Sunbury, Pa., on September 26, 1776. Later he served as a Lieutenant in Captain John Moll's Com-

pany of the Northumberland County Militia, and at another time he was a Lieutenant in command of a Party of Northumberland County Rangers on the Frontier.

NOTE: The compiler is very anxious to learn the names of the children of Harman and Jacob Speece, mentioned above, as well as those of John, mentioned below. Also, he would like to know the parentage of John Speece, 1789-1851, buried at Liverpool, Pa. Who was Hannah Speece who died in what is now Washington, Snyder County, Pa., in 1838?

JOHN SPEECE was assessed in Penn Township for the first time in 1782. The John who is buried at Liverpool, Pa., may have been his son. Some think the John buried at Liverpool in 1851, was a son of Harman.

FREDERICK STAHL was assessed in Mahantango Township for the first time in 1796. The compiler believes that he was a son of John Stahl and his wife, Susanna, had their son, Peter, born October 28, 1823, baptized at Grubb's church in Chapman Township.

CAPT. JOHN STAHL, was born in 1755, and died in what is now Chapman Township. Snyder County, on June 25, 1840. The compiler does not know when he first came to what is now Snyder County, but he was on the Mahantango Township tax list in 1796. Frederick seems to have been his son. It is thought that John was Captain of the 5th Company, 4th Battalion of the Northampton County Militia during all or part of the Revolution.

MATHIAS STAHL (also Stall, Stoll, Stull, Stohl, etc.) was assessed in Penn Township for the first time in 1783. In 1787, he was taxed with 100 acres and personal property. When Beaver Township was formed from the western part of Penn, in 1787, and thereafter, he was assessed there, under the name of Mathias Stull. In 1790, his family consisted of two males over and two under 16 years, and two females.

ADAM STAUB was assessed with 20 acres and personal property in Heidelberg Township, York County, in 1779. Soon thereafter he came to what is now Snyder County. In 1784, he and his wife, Eva, had their son, John George, baptized at the old Zion Lutheran Church, north of Freeburg. Adam served as a private in Captain Charles Meyer's (Moyer's Company of the Northumberland County Militia.

ADAM STEEL was assessed in

Beaver Township for the first time in 1799.

JACOB STEEL seems to have been a non resident landowner in Penn Township. It is believed that he lived in Philadelphia or Chester County. A Jacob Steel was a Lieutenant in the Chester County Militia.

JOHN STEEL seems to have been a non reisdent landowner in Penn Township. He was assessed only in the year of 1776. He may have been a native of Chester County. One of his name served in the 4th Company, 8th Battalion of the Chester County Militia.

HONORABLE FREDERICK STEESE (also Stees, Steece, Sties, Stiess, Steise, etc.) was a son of John Jacob Stiess and his wife, Margaret Eckbert. Frederick was born in 1767, probably in Lancaster County, Pa., and died at Oakland Mills, Juniata County, Pa., in August, 1839. He was buried at McAllisterville, Pa., and some years ago a church was built over his resting place. His first wife was Anna Barbara, daughter of Andrew Morr, Jr. She was born on November 7, 1772, and died in the year 1804. She is interred in one of the cemeteries at or near Freeburg. His second wife was Mary Magdalene Riblett, widow of —— ——Worthington. He had children with both wives. Frederick's parents came to what is now Snyder County in 1776, or before. and Frederick was assessed in Penn Township for the first time in 1788, and when Mahantango Township was formed, in 1796, he was assessed there. His home was at what is today Mt. Pleasant Mills. He was a mill builder and contractor and built many mills in what is now Snyder and adjoining counties. He built the mill at Mt. Pleasant Mills, and about the year 1810, sold this property to John Schnee of Lebanon County. Frederick also owned a sawmill and about 400 acres of land at the same location. In 1790, Frederick's family consisted of three males over 16. two under that age, and four females. On June 7, 1796. he was appointed a justice of the peace for Mahantango Township. Frederick owned many mills and factories driven by water power and operated by his sons and relatives, and established a big trade for his products in Reading and Philadelphia, in this he merely followed in the footsteps of his father, who had done the same. Frederick owned huge wagons drawn by teams of six horses. and many were the fatiguing trips made overland to the above mentioned cities with his products. It is said, that he fattened as many as 300 hogs in a year, and killed as many as 60 of them in one day. It is estimated that at one time he was the richest man in what is now Snyder County, with property conservatively estimated to be worth at least $200,000, but thru his generous nature, and abiding faith that does not take into consideration the frailties of human nature. He lost all, and died in actual want. He was one of the first Lutherans to settle in the Mt. Pleasant Mills section. He built a school house on the spot where the present one stands, and had it arranged with a movable partition, so that the whole could be used for church purposes. This building was constructed about 1810, and in 1818 sold to the present Lutheran congregation at that place. He owned the land on which the village of Mt. Pleasant Mills, or Fremont, now stands. He moved to what is now Paxtonville and built a grist mill and saw mill there, and some time afterward moved to Middleburg, where he operated a store. This store was later owned by his son, Frederick, who became Middleburg's first postmaster. In 1817 and 1818, he was a member of the Pennsylvania State Legislature. In 1827, in partnership with his son-in-law, "Colonel" John George Herrold, they built a one mile section of the Pennsylvania Canal from Witmer's (Dundore's) northward. In 1828, he moved to what was formerly the John George Morr farm, near Freeburg, where he operated a farm and built a grist mill. After a few years he moved to the Lost Creek Valley in Juniata County, and it is believed that he built the mill still standing at Oakland Mills, in that county. His children by his first wife were: Jacob, 1788-1833 (lived at Uniontown, Ohio); John, 1792-1862 (unmarried, lived at Pine Grove, Pa.); Frederick, 1794-1864 (in latter years he lived at Dauphin, Pa.); Mary (Mrs. John George Herrold), Benjamin, 1798-1869, (married Lydia Shaffner Greenawalt. He died in Philadelphia, Pa.); Catherine, 1800-1862 (Mrs. John Bollender. She died at Monroe, Wisconsin); Elizabeth, 1803-1852, (Mrs. Thomas Stackpole. Thomas was a native of Huntingdon County). The children by the second wife were: Henry, William, Matilda, Elijah, Thomas, Amelia, Barbara, Harriet, Sarah, Lydia, and Reuben.

Frederick was Captain of the 3rd Company, 3rd Regiment, Northumberland County Militia, on February 28, 1794. His son, Frederick, Jr., served in the War of 1812. (The compiler is a great-great-grandson of the subject of this sketch.)

JOHN JACOB STEESE (STIESS) was born in Germany and embarked for America at Rotterdam, Holland, on the British ship "Chance," Captain Charles Smith, Master, arriving at Philadelphia, where he took the English oath of allegiance on August 8, 1764. His wife was Margaret Eckbert, who was born in 1741, and died in 1824, and is buried in the Old Hassinger Cemetery, west of Middleburg. "Jacob," as he was commonly called, was born about 1738, and is supposed to have died in Philadelphia, of yellow fever, while on a business trip there. The Steese family had three children, but only two are known to the compiler, they were; Frederick and Mary, first wife of Colonel Henry Meyer of Brush Valley, Center County, Pa. Mary was born about 1765, and died in August, 1801. It is supposed that she was buried at Rebersburg, Pa. It is supposed that Jacob came to what is now Snyder County before the Revolution. In 1776, he was assessed as a resident, but not a landowner in Penn Township. It is supposed that he returned to one of the eastern counties during the Indian uprisings, but he must have returned about 1780, because. in 1781 and in 1782, he was taxed with 100 acres, a gristmill, sawmill, and personal property. After his death, in 1782, his widow was taxed with this property for a few years, and about the time their son, Frederick, became of age, 1788, he was assessed with the same property. The compiler believes that this pioneer served during the Revolutionary period, but does not know his military record. Later information indicates that the third child of John Jacob Stiess and his wife, was a daughter named Margaret, who is said to have married a man named Wining or Vining, and moved to the state of Ohio. Mary Stiess, who was the first wife of Colonel Henry Meyer, is said to have been a very strong woman, and that she personally operated a gristmill before the days of her marriage to Henry. Jacob Steese served in the Northumberland County Militia, but the poor penmanship of the time gave the name as "Jacob Stiers."

FREDERICK STEFFEN (also Steffy, Steffin, Stephen, Steffey,

etc.) was assesesd as a single freeman in Mahantango Township in 1796. He was a carpenter. If he was a son of John Adam Steffen, Sr., he was not mentioned in his will.

LEONARD STEFFEN was a son of John Adam and Agnes Steffen, mentioned below. He was assessed in Mahantango Township for the first time in 1796.

JOHN STEFFEN was a son of John Adam and Agnes Steffen. He was born about 1780, and died in Mahantango Township. His will was recorded at Sunbury, Pa., on March 12, 1810. It mentioned his wife, Elizabeth, and the following children; David, Maria, Susan.

JOHN STEFFEN (also given on the records as STEPHEN and STEPHENS) was a resident of Penn Township. He died in the year 1794, and letters of administration were granted to John Karner maybe Barner). Peter Server (Zerbe) and Peter Clemens (possibly neighbors), wrere surety for the administrator. Judging from the known residence of Clemens and Zerbe, the subject of this sketch must have lived in what is today Chapman Township.

JOHN ADAM STEFFEN was born about the year 1745, and died in what is now Chapman Township, Snyder County, Pa., in the year 1822. He was one of the earliest settlers in what is today Snyder County. His name appeared on the first tax list made for that district in 1768, and continued until 1776, when it disappeared for some years, possibly because he and family may have returned to some eastern county during the Indian uprisings in the Middle Creek and Penns Valleys. It is believed that the Steffens came from Northampton County. In 1782, he was assessed with 100 acres and personal property in Penn Township, the same was true in 1787. In 1790, his family consisted of one male over and five under 16 years. and two females. When Mahantango township was formed in 1796, he lived there. It is believed that the John Stephen who died in Penn Township in 1793 was his father. Adam's will was probated at Lewisburg, Pa., on June 12, 1822. It mentioned his wife, Agnes, and these children; Catherine (Mrs. Mathias Winkelman), John Adam Jr., Elizabeth (Mrs. Jacob Reichenbach), Leonard, Jacob, Mary, and John (whose wife was Mary ———. He died in 1810). An Adam Steffen was a Corporal in the 8th Company, 1st Battalion of the Northampton County Militia during part of the Revolution. Marand

Steffen and Prof. Harry Steffen of Selinsgrove, Pa., are descendants of this pioneer. Adam's son Jacob married Barbara ———, and they had a son Jacob, born Feb. 20, 1821, and baptized at Grubb's Church.

JOHN ADAM STEFFEN, JUNIOR, was a son of the man mentioned just above. He was born about 1785 and died in what is now Washington Township, Snyder County. His will was probated at Lewisburg, Pa., on April 18, 1826. It mentions his wife, Margaret, and the following children: Barbara (Mrs. Michael Sheffer, or Shaffer), Elizabeth, Catherine, Anna Maria, John, and Jacob.

ERNEST STEPHENSON, weaver, was assessed in Mahantango Township for the first time in 1796.

DEWALT STEININGER was assessed in Beaver Township for the first time in 1799.

JACOB STIGELMAN (also Stigleman, Steigleman, etc.) was born in 1728, in Germany. He embarked for America at Rotterdam, Holland, in the British ship "Peggy," Captain James Aber-Crombie master. They arrived at Philadelphia where Jacob took the English oath of allegiance on September 24, 1753. At the time of his arrival he was 25 years old. He was assessed as a non resident landowner in Penn Township between 1776 and 1787, and during most of the period was taxed with 200 acres. The compiler can find no evidence that he lived in the township at any time.

DANIEL STIMELY (also Stimley, Stinely, probably the name STIMELING today) was granted a warrant of survey for 100 acres of land in Northumberland (now Snyder) County on September 30, 1772. Soon thereafer he must have become a resident on it because his name was given on the Penn Township tax list in 1776. He must have been a native of Tulpehocken Township. Berks County. From 1782 to 1785. he was assessed as a non resident landowner in Penn Township, and as a resident. but not a landowner, with occupation of laborer, in Tulpehocken Township. In 1785. he was taxed with 100 acres and personal property in Penn Township, and in 1790, his family consisted of one male over and two under 16 years and two females. The Benjamin Stimely who died in Center Township in 1826 was probably his son. He served as a private in Captain Michael Weaver's Company of the Northumberland County Militia, and in Lieutenant Jacob Bard's Party of Rangers from the same

county. Descendants of his still live in Snyder County.

CONRAD STOCK (also Stuck, Stoch, etc.) is supposed to have been a relative of the other Stocks of the section. Some think he may have been a son of Melchoir Stock, Senior, if so, he died before his father, who died in 1798. He was not mentioned in the elder Melchoir's will. Conrad served in the companies of Captain John Moll and Capain John Black of the Northumberland County Militia.

GEORGE STOCK was a son of Melchoir Stock, Senior. George was born in 1754, probably in Lancaster County, Pa. He was assessed in Penn Township for the first time in 1778. In 1786, he was taxed with 100 acres and personal property, and in 1789 he was assessed in the newly fromed township of Beaver. In 1792, he received warrants for additional land in Northumberland (now Snyder) County. He served as a private in Captain John Moll's Company of the Northumberland County Militia, and in 1780, in the Ranger Parties of Lieutenant John Coleman and Lieutenant Jacob Spees. In 1833 he was a pensioner.

JOHN STOCK was a relative of the other Stocks of the section. He served as a private in Captain John Moll's Company of the Northumberland County Militia.

NATHAN STOCK was a son of Melchoir Stock, Senior. In 1790, his family consisted of one male over and three under 16 years, and four females. He lived in Penn Township at that time.

MELCHOIR STOCK, SENIOR, was granted a warrant of survey for 120 acres in Cumberland (now Snyder) County, Pa., on October 30, 1765. It is evident that he occupied it soon after this, because he was assessed as a resident of Penn Township in 1772. On May 29. 1772, he was granted a warrant of survey for 50 acres, and in 1776, one for 60 acres in Northumberland (now Snyder) County. He was one of the large landowners of the section. In 1774, he was a road cupervisor, and in 1777, a constable for Penn Township. Prior to 1790, he was one of the members of the Row's (Salem) Lutheran Church, and it is believed that he is buried in that cemetery in an unmarked grave. He died in Penn Township and his will was probated at Sunbury, Pa., on May 5. 1798. It mentions his wife, Anna Mary, and these children: Peter (who died in 1797, Melchoir, Jr. (who had

a daughter, Elizabeth, and a son, Melchoir.) Mathias, George, and Michael. Melchoir, Jr., and Daniel Rush were the executors of the will.

MECHOIR STOCK, JUNIOR, was a son of Melchoir Stock, Senior. He was assessed in Penn Township for the first time about the year 1781. In 1803, he was a road viewer, and in 1816, a road supervisor in Penn Township. In 1790, his family consisted of one male over and two under 16 years, and two females. His will was probated at Lewisburg, Pa., in 1832. It mentious his wife, Margaret, and these children; Elizabeth (Mrs. Abraham Swartzlander), Christian Conrad, and Frederick. Melchoir, Sr., in his will made in 1797, stated that Melchoir, Jr., had a son Melchoir, but this Melchoir, the third, must have died before his father because he is not mentioned in this will. Melchoir, Junior, and his wife are buried in the cemetery of the First Lutheran Church at Selinsgrove.

MICHAEL STOCK seems to have been the oldest son of Melchoir Stock, Senior, and his wife Anna Mary. Michael was assessed in Penn Township for the first time in 1771, a year before his father, and since his father was granted land in the Middle Creek Valley as early as 1765, it is supposed that Michael was his father's tenant. It is supposed that the Stocks came from Bucks or Berks County. Michael lived about halfway between the present village of Kreamer and Globe Mills, several hundred yards south of the present highway. His home was the usual log cabin. One morning in the spring of 1781, while the men and boys were at work in the fields a band of marauding Indians appeared at the cabin and killed and scalped four or five of the inmates. The pioneer, Mathias Schoch, is said to have been the first to discover the murder, and coatless, with rifle in hand, he ran to the neighbors shouting "Come quickly, the Indians have killed the Stocks." The late Mathias Dauberman stated that in childhood he heard his grandfather (probably the Revolutioner, Christian Dauberman) often relate this story. The family was buried at the place of their demise, and their graves were rudely marked, but with the changes of ownership, the small graveyard and the markers disappeared years ago. About thirty years ago the excavations where the cabin stood was still visible, but now even that seems to have been forgotten. It seems that only female members of the family were killed. History does not seem to have recorded their names, nor have relatives, or others, marked the resting place of those whose lives were sacrificed in the forward march of colonization. Michael served as a private in the companies of Captain Michael Weaver and Captain John Moll of the Northumberland County Militia, he also served in the party of Lieutenant Jacob Spees of the Northumberland County Rangers.

PETER STOCK was a son of Melchoir Stock, Senior, and his wife, Anna Maria. He was born about the year 1760 and died in 1797, just a short time after his father. It is evident that he left heirs, or he would not have been mentioned in his father's will which was made on December 25, 1797. He was assessed in Penn Township for the first time in 1778, and in 1781, was taxed with 235 acres and personal property. He served in the organizations of Captain John Black and Lieutenant John Coleman of the Northumberland County Militia and Rangers.

ADAM STOVER was born in 1751 and died in what is now Haines Township, Center County, Pa., in 1824. He lived in Penn Township before 1780, but presumably only for a short time. He was one of the earliest settlers in the Penns Valley. The "Lower Fort" was built on his farm, not far from Woodward. He is buried in the Wolf's Chapel Cemetery and his grave is marked. He served in Captain Charles Meyer's (Moyer's) Company of the Northumberland County Militia.

ANDRIES STOBER (ANDREW STOVER) was born on July 5, 1750, and died in or near Selinsgrove, Pa., on November 17, 1817. He is buried in the cemetery of the First Lutheran Church in Selinsgrove. It is believed that he did not come to what is now Snyder County until after the Revolution. An Arnst Stober served in Captain Samuel Roberts Company of the Chester County Militia, in 1782.

FREDERICK STOVER was born on June 21, 1759, and died in what is now Haines Township, Center County, Pa., on September 9, 1837. He lived near the village of Aaronsburg, and is buried in the cemetery at Wolf's Chapel, near that place. He came to Penn Township before 1780, and moved into the Penns Valley in 1786. He served in Captain Charles Meyer's Company of the Northumberland County Militia.

JOHN STOVER was born on July 3, 1753, and died in or near Selinsgrove, Pa., on July 20, 1823. He is interred in the cemetery of the First Lutheran Church in Selinsgrove. John lived in what is now Penn Township before 1780, and is supposed to have been a brother of the men mentioned above. He served ed as a private in the 2nd Company, 4th Battalion of the Northumberland County Militia.

WILLIAM STOVER was assessed in Penn Township for the first time in 1794. He may have been a son of John Stover (1753-1823).

ADAM STRAUB (also Straub, Stroup, Straup, Stroop, etc.) lived in Penn Township in 1790, and his family consisted of one male over and three under 16 years, and six females.

ANDREW STRAUB is believed to have been an older son of Peter Straub (1724-1804). When or where he was born or when he died is unknown to the compiler. However, it is known that about 1796, he laid out the village of Freeburg, Snyder County, Pa., which at first was known as "Straubstown" but later changeu to Freeburg (probably from Freiburg the supposed ancestral home, in Germany, of his father, Peter). When the plot of Freeburg was surveyed. Andrew gave several acres of ground for a church and cemetery in the center of the town. This is today known as St. Peters Lutheran and Reformed Church. He is buried in the cemetery which he donated to the church, and a grateful posterity has erected a small monument to his memory.

ANDREW STRAUB. An Andrew Straub was assessed in Beaver Township for the first time in 1789, and the compiler believes that this was a different man. In that year he was taxed with a gristmill and two stills. An Andrew Straub had served in the Northampton County Militia, during the Revolution. He may have been a son of Jacob, and nephew of Peter.

CHARLES STRAUB. SENIOR. was assessed as a resident of Lynn Twp., Northampton Co., in 1786. In 1790, his family consisted of two males over and three under 16 years and four females. He served in Captain Henry Geiger's Company of the Northampton County Rangers.

CHARLES STRAUB, JUNIOR. was assessed in Penn Township for the first time in 1787, and in that year was designated as a single freeman. In 1790, he was married and he and his wife had two daughters. In 1796, when Mahantan-

go township was formed he was assessed there. It is supposed that he was a son of Charles, Senior, who came to Penn Township before 1790.

GEORGE P. STRAUB was a son of Peter Straub, Sr. George was born in what is now Washington Township, Snyder County, Pa., on June 13, 1769, and died in the same section on September 9, 1853. His wife, Catherine, was born on June 25, 1769, and died on December 4, 1837. Both are interred in the St. Peter's Cemetery in Freeburg.

JACOB STRAUB was assessed in Beaver Township for the first time in 1789. He may have been a son of Peter, Senior.

JOHN STRAUB seems to have been one of the older children of Peter Straub, Senior. John was probably born about the year 1754, and was assesstd in Penn Township for the first time in 1776. He was a single freeman at the time. In 1787, he was taxed with 100 acres and personal property. He died in Penn Township in 1824. He served as a private in Captain Benjamin Weiser's Company of the German Regiment, Continental Line, stationed at Philadelphia, Pa., on January 30, 1777. He served in the companies of Captain Michael Weaver and Captain Charles Meyer of the Northumberland County Militia, and in the Northumberland County Ranger organizations of Captain John Snyder and Lieutenant John Coleman.

PETER STRAUB, JUNIOR, was a son of Peter Straub, Senior. The younger man was born in what is now Washington County, Pa., on March 18, 1776, and died on October 10, 1845. His wife was Anna Marie, daughter of John Haines and his wife, Regina Schuster. Anna Marie was born on July 4, 1772, and died on January 28, 1845. Both are buried in St. Peters Cemetery in Freeburg. They had no children of their own, but raised Jacob Haines a nephew of Mrs. Straub. Jacob was the grandfather of Mrs. Dennis R. Fisher, of Selinsgrove.

PETER STRAUB, SENIOR, was the son of Peter Straub who was born in Germany and embarked for America in the British ship "Pennsylvania Merchant," Captain John Stedman, master, at Rotterdam, Holland, with his wife and sons Peter (1724-1804) and Jacob. The wife was named Maria. They arrived at the port of Philadelphia where the older Peter took the English oath of allegiance on September 18, 1733. The Peter of this sketch was born in Germany on November 8, 1724. came to America with his parents in 1733, and lived in one of the eastern counties, and prior to 1768, came to what is now Washington Township, where he died on September 15, 1804. He is buried in the St. Peters Cemetery in Freeburg, on land donated by his son, Andrew. In 1770, Peter Straub, Andrew Morr, and Casper Roush applied to the proprietors of the colony for land for a church and school, and in 1774, a tract of 43 acres was granted to them, about a mile north of the present site of the village of Freeburg. Soon thereafter they built a combined church and school building. which, however, was never fully completed, but regular services were held there from about 1781 on, at least a baptismal record was kept from that date. Peter was overseer of the poor for Penn Township in the years 1773, 1774, and 1775. In 1781, he was taxed with 200 acres of land and personal property. In 1785, he lived about three miles north-west of the present site of Freeburg, where later Jacob Haines lived. He had a one-story weatherboarded house, painted red. It is said that he had many unique characteristics, such as wearing home-made clothing only, he made his own straw hats, used strings instead of buttons on his clothes, cooked before an open fire on the hearth, made his own hickory splint chairs. used wooden spoons and bowls of his own manufacture. etc. His known sons were: Andrew, John, George P., and Peter, Jr. He served as a private in Captain Charles Meyer's (Moyer's) Company of Militia and Rangers from Northumberland County. In 1790, his family consisted of two males over and two under 16 years and two females, and indication that one of his sons and wife, with two chldren lived with him.

JOHN NICHOLAS STRAUSSER (also Strawser, Strauser, Strouser, Strousser, Strosser, etc.) was commonly called "Honnickle." He was assessed in Penn Township form an early date and in 1796, he was assessed in Mahantango Township and his occupation stated as jockey. It is supposed that he was born about 1754 and died in 1814. The place of his burial is supposed to be the pioneer cemetery oppisite the lower Herrold schnolhouse in Union Township. He served in Captain Ritter's Company of the Berks County Militia in 1780.

MATHIAS STRAYER (also Straier, Straher Streer, Straer, Strehr,

etc.) was assessed in Penn Township for the first time in 1776, In 1781, he was taxed with 200 acres and personal property. The same was true in 1787. In 1789, he was assessed in Beaver Township, and in 1790, his family consisted of three males over 16 years and five females. He died in Beaver Township in 1791, and his will is on record at Sunbury, Pa. It mentions his wife, Mary Margahet, and son, Andrew, who was the executor of the will. It refers to other children, but does not give their names. He served as a private in Captain Michael Motz's Company of the Northumberland County Militia.

CHRISTIAN STROAM (also Strom, Strohm, Strome, etc.,) in 1774. was listed as owning 200 acres and personal property in Lebanon Township, Lancaster Co., Pa. In 1776, he was a nonresident landowner in Penn Township. The same was true in 1788. He may never have lived in the township.

JOHN STROAM seemingly was a son of Christian, mentioned above. It is believed that he was a tenant on his father's land for a short time.

ABRAHAM STUMP, SENIOR, in 1771, lived in Heidelberg Township, Lancaster County, Pa., and on Dec. 2, 1773, was granted a warrant of survey for 100 acres in Northumberland (now Snyder) County. His name appeared on a tax list in Penn Township for the first time in 1778, but it is believed that he was a nonresident landowner at the time, andthat he never resided in the district.

ABRAHAM STUMP (also Stumpf, Stumph, etc.,) was a son of Abraham Stump, Senior. He came to Penn Township prior to 1785, and in that year was taxed with 150 acres and personal property. In 1801, he contributed to the fund for the erection of the First Lutheran Church of Selinsgrove. In 1802, he lived in the village of Freeburg. In 1790, his family consisted of one male over and four under 16 years, and three females.

CASPER STUMP was assessed as a laborer in Tulpehocken Township, Berks County, Pa., in 1767, and for a number of years thereafter. In 1776, he was a nonresident landowner in Penn Township. In 1781, he served as a private in Captain Jonathan Reigle's Company of the Berks Co. Militia.

FREDERICK STUMP lived in what is now Snyder County before

1768. His name was on the tax list for that year. On January 10, 1768, he and John Eisenhauer (Ironcutter,) in a drunken brawl, murdered six friendly Indians at the mouth of Middle Creek. The following day he and Eisenhauer ascended the Middle Crek to the present site of Middleburg, and murdered four more in cold blood. A day or two later, while visiting George Gabriel's tavern on the bank of the Susquehanna near the present site of Selinsgrove, Stump William Blythe, a former officer in the service of the Province of Pennsylvania, then living near the place of the murder, made an investigation and discovered the bodies of some of the dead. He made a report to the Provincial Council at Philadelphia, and the council sent Captain William Patterson and a party of men to arrest the culprits. They were lodged in the Cumberland County jail at Carlisle, for Snyder County was then still a part of that division. It seems that friends released the murderers, and Governor Penn offered a reward of two hundred pounds for their recapture. Tradition has it that Stump went to Virginia, and that he died there many years later. Probably no more dastardly crime was ever enacted against peaceful Indians in any section. Frederick according to tradition founded the town of Fredericksburg, Lebanon Co., Pa., in 1758.

JACOB STUMP, shoemaker, was a native of Albany or Greenwich Township, Berks County, or he may have been a son of William Stump of Beaver Township. He was assessed in Penn Township for first time in 1799.

WILLIAM STUMP was assessed in Penn Township for the first time in 1785. In 1787, he was taxed with 350 acres and personal property. In 1789, he lived in Beaver Township and was taxed with a distillery in addition to other property. The same year he was one of the petitioners for the election of a justice of the peace for Beaver Township. In 1790, his family consisted of one male over and three under 16 years, and five females.

HENRY STYERS (also Stiers, Stires, etc.,) was assessed in Penn Township before 1780. In 1783, a Henry Styers was assessed in Whitpain Township, Philadelphia County. It is believed that they were the same man, and that he was a nonresident landowner in Penn Township.

JACOB STYERS was assessed

in Penn Township in 1780 and 1781 but there is evidence to indicate that he lived there at an earlier date. He may have been a son of Henry, mentioned above, and been a tenant on his father's land. He served as a private in the companies of Captain John Moll and Captain John Black of the Northumberland County Militia or Rangers.

HENRY SUMMEROUSER was assessed in Penn Township only in the year of 1776.

ELIJAH SUTTON was probably a son of Stephen Sutton of the city of Lancaster, Pa. It seems that he was a tenant on his father's land in what is now Snyder County in 1778. He served as a private in Captain John Moll's Company of the Northumberland County Militia.

ISAAC SUTTON seems to have been a brother of Elijah, mentioned above, and probably a tenant on the Stphen Sutton land, too. He served in Captain John Moll's Company from Northumberland County.

IZAIAH SUTTON was taxed in Penn Township in 1781. It ns believed that he was a brother of the man named above.

STEPHEN SUTTON was taxed in Lancaster, Pa., in 1771, and on December 3, 1774, he was granted a warrant of survey for 300 acres in Northumberland (now Snyder) County. In 1776, he was taxed as a nonresident landowner in Penn Township. It is supposed that his four sons became tenants on his land in what is now Snyder County for a short time.

ZACHRIAH SUTTON was taxed in Penn Township in 1781, and seems to have been one of the four sons of Stephen Sutton.

JOHN SWARTZ, SENIOR, (also Schwartz, Schwerz, Swartz, etc.) The name Schwartz translated into English is Black, and he may have been the man whose name appears on the Revolutionary rolls as Captain John Black. John Swartz was assessed in Penn Township for the first time in 1772, he was listed as the owner of 50 acres of land and personal property. In 1796, when Mahantango Township was formed he and Martin, Abraham, Peter, and John, Jr., probably his sons were assessed there. It is believed that he is buried in an unmarked grave in the Grubb's Church Cemetery. In 1780, he was a private in Ensign Simon Herrold's Party of the Northumberland County Rangers serving on the Frontier.

JOHN SWARTZ, JUNIOR, seems

to have been a son of John Swartz Senior. He was assessed in Penn Township for the first time about 1792, and when Mahantango Township was formed, in 1796, he lived there. His wife was named Maria, and she is supposed to have been a daughter of Henry Meiser. Three of their children were baptized at Grubb's Church. The dates of their birth were John Philip, April 30. 1792; Anna, Feb. 22, 1795, and Henry, April 15, 1797.

MARTIN SWARTZ was probably a son of John Swartz, Sr. He was assessed in Penn Township for the first time in 1783. In 1796, when Mahantango Township was formed, he was taxed there. He died in that township and letters of administration in his estate were granted to John Swartz on October 31, 1804. Maria Eva, a daughter of Martin and his wife was born on March 16, 1800. and baptized soon thereafter at Grubb's Lutheran Church in what is now Chapman Township. Two of their sons were named Fred and Martin.

PETER SWARTZ seemingly was a son of John Swartz, Senior. He lived in Penn Township as early as 1780, and when Mahantango Township was formed in 1796, he was assessed there. His wife was Margaret, probably Margaret, daughter of Jacob Haffich, Senior. Peter served as a private in the companies of Captain John Snyder and Captain Michael Weaver of the Northumberland County Militia.

JOHN SWIFT was a nonresident owner of Snyder County lands. As early as 1760 he held a patent for the land where Beavertown now stands. As early as 1776, he was taxed with these lands and in 1781, he owned 900 acres. About 1800, he soon thereafter, Jacob Lechner, surveyor, and first postmaster in Selinsgrove, plotted a townsite for Swift and the place was named "Swifttown," but later it was changed to Beavertown. One of the streams in the vicinity still bears the name of "Swift Run." At least three men of the name of John Swift served in the Revolutionary Forces from Pennsylvania.

ALBRIGHT SWINEFORD (also Schweinford, Schweinfurth, etc.) was born in Germany on February 16, 1728. He sailed for America from Rotterdam, Holland, in the British ship "Henrietta," Captain John Ross, master, and arrived at Philadelphia, where he took the English oath of allegiance on October 22 1754. He died in the village of Swineford (part of Middleburg,) Pa., on October 15,

1810. His wife was named Margaret. He and a number of the members of his family are buried in the Swineford Private Cemetery on the land which he once owned, but now the property of Thomas Bower. In 1773, Albright lived at Middletown, Lancaster (now Dauphin) County, Pa. His name appeared on the Penn Township tax list for the first time in 1778, and in 1781, he was taxed with 670 acres of land, personal property, a sawmill. and a gristmill. In 1790, his family consisted of one male over and one under 16 years, two females, and three slaves. In 1794, he was granted a warrant of survey for an additional 400 acres of land in Northumberland (now Snyder) County . In 1789, he was appointed a member of the board for the removal of debris from the Middle Creek. In 1792, he was a road viewer, and in 1802, one of the overseers of the poor for Penn Township. The children of Albright were: John (1758-1805); George Michael (1764-1812); Jacob (1769-1826); Peter (who had a son Samuel,) and Catherine (Mrs. John Cummings.) In September, 1777, Albright enlisted in Captain John Rutherford's Company, 4th Battalion, of the Lancaster County Militia. His son George Michael was a drummer boy in the same company.

GEORGE MICHAEL SWINEFORD, was a son of Albright Swineford, mentioned above. He was born in what is now Dauphin County, Pennsylvania, in 1764. He came to what is now Snyder County with his parents in 1778. He was assessed in Penn Township for the first time in 1786. and was designated as a single freeman. A year later he owned some land but was still unmarried. In 1790, his family consisted of one male over and one under 16 years, and two females. In 1795, he was one of the petitioners asking for the formation of Mahantango Township. George died in what was then Center Township on April 5, 1818. His will is on record at Lewisburg, Pa., and mentions his wife, Susanna, and the following children: Polly (Mrs. Henry Smith), Elizabeth (Mrs. John Bachman), John, George, Philip, Israel, and Margaret. On August 12. 1777, when only thirteen years old, he enlisted as drummer boy in Captain John Rutherford's Company, 4th Battalion of the Lancaster County Militia. This company marched from Middletown to Philadelphia to enter the Continental Service. His father and brother, John, were members of the same company. In May, 1780, he served as a private in Lieutenant Jacob Bard's Party of the Northumberland County Rangers. George is buried in the Swineford Private Cemetery at Middleburg, and his grave is marked.

JACOB SWINEFORD was a son of Albright Swineford. He was born about the year 1769, probably in what is now Dauphin County, Pa. He came to what is now Snyder County with his parents in 1778. He was murdered in Lebanon, Pa., on July 4, 1826. He and his son had taken 380 sheep to that city, most of whom had been sold. He was struck down and killed, at an alley on Hill Street. by three men, who robbed him of between $400 and $500. A purse containing $80 was overlooked by the assailants. He was assessed in Penn Township for the first time about the year 1792. Letters of administration in his estate were granted to George Aurand and Jacob Fryer (supposedly his sons-in-law) on July 19, 1826.

JOHN SWINEFORD was one of the older children of Albright Swineford. He was born in what was then Lancaster County, Pa., on April 16, 1758, and died near what is now Middleburg, Pa., on January 15, 1805. He came to what is now Snyder County with his parents in 1778, and was assessed in Penn Township for the first time in 1780. For a number of years he did not own any land himself, but assisted his father in his numerous enterprises. In 1790, John's family consisted of one male over and one under 16 years, and six females. In 1795, he was one of the petitioners for the formation of Mahantango Township. About 1800, he laid out the village of Swineford. which was named for him. He died and is buried in the village which he founded. On August 12. 1777, he was a corporal in Captain John Rutherford's Company, 4th Battalion of the Lancaster County Militia. This was the same organization in which his father and brother George served.

PETER SWINEFORD was one of the younger sons of Albright Swineford. He is supposed to have been born in what is now Dauphin County, Pa., and came to what is now Snyder County in 1778, with his parents. He was assessed in Beaver Township in 1790, and at that time his family consisted of one male over and one under 16 years, and one female. He had a son named Samuel.

MICHAEL SWINGLE, SENIOR. (the present day spelling of this name is Swengle) was born about

the year 1720, in Germany, and died in what is now Snyder County, in 1794. He was a son of Nicholas Swingle, born in 1696. and a brother of George, born in 1726. Nicholas sailed for America from Rotterdam, Holland, in the British ship "Samuel," Captain Hugh Percy, master, arriving at Philadelphia, Pa., where he took the English oath of allegiance on December 3, 1740. Michael's wife was Elizabeth ————. She was born on October 26, 1745, and died on October 26, 1823. Both are buried in the Hassinger Old Cemetery, west of Middleburg. Michael's name appeared on the Penn Township tax list for the first time in 1771. On November 11. 1772, he was granted a warrant of survey for 50 acres in Northumberland (now Snyder) County. On September 12, 1792, he was granted a warrant of survey for 60 acres in Snyder County. On January 2, 1795, his wife was appointed administrator of his estate.

MICHAEL SWINGLE, JUNIOR, (now Swengle) was a son of Michael Swengle, Senior, and his wife, Elizabeth. The younger Michael was born on July 13, 1774, in what is now Snyder County, Pa., and died on April 6, 1851. His wife. Esther ————, was born on May 28, 1777, and died on March 3, 1858. Both are buried in the Hassinger Old Cemetery, west of Middleburg. Michael, Junior, was assessed in Beaver Township for the first time in 1796. John (1805-1875) seems to have been a son of Michael, Junior.

GEORGE SWOPE (also Swobe, Swoab, Swob, Swop, etc.) was a resident of Longswamp Township. Berks County, Pa., in 1767. His name appeared on the Penn Township tax list for the first time in 1776. In 1781 and 1782 he was taxed with 50 acres and personal property. His name does not again appear. A George Swope was a private in Captain Henry Shade's Company of the Pennsylvania Troops at Kings Bridge. New York, on August 1, 1776.

ISAAC TAYLOR was assessed in Beaver Township in 1790, and his family consisted of one male over and one under 16 years, and four females.

GEORGE THOMAS lived in Penn Township before 1780. In 1789, he lived in Beaver Township. It is supposed that he was a brother of John Thomas. In 1790, his family consisted of one male over and three under 16 years, and three females. He served as a private in the companies of Captain Michael Weaver and Captain Mich-

ael Motz of the Northumberland County Militia, and in the command of Lieutenant Jacob Spees of the Northumberland County Rangers.

SERGEANT JOHN THOMAS was assessed in Penn Township for the first time in 1778, and it is believed that he was a brother of George Thomas, mentioned above. In 1781, he was taxed with 200 acres and personal property in Penn Township. and in 1787, with 380 acres and personalty. In 1790, his family consisted of two males over and one under 16 years, and seven females. He died in Penn Township in 1812. He served as a private in Captain Michael Motz's Company of the Northumberland County Militia, and as a Sergeant in Lieutenant Jacob Spees' Company of Rangers from the same county. He was a pensioner.

JOHN THORNTON came to Penn Twp., after 1790. It is believed that he was the father of John Thornton, the Revolutionary soldier. The elder John died in Penn Township in 1798.

JOHN THORNTON, believed to have been the son of John Thornton, mentioned above, was assessed in Penn Township for the first time in 1791. In 1796, when Mahantango Township was formed, he was assessed there. He lived in the vicinity of the present village of Dundore in Union Township. He married Magdalene, the daughter of Peter Witmer, Senior. John died in 1816, and his wife was appointed administrator of his estate. In 1777. he served as a private in the Pennsylvania Artillery Regiment. In 1790 his family consisted of one male over and three under 16, and one female. A John Thornton and Jacob Keiser were sureties for the administrator. Mrs. Thornton.

JOHN TRAUB, SENIOR, (also Troub, Troup, Traup, Troop, etc.) lived in Penn Township before 1790. When Mahantango Township was formed in 1796, he lived there. His wife was Anna Maria Hupman (or Hoffman.) and their daughter, Christina, born on May 15, 1791, was baptized at Grubb's Church in what is now Chapman Township. In 1790, Peter's family consisted of one male over and two under 16 years, and four females.

GEORGE TREASTER was assessed in Penn Township for the first time in 1778. He may have been a son of Martin Treaster who died in 1782.

JACOB TREASTER may also have been a son of Martin. He was assessed in Penn Township for the first time in 1778. He lived in what is now Monroe Township, and in 1789, he was one of the petitioners for having that part of Buffalo Township annexed to Penn Township. In 1801, he contributed to the fund for the erection of the First Lutheran Church of Selinsgrove. He served in the companies of Captain Michael Motz and Captain Michael Weaver of the Northumberland County Militia.

JOHN TREASTER lived in Beaver Township in 1790, and his family consisted of one male over and one under 16 years, and five females.

MARTIN TREASTER (also Trester, Treester, Troester, etc.) was a native of Lancaster County, Pa. He came to Penn Township in 1771 or 1772, and in the latter year was granted a Tavern license in Penn Township, along with Peter Hosterman and George Wolf. He died in Penn Township in 1781, and Elizabeth Treaster, probably his wife, was appointed administrator of his estate. It seems that she refused to serve, and Jacob Treaster and George Wolf were appointed in her stead. If this is not true, then there must have been two Martin Treasters living in Penn Township, probably father and son, and they died within a year of each other. Later infromation proves that Martin, Jr., died in October 1781, leaving six children: Christina, Mary, George, Martin, John, and Catherine.

MICHAEL TREASTER, SENIOR, lived in the western part of Snyder County. In 1790, he lived in what is now Beaver Township, and his family consisted of three males over and two under 16 years, and six females.

MICHAEL TREASTER, Junior, may have been a son of Michael, Senior. On October 24, 1771, he married Rosina Bickle (maybe a daughter of Tobias Bickle, Sr.), according to the records of the Christ Lutheran Church of Stouchsburg, Berks County, Pa. This would indicate that he was a native of Berks County. Michael was assessed in Penn Township for the first time in 1776. In 1781, he was taxed with 200 acres and personal property. In 1790, his family consisted of one male over and five under 16 years, and two females. He served as a private in Captain Charles Moyer's Company and in Lieutenant Jacob Spees' Party of the Northumberland County Rangers.

WILLIAM TREASTER was a son of Martin Treaster or of Michael Treaster, Senior. He lived in Penn Township before 1780. In 1790, his

family consisted of one male over and two under 16 years, and two females. He served as a private in Captain Michael Motz's Company of the Northumberland County Militia.

PETER TREMGEL was assessed in Penn Township only in the year 1780.

MATHIAS TRENKLE was assessed in Penn Township only in the year 1780.

CONRAD TREWITZ was born in 1750, and died in 1830. He is buried in the Portzline Cemetery in Perry Township, and his grave is marked "C. T." He came to Penn Township in 1776, or before. He enlisted in Captain Benjamin Weiser's Company, German Regiment, Continental Line, on August 15, 1776, and served under Colonel Hunsicker until Hunsicker deserted to the British. Later Colonel Weldner commanded this regiment, and Conrad served with him until January, 1781, when he was discharged by General Muhlenberg in New Jersey. Trewitz applied for a pension. Michael Yeisley stated that he and Trewitz were messmates in Weiser's Company, and it seems that the pension was granted.

FREDERICK TRIAN (also Trion, Tryon, Tryan, etc.) was assessed in Penn Township for the first time in 1794. In 1801 he contributed to the fund for the erection of the First Lutheran Church of Selinsgrove. In 1802, he was one of the overseers of the poor in Penn Township.

JACOB TRIAN seems to have been a relative of Frederick Trian, mentioned above. Jacob lived in Penn Township in 1786, or before. Mary Magdalene, daughter of Jacob and Barbara "Trigan" was baptized at the old Zion Lutheran Church, north of Freeburg, in 1786. Jacob died in Penn Township and letters of administration in his estate were granted to Daniel Pennebacker (a son-in-law) and Daniel Hackenberg on January 24, 1814. Jacob and Barbara Trian had these daughters: Susanna Barbara (Mrs. Christian Mowerer of Spring township, Adams County, Ohio); Mary, (Mrs. Philip Roush of Penn Township, now Snyder County); Polly, (Mrs. Jacob Repass of Center Township, now Snyder County, Pa.); Sarah (Mrs. Daniel Wittenmeyer, or maybe Pannebacker, of Freeburg, Pa.); Elizabeth (Mrs. Abraham Mertz of Penn and Mahantango Townships, now Snyder County, Pa.), and Margaret Trion (who lived in Adams County, Ohio, in 1816).

PAUL TRIMMER was assessed in Beaver Township for the first time in 1789. The same year he was one of the petitioners asking for the eelction of a justice of the peace in that district. In 1790, his family consisted of one male over and three under 16 years, and three females.

GEORGE TROUTNER, SENIOR, (also Scroutner). It is sometimes believed that this is the same name as Troutman today. George was an early settler in Penn Township, and in 1774, held the office of constable. In 1784, he was assessed with 300 acres of land and personal property. It is believed that he is the man who served in Captain Michael Weaver's Company of the Northumberland County under the name of "George Scroutner."

GEORGE TROUTNER, JUNIOR, evidently was a son of the man mentioned above. In 1781, he was assessed in Penn Township for the first time, and designated as a single freeman. In 1790, he lived in Center County, and his family consisted of two males over 16 years, and one female. It is believed that his father lived with him at the time. On January 30, 1777, he was a private in Captain Benjamin Weiser's Company of the German Regiment, Continental Line. In 1780, he served in the Northumberland County Rangers under Lieutenant Jacob Spees.

JOHN TROXEL seems to have been a native of Lancaster County, Pa. He was assessed in Beaver Township for the first time in 1794. In 1790, he lived elsewhere in Northumberland County and his family consisted of three males over and one under 16 years, and four females. The village of Troxelville was founded by this man, or his son of the same name. He served as a private in the Colonel's Company of the 10th Pennsylvania Regiment, Continental Line, in August, 1778.

JOHN TUCK (also Duck, Dock, etc.) lived in Penn Township in 1790, and his family consisted of two males over and three under 16 years, and four females. One of his sons was Benjamin Duck, who died in 1848. Benjamin was married to Mary Margaret, daughter of Jacob Menges and Catherine, daughter of the pioneer, John George Roush.

JOHN GEORGE ULRICH, SENIOR, was assessed as a resident and landowner in Tulpehocken Township, Berks County, Pa., in 1767 and 1768. It is believed that he is the same man to whom a warrant of survey for 150 acres was granted in Lancaster County, Pa., on October 10, 1738, this was before the formation of Berks County. There is no evidence that this man ever lived in what is now Snyder County, but it is believed that he was one of the earliest non resident landowners in what is now Penn Township, and that his son of the same name became a tenant on this land.

LIEUTENANT JOHN GEORGE ULRICH, JUNIOR, was born on February 3, 1753, supposedly in Tulpehocken Township, Berks County, Pa., and died on April 17, 1824, near Selinsgrove, Pa. He married Catherine Laudenslager, who survived him. He came to what is now Penn Township before 1776. A sketch in a local history states that when he settled in the township some of the Indians still remained, and that he had sufficient prudence and foresight to extend to them a friendly welcome whenever they approached his cabin. This friendly relation seems to have stood him in good stead, because an attack on him and his family was planned by hostile Indians, but a friendly one told him of the anticipated attack and advised him and his family to leave. Not desiring to lose his crops, he sent his family to a place of safety and himself remained on the farm. The attack was made, as planned, but no harm came to him. The Ulrich spring, just west of the town of Selinsgrove, and about a fourth of a mile north of the Susquehanna University campus, was frequently visited by the Indians. An Indian path led from the Middle Creek, past the spring, and over the hills to the Buffalo Valley. Part of the campus of Susquehanna University and the ground on which the home of the compiler stands was once part of the Ulrich holdings. Descendants of the original owner still occupy part of the original acres. In 1789, George was a fence viewer in Penn Township. In 1790, his family consisted of one male over and four under 16 years, and three females. In 1801, he and his son contributed to the fund for the erection of the First Lutheran Church in Selinsgrove, Pa. His will was made on March 25, 1825, and probated at Lewisburg, Pa., on April 6. 1826. This would indicate that the date of his death as shown on his tombstone in the cemetery of the First Lutheran Church in Selinsgrove must be incorrect. He and his wife are both buried in the old cemetery of the above mentioned church. George's will mentions the following children: Benjamin, John, George, Daniel, Jonathan, Margaret, born Oct. 16, 1778, (Mrs. Adam Good), and Elizabeth (Mrs. Peter Bergstresser). His son, John, and son-in-law, Peter Bergstresser, were executors of the will. In 1776, John George was a private in Captain John Clark's Company of the Northumberland County Associators. At a later date he was a Lieutenant in Captain Michael Weaver's Company of the Northumberland County Militia. Descendants of this pioneer are numerous in Snyder and surrounding counties, and in the western states.

ANDREW ULSH, (also Ulce, etc). was assessed in what is now Snyder County in 1771, but due to indefinite township and county lines, he probably lived in what was then Greenwood Township of Cumberland County. He was assessed there with 61 acres and personal property in 1778. John and Jacob, who lived in what is now Snyder County in 1790, are believed to have been his sons.

ROBERT VANCE seems to have been a native of Cumberland County. He was assessed in Mahantango Township for the first time in 1796.

DANIEL VAN HORN was assessed in Penn Township for the first time in 1785, when he was taxed with 50 acres and personal property. In 1789, he lived in Beaver Township, and in that year was one of the petitioners praying for the election of a justice of the peace for the new township of Beaver. In 1790, his family consisted of one male over and five under 16 years, and seven females. Some of the Van Horn family still lived in Snyder County in 1935.

JACOB WAGNER was a brother of Peter Wagner, Senior. He lived in Beaver Township before 1800.

PETER WAGNER, SENIOR, was a resident of Beaver Township before 1800. He had a brother named Jacob. Peter was a son-in-law of Adam Regar, of Beaver Springs. Peter died in Beaver Township and his will was probated at Sunbury, Pa., on July 6. 1804. It mentions his wife, Marie Margaret Regar, and their children, Susanna and Peter, Junior.

JAMES WALES was one of the older children of John Wales. He was a millwright, and probably was born about 1777. He was assessed in Penn Township for the first time in 1799. His father was a Revolutionary soldier and is buried at New Berlin.

JOHN WALES (also given as Walls and Wallis, etc.) seems to have been a native of York County. He was assessed in Penn Township for the first time in 1776. He seems to have left what is now Snyder County in 1782, and in 1783 lived in Dover Township, York County. He returned at a later date and died in 1798. His will was probated at Sunbury, Pa., on December 12, 1798, and mentions his wife, Anna Mary, who died in Center Township on February20, 1827, and the following children: James, John, Joseph, Jacob, Sarah, and Susanna (who had died prior to the making of his will on November 22, 1798). John was a farmer. In 1795, he was one of the petitioners for the formation of Mahantango Township. He received depreciation pay for services in the Northumberland County Militia. John, his wife, and some of their children are buried in the old cemetery at New Berlin.

SAMUEL WALLIS (also Walles, Wallace, etc.) was assessed as a non resident landowner in Penn Township from 1776 to 1787, and possibly later. In 1785, he was taxed with 900 acres. He lived in Sunbury. He served in Captain Hepburn's Company of the Northumberland County Militia, or Rangers.

DAVID WALTER was a son of Jacob Walter, Senior. He was born on February 10, 1761, and died in what is now Center Township of Snyder County, on October 9, 1838. Frederick and John D. Walter, probably sons, were administrators of his estate. He was buried in the Fry (Salem) Church cemetery in Center Township. He was assessed in Penn Twp., for the first time in 1786, and at the time was designated as a single freeman. In 1790, his family consisted of one male over and two under 16 years, and one female. In May, 1780, he served in Lieutenant John Coleman's Party of Northumberland County Rangers, and at another time he served in the company of Captain John Black. On Maf 2, 1833, he was granted a pension for his services as a ranger and in the militia.

JACOB WALTER, SENIOR, was born in Germany on January 15, 1729, and died in what was then Beaver Township of Northumberland (now Snyder) County on January 23, 1803. He married Marie Kauffman in July, 1757. Both are buried in the Hassinger Old Cemetery, west of Middleburg, Pa. The above data was taken from tombstones in existence in 1884, but since have become indecipherable. On June 24, 1772, Jacob was granted a warrant of survey for 200 acres about a mile west of the present town of Middleburg, and soon thereafter he and his family became residents on it. In 1787, he was assessed with 400 acres and personal property. Because of the changing township lines he lived in Beaver Township in 1789. His land adjoined that of John Yost Kern, also one of the earliest pioneers in the Middle Creek Valley. It is said that for many years, when a minister came into that valley, divine services were held at the home of Jacob Walter. In 1790, Jacob's family consisted of five males over and five under 16 years, and one female. A Jacob Walter was listed among the New Levies, and an other served in Captain Peter Grubb's Company of the Lancaster County Militia. Neither of these may have been the subject of this sketch.

JACOB WALTER, JUNIOR, was a son of Jacob Walter, Senior. He was assessed in Penn Township for the first time in 1786, and was designated as a single freeman at the time.

JOHN WALTER seems to have been a son of Jacob Walter, Senior. He was assessed in Penn Township for the first time in 1793.

LUDWIG (LEWIS) WALTER (also Walther, Wallter,) etc. was assessed as a freeman in Cocalico Township, Lancaster County, Pa., in 1772, and later seems to have lived in York County. In 1776, but not thereafter he was assessed as a non resident landowner in Penn Township. It is believed that he was a brother of Jacob Walter, Senior.

PHILIP WALTER is believed to have been a son of Jacob, Senior. He was assessed in Penn Township for the first time in 1793. He died in Center Township in 1819. Henry and John were his sons.

CASPER WANNAMAKER was a resident of Beaver Township before 1790, in that year, his family consisted of one male over and two under 16 years, and three females. He died and his wife, Mary, and Adam Regar were appointed administrators of his estate on October 7, 1801. It is believed that his wife was Adam Rogar's daughter.

HENRY WARFEL (also Warfle, Warford, etc. was a native of Lancaster County. In 1776, he was assessed as a non resident landowner in Penn Township. He may never have lived in what is now Snyder County. In 1780, he was a private in the 8th Company, 6th Battalion of the Lancaster County Militia.

DAVID WEAVER was born in 1758, and died in Haines Twp., Center Co., Pa., in June, 1813. He married Eva Wolf, and in 1783, they had their son, David, baptized at the old Zion Lutheran Church, north of Freeburg, Pa. In the same year, he was taxed with 100 acres of land and personal property in Potter (now Haines) Township, Center Co., Pa. He and his wife are buried in the cemetery at Wolf's Chapel, near where they lived, and their graves are marked. They had the following children: David, Jr. (1783-1864); Elizabeth, born about 1785. who married Jacob Musser; Philip, born about 1789; Catherine, born about 1792, married John Brown; George, born Oct. 22, 1794 (was the first child baptized at the Salem Lutheran Church, Aaronsburg, Pa.). He married Sarah Harper, and later Margaret Moyer; Sarah, born about 1797, married Henry Bower; Michael, born April 5, 1800, died Aug. 3, 1876, and is buried at St. Paul's Cemetery at Woodward, Pa.; Christina, born about 1802, married Thomas Hubler, and Thomas, born about 1804, married Lydia Meyer. In 1776, David enlisted as a private in Capt. John Clark's Company at Sunbury, Pa., and served with the Continental Forces for some four months. Later, he served as a Private in Capt. Charles Meyer's company of the Northumberland County Militia.

CAPTAIN MICHAEL WEAVER (also Weber, Weaber, etc.) was born in Germany about the year 1722. He came to America either in 1741 or 1751, and was naturalized by the Supreme Court at Philadelphia, Pa., Sept. 24, 1762. Egle says that Michael Weaver and his wife, Anna Barbara, presented a communion service to the Lutheran Church of Heidelberg Township, Lancaster Co., Pa., in 1764. He was assessed in Penn Township for the first time in 1771. In 1775, he was one of the road supervisors of the township. In 1787, he was assessed with 200 acres and considerable personal property in the township. The same year, he was granted a warrant of survey for 250 additional acres. In 1789, he and his wife, Barbara, were members of the Row's (Salem) Lutheran Church. According to the U. S. Census of 1790, his family at that time consisted of one male, over 16 years, and two females. About 1797, he followed some of his sons to what is now Haines Twp. Center County, Pa., where he died in May, 1801. His will is recorded at Bellefonte,

Pa. It is believed that he is buried at Wolf's Chapel n Center County. On Oct. 8, 1776, Michael was commissioned Captain of the 2nd company, 4th Battalion of the Northumberland County Militia, and held the commission for at least two years. It is believed that Michael lived 'between the villages of Salem and Kantz, in Penn Township. The children of Michael and his wife were: David (1758-1813), who married Eva Wolf; Michael, Jr., who married Catherine Elizabeth, daughter of the pioneer, Andrew Morr; Andrew; Margaret, who married one of the Row's of the Salem section; Christina, who married a Brown, and died before 1801; Elizabeth, who married a Wolf, and died before 1801; and Juliana (1760-1813), who married a Stover (Stober) and is buried at Wolf's Chapel Cemetery in Center County, Pa.

JOHN WEAVER was listed as a single freeman in Penn Township for the first time in 1776. He was a son of Capain Michael Weaver. He lived in what is now Haines Township, Center County, Pa., from 1793 to 1810. In September, 1776, he was a private in the 1st Company, 4th Battalion of the Northumberland County Militia.

MICHAEL WEAVER, JUNIOR, was a son of Captain Michael Weaver. He married Catherine Elizabeth, daughter of Andrew Morr, Jr. Catherine Elizabeth was born on Decemebr 25, 1768. In 1790, his family consisted of one male over 15 years, and four females. In 1802, Michael and his wife lived in the village of Freeburg, later they moved to Canton, Ohio, where it is supposed they died and are buried. Catherine was blind for a number of years before her death.

JOHN WEBER was listed as a single freeman in Beaver Township for the first time in 1799.

GEORGE WEIAND (also Weyand, Weiant, Wiant, etc.) lived in Mahantongo Township prior to 1800. Marie, born August 2, 1797, and Sarah, born January 15, 1815, daughters of George, were baptized at Grubb's Church, soon after birth. Catherine Hahn, single, was sponsor for the first child, and the parents for the second. George and Jacob seem to have been brothers.

JACOB WEIAND probably came from Berks County. He was assessed in Penn Township for the first time in 1795. In 1787, he lived in Beaver Township and was taxed with 50 acres of land and personal property. In 1796, he and John

Weiand were assessed in Mahantango Township. From October 17 to December 18, 1781, he was a private in Captain Nicholas Selbert's Company of the Berks County Militia.

CHRISTIAN WEIKEL, tailor, was assessed in Penn Township for the first time in 1799.

JOHN WEIRICK lived in Center Township and died there. Letters of administration in his estate were granted to Henry Weirick and John Wales on August 8, 1810. It is supposed that he lived in what is now Snyder County before 1800.

LIEUTENANT PETER WEIRICK (also Wirick, Wirich, Weirich, Werig, Weirig, etc.) was taxed in Penn township for the first time in 1776, but it is believed that he lived there before that date. He may have been a son of John Jacob Weirick who came from Germany on the British ship "Patience" and took the oath of allegiance at Philadelphia on August 11, 1750. It is believed that Peter came from either Berks or Lancaster County. In 1781, he was assessed with 200 acres and personal property in Penn Township. Later tax lists do not seem to carry his name. It is believed that he was a brother of Captain William Weirick, and a relative of Colonel George Weirick of the War of 1812. On October 8, 1776, Peter was Second Lieutenant of the 6th Company, 4th Battalion of the Northummberland County Militia. In 1819, he lived in Guernsey Co., Ohio, and was a pensioner.

CAPTAIN WILLIAM WEIRICK was assessed in Penn Township for the first time in 1776, but evidently came there an earlier date. He seems to have been a brother of Peter Weirick, mentioned above, and of Colonel George Weirick of the War of 1812, and of the Hon. Samuel Weirick of Union County. On September 25, 1795, letters of administration in the estate of William Weirick were granted to Catherine Weirick (probably his wife), and a William Weirick and Frederick Stein were her sureties. On October 8, 1776, he was Captain of the 4th Company, 4th Battalion of the Northumberland County Militia .

LIEUT. COL. BENJAMIN WEISER was the thirteenth cild of Col. John Conrad Weiser, the interpreter and Indian agent. He was born at Womelsdorf, Berks County, Pa., on August 12, 1744. Little is known of his early life, but in 1767, he was assessed with 200 acres of land and personal property in Heidelberg

Township, Berks County. Prior to his death in 1760, Colonel Weiser had received from the proprietors of the colony of Pennsylvania some 2600 acres of land on both sides of the Susquehanna River between Selinsgrove and Port Trevorton. When he died, this land fell to his heirs. They tried to sell the land, but were unsuccessful, and some of his heirs, including Benjamin, as early as 1770 became tenants on it. In 1773, by a deed of partition, this land was divided among the Weiser heirs, and Benjamin received for his share about 250 acres on the Isle of Que, just south of the present town of Selinsgrove. His sister, Mary, wife of the Rev. Henry Melchoir Muhlenberg, received a tract of about 170 acres just south of his at the lower end of the island. In the summer of 1771, Rev. Frederick A. Muhlenberg, nephew of Benjamin, made a missionary journey into the Middle Creek Valley and stopped to hold services at the house of Benjamin. This data was taken from Rev. Muhlenberg's diary, and indicates that Benjamin had lived there long enough to construct a permanent dwelling place. People living before 1920, will remember the old log house just east of the stone mansion built by John George Fisher about 1825. This log house was the Weiser dwelling, and the compiler remembers how when he was a boy, it was used by the Norman Fisher family as a storage place. On March 24, 1772, shortly after the formation of Northumberland County, Benjamin was appointed a justice of the peace for Penn Township. On January 1, 1778, he was again appointed to the office. In 1781, he was taxed with 230 acres and personal property in Penn Township. On March 2, 1787, Sheriff Thomas Grant sold Captain Weiser's property under a foreclosure sale to John Adam Fisher who owned the land on Weiser's south. On July 8, 1776, he was commissioned as a Captain in the German Regiment of the Continental Line, and he raised a company of volunteers among his neighbors in what is now Snyder County. On January 30, 1777, he was on duty with his company and regiment at the city of Philadelphia. Captain Weiser seems to have had numerous misfortunes in his life. first, his commission in the German Regiment seems to have been taken from him, soon thereafter, however, he was commissioned a captain in the Northumberland County Militia. Then he, and others, who served in

the office of justice of the peace were impeached, and finally his property was taken from him for debts. One of his descendants states that he was "Pursued by the phantom of recovering his grandfather's possessions in the State of New York." In a letter to Simon Snyder (later Governor of Pennsylvania), he refers to progress made in that direction. Benjamin at one time was a Lieutenant-Colonel in command of a battalion of the Northumberland County Militia.

JOHN WEISER was born in Berks County, Pa., in 1757, and died in Cumberland County on September 16, 1827. He was assessed in Penn Township only in the year 1778, and may have been a nonresident landowner. In 1780, he was a resident and landowner in Heidelberg Township, Berks County. He served as a private in Captain George Nagel's Company of Riflemen from Berks County, and was a pensioner.

CAPTAIN JOHN CONRAD WEISER, commonly called "Conrad" was a son of Philip Weiser (1728-1761,) and a grandson of the Indian agent, Colonel Conrad Weiser. Captain Weiser became a resident of Selinsgrove in 1796, and was the owner of the part of Selinsgrove which at one time was called Weiserburg. He died in Selinsgrove on January 30, 1803, and is buried in the old cemetery of the First Lutheran Church. His wife was Barbara Boyer. Rev. Daniel Weiser, the Reformed minister of Selinsgrove from 1824 to 1833, was a son. Daniel's son the Rev. C. Z. Weiser was the Reformed minister of the Selinsgrove congregation from 1853 to 1861. Benjamin Weiser, tailor, was a son of Captain Conrad Weiser. Benjamin's son, the Rev. Reuben Weiser was a Lutheran minister and served in Selinsgrove from 1846 to 1848. Captain Weiser and wife also had two daughters, Catherine (Mrs. John Bassler of Selinsgrove) and Mary (Mrs. George Holstein.) Barbara Boyer, wife of Captain Weiser, was born on February 8, 1753, and died in Selinsgrove on December 15, 1825 Her will was probated at Lewisburg, Pa., and mentions these children: Daniel, Sophia (Mrs. John Shaver — probably Shaffer,) ` Benjamin (who died before his mother and left these children: Henry, Susanna, Jonathan and Francis,) Frederick and Hannah (Mrs. Peter Rhoads, who died before her mother.) From the above you will note that there are some discrepancies as to who really were the children of Conrad and his wife.

PETER WEISER was a son of Col-

SNYDER COUNTY PIONEERS

98

onel Conrad Weiser. He was born in the Tulpehocken section of Berks County, Pa., on February 27, 1730. When his father died in 1760, he became one of the heirs to his estate and he received 229 acres of land at the head of the Isle of Que, which he later sold to John Snyder. He was assessed in Penn Township as a non resident landowner from 1776 to about 1783. There is no evidence that he ever lived in what is now Snyder County. In 1787, he lived in Reading and was listed as a saddler. It is supposed that he died in Reading. His wife was named Catherine.

LIEUTENANT PETER WEISER, son of Philip Weiser, and a nephew of the Peter, mentioned above, became a one-third heir to his father's land, when the latter died in 1761. It is not known when the younger Peter first came to what is now Snyder County to live, but he lived there in 1790, and his family consisted of one male over 16 years, and three females at the time. There are indications that he may have lived in the section of Selinsgrove at two different times, returning to Berks County between them. Peter was Third Lieutenant in Captain George Nagle's Company of the Berks County Militia. He took part in the battle of Long Island and was wounded at the battle of Germantown, on November 5, 1777.

PHILIP WEISER was assessed in Penn Township only in the year of 1776. The indications are that he was a nonresident landowner at that time. A Philip Weiser received depreciation pay for services in the Berks County Militia.

JACOB WELSH (also Welch) lived in Penn Township before 1780. In 1783, he was assessed as a resident and landowner in Augusta Township of Northumberland County. In 1780, he served as a private in Captain John Moll's Company, and in Ensign Simon Herrold's Party of Rangers from Northumberland County.

JOHN WELSH was assessor in Penn Township for the first time in 1778. The name disappeared after 1782. He was taxed with 50 acres of land and personal property. In 1780, he served in Ensign Simon Herrold''s Party of the Northumberland County Rangers, on the Frontier.

MICHAEL WERLEIN lived in Maxatawney Township, Berks Co., Pa., in 1784. In 1799, he was taxed with a ferry and a sawmill in Penn Township. He died in 1804, Solomon is supposed to have been his son.

JACOB WESTMAN, carpenter, was assessed in Penn Township for

the first time in 1799.

PHILIP WETZEL, SENIOR, seems to have been a son of Jacob Wetzel, Sr. He was born on December 19, 1751, probably in Berks County, Pa., and died in Center Township, Union (now Snyder) County, Pa., on September 4, 1826. He is buried in the Hassinger Old Cemetery, west of Middleburg, Pa., In 1780, he was assessed as a single freeman in Hereford Township, Berks County. In 1784, he lived in the same township but owned no land. His occupation at the time was that of blacksmith. He was assessed in Penn Township for the first time in 1794. Letters of administration in his estate were granted to Philip Wetzel on November 17, 1826, and Henry Wetzel and Peter Decker were given as sureties. A deed given by the heirs of Philip Senior, dated on Dec, 2, 1828, contained these names of the supposed children of Philip; Philip of Middleburg, Pa., Daniel of Center Township, Solomon of Fayette Seneca Contuy, New York, and Jonathan of Center Township. Eva, wife of Philip (Junior or Senior) born Dec. 28, 1788, died Feb. 18, 1832, is buried in the Hassinger Old Cemetery. Philip Wetzel, Senior, served as a Sergeant in the Pennsylvania Artillery. His father Jacob served as a private, 8th Class, in Captain John Miller's Company of the Berks County Militia, in 1783.

JOHN WIANT was assessed in Mahantango Township for the first time in 1796. His wife was named Catherine. In 1794, they had their son, Philip, baptized at the old Zion Lutheran Church, north of Freeburg. George. Jacob. and Michael, may have been brothers of John.

MICHAEL WIANT was assessed in Mahantango Township for the first time in 1796.

JOHN WLKESON seems to have lived in Penn Township before 1780. In 1785, he lived in Catawissa township and was taxed with 50 acres and personal property. In the same year a John Wilkeson was a non resident owner of 900 acres in Turbot Township of Northumberland County. In the summer of 1780, he served in Ensign Simon Herrold's Party of Northumberland County Rangers.

JOHN WILLIS seems to have been a native of Philadelphia County. He was assessed in Penn Township for the first time in 1778 and his name remained on the lists until 1785. The indications are that he was a non resident landowner, and that at a later date he lived in York County.

MOORE WILSON was assessed in Beaver Township for the first time in 1794. In 1790, he lived in Bedford County, and his family consisted of one male over and one under 16 years, and one female.

DANIEL WINES (sometimes given as Vines) lived in Beaver Township before 1790. There are indication that there were two men of the same name there, and both had families. The one had two males over and three under 16 years, and three females, in 1790.

HENRY WINKLEBLECH was assessed as the nonresident owner of 100 acres of land in Penn Tonwship in 1785 There is no evidence that he ever lived in the township.

LEONARD WINKLEBLECH seems to have been a native of Lancaster County. He was assessed in Penn Township for the first time in 1786, and in that year was taxed with 150 acres and personal property. It is believed that Leonard married Elizabeth, daughter of the pioneer, John George Herrold. It is believed that he was the son of the Leonard Winklblech who was a private, 8th class, 8th Company, 2nd Battalion of the Lancaster County Militia, in 1782.

CHRISTOPHER WISE (also Weiss, Weis, etc.) seems to have been a native of Cumberland County. He lived in Beaver Township in 1789, and in that year was one of the petitioners asking that an election for a justice of the peace be held in Beaver Township. In 1790, his family consisted of one male over 16 years, and three females. He was born on October 30, 1761, and died on September 14, 1826. He is buried in the old cemetery at Beaver Springs. In 1778, he served in the 7th Company, 8th Battalion of the Cumberland County Militia.

GEORGE WISE (also Weis) lived in Lancaster, Pa., in 1771. He was assessed in Penn Township for the first time in 1776. In 1782, he and his wife, had their daughter Elizabeth Barbara, baptized at the old Zion Lutheran Church, north of Freeburg. Fred and Margaret Arbogast were the sponsors. In 1793, and as late as 1801, he lived in what is now Haines Township, Centre. He served as a private in Captain Bowen's Company of the 9th Pennsylvania Regiment. A man of the same name was a private in Captain William Heyser's Company of the German Regiment, May 22, 1777. A George Wise was a Sergeant in Captain Andrew Groff's Company, stationed at Phiadelphia, July 16. 1776.

FREDERICK WISE lived in Penn Township in 1778, or before. On

November 25, 1778, he and about a hundred others from what is now Snyder, Union, and Northumberland Counties petitioned the Provincial Council to exonerate them of their taxes, due to the ravages of an Indian war and the destruction of their crops and property. In 1787, Frederick became a resident of Lewisburg, Pa.

JOHN WISE was assessed in Beaver Township for the first time in 1791. From 1793 to 1801, he lived in what is now Haines Township, Center County. A John Wise served in the 6th Battalion of the Northampton County Militia during the Revolution.

ABRAHAM WITMER, SENIOR, was a brother of John Witmer who lived just south of Mahantango Creek. John was a son of Michael Witmer of Earl Township, Lancaster County, Pa. It was said that he was the first one of the Witmer family to live north of the Mahantango Creek, but the date of his moving there is unknown to the compiler, however, he did live there when Mahantango Township was formed in 1796. He died in Chapman Township and his will was probated at Lewisburg, Pa., on February 21, 1826. The will mentions his wife, Mary, and these children: Abraham, Jacob, John, Anna, Mrs. George Leiter), Barbara (Mrs. John Leiter), Elizabeth, (Mrs. John Miller,) and Frances (Mrs. John Leiter). The executors of the will were Abraham Witmer, Jr., and John Ebright.

CHRISTOPHER WITMER seems to have been a son of John Witmer Just when and how long he lived in Penn Township is unknown to the compiler. The evidence indicates that he lived across the river in Mahanoy Township, where he was taxed with 30 acres of land and personal property in 1781. He married Hannah, daughter of Captain Casper Reed. Captain Reed lived on the present site of the village of Port Trevorton. Christopher served as a private in Capt. John Moll's Company of the Northumberland County Militia.

HERMAN or HENRY WITMER was assessed with 100 acres and personality in Mahanoy Twp., in 1781 and again in 1786. Prior to the first date he seems to have lived in Penn Township. He served as a as a private in Captain John Moll's Company of the Northumberland County Militia. He was a son of Michael.

JACOB WITMER was a son of Abraham Witmer, Senior. He was assessed in Mahantango Township in 1796. He lived in what is now Snyder County as early as 1790, and in that year his family consisted of one male over 16 years and three females. He may have been the Jacob Witmer, who married Mary, daughter of Captain Casper Reed.

JOHN WITMER was a son of Michael Witmer of Earl Township, Lancaster County, Pa. About 1770, or soon thereafter, he became a tenant on his father's land, which the father had secured a short time before. Some of this land lay along the Mahantango Creek, and had previously been owned by Thomas McKee, the Indian Trader, who died in 1772. John or his father built a stone grist mill near the site where the present Susquehanna Trail crosses the Mahantango Creek, and when Michael died, John inherited the mill. Later this mill became known as Weiser's mill. John may not have lived in what is now Snyder County, but he owned land in what is now Chapman Township. His son Abraham is said to have been the first of the Witmers to live north of the Mahantango Creek. Abraham Witmer, Junior, who lived in Port Trevorton in 1885, is supposed to have been a grandson of John.

JOHN WITMER, son of Peter Witmer, Sr., and his wife, Maria Salome, was born in what is now Union Township, Snyder County, Pa., on Ferbuary 8, 1778 and died in the same township on May 11, 1853. His wife, Elizabeth, daughter of Captain Simon Herrold, was born in the same section on April 2, 1781 and died on September 4, 1857. Both are buried in the old cemetery at Witmer's Church in Union Township. One of their children, Frederick Witmer, was baptized at the Grubb's Church in Chapman Township on June 29, 1815. Frederick Herrold, Sr. (uncle of the mother), and his wife, Catherine, were the sponsors. John was assessed in Mahantango township for the first time in 1799.

MATHIAS WITMER was assessed with 100 acres and personal property in Mahanoy Township in 1781. At an earlier date he seems to have lived on the west side of the Susquehanna River, probably in what is now Chapman Township. On January 30, 1777, he was a private in Captain Benjamin Weiser's Company of the German Regiment, Continental Line, stationed at Philadelphia.

MICHAEL WITMER was born about 1728 and died in Manor Twp., Lancaster Co., Pa., in 1789.

In 1771 he was assessed with 300 acres in Earl Township, Lancaster County, Pa. About 1770, he purchased a tract fo land along the Mahantango Creek lying in what is now Juniata and Snyder Counties. Some of this land at one time had been owned by Thomas McKee. Michael's name appeared on the Penn Township tax list of 1776, or before, and remained until 1782, when his son John probably bought the land on which he had been a tenant for some years. There is no evidence to indicate that Michael ever lived in Chapman Township. Abraham Witmer, living in Selinsgrove in 1910, and his descendants, John and Charles Witmer, are descendants of this pioneer. It is thought that Michael may have been a son of Christopher Witmer who sailed from Rotterdam, Holland with the Palatines, on the British ship "William and Sarah" and took the oath of allegiance at Philadelphia, on September 18, 1727. Michael was a private, 8th Class, 3rd Company, 3rd Battalion of the Lancaster County Militia. His sons were: John, Abraham, and Herman.

PETER WITMER, SENIOR, was born in Herzheim, Nassau, Dillsburgishaft, Germany, in 1737. It is believed that his father was also named Peter, and that he came on the ship "Muscliff" in 1744, or on the ship "Restauration" in 1747. The Peter of this sketch married Marie Salome ———in Philadelphia, Pa., in 1757. On June 8, 1759, he was granted a warrant of survey for 50 acres of land in Lancaster County. In 1773, he lived in Manor Township, Lancaster County, and was taxed with 140 acres and personal prope rty. In 1775 or 1776, he loaded his family and goods in a flat boat at Columbia, Pa., and came up the river with them to the site of the present village of Dundore, in Union Township, where he built his first cabin. He was assessed in Penn Township for the first time in 1776, and in 1786, was assessed with 120 acres of land, a fulling mill, and considerable personal property. In 1785 he was one of the road supervisors of Penn Township. In 1790, his family consisted of four males over 16 years, and three females. In 1791, he established a ferry across the river to the foot of the Mahanoy Mountain. Peter died in what is now Union Township in July, 1793 and his will was probated at Sunbury, Pa., on August 3, 1793. The will mentions his wife, Maria Salome, and some of their children;

Peter, Junior, Susanna, Magdalene, (Mrs. John Thornton), and Mary (Mrs. John Motz). Mary was born in Lancaster County, Pa., on October 9, 1767, and died at Woodward, Center County, Pa., on March 12, 1839. Other known children of Peter, Senior, were John and Samuel. Peter, Senior, was buried in the Row's (Salem) Cemetery in Penn Township. Peter, Senior, and his son, Peter, Junior, received depreciation pay for services in the Northumberland County Militia. Ralph Witmer and Frank A. Eyer, both of Selinsgrove, Pa., are descendants of this pioneer.

PETER WITMER, JUNIOR, was born in Lancaster County, Pa., about 1760 and was presumably the oldest son of Peter, Senior, and his wife, Maria Salome. He was assessed in Penn Township for the first time in 1781, and in that year was listed as a single freeman. About 1776, he came to what is now Union Township of Snyder County with his parents, who had previously lived in Manor Township, Lancaster County. Peter and his father owned large tracts of land near the present village of Dundore, and after the elder Peter's death, in 1793, his son inherited much of the estate. Peter, Jr., and his brother-in-law, John Motz, were executors of the will of the older Peter. In 1790, Peter, Junior's family consisted of one male over and two under 16 years, and one female. In 1796, when Mahantango Township was formed from the southern part of Penn, he was assessed there. H's brothers were John and Samuel, and his sisters, Susanna, Magdalena (Mrs. John Thornton), and Mary (Mrs. John Motz). Peter, Junior, served in Captain John Moll's company of the Northumberland County Militia. Peter married a daughter of Capt. George Overmire, and moved to Belmont County, Ohio, in 1801. He died on Nov. 19, 1835, and is buried near New Reading, Perry Co., Ohio.

SAMUEL WITMER was one of the sons of Peter Witmer, Senior. He was born in Manor Township, Lancaster County, Pa., on April 4, 1771, and died in what is now Union Township, Snyder County, on October 4, 1829. His wife, Sarah ———, was born on May 6, 1776, and died on June 9th, 1848. He is buried in the cemetery of Keiser's Church in Union Township, and she in the old cemetery at Witmer's Church in the same Township. Samuel came up the river with his parents in a flatboat in 1776 and settled where the present hamlet

of Dundore now stands. Samuel built the old house near the Dundore store about the year 1800, and it is still in every day use. Samuel was assessed as a single freeman in Mahantango Township for the first time in 1796. His will was probated at Lewisburg, Pa., on September 21, 1829. His wife, Sarah, and George Herrold, were executors of his will. Associate Judge, Daniel Witmer, born February 10, 1812, died December 14, 1896, was one of his children. David, Isaac, and Saul were other sons.

ANDREW WITTENMEYER, SENIOR, came from Berks or Lancaster County. His name appeared on the Penn Township tax list for the first time in 1776. In 1781, and for a number of years thereafter, he was taxed with 400 acres of land and personal property. In 1790, his family consisted of two males over and one under 16 years, and three females. In 1795, he was one of the road supervisors of Penn Township. He lived in the vicinity of Middleburg, and it is believed that he is interred in the old cemetery at Hassinger's Church, west of Middleburg. He died in Penn Township, and his will was probated at Sunbury, Pa., on April 11, 1800. It is thought that his wife's name was Susanna, and that she preceded him in death, because she is not mentioned in the will. His children were: Anna Mary, Andrew in Jacob, Catherine Miller, Barbara (Mrs. Jacob Roush), and Susanna (wife of either Peter or Jonas Apple). The sons were executors of his will. It is believed that Andrew was a Revolutionary soldier. A Ludwig and an Andrew Wittenmeyer sailed for America from Rotterdam, Holland, in the British ship "Phoenix." They arrived at Philadelphia where they took the oath of allegiance on August 28, 1750. It is believed that Andrew was the son of Ludwig.

ANDREW WITTENMEYER, JUNIOR, was a son of Andrew Wittenmeyer, Senior, mentioned above. He was born on October 7, 1767, probably in Lancaster County, Pa., and died near what is now Middleburg, Snyder County, Pa., on June 15, 1848. His wife, Maria Catherine ———, was born on March 22, 1776, and died on April 22, 1851. Both are buried in the cemetery at Middleburg, Pa. Andrew, Junior, came to what is now Snyder County with his parents, before the Revolution. He was assessed in Penn Township for the first time in 1789. In 1801, he was the executor of his father's will. Andrew

(1793-1875) was probably his son.

LUDWIG (LEWIS) WITTENMEYER was a resident of Lancaster County. He was born in Germany, and set sail for America from Rotterdam, Holland, in the British ship "Phoenix," John Mason, master. He arrived at Philadelphia where he took the English oath of allegiance on August 28, 1750. An Andrew Wittenmeyer was on the same ship, and the compiler believes that he was Ludwig's son. Ludwig's name appeared on the Penn Township tax list from 1776 to 1787, but he was always designated as a non resident landowner. In the latter year he was taxed with 200 acres. There is no evidence that he ever lived in what is now Snyder County.

MICHAEL WITTENMEYER may have also been a son of Ludwig, mentioned above, or he may have been a son of Andrew, Senior. He was born on December 13, 1772, and died on July 29, 1850. His wife, Magdalena, was born on September 16, 1772, and died on May 30, 1849. Both are buried in the Hassinger Old Cemetery, west of Middleburg. He was assessed in Penn Township for the first time in 1799. It is believed that John G. Wittenmeyer (1774-1824), buried in the same cemetery, was his brother.

CAPTAIN GEORGE WOLF was one of the early settlers of Penn Township. In 1772, he was granted a tavern license, and at one time he had a tavern near where the Snyder County State Bank stands at Hummel's Wharf. In 1774, he was still operating his tavern. In 1773, he was a member of the first grand jury to convene in Northumberland County. In 1776 and 1777, he was Sub-Lieutenant of the Northumberland Co. Militia. In 1787, he was assessed as the nonresident owner of 400 acres in Penn Township. In 1789, he was one of the petitioners asking that the lower part of Buffalo Twp., be annexed to Penn Township. In 1790, his family consisted of two males over and one under 16 years, and two females. It is believed that he later moved to Center County. George, Henry and John seem to have been his sons. On October 8, 1776, he was Captain of the 5th Company, 4th Battalion of the Northumberland County Militia.

GEORGE WOLF, Junior, was a son of Captain George Wolf, mentioned above. He may have been born in Penn Township. He was assessed in Penn Township for the first time in 1793.

HENRY WOLF seems to have

been a son of Captain George Wolf. He lived in what is now Monroe (but then Buffalo) Township in 1789, and was one of the petitioners praying that the lower part of Buffalo Township be annexed to Penn Township. This was done in the same year.

JOHN WOLF evidently was a son of Captain George Wolf. He was assessed in Penn Township for the first time in 1793.

JOHN WOODLING was born on January 31, 1776, presumably in Frederick Township, Montgomery County, Pa., and seems to have been a son of John Woodling who lived in Philadelphia, later Montgomery County. He died in what is now Penn Township, Snyder County, and is buried in the cemetery of the First Lutheran Church in Selinsgrove, Pa. His tombstone indicates that he died on September 19, 1860, but due to the fact that his will was probated at Lewisburg, Pa., on March 1, 1853, the date of "1860" must be incorrect. His wife was named Susanna ——————. John seems to have come to what is now Snyder County with his brother, John George, on cattle buying trips as early as 1790, and some time prior to 1800, both brothers settled in the Middle Creek Valley. John bought and sold various tracts of land in what is now Penn and Washington Townships. John mentions these children in his will: Isaac (1809-1873), John, Elizabeth (Mrs. Samuel Pawling), Catherine (Mrs. John Wise), Polly Mrs. Peter Bowman), Abraham, Lydia (Mrs. Henry Wittenmeyer), David, and Jacob. who married Hannah Pawling, and died before his father. Isaac, son of John and Susanna Woodling was baptized at the old Zion Lutheran Church, north of Freeburg, in 1809.

JOHN GEORGE WOODLING (also Woodly, Woodley, Watling, Wodley, Wodly, etc.) was born on January 16, 1761, probably in what is today Frederick Township, Montgomery County, Pa. His father seems to have been John Woodling. He also had a brother named John. Hannah Herb (?), wife of John George Woodling, was born on October 23, 1762, and died near Freeburg, Snyder County, Pa., on September 18, 1831. He died about the year 1845, and is supposed to have been buried at her side in an unmarked grave in the St. Peter's Cemetery in Freeburg. According to tradition, "George Woodling" as he was commonly called, first came into the Susquehanna Valley about

the year 1790 to buy cattle for the Philadelphia butchers. These he drove overland via the "Reading Road." His younger brother, John, mentioned above, accompanied him on these trips. After a number of trips to the section, they became interested in land in what is now Penn and Washington Townships, and at one time they owned the greater part of what is now known as the "Sand Hill" and the "Flintstone Valley." George bought the Flintstone tract about the year 1798. George Woodling, a great grand son of the pioneer, aged 80 years in 1934, was the owner of part of the original purchase of 1798. Irwin Steffen is at present the owner of most of the remainder of the original purchase. Not any of the "Sand Hill" land is in the hands of a Woodling descendant at this date. About 1795, George and his brother built the stone gristmill, near Pawling's Station on the Middle Creek in Penn Township. This mill was still standing in 1934, but was no longer in active use. It has variously been known as Woodling's, Kantz's, Pawling's, Glass', Renninger's and Boyers' Mill. The compiler is a great-great-grandson of this pioneer and has in his possession a sheet of paper on which George in his own penmanship in German script, wrote the names of himself, wife, and children, with the dates of their births. The writer also has numerous other papers which were written or signed by the pioneer. He also has a German Bible published in Nuremberg, Germany, in 1736, on the flyleaf of which is written the name of "George Woodling"' and the fact that he was an officer of the Freeburg Church. The children of George and Hannah Woodling were: George, born March 14, 1785, Daniel (April 8, 1788), Magdalena, (Oct. 25, 1790), Henry (Sept. 5, 1793), Jonas Jan. 26, 1795), Joseph (June 20, 1796), Samuel (Sept. 27, 1797), and William Aug. 20, 1802). Daniel lived near Millersburg, Pa., in May, 1835. Henry was a soldier in the War of 1812. Joseph moved to Center County about 1850, and died near Millheim or Rebersburg. William lived most of his life in Washington Township and is buried at Freeburg. George, born 1785, had a son named George, who was baptized at the old Zion Lutheran Church, north of Freeburg, in 1808. His wife was named Elizabeth, according to the baptismal records. George "Wodly" of Frederick Township, served as a private in Captain Michael Gaugler's Com-

pany of the Philadelphia County Militia. Frederick Township at that time was part of Philadelphia County, later it belonged to Northampton County, and now to Montgomery County. It seems that in 1845, George was living with his nephew, Jacob Woodling, in Selinsgrove. In that year, Jacob wrote to Colonel Henry C. Eyer, State Senator, at Harrisburg, asking if he could not secure a pension for the "old man," and on January 15, 1845, Senator Eyer replied that at the time he was unable to locate the service record, but that he would do what he could. Since nothing more came of this, it is presumed that George died soon after. Jacob ran a tavern on the Isle of Que, and died in Selinsgrove in 1847.

ABRAHAM WOODS lived in Beaver Township before 1790. The U. S. Census of 1790, states that his family consisted of one male over and one under 16 years, and three females.

JEREMIAH WOODS lived in Beaver Township in 1790, and his family consisted of one male over and one under 16 years, and three females.

JOHN WOODS, SENIOR, was assessed in Penn Township for the first time in 1785. From 1778, he seems to have lived in Turbot Township of Northumberland County, and until 1785, he was assessed with only personal property there. In 1789, he was assessed in Beaver Township, and in the same year he was one of the petitioners asking that an election for a justice of the peace be held in that district. In 1790, his family consisted of one male over 16 years, four females, and one other person. He received depreciation pay for services in the Northumberland County Militia

JOHN WOODS, JUNIOR, evidently was a son of John Woods, Senior. The younger man was assessed in Beaver Township for the first time 1789. In 1790, his family consisted of one male over and four under 16 years, and one female.

JOSEPH WOODS was assessed in Penn Township for the first time in 1781. In 1790, his family consisted of one male over and three under 16 years, and two females. He did not become a landowner until 1787. He served as a private in Captain Ephraim Blackburn's Company (the West Nottingham) of the Chester County Militia.

LEVI WODS lived in Beaver Township in 1789. In 1790, his family consisted of one male over and one under 16 years, and three 'females.

LUDWIG WOODROW (also Woodroe, Woodro, Worrah, etc.) was a non resident landowner in Penn Township, and was assessed only in the year of 1776. Simon Woodrow, whose name appeared at the same time, seems to hav been his son.

SIMON WOODROW was a resident of Colerain Township, Lancaster County, Pa., in 1771, 1772, and 1773, and the indications are that he came to what is now Snyder County in the year of 1774. He was assessed in Penn Township for the first time in 1776, under the name of "Simon Worrah." In 1781, he was taxed with 150 acres of land and personal property, and he was assessed in Penn until Mahantango was formed in 1796, when he was assessed there until his death in 1812. His will was probated at Sunbury, Pa., on January 21, 1812. Valentine Haas was the executor. Legacies were given to his grandchildren; Rebecca, Reuben and Isaac Foutz (probably children of Michael Foutz, who was assessed as a single freeman in what is now Snyder County as early as 1771). Other legatees were; Hannah Cogan, John Woodrow (nephew), and Sarah Woodrow (daughter of John). Simon Woodrow was a member of the Committee of Safety from Penn Township in 1776, and for this was credited as having served during the Revolutionary period. A Simon Woodrow served in the Chester County Militia, but it is believed that this was a different man.

CHRISTIAN WORTH also (Wirth Werth, etc.) was born on December 7, 1760, and died on September 22, 1819. He seems to have lived in York County before he came to what is now Snyder. In 1790, in one of the upper townships of Adams or York County, and his family consisted of one male over and three under 16 years, and six females. Adam Wirth who lived in the vicinity of Grubb's Church between 1817 and 1829, probably was his son, Christian is probably buried in the old part of the Grubb's Cemetery. He served as a private in the 2nd Company, 2nd Battalion of the Lancaster County Militia.

JOHN YEAGER (also Jaeger, Yager, Jager, etc.) lived in Beaver Township in 1790, and his family consisted of one male over and five under 16 years, and one female. In 1808, a John Yeager and his wife, Catherine, lived in the vicinity of Grubb's Church.

PHILIP YOCHIM was assessed in Penn Township for the first time in 1793. It is believed that he married Elizabeth, daughter of Captain Casper Snyder. Philip seems to have died soon after 1800 and left a widow and two children, a son and a daughter. About 1812, Philip's widow married Christian Fisher, Senior, and became the mother of three or four children with her second husband. Christian had previously been married to Hannah Snyder, Elizabeth's older sister. Anna Yochim, daughter of Philip Yochim and his wife, Elizabeth Snyder, married David, the youngest brother of Christian Fisher. Elizabeth Snyder-Yochim- Fisher was born on April 27, 1779, and died on April 13, 1851. She is buried in the old Lutheran Cemetery in Selinsgrove, by the side of her second husband.

HENRY YODER, carpenter, was assessed in Penn Township for the first time in 1799. He seems never to have married, or if he did, he did not have any children. He died in Center Township in 1816, and his nephews, Peter, Jacob, John and Melchoir, were his heirs. He was one of the builders of the first school house at Globe Mills, in 1805.

JACOB YODER, potter, was as-first time in 1799. He seems to have been a son of Melchoir Yoder, Senior, and a brother of Peter, John, and Melchoir, Junior. Jacob also helped to build the first school house at Globe Mills, which for a time was used as a church.

JOHN YODER was born on November 27, 1768, and died on October 20, 1833. His wife, Catherine Hirt (or Hert), was born on April 17, 1769, and died in 1843. Both are buried in the cemetery at Globe Mills in Middle Creek Township. His tombstone states that they were married on November 14, 1790, and that they had one son and one daughter. In 1799, John Yoder and others associated themselves together for the purpose of securing a church and school for their locality. The beginning made at this time eventually led to the formation of Seiber's or Globe Mills Lutheran Church, and a public school located at the same place. When the first building was built there in 1805, he was one of the largest contributors of work, money, and material for its erection.

MELCHOIR YODER, SENIOR, came to the section now known as Globe Mills before 1800. He seems to have had a brother named Hen-

ry. Melchoir and Henry were born in Germany and after coming to this country settled in Montgomery County. In 1796, Melchoir, Junior, and his wife, Anna, came to the Middle Creek Valley and bought some land from Judah Roberts in what is now Middle Creek Township. In a short time his father, brothers, and uncle also came to the section. Melchoir, Senior's children were: Peter, Jacob, John and Melchoir, Junior. Some think he also had a son named Abraham. There is evidence which indicates that Melchoir died in 1802. John succeeded to the ownership of his father's estate. In 1790, his family consisted of three males over and three under 16 years, and two females.

MELCHOIR YODER, JUNIOR, came to what is now Middle Creek Township in the year 1796, and bought from Judah Roberts a tract of 103 acres. Melchoir's wife was named Anna. Before 1800, his father, uncle and brothers also located in the same community.

PETER YODER was a son of Melchoir Yoder, Senior. He came to what is now Middle Creek Township with his parents before 1800. In 1805, he was one of the contributors in work and material for the erection of the first school and church building at Seiber's, now known as Globe Mills.

LIEUTENANT JACOB YONER seems to have lived in Penn Township at some time during the period prior to 1800. It is supposed that he died at Selinsgrove, and that he is buried in the old cemetery of the First Lutheran Church. He was a Lieutenant in Captain Paul Baulty's Company of the Northumberland County Militia, on April 29, 1782.

MAJOR CASPER YOST (also Jost, Youst, Yoost, etc.) was a son of John Yost and his wife, Mary Foster. John was a Revolutionary soldier. Major Yost was born in Hanover, Pa., in 1748, and died in Penn Township in the year of 1781. In 1765, he married Catherine, daughter of Colonel Philip Cole and his wife, Elizabeth Edie. From 1771 to 1773, Major Yost was a resident, but not a landowner in Lebanon Township, Lancaster County, Pa. Soon thereafter, he became a resident of Penn Township. On October 8, 1776, he was Second Major of the 4th Battalion of the Northumberland County Militia, which at that time was commanded by his father-in-law. Colonel Cole.

CASPER YOST, JUNIOR, was a

son of Major Casper Yost and his wife, Catherine, daughter of Colonel Philip Cole. Casper, Junior, was born about the year 1770, and in 1811 he was living in New Berlin, Pa.

CHRISTIAN YOST, SENIOR, seems to have been a brother of Major Casper Yost. Christian lived in Penn Township prior to 1780. In 1790, his family consisted of himself and wife. He served as a priva.e in Captain Michael Weaver's Company, 4th Battalion of the Northumberland County Militia.

CHRISTIAN YOST, JUNIOR, lived in Penn Township from before 1780. In 1790, his family consisted of one male over and one under 16 years, and two females.

GEORGE YOUNG was assessed in Penn Township for the first time in 1793.

MATTHEW or MATHAS YOUNG (also Jung, Yung, etc.) was assessed in Buffalo Township from 1778 to 1787, and in Beaver Township from 1789. One record states that he died in 1787, but the compiler can find no confirmation of this. Should it prove true, then it may have been his son, of the same name, who lived in Beaver Township. In 1790, the family consisted of one male over 16, and four females. His daughter, Margaret, was captured by the Indians. She was still alive in 1787. Matthew served as a private in the Northumberland County Militia.

JACOB ZEARNS (also Zerns, Zurns, Zirns, etc.) papermaker, was assessed in Beaver Township for the first time in 1799. People of the same name lived in the vicinity of Richfield at a later date.

FREDERICK ZELLER (also Seller, Zellers, Sellers, etc.) is supposed to have lived in what is now Snyder County before 1800. His wife was named Catherine. He died in what is now Perry Township, and his will was probated at Lewisburg, Pa., on April 4, 1820. His will mentioned his wife, and these children; Henry, Andrew, Mary, Catherine, and Lydia.

HENRY ZELLER was granted a warrant of survey for 150 acres in Northumberland (now Snyder) County, on Nov. 11, 1772, and in 1776, he was listed as a single freeman in Penn Township for the first time. His name does not appear after 1776. It is supposed that he was a relative of John Zeller who owned land on both sides of the Mahantango Creek. A Henry Zeller served in the Northampton County Militia, and one in Captain Orth's Company of the Lancaster County Militia.

JOHN ZELLERS was assessed as a laborer in Williams Township, Northampton County, Pa., in 1772. On June 9, 1774, he was granted a warrant of survey for 307 acres in Northumberland (now Snyder) County. He was assessed in Penn Township for the first time in 1776. In 1778, his name was given on the tax list as "Zellerman." In 1781, he was assessed with 500 acres and personal property, and in 1785, with 800 acres and personality. In 1796, when Mahantango Township was formed from the southern part of Penn, he was one of the largest land holders in the new district. He died in Mahantango Township in 1809, and Adam Light and Adam Wilt were administrators of his estate. Frederick, George, Benjamin, and Henry, may have been his sons. On May 13, 1780, he was a private in Captain John Snyder's Company of the Northumberland County Militia, or Rangers.

JOHN ZERBE was a laborer in Tulpehocken, Berks County, Pa., in 1779. He was assessed in Penn Township for the first time in 1793. His ancestor, John Zerbe, was head of one of the families which came down from New York state in 1723 or 1725. The Zerbes were of French Huguenot origin, but had lived in Germany for several generations, and came to America with the Palatines. The Zellers, Herrolds, and Pontius' were also Huguenots. In 1790, John seems to have lived in Robeson Township of Berks County, and his family consisted of one male over and two under 16 years, and one female.

PETER ZERBE was a single freeman in Tulpehocken Township, Berks County, Pa., in 1779. It is believed that he was a brother of John, mentioned above. He was assessed in Penn Township for the first time in 1790.

CHRISTIAN ZIMMERMAN lived in Penn Township in 1790, and his family consisted of two males over and one under 16 years, and two females.

CHRISTOPHER (STOPHEL) ZIMMERMAN may have been a native of Berks County. He was assessed in Penn Township for the first time in 1776, but it seems that he was not a resident at that time. In 1787, he was taxed with 50 acres and personal property. In 1790, his family consisted of three males over and four under 16 years, and three females. In 1796, when Mahantango Township was formed, he lived there. William and Jacob, who lived in the same district at the same time probably were relatives. A Christopher Zimmerman served as a private in Lieutenant James Gleave's Company of Rangers from Berks County. A Christopher Zimmerman was a Sergeant in the 5th Pennsylvania Regiment, Continental Line.

JACOB ZIMMERMAN, single freeman, was assessed in Mahantango Township in 1796.

WILLIAM ZIMMERMAN was assessed in Mahantango Township in 1796. It is believed that he was a brother of Jacob. In 1790, he lived in Penn Township and his family consisted of one male over and one under 16 years, and one female.

JOHN ZWALLY (also Zwalley, Zually, etc.), weaver, was assessed in Mahantango Township in 1796. He married Barbara, daughter of John and Catherine Arbogast. John Arbogast died in Penn Township in 1811.